INTERNATIONAL ADJUSTMENT AND FINANCING: THE LESSONS OF 1985–1991

C. FRED BERGSTEN, EDITOR

International Adjustment and Financing: The Lessons of 1985–1991

INSTITUTE FOR INTERNATIONAL ECONOMICS
WASHINGTON, DC 1991

C. Fred Bergsten is the Director of the Institute for International Economics. He was formerly Assistant Secretary for International Affairs at the US Treasury, Assistant for International Economic Affairs to the National Security Council, and a Senior Fellow at the Brookings Institution, the Carnegie Endowment for International Peace, and the Council on Foreign Relations. He is the author or coauthor of numerous books and articles on a wide range of international economic issues, including *America in the World Economy: A Strategy for the 1990s*, *The United States–Japan Economic Problem*, and *The Dilemmas of the Dollar*.

INSTITUTE FOR INTERNATIONAL
ECONOMICS
11 Dupont Circle, NW
Washington, DC 20036-1207
(202) 328-9000 Telex: 261271 IIE UR
FAX: (202) 328-5432

C. Fred Bergsten, *Director*
Linda Griffin Kean, *Director of Publications*

Printed in the United States of America
95 94 93 92 91   5 4 3 2 1

Library of Congress Cataloging-in-Publication Data

International adjustment and
   financing : the lessons of 1985–1991 /
   C. Fred Bergsten, editor. p.   cm.
   "November 1991."
   Includes bibliographical references
   and index.
   1. Balance of trade—Congresses.
   2. Foreign exchange administration—
   Congresses.
I. Bergsten, C. Fred, 1941-
HF1014.I47   1991   91-40029
382'.17—dc20   CIP

ISBN cloth 0-88132-142-7
ISBN paper 0-88132-112-5

Contents

Tables

Figures

INTERNATIONAL ADJUSTMENT AND FINANCING:
THE LESSONS OF 1985–1991

Preface

The large trade imbalances that emerged among the world's major economies in the 1980s have been a focal point of the research program of the Institute since its inception in 1981. I began calling attention to the problem in the early 1980s and, with William R. Cline, addressed its most crucial geographical dimension in *The United States–Japan Economic Problem* (1985). Stephen Marris provided a comprehensive analysis that included the financial dimension of the issue in *Deficits and the Dollar: The World Economy at Risk* (1985, revised in 1987). Cline reviewed the results of the first phase of the policy response in *United States External Adjustment and the World Economy* (1989), and I drew on his preliminary analyses in my *America and the World Economy: A Strategy for the 1990s* (1988).

On the basis of these studies, I and others at the Institute have participated actively in the national and international debate on the adjustment issue. Hence we have felt a responsibility to continually assess the progess or lack thereof in the realization of our analytical projections and policy prescriptions. The need to reassess became especially acute in the late 1980s as widespread disappointment emerged over the continuation of sizable imbalances despite large changes in exchange rates and other policy measures aimed at reducing the imbalances. This study derives from a conference organized by the Institute in late 1990 to analyze the extent to which actual trade shifts had tracked the expectations of both economists and policymakers, and to draw lessons for both from the dramatic swings of the period.

The conference was organized in four parts; this volume maintains that organization. First, Paul R. Krugman presented an overview paper that framed the adjustment problem and asked a series of questions to be addressed in each of the country studies and other analyses. Two particular issues were identified as the focus of the project: Had the economic models used to predict the outcome of adjustment efforts performed as expected? And did the policy measures adopted by governments achieve the desired results?

Second, leading economists from the three countries with the largest imbalances examined the adjustment record of each in detail. For the United States, William R. Cline offered a macroeconomic perspective and Allen J. Lenz a sectoral view. Masaru Yoshitomi analyzed the experience of Japan. Norbert Walter did the same for Germany. These country studies assess the causes of the surpluses and deficits that emerged in the middle of the 1980s, trace the reduction of those imbalances toward the end of the decade, and offer answers to the central questions concerning the efficacy of the adjustment models and policy measures. The original papers for the conference covered these events through the middle of 1990, but the revised versions published here provide an update through the middle of 1991.

A third component of the volume addresses the systemic implications of the experience of the 1980s. Robert A. Mundell and John Williamson draw lessons for the exchange rate regime and for the global adjustment mechanism more broadly. Stephen Marris, who originated the "hard landing" scenario in the mid-1980s, describes how that outcome was avoided and draws inferences for the international financing of future imbalances. Peter B. Kenen draws a number of lessons for both adjustment and financing from the other papers and from his own analysis of the events of the 1980s.

Fourth, and subsequent to the conference, Paul Krugman reflected on the numerous strands of analysis presented there and produced a concluding overview chapter that sought to answer the basic questions posed at the outset. His primary focus in that chapter is to determine who the conference's deliberations had proved correct—the conventional economists or the various skeptics, which Krugman divides into three schools of thought that he labels structuralists, shmooists, and secularists. He rejects each of these critiques and reaches three basic conclusions: exchange rate changes work, they are in fact necessary components of an effective adjustment process, and the relationship between exchange rate changes and trade is reasonably stable (and thus predictable).

As with several earlier Institute studies, we decided to release the results of this project in two different formats in an effort to meet the needs of different groups of readers. In addition to this volume, which contains all of the papers presented to the conference and comments on them, in October 1991 we published Paul Krugman's final chapter separately as the 34th in our series of POLICY ANALYSES IN INTERNATIONAL ECONOMICS under the title *Has the Adjustment Process Worked?* Krugman answers that question strongly in the affirmative, and we hope that this volume will make a useful contribution to the ongoing effort to understand, and draw policy lessons from, one of the central international economic issues of the past decade.

The Institute for International Economics is a private nonprofit institution for the study and discussion of international economic policy. Its purpose is to analyze important issues in that area, and to develop and communicate practical new approaches for dealing with them. The Institute is completely nonpartisan.

The Institute is funded largely by philanthropic foundations. Major institutional grants are now being received from the German Marshall Fund of the United States, which created the Institute with a generous commitment of funds in 1981, and from the Ford Foundation, the William and Flora Hewlett Foundation, the William M. Keck, Jr. Foundation, the Alfred P. Sloan Foundation, the C. V. Starr Foundation, and the United States–Japan Foundation. A number of other foundations and private corporations also contribute to the highly diversified financial resources of the Institute. No funding is received from any government. About 12 percent of total resources in our latest fiscal year were provided by contributors outside the United States, including about 2 percent from Japan.

The Board of Directors bears overall responsibility for the Institute and gives general guidance and approval to its research program—including identification of topics that are likely to become important to international economic policymakers over the medium run (generally, one to three years), and which thus should be addressed by the Institute. The Director, working closely with the staff and outside Advisory Committee, is responsible for the development of particular projects and makes the final decision to publish an individual study.

The Institute hopes that its studies and other activities will contribute to building a stronger foundation for international economic policy around the world. We invite readers of these publications to let us know how they think we can best accomplish this objective.

C. FRED BERGSTEN
Director
November 1991

1

Introduction

Introduction

Paul R. Krugman

In his book on the German hyperinflation of the 1920s, Frank D. Graham (1930/1967) pointed out that since the social sciences cannot perform controlled experiments, we must rely instead on "disorder": variation in the data given us by history. From a scientific point of view, if not otherwise, the disorderly 1980s were an edifying decade. As figure 1 shows, the United States in particular engaged in what amounts to an experiment in the consequences of massive but temporary currency appreciation. The decade's record of huge swings in exchange rates and trade balances gives us the best opportunity ever to sort out competing schools of thought in the economics of international adjustment, and perhaps even to get reasonably solid estimates of some key economic parameters.

This book consists of papers presented at a conference held at the Institute for International Economics in October 1990. The purpose of the conference was to provide an assessment of what the second half of the 1980s taught us about one crucial set of issues: the process of trade adjustment and the role of exchange rates in that adjustment. This paper provides a brief introduction to the subject, laying out a short list of what I regard as the central questions. I would suggest that discussion of the problem of trade adjustment can usefully be characterized under five main themes.

The first theme is the role of real exchange rates in determining the trade account. Traditional econometric approaches to trade take it for granted that trade flows may be regarded as functions of relative prices, among other things, and therefore give some measure of the real exchange rate an important role in the adjustment process. For much of the past decade, however, an influential school of thought has argued that real exchange rate changes are either irrelevant for the trade balance or at any rate unnecessary to change trade balances.

The second theme is the effectiveness of *nominal* exchange rate changes in promoting or facilitating real exchange rate changes. The traditional "elasticities

Paul R. Krugman is a Visiting Fellow at the Institute for International Economics and Professor of Economics at the Massachusetts Institute of Technology.

Figure 1 United States: real exchange rates and current account deficits, 1980–90

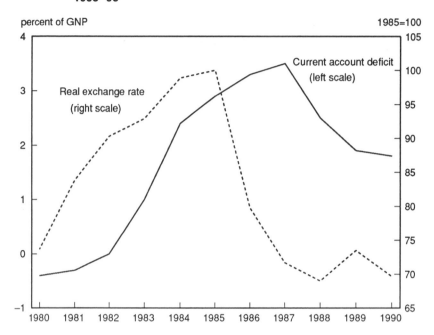

percent of GNP   1985=100

Current account deficit (left scale)

Real exchange rate (right scale)

1980 1981 1982 1983 1984 1985 1986 1987 1988 1989 1990

Sources: International Monetary Fund, *International Financial Statistics,* various issues; Organization for Economic Cooperation and Development, *Main Economic Indicators,* various issues.

approach" took it for granted that currency adjustment shifted relative goods prices. In the 1970s, however, a rallying cry of the "monetary approach" to the balance of payments and exchange rates was the statement that the exchange rate is the relative price of two moneys, *not* of two goods. Yet in the 1980s nominal and real exchange rates moved in striking parallel. Was the old view right, or is there another explanation?

A third theme is the role of dynamic factors in trade adjustment. During the 1980s, a large theoretical and empirical literature arose that essentially proposed or tested for a variety of exotic obstacles to trade adjustment, such as the alleged willingness of Japanese firms to hold dollar prices fixed no matter what the exchange rate, and the phenomenon of "hysteresis," in which market shares once lost during a period of currency overvaluation prove hard to regain. When the US trade deficit and the Japanese surplus remained stubbornly high in the face of a plunging dollar and a soaring yen, exotic stories gained wide currency; now that trade imbalances have narrowed, there is a visible resurgence of plain vanilla trade modeling.

A fourth theme is that of "competitiveness": long-run trends that shift the trade balance for any given (real) exchange rate, or that shift the exchange rate needed to achieve any given trade balance. By the end of the 1980s, the dollar was in real terms roughly back where it started; but the trade deficit, although narrowed sharply from its peak, was not. The yen had meanwhile risen to unprecedented heights, despite which Japan had established a persistent surplus position. Clearly something was going on—but what?

The final theme is very different from the others: How willing are capital markets to finance sustained large current account imbalances among major industrial countries? Here, as in the discussion of trade adjustment, there has been a visible resurgence of plain vanilla thinking. After a period of unusually large current account imbalances, which led to speculation that the newly integrated world economy will no longer operate under the traditional constraints, does the narrowing of these imbalances mean that normalcy has returned?

This introduction is in five parts, corresponding to the five main themes. A final section tries to set some ground rules for debate.

The Role of the Real Exchange Rate

Between February 1985 and January 1988 the prices of goods and services produced in the United States fell by an astonishing amount relative to those produced in other industrial countries—more than 40 percent against Japanese and German goods. Was this fall a necessary precondition for the subsequent decline in the US trade deficit? Or did it represent a gratuitous "fire sale" of US goods (and, in the wave of inward direct investment that followed, of US assets)?

The sides in this debate may be briefly summarized. One side argues that the deficit fell purely and simply because US domestic demand fell relative to US output, freeing resources for export and to replace imports. This is the position that has been argued in particular by Robert A. Mundell (1989) and Ronald I. McKinnon (1984). The other side, while granting that such a fall in domestic demand was necessary, argues that a real depreciation was also necessary, in order to provide the incentive to switch both US and foreign spending onto US products. This is the traditional view (presented, e.g., in Swan 1963 and Johnson 1958), which I suppose I have most aggressively restated (Krugman 1988).

Figure 2 may be a useful way to present the issue. It shows the real exchange rate (by some measure) and the level of domestic spending (real domestic demand) affecting two variables: the trade balance and the overall (domestic and foreign) demand for domestic goods. Other things equal, a real depreciation would tend to reduce the trade deficit and to increase the demand for domestic goods. An increase in real domestic demand would tend to increase both the trade deficit and the demand for domestic goods.

Figure 2   Impact of the exchange rate and domestic demand on the trade balance and demand for domestic goods

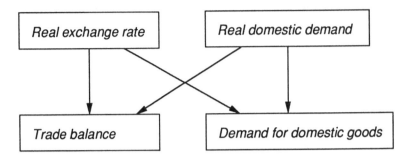

One thing on which all serious discussion agrees is that unless an economy is able to draw unemployed resources into production, a real depreciation by itself cannot achieve a sustained reduction in the trade balance. The reason is that such a depreciation would lead to excess demand for domestic goods, which would have to be corrected somehow, most probably by an inflation that would restore the original real exchange rate.

The real issue, however, is whether a reduction in domestic demand needs to be accompanied by a real depreciation to translate fully into a trade balance improvement. The reason for supposing that it must is immediately apparent from figure 2: other things equal, a reduction in domestic demand will fall in part on domestic rather than imported goods, and thus tend to produce an excess supply of domestic goods. In Harry Johnson's terminology, such expenditure reduction must be accompanied by the "expenditure switching" that a real depreciation can provide.

Why isn't this view universally accepted? I suspect that some analysts have simply forgotten about the market for domestic goods: as economic analysis gets ever more theoretical and mathematical, simple things can get lost. But there is a deeper justification for challenging the need for a real exchange rate change. It runs as follows: when US domestic demand falls, this fall is necessarily accompanied by a corresponding rise in spending abroad. Part of this additional spending abroad will fall on US products, even at unchanged relative prices, so that overall the demand for US products need not fall. Hence the real exchange rate may not need to change. To this the conventionalists reply that world markets for goods and services are just not that well integrated—that even today the marginal propensity of non–US residents to spend on US goods is much less than that of US residents.

We are of course in very honorable company in this argument, whichever side we take, because this is simply a restatement of the debate between John Maynard Keynes and Bertil Ohlin on the German transfer problem after World War

I, with McKinnon as Ohlin and myself as Keynes. There is one difference, however. Germany never really made its transfer, but global payments imbalances have indeed been narrowed. So maybe this time we can really settle the debate (until next time).

Nominal Versus Real Exchange Rate Changes

The 1970s saw the rise of the new classical macroeconomics, which rejected the ad hoc assumption of sticky prices and sought to ground business cycle analysis in a framework of continuously clearing markets. At first, the new classicism was centered around what we may call the Lucas Project (Lucas 1981): an effort to explain how nominal shocks could have real effects in a world of imperfect information. By the mid–1980s, this project had effectively collapsed both as a theoretical effort (introducing capital markets seemed to put too much information into the model) and as an empirical project (too many of the initially supportive results turned out to be highly sensitive to changes in specification and/or data set). Today the new classical economists have turned to real business cycle theory, which holds that real fluctuations have real causes, and that correlations with nominal variables are cases of reversed causation.

In the international sphere, a new classical view would hold that an exchange rate change, as a nominal event, should have no real consequences. In particular, nominal depreciation should be offset by some combination of inflation in the depreciating country and deflation abroad, so that the real exchange rate does not change.

The facts of the 1980s have, of course, run strikingly counter to this presumption (figure 3). To an extent that has surprised even the most Keynesian of Keynesians, nominal exchange rate changes have translated one-for-one into real changes. This observation has potentially serious implications not only for international macroeconomics but for economics in general. Charts like figure 3 have indeed started to become "exhibit A" for the case that prices are sticky after all.

But the new classical economists have not given up. At least among academics, it is popular to argue that the correlation between real and nominal exchange rate changes reflects causation from real to nominal, not the other way around—that central banks try to stabilize domestic price levels while shocks bounce the real exchange rate around, and that a close correlation between the real and nominal rates is the result. (See Stockman 1989 for a notable exposition.)

What have we learned? Is there enough evidence in the experience of the 1980s to refute the new classical view of exchange rates and, by implication, of everything else? Or can the data be effectively explained within a market-clearing model?

Figure 3   United States: nominal and real exchange rates, 1980–90

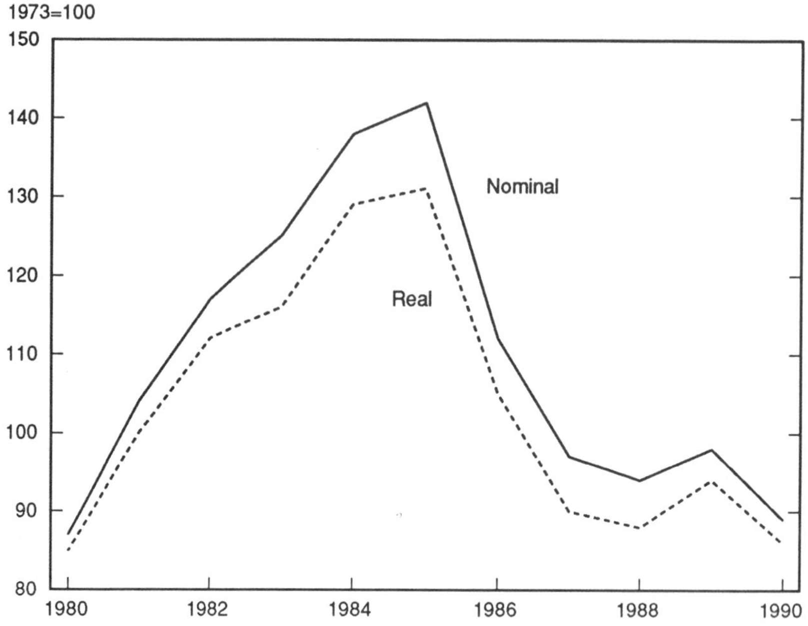

1973=100

Source: International Monetary Fund, *International Financial Statistics,* various issues.

Dynamics of Trade Adjustment

Among those for whom the idea that nominal exchange rate changes alter relative prices poses no problem, there has still been a wave of rethinking of the process of adjustment. In particular, two concepts have attracted a great deal of attention. The first is that of "pricing to market": the alleged tendency of firms to hold prices in foreign currency constant in the face of volatile exchange rates. The second is that of "hysteresis": the alleged difficulty of reversing changes in trade shares once they have happened.

A number of observers noted that during the dollar's rise import prices in the United States fell less than one might have expected. Rudiger Dornbusch (1987) was the first to suggest that this observation might require a new effort to model markets for manufactured goods as imperfectly competitive. As the dollar fell, the mildness of the import price shock (and the failure of the feared Marrisite hard landing to materialize) attracted much more attention, together with extensive empirical work.

Some of these studies appeared to show pricing to market, especially by Japanese firms, to a striking degree. Important questions remain, however.

Above all, there is the worrisome question of the data. There is a growing sense that many of the exotic phenomena of the 1980s had little to do with deep issues of market structure and firm pricing strategy, and a lot to do with two prosaic issues: sharp fluctuation in the prices of raw materials, and dubious price and quantity indices for computers. Some studies, notably Richard C. Marston's work (1989, 1990), seem to be relatively invulnerable to these problems. In general, however, there is the real question of whether we have been taking a kind of international economics Rorschach test, trying to read meaning into random patterns created by the US Commerce Department.

Related to the pricing to market issue is that of hysteresis. The hysteresis story is perhaps better conveyed by the alternative term "beachhead effects": just as it would have required a smaller force to defend Kuwait from invasion than it did to liberate it once invaded, we may need a much weaker dollar to regain the markets lost in the 1980s than we would have needed to hold on to them. The implication of this line of thought is that there may have to be a period of dollar undershooting to make up for the persistent effects of the high dollar of the 1980s. Some initial crude theoretical modeling of this issue by Baldwin and Krugman (1989) was followed by a clever demonstration by Avinash Dixit (1989) that quite modest costs of entry and exit could, when combined with uncertainty about the future exchange rate, make firms very reluctant either to abandon the markets they have or enter markets they were not in.

The question is again whether this is a clever explanation of something that does not need explaining. Some lags in the adjustment of trade to the exchange rate are standard even in traditional analysis; have the events of the 1980s indicated that there are either longer lags than we used to think, or dynamics that go beyond the idea of a simple lag?

Competitiveness

Figure 1 shows that when the dollar went up, the US current account deficit followed with a lag; when the dollar went down, the deficit eventually turned around. But while the dollar went more or less back to where it started, the deficit did not: with US relative prices back to historical levels, we end with a deficit that is 1.5 percent or so of GNP, not the rough balance of a decade ago.

This apparent secular downward trend in the US trade balance associated with any given real exchange rate has its counterparts abroad, especially in Japan. The question is what it means, and what it says about the international adjustment mechanism.

The conventional trade modelers' approach is simply to estimate income elasticities; if the ratio of the income elasticity of export demand to that of import demand is less than that of domestic to foreign growth, a country will need a secular real depreciation to keep trade balanced. This is ultimately an unsatisfactory approach, however: surely one would not have thought *a priori* that Japan's export mix in, say, 1955 consisted of goods with especially high income elasticity of demand. What these apparent income elasticities are surely capturing is something about the supply side of economies, about their ability to open up new export markets.

The question is whether something useful can be said about the sources of secular trends in real exchange rates. At the moment, it seems reasonable to conclude that over the past twenty years there has been an ongoing 1 percent to 2 percent annual decline in the real dollar consistent with any given trade balance, and a similar upward trend of 2 percent to 3 percent per year in the real yen. Presumably these trends are ultimately traceable to the broader issues of "competitiveness" in terms of technology, productivity, and all that. But can we model the linkage between commonsensical notions of competitiveness and the trade balance? And will these trends continue?

World Capital Markets and Current Account Financing

During the postwar period up through about 1980, large current account imbalances on the part of industrial nations were rare and short-lived. In their famous, much maligned paper, Feldstein and Horioka (1980) essentially argued from this observation that international capital markets are not well integrated in terms of their willingness to transfer resources on a sustained basis, however well linked short-term securities markets may appear to be.

Then came the 1980s. For a time current account imbalances among industrial nations ballooned, with no apparent qualms on the part of the markets. There was a growing belief among economists that this marked a new era in capital mobility, perhaps even a return to the pre–World War I world of massive capital flows for decades on end. The surge in foreign direct investment after 1985 reinforced the view that something fundamental had changed.

But now the current accounts have converged again (figure 4). Are we still in the Feldstein-Horioka world, with the mid–1980s an aberration?

Summary Thoughts

In 1970, economists had a fairly straightforward view about how international adjustment worked. Trade flows depended on relative prices and incomes; depreciation lowered the relative price of a country's goods; there were moderate lags leading to a J-curve, but in the medium term depreciation would move trade toward surplus. Underlying this view was a geared-up Keynesian macroeco-

Figure 4 Current account balances in the G-3 countries, by quarter, 1985–90

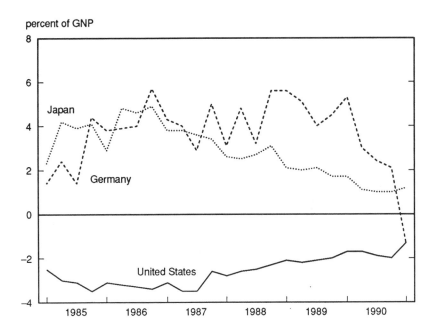

percent of GNP

Source: Organization for Economic Cooperation and Development, *Main Economic Indicators,* various issues.

nomic model, in which changes in nominal variables like the exchange rate had real effects because of sticky prices.

By 1980, this view was largely discredited, at least among academics. Rightly or wrongly, stagflation was taken to have refuted the Keynesian model. Equilibrium models were in fashion; the conventional wisdom on international adjustment was widely viewed as sheer nonsense because of its lack of microeconomic foundations.

Now we have experienced a great, if unintended, experiment. And the old conventional wisdom looks pretty good. On the face of it, the great surprise of international adjustment in the 1980s was that there were so few surprises. Once we clean up the data, it seems possible to argue that trade flows have responded to exchange rates in just about the way that an economist who had avoided listening to any new ideas between 1970 and 1980 would have expected.

Let me therefore suggest that the central theme of this conference is, in effect, whether the international adjustment experience of the 1980s should make us comfortable with a good old-fashioned income-and-price-elasticity view of international trade—and with old-fashioned ad hoc Keynesianism.

References

Baldwin, Richard, and Paul R. Krugman. 1989. "Persistent Trade Effects of Large Exchange Rate Shocks." *Quarterly Journal of Economics* 104, no. 4 (November):635–54.

Dixit, A. 1989. "Hysteresis, Import Penetration, and Exchange-Rate Pass-Through." *Quarterly Journal of Economics* 104:205–28.

Dornbusch, Rudiger. 1987. "Exchange Rates and Prices." *American Economic Review* 77:93–106.

Feldstein, M., and C. Horioka. 1980. "Domestic Saving and International Capital Flows." *Economic Journal* 90:314–29.

Graham, Frank D. 1930. *Exchange, Prices, and Production in Hyper-Inflation: Germany, 1920–1923.* (Reprinted 1967 New York: Russell and Russell.)

Johnson, Harry. 1958. "Toward a General Theory of the Balance of Payments." In *International Trade and Economic Growth: Studies in Pure Theory.* London: George Allen and Unwin.

Krugman, Paul R. 1988. *Exchange-Rate Instability.* Cambridge, MA: MIT Press.

Lawrence, R. 1990. "US Current Account Adjustment: An Appraisal." *Brookings Papers on Economic Activity* 2:343–82.

Lucas, Robert E., Jr. 1981. *Studies in Business Cycle Theory.* Cambridge, MA: MIT Press.

Marston, R. 1989. "Pricing to Market in Japanese Manufacturing." *NBER Working Paper* 2905. Cambridge, MA: National Bureau of Economic Research (March).

Marston, R. 1990. "Price Behavior in Japanese and US Manufacturing." Philadelphia: Wharton School (mimeographed).

McKinnon, Ronald I. 1984. *An International Standard for Monetary Stabilization.* POLICY ANALYSES IN INTERNATIONAL ECONOMICS 8. Washington: Institute for International Economics.

Mundell, Robert A. 1989. "The Global Adjustment System." *Rivista di Economica Politica* (December): 351–466.

Stockman, A. 1988. "Real Exchange Rate Variability Under Pegged and Floating Nominal Exchange-Rate Systems: An Equilibrium Theory." *Carnegie-Rochester Conference Series on Public Policy* 29:259–94.

Swan, T.W. 1963. "Longer-Run Problems of the Balance of Payments." In H.W. Arndt and W. M. Corden, eds., *The Australian Economy.* Melbourne: Cheshire.

2

The United States

The United States

US External Adjustment: Progress, Prognosis, and Interpretation

William R. Cline

The Plaza Agreement of September 1985 established a policy of reducing the value of the dollar to achieve a correction of the large US external deficit. By now, many in the American public, Congress, and even academia have concluded that this process has failed. In the words of the *Washington Post*:

> The dollar has been dropping for five years, and the trade deficit is hardly lower now than it was then. It doesn't look as though a lower dollar is going to bring American trade into balance.[1]

Frustration with the exchange rate approach to external adjustment could eventually induce Congress to take protectionist measures to deal with the trade deficit, especially in the face of higher unemployment. Already many analysts have concluded that the United States must have an underlying problem of declining industrial competitiveness and call for industrial policy and even managed trade.

This paper first examines the extent of US external adjustment to date and considers whether the observed performance is consistent with what the econometric models had predicted. The answer is in the affirmative: there should be no great surprise that the external accounts stand where they do. The analysis

---

1. *Washington Post,* 11 October 1990.

William R. Cline is a Senior Fellow at the Institute for International Economics. He was formerly Senior Fellow at the Brookings Institution and Deputy Director for Development and Trade Research at the US Treasury.

Table 1   United States: changes in trade and the exchange rate of the dollar, 1978–89[a] (percentages)

	1980–87	1987–89
Real effective exchange rate[b]	5.0	− 12.0
Exports		
Total	1.6	20.0
Nonagricultural	2.1	20.0
Imports		
Total	5.7	7.7
Agricultural	10.5	7.5

a. Annual averages.

b. With a two-year lead (i.e., 1978 figure for 1980 and 1985 for 1987), unit volume of equal deflation.

Source: International Monetary Fund, *International Financial Statistics,* various issues.

then examines the prospects for the period 1990–95. It finds that whereas the previous outlook had been for the external deficit to follow a U-shaped curve and become larger once again after 1990, the renewed decline of the dollar in 1990 and the slide of the US economy into zero or even negative growth alter that prospect, and instead leave a horizon of a flat current account deficit that decreases gradually as a percentage of GNP.

The paper then addresses certain theoretical issues, especially the roles of the real exchange rate and the saving-investment identity. It considers the implications of prospective US action on the fiscal deficit, and concludes with brief observations on the financial markets.

Has Adjustment Occurred?

Even the most cursory look at the US external accounts makes it obvious that some, indeed considerable, adjustment has taken place following the decline in the dollar. Table 1 shows the annual growth rates of nominal trade values and the real value of the dollar during the overvaluation period in the first part of the 1980s and then during the period of initial correction. The exchange rate measure whose course is depicted here is the International Monetary Fund's real effective exchange rate index of the dollar against the currencies of 16 industrial countries, deflating by export unit values (discussed below). Its period is set with a two-year lead for comparison with the trade data, as most models indicate a response period of this magnitude from exchange rate change to trade change.

From 1978 to 1985 the real value of the dollar rose 48 percent, for an average annual increase of 5 percent. During the corresponding trade period of 1980 to 1987, US nonagricultural exports rose at an anemic 2.1 percent annual (nominal) rate, whereas nonoil imports rose at a rapid 10.5 percent. Then, in the second phase, the real value of the dollar declined by 20 percent from 1985 to 1987. The trade consequences were an explosion of US export values, which rose at an annual rate of 20 percent during 1987–89, and a moderation of (nonoil) US import growth rates to 7.5 percent annually.[2]

The "bottom line" of the US external accounts also showed improvement. The trade deficit rose from $25 billion in 1980 to $160 billion in 1987, and then declined to $115 billion in 1989. The current account moved from a surplus of $1 billion in 1980 to a deficit of $162 billion in 1987, and then fell to $110 billion by 1989.[3] Relative to total production, the current account deficit fell from a peak of 3.6 percent of GNP in 1987 to 2.1 percent in 1989.

The persistence of an external deficit despite the impressive reversals in export and import growth rates reflected the enormous "gap factor" that had developed by 1987. By then, imports had risen to a level 64 percent above exports, whereas the gap had been only 11 percent in 1980. If import and export growth rates had remained unchanged in 1987–89 at their 1980–87 rates, by 1989 the trade deficit would have reached almost $300 billion.[4] In short, there has been far more progress on external adjustment than meets the naked eye; without the decline in the dollar, the deficit would have risen far beyond its peak of $160 billion in 1987.

How Much Adjustment?

There should be little doubt that some adjustment has taken place. A more subtle question is whether the amount of adjustment that has occurred has been as much as economists, particularly the model builders, expected.

---

2. The much greater response on the export side than for imports was in keeping with the typical empirical finding of near-unity price elasticity of import demand, such that for imports the rise in prices offsets the decline in volume.

3. *Survey of Current Business*, June 1990, 77.

4. From their 1987 base, at 1.6 percent annual growth (table 1) exports would have risen to $258 billion. At their 10.5 percent growth rate, nonoil imports would have expanded to $500 billion. Adding the actual figure for oil imports in 1989, the trade deficit would have stood at $293 billion. More formally, simulation of the HHC model (described below) estimated that if the real value of the dollar had stayed at its level of the first quarter of 1985, the current account deficit would have reached $339 billion by 1990 (Cline 1989b, 111).

Stylized Facts

Paul R. Krugman's overview paper for this volume (chapter 1) postulates what is becoming a stylized paradox: "If the dollar is back to its 1980 level, why isn't the trade balance?" His figure 1 shows a close fit between the trade deficit (nonoil imports, nonagricultural exports) as a percentage of GNP and the real exchange rate when both were rising, from 1980 to 1985, but a much weaker response of the trade deficit to the dollar during the currency's subsequent decline. Krugman alludes to the Houthakker-Magee asymmetry between the income elasticities of imports (higher) and exports (lower) as an explanation, but he considers it unsatisfactory because it does not reflect meaningful product elasticity differences, and he suggests that shifting supply is responsible instead.[5] He concludes merely that there seems to be a systematic decline in US competitiveness that requires a secular real depreciation of the dollar by 1 percent to 2 percent annually to hold the trade deficit constant relative to GNP. He suggests a corresponding secular appreciation of 3 percent to 4 percent annually for the yen.

Before writing this stylized fact into concrete, it is worth taking another look at the data. In the same spirit as Krugman's, figure 1 below reports the ratio of nonoil imports to nonagricultural exports for the United States from 1980 to 1990. It also shows the IMF's export unit value–deflated real effective exchange rate index for the United States. The exchange rate index has a lead of two years (i.e., the period covered is 1978 to 1988) in the figure, so that the trade year corresponds to the period when the causal exchange rate signal was emitted.

The figure shows a much closer adherence between the real exchange rate and trade performance in the correction phase of the cycle (after 1987) than does the Krugman diagram. In part this improvement is simply due to allowance for the two-year lag. More importantly, however, *the IMF export unit value–deflated index does not show the dollar back at its 1980 level by 1988 (or 1989)*. Instead, with 1978 = 100 (and 1980 = 101.8), by 1988 the real exchange rate was only back to 115.2, or 15 percent above the base (and in 1989 it rose again to 117.7).[6]

This challenge to the by-now nearly conventional wisdom that the dollar has returned whence it started is given support in figure 2. This figure plots four alternative IMF real effective exchange rate measures for the dollar: the deflators are the unit value of (manufactured) exports, the normalized unit labor cost of manufactures, the wholesale price index, and the consumer price index. It is

---

5. Krugman could add as evidence his own earlier finding of the "45-degree-line rule": countries with faster growth tend to have a higher ratio of export demand elasticities to import demand elasticities. Korea and Taiwan are cases in point. The measured elasticities are thus almost certainly capturing supply-shift phenomena rather than meaningful differences in foreign demand for the type of products exported by each country.

6. Calculated from IMF, *International Financial Statistics Yearbook* 1990, 111.

Figure 1 United States: real effective exchange rates and ratio of nonoil imports to nonagricultural exports, 1978–90

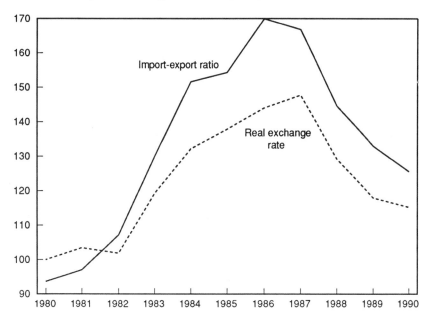

Note: The exchange rate measure is the International Monetary Fund's multilateral effective index for the United States deflated by unit value of exports; it is plotted with a two-year lead (1978 = 100). The import-export ratio is that for nonoil US imports and nonagricultural US exports and is given in percentages. The estimate for 1990 is based on trend from data for the first seven months.

evident that the export price deflator shows much less correction of the dollar than do the wholesale and consumer price–deflated series. The unit labor cost measure hints that these series may overstate the dollar's real decline, although it too shows more decline than the export price–deflated series.

Of the four series, the most directly relevant for trade is the unit value of manufactured exports. The other measures encompass the domestic economy, whereas the unit value deflator refers explicitly to trade. There is of course the issue of whether the unit value deflator based on trading partners' exports accurately reflects their pricing in the US market, as it has been argued that firms in partner countries discriminate in their marketing. However, if such discrimination had occurred, the unit value deflator index shown in figure 2 would *overstate* the decline of the dollar (by overstating the rise of trading-partner prices of goods sold in the US market).

The discrepancy of 15 percent in the real dollar indices has enormous implications. My models indicate that a 1 percent change in the real exchange rate

Figure 2 United States: real effective exchange rates calculated using alternative deflators, 1978–89

1978=100

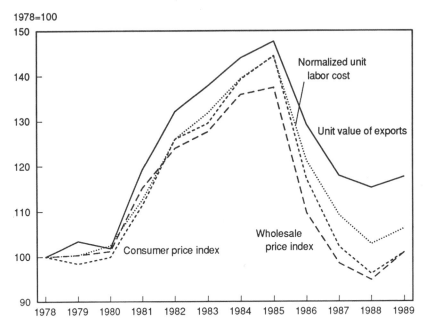

Source: International Financial Statistics, various issues.

changes the trade balance by $5 billion to $7½ billion.[7] On this basis, if the real dollar remains 15 percent or so above its 1978–80 level, a return to that level would largely eliminate the trade deficit (estimated below at $112 billion for 1990).

Conceptually, the export price (or unit value) index, rather than the wholesale price index, is the proper one to use for evaluating the real exchange rate.[8] There can be a systematic difference in productivity growth between export industries

---

7. Cline (1989b, 209). If the decline is just against the currencies of the industrial countries plus Korea and Taiwan, the range is $4½ billion to $6½ billion per percentage point change in the exchange rate.

8. The IMF notes that, because goods that can no longer compete as the exchange rate rises will drop out of the export basket, and goods actually exported must retain a certain adherence to international prices, the unit value export price may not fully capture competitiveness trends. However, by this argument the unit export value–deflated real exchange rate should have lagged well behind the rise of the index based on wholesale prices when the dollar rose; as indicated in figure 1, it did not do so, suggesting that this consideration is not dominant.

Figure 3   United States and Japan: ratio of export unit value index to wholesale price index, 1978–89

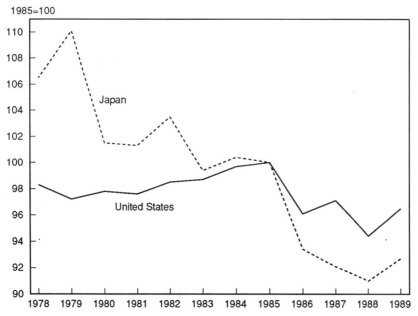

Source: International Financial Statistics, various issues.

and those producing for the home market. Figure 3 shows, for example, that the ratio of the export unit value index to the domestic wholesale price index for Japan has persistently declined over the past decade, while that for the United States has remained relatively unchanged.

Unfortunately for researchers, the index of relative export prices for manufactures constructed by the Organization for Economic Cooperation and Development (OECD) shows just the opposite of the IMF index. By 1988, US manufactured export prices relative to those of 23 OECD and 6 developing countries stood more than 10 percent below their 1980 level on the OECD measure.[9] It seems unlikely that the difference between the IMF series (which is for exchange rates against those of 16 other industrialized countries) and the OECD series can be accounted for by the broader country composition of the latter. Until the two organizations resolve their differences, the discussion here should be interpreted as raising doubt about the stylized fact of a complete return of the dollar to 1980 levels, rather than refuting it. Krugman's Rorschach sample remains clouded.

---

9. *OECD Economic Outlook*, June 1990, 146.

Even with incomplete reversal of the dollar, there is probably still some room for the Houthakker-Magee phenomenon in explaining the incomplete reversal of the US external deficit. My External Adjustment with Growth (EAG) model estimated the weighted-average income elasticity of US imports at 2.4, and that of exports at 1.7; the difference would provoke an annual erosion of some $8 billion in the trade balance with US and foreign growth both at 3 percent (Cline 1989b, 153). I agree with Krugman (and Helkie-Hooper) that supply-side shifts are more likely to be the cause of this phenomenon than underlying differences in income elasticities of demand. In my projections, I applied a weighted average of country-specific elasticities and global average elasticities; this reduced the US asymmetry to an income elasticity of 2.2 for imports and 1.85 for exports. With the corresponding annual trade erosion for equal domestic and foreign growth cut to $4 billion, it would require annual real dollar depreciation of ⅔ percent to neutralize the adverse trend (versus Krugman's 1 percent to 2 percent annually).[10]

Especially if the elasticities are asymmetrical, but even if they are not, consideration of the activity variable in the trade equation helps explain US trade erosion in the 1980s, when relative US growth accelerated. During the period 1971–80, real GNP grew more slowly in the United States than in other industrial countries, at 2.8 percent versus 3.4 percent (annual averages), respectively. In contrast, from 1981 through 1989, US growth was slightly faster than that in other industrial countries (annual averages of 2.9 percent and 2.8 percent, respectively).[11]

Tracking the Models

The summary concepts reviewed above can provide only an overall guide as to whether the trade accounts have behaved as might have been expected. A more complete test requires comparison of the actual results in 1989 and 1990 with the trade forecasts. The impression is widespread that the models were seriously in error in projecting the response of the external accounts to the dollar. Ironically, besides the general impression among the informed public that the econo-

---

10. In the other model I applied, based on the Helkie-Hooper model, there is no Houthakker-Magee elasticity asymmetry. Helkie and Hooper estimated an equation with a term for relative capital stock, which removed the difference in the income elasticities. However, in principle it is necessary to project future differences in the rate of capital formation, and if the foreign rate remains above that of the United States, an adverse trend in the external balance will persist despite similar income elasticities on the export and import sides.

11. Calculated from IMF, *World Economic Outlook*, October 1989, 74, and October 1990. The calculations apply 1980 GNP weights.

mists' models overpredicted the adjustment (as discussed above), the opposite critique has been heard as well. Thus, at least through mid–1989 the US Treasury Department's semiannual reports to the Congress on the external sector argued that the conventional models were too pessimistic because they allowed neither for "increased efficiency" of US manufacturing following "intense competitive pressure" during the period of dollar strength, nor for the favorable trade shifts to be expected from direct investment.[12]

Marris

One of the earliest and best-known studies of the problem of the US external deficit was that by my colleague Stephen Marris. His model for the US external accounts was based on relatively standard trade equations driven by US and foreign growth and relative trade prices as influenced by the real exchange rate. Figure 4 reproduces the fan diagram Marris used to project the US current account deficit under alternative assumptions about the decline of the dollar (Marris 1987, 107). The figure shows alternative average annual rates of decline in the real dollar exchange rate for a 3½-year period beginning in the fourth quarter of 1985.

The rib of the fan closest to actual developments is the one with an annual decline of 12 percent and a total decline of 32 percent.[13] Interpolating for the actual decline (slightly less than this rib), Marris's prediction for the 1989 current account deficit would have been $80 billion (the vertical axis intercept of the superimposed grid). At least in qualitative terms, that predicted outcome was relatively close to the actual result of a deficit of $110 billion; Marris correctly foresaw the persistence of a large deficit despite a major depreciation. Marris stressed that the adverse initial trade gap factor would require a very large depreciation to achieve an eventual elimination of the current account deficit.

---

12. US Department of Treasury, *Report to the Congress on International Economic and Exchange Rate Policy,* April 1989. However, by October 1989 the Treasury had become less optimistic, as it concluded that "On balance, it would appear that further improvement in the US current account position in 1990, if any is to occur at all, is likely at best to be very modest." US Department of Treasury, *Report to the Congress on International Economic and Exchange Rate Policy,* October 1989, 14.

13. With 1985 = 100, the MERM (multilateral exchange rate model) effective exchange rate index of the IMF showed an average of 103.6 for the baseline used by Marris (fourth quarter 1984 to first quarter 1985). For 1989 the index stood at 71, indicating a cumulative depreciation of 31.5 percent.

Figure 4 Marris in retrospect: time profile of the US current account balance under alternative exchange rate assumptions, 1984–92

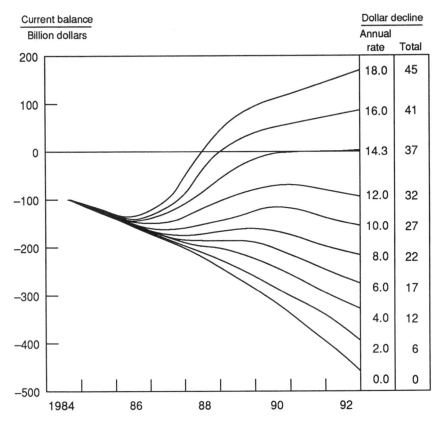

Note: Simulation of D&D model using baseline growth and inflation assumptions. Dollar declines at constant rate from 1985:3 to 1989:1 form its 1984:4–1985:1 baseline. On October 31, 1985, the dollar was 11.4 percent below this baseline. Dollar measure by IMF index.

Source: Marris, Stephen. 1987. *Deficits and the Dollar: The World Economy at Risk,* rev. ed. POLICY ANALYSES IN INTERNATIONAL ECONOMICS 14. Washington: Institute for International Economics, 107.

Brookings Survey

Like Marris, other trade modelers came to the conclusion that in the absence of much more significant depreciation the US current account deficit would plateau at a high level of over $100 billion and then begin to widen once again. Five major macroeconomic models surveyed by Ralph C. Bryant at the Brookings

Institution estimated that, with the dollar unchanged in real terms from its level of 22 December 1987, the US current account deficit would decline to $125 billion in 1988 and $108 billion in 1989, but then rise again to $113 billion in 1990 and $127 billion by 1991 (Bryant 1988, table 3). The actual outcome in 1989 was extremely close to the projection, and if the current account deficit proves to be lower than the estimate for 1990, the divergence should easily be explained by lower-than-expected US growth.[14]

EAG and HHC Models

In early 1989 I published projections of the US external accounts based on the assumption that the real exchange rate would remain constant at its level of the fourth quarter of 1987 (Cline 1989a, b). The central finding of my analysis was that US external adjustment was far from complete, and that under base-case growth rates (assumed at 2½ percent for the United States), the US current account deficit would not fall below $115 billion and by 1992 would be back up to the range of $155 billion. The study called for US fiscal correction and further dollar depreciation, configured heavily toward realignment relative to the deutsche mark and the yen, so that the corresponding foreign adjustment would be well distributed. The analysis showed that otherwise large German and Japanese surpluses would persist and widen, not only in the baseline but also if the dollar depreciated simply proportionately against all foreign currencies, with no beyond-proportional movement against the mark or the yen.

The analysis applied two alternative models. The first, the EAG (External Adjustment with Growth) model, was a multicountry model dividing the world into 17 major countries and regions. Equations were estimated for the trade of each country (or region) with each other country (or region). US exports to a given trading partner depended on the price of the US export (unit value) relative to the price of the partner's competing domestic good (wholesale price index); the US export price relative to that of competing third countries (export unit value); and the real growth rate in the importing country (activity variable). US imports were estimated similarly but from the standpoint of each trading partner's exports to the US market. The model provided special treatment of oil trade, considering OPEC as a separate region as well as "UK oil" and "Mexico oil" as

---

14. The Brookings group assumed US growth of 3 percent. Actual growth was 3.5 percent in 1988, but only 1.8 percent in 1989. It is likely to reach only 1.5 percent in 1990. One year-percentage-point cut in growth reduced the current account deficit by $8 billion in the models surveyed by Brookings. On this basis, with a 2.2-percentage-point cumulative shortfall in growth, the 1990 current account based on these models would have been expected to stand at about $95 billion in 1990 (113—[8 x 2.2] = 95).

separate "countries." Proportionate relationships of nonfactor to merchandise trade, and the assumption of a simple 7 percent nominal return applied to cumulative current account deficits after 1988, translated the trade projections into current account estimates.

The second model (HHC) was an adaptation of the Helkie-Hooper model of the US current account, developed at the Federal Reserve Board. The adaptation simplified the agricultural and oil equations and imposed an adjustment to trade prices that set them halfway between the observed and the predicted levels for the fourth quarter of 1987.

For purposes of evaluating the performance of the EAG and the HHC models for the period 1988–90 the prospective "actual" outcome for 1990 can be estimated as follows: Exports rise by 7.4 percent, based on levels in the first seven months compared with those in the same period of 1989. Nonoil imports rise by 2.2 percent, based on an actual increase of 1.3 percent in the first quarter over the first quarter of 1989 (balance of payments basis), 1.5 percent in the second (customs basis), and an assumed 3 percent in the second half. The recovery to a still-weak 3 percent rate is based on the actual outcome for April to July (3.1 percent, customs basis) and the J-curve effect from a falling dollar. Overall, of course, 1990 nonoil imports are extremely weak (and probably will decline in real terms), a reflection of the slide of the economy toward recession.

Oil imports for 1990 are based on actual data for the first seven months, plus spot market oil prices with a one-month lag (the pattern that most closely relates average oil trade prices to spot prices for monthly data for the last three years) for the final five months.[15] For the year, oil imports surge from $50.9 billion in 1989 to $64.9 billion, or by 28 percent.

Data for nonfactor services are actual data for the first half; it is assumed that they continue their ratios to merchandise exports and imports, respectively, during the second. Factor services showed a surplus of $1.4 billion in the first half. However, the projection for 1990 arbitrarily imposes a deficit of $5 billion for the year, on the grounds that a surplus or even zero balance is inconsistent with the cumulating current account deficit. As discussed below, factor services pose one of the largest puzzles for the outlook over the medium term.[16]

---

15. August oil imports are assumed equal to those for July. Average oil prices are then $25 per barrel for trade in September, $33 in October, and an assumed $30 in November and December.

16. In the event, the 1990 outcome showed a $5 billion surplus on factor services rather than a deficit. Nonfactor service exports were $7 billion higher than projected here. As all the other projections were very close to the actual results, these two categories accounted for the bulk of the divergence between the $113 billion deficit anticipated in table 2 and the final outcome of only $92 billion (US Department of Commerce, "Summary of US International Transactions: First Quarter 1991," BEA 91-26, 11 June 1991).

The projected external accounts using the EAG and the HHC models, and applying actual growth rates and exchange rates during the period from 1988 to the third quarter of 1990, are shown in table 2. The two models moderately overstate the current account deficit in 1988, lie on either side of the actual outcome in 1989, and moderately overstate the deficit in 1990. The EAG model comes extremely close to the actual outcome, as its cumulative current account deficit for the three years is $353 billion compared with $352 billion in the actual results.

For the components of the external accounts, the EAG model tracks both exports and imports well. It tends to understate the levels of nonfactor services, but slightly overstates their surplus. The model strays the furthest on factor services, where its deficit of $27 billion for 1990 is far off the mark. Moderate overstatement of the trade and nonfactor service surpluses brings the model's current account balance close to the actual.

The HHC model shows a serious upward bias in the nominal values of both exports and imports, but fortuitously the resulting nominal trade deficit is not far from the actual one. The model also substantially understates both the level of nonfactor services and their resulting balance. The model does a much better job than the EAG model, however, in predicting how small the factor services deficit remains despite rapid cumulation of external deficits (and by implication external debt).

The difficulties in the HHC values for trade stem in part from the use of consumer prices for foreign price indicators, but more importantly from the bias incorporated in the US balance of payments measures of trade because of the questionable deflator for computers (see Cline 1989b, 85–86; Lawrence 1990; Meade, cited in Lawrence 1990). That something is seriously wrong with the Bureau of Economic Analysis (or BEA) estimates is evident from a simple examination of estimates of trade at constant values. According to the estimates, the average price of nonoil imports rose by only 6.5 percent from 1982 to 1989, and the average price of nonagricultural exports actually declined by 6 percent.[17] The BEA data thus show much larger volume increases and smaller price increases than are likely to have occurred.

The main culprit is computers. The BEA index treats their computing capacity (e.g., in millions of instructions per second, or MIPS) as their real output. As MIPS have risen far more rapidly than the value of computer sales, the result is a falling price index for computers.[18] This treatment affects both imports and

---

17. Calculated from *Survey of Current Business*, July 1990, 69, table E.

18. The "truth" would seem likely to show a lesser quantity increase and a higher price increase. Essentially, for the tasks users have at hand, the excess capacity of the typical microcomputer (for example) has risen sharply, and it is utilized capacity rather than total capacity that is relevant for the market value.

Table 2 United States: external accounts, 1988–90 (billions of dollars)

Account	1988	1989	1990[a]
Total merchandise exports			
EAG	306.2	361.1	396.0
HHC	336.8	397.7	427.2
Actual	320.3	360.5	387.0
Nonagricultural exports			
HHC	307.7	366.5	393.7
Actual	282.1	319.0	
Total merchandise imports			
EAG	430.9	450.3	498.0
HHC	473.6	511.9	545.9
Actual	447.3	475.3	498.7
Nonoil imports			
HHC	435.0	461.0	481.0
Actual	407.7	424.4	433.8
Trade balance			
EAG	− 124.7	− 89.2	− 101.9
HHC	− 136.8	− 114.2	− 118.7
Actual	− 127.0	− 114.9	− 111.7
Nonfactor services exports			
EAG	87.7	103.5	113.5
HHC	71.9	75.6	79.0
Actual	103.1	115.2	126.5
Nonfactor services imports			
EAG	75.8	79.2	87.6
HHC	78.1	86.0	92.4
Actual	91.5	94.7	105.2
Factor services income			
HHC	100.6	98.6	113.3
Actual	110.0	127.5	125.0
Factor services payments			
HHC	104.5	113.3	121.1
Actual	108.4	128.4	130.0
Factor services balance			
EAG	− 10.0	− 19.5	− 27.2
HHC	− 3.9	− 14.8	− 7.8
Actual	1.6	− 0.9	− 5.0

Account	1988	1989	1990[a]
Current account balance			
EAG	− 136.6	− 98.8	− 118.0
HHC	− 147.5	− 132.2	− 127.3
Actual	− 128.9	− 110.0	− 112.8[b]

a. Data for 1990 are trend estimates based on trade data for the first seven months (six months for services), and assuming an average oil price of $30 per barrel in the last four months. The factor services balance is arbitrarily set at a $5 billion deficit for the year.

b. The International Monetary Fund projects the 1990 current account deficit at $97 billion.

Source: Actual data from US Department of Commerce, "Summary of U.S. International Transactions," various issues.

exports, and the importance of computers has been rising in both. Lawrence shows that when computers are removed, nonoil import and nonagricultural export prices behave much more as expected.

With trade volumes calibrated to the BEA base, and trade price equations sensibly linked to foreign and US wholesale prices, the HHC model ends up close to the mark for quantities but substantially overstates prices as against the (doubtful) BEA benchmark. The result is an overstatement of nominal values predicted for both exports and imports. As Lawrence notes, however, the damage, at least on the import side, is limited by the fact that the price elasticity is near unity, so an overstated rise in the price (relative to BEA) is offset by an understated decline in volume (relative to BEA).

The EAG model is free of the computer price problem, because it employs only unit values of exports and wholesale prices—not the BEA price indices used in the national accounts and the calculation of real balance of payments trade series. Sometimes the Rorschach sample data base breaks your way.

Lawrence

Robert Z. Lawrence (1990) has also recently examined the question of whether US external adjustment has been consistent with what would have been expected from the economic models. He emphasizes the distortion caused by the computer price problem. Estimating trade equations excluding computers, he finds that US trade behavior has been closely on track with what would have been predicted from equations estimated during the period 1976–84. His results confirm the conclusion that there is no major surprise in the path of the US external accounts through 1990 (with the possible exception of factor services).

Lawrence's estimates do revive the nagging question of the Houthakker-Magee asymmetry. His activity elasticity for US imports is 2.77, whereas that for US exports is only 1.53. Moreover, his "foreign" activity is that for the rest of the OECD only (ROECD). Activity in ROECD would have to grow at 4.5 percent annually for the United States to be able to avoid trade deterioration in the face of 2½ percent domestic growth (even with exports initially at equilibrium with imports). As only Japan is likely to grow at such a high rate, Lawrence's results are essentially pessimistic. For the reasons discussed above, it would seem at least premature to conclude that there is such an adverse structural bias to US trade elasticities.

Changing the Outlook

Conventional models can thus explain what has happened to date, at least if they avoid (or are corrected for) the computer pricing problem. For policy purposes, it is important to consider what the models say about the future outlook for the US external accounts.

Table 3 reports projections of the EAG model and a revised version of the HHC model (HHCR) for the period 1991–95. The HHCR estimates apply adjustment scalars to exports, nonoil imports, and nonfactor services equal to the respective ratios of actual to model-estimated values in the period 1988–89. These adjustments shrink the nominal values predicted for imports and exports. Similar adjustment factors are applied to the implicit rates of return on domestic and foreign assets.[19]

The projections through 1995 assume that the real exchange rate remains at its level of 15 August 1990, except for the yen-dollar rate, which is frozen at its real level at the end of September to incorporate the yen's further appreciation.

---

19. As there would appear to be a significant bias in the longer-term projections of the HHC model toward overstatement of capital service earnings relative to payments, further corrections are added. The model estimates of the asset and liability positions are replaced by actual levels for the 1987–89 base period. Exogenous projections are made for the stocks of direct investment and for foreign holdings of US government liabilities, at 7 percent nominal growth by 1993 and after but trending down from 17 percent for foreign direct investment in the United States and 10 percent for US direct investment abroad in 1990. The positions of private assets and liabilities are determined residually by allocating one-third of the current account deficit to reduction of US portfolio assets abroad and two-thirds to buildup of foreign portfolio holdings in the United States. Furthermore, the high model-based rate of return on direct investment (for example, 17.4 percent in 1991 even after application of the 1988–89–based adjustment factor) are assumed to continue only for the stock of direct investment through the end of 1992. Incremental real direct investment stock thereafter is assumed to have a return of only 10 percent. The adjustment reflects the fact that the high apparent rate of return stems largely from low, historically based estimates of the existing capital stock.

Real GNP growth rates are projected on the basis of the IMF's October 1990 *World Economic Outlook* estimates for 1990 and 1991. For the United States, however, actual growth is applied for the first half of 1990, and *zero growth is assumed for the second half*, followed by weak recovery in 1991 (1½ percent growth). US growth is assumed to rebound to 3½ percent in 1992 and then plateau at 2½ percent. For 1992–95, growth is assumed to average 3½ percent in Germany (from the stimulus of reunification), 3 percent in France and Italy, 2½ percent in the United Kingdom, 4 percent in Japan, and 2½ percent in Canada. Otherwise growth rates are as originally projected for 1990–92 in Cline (1989b). The price of oil is assumed to moderate to $25 per barrel in 1991 and remain flat in nominal terms.

Table 3 reports the revised projections as well as my earlier projections. The first panel repeats the baseline forecasts of my 1989 study, which were essentially a 1988 outlook assuming the dollar would remain unchanged at fourth-quarter 1987 levels. The estimates showed the adverse U-shaped curve typical of the conventional models, with the average of the HHC and the EAG models' predictions showing the current account rising again to $153 billion by 1992.

The center panel of table 3 reports projections made in June 1989 on the basis of the "strong dollar" path of actual exchange rates through that period (Cline 1989c). Those projections assumed continued US GNP growth at 2½ percent and assumed that the dollar would remain at its real level of May 1989. It is evident that the higher value of the dollar at that time than in the fourth quarter of 1987 meant potentially a serious additional deterioration in the external accounts from the original projections. Both models showed that under the strong dollar scenario the current account deficit could reach over $190 billion by 1992.

The third panel of the table provides greater detail on the five-year outlook as of October 1990. The striking change is that both the EAG and the HHCR models show the current account stabilizing in the range of $100 billion deficits "as far as the eye can see." The downgrading of the US growth rate for 1990–91 amounts to 2 percentage-point-years loss relative to the earlier baseline of steady 2½ percent growth. Each percentage-point-year of lost growth cuts approximately $15 billion off of the US current account deficit (Cline 1989b, 209), so the change provides an improvement of about $30 billion from the deficit in the old baseline.

The rest of the gain is from the real depreciation of the dollar. From the fourth quarter of 1987 to the second quarter of 1989, the real value of the dollar rose 11.3 percent against the currencies of the other G-7 countries on a multilateral trade-weighted basis, and by 4.6 percent on a US–bilateral basis (deflating by wholesale prices). Then, by the third quarter of 1990, the real value of the dollar had fallen from its fourth-quarter 1987 base by 7.3 percent on a multilateral

Table 3 United States: external accounts, alternative projections, 1990–95 (billions of dollars except where noted)

	1990	1991	1992	1993	1994	1995
	Outlook as of mid–1988					
Trade balance						
EAG	−115.4	−123.9	−132.6			
HHC	−107.4	−115.7	−116.4			
Current account balance						
EAG	−134.7	−150.7	−168.0			
HHC	−124.4	−135.6	−138.4			
	Outlook as of June 1989					
Trade balance						
EAG	−119.0	−141.8	−152.7			
HHC	−112.7	−140.6	−158.6			
Current account balance						
EAG	−138.7	−172.6	−194.1			
HHC	−132.3	−167.7	−194.2			
	Outlook as of October 1990					
Exports						
EAG	396.0	451.5	512.6	571.8	637.6	711.5
HHCR	394.6	451.3	512.1	566.2	628.0	697.0
Imports						
EAG	498.0	545.7	594.4	658.2	724.1	796.4
HHCR	512.2	558.7	609.4	669.6	733.1	800.7

	1990	1991	1992	1993	1994	1995
Trade balance						
EAG	−101.9	−94.2	−81.8	−86.4	−86.5	−84.9
HHCR	−117.6	−107.4	−97.3	−103.4	−105.1	−103.7
Nonfactor services						
EAG	25.9	33.4	42.3	48.0	55.3	63.8
HHCR	23.4	29.2	32.6	34.0	36.0	38.2
Factor services						
EAG	−27.2	−36.7	−46.4	−56.0	−66.8	−78.6
HHCR	−7.6	−14.4	−16.6	−20.3	−23.1	−25.4
Current account balance						
EAG	−118.0	−112.6	−101.5	−110.4	−114.6	−116.7
HHCR	−116.0	−107.4	−96.8	−105.9	−109.2	−108.8
Current account balance as a percentage of GNP						
EAG	−2.2	−2.0	−1.7	−1.7	−1.7	−1.6
HHCR	−2.1	−1.9	−1.6	−1.7	−1.6	−1.5
Current account balance as a percentage of XGS						
EAG	−23.2	−19.4	−15.4	−15.0	−14.0	−12.7
HHCR	−22.4	−18.4	−14.7	−14.7	−13.8	−12.4

EAG = External Adjustment with Growth model; HHC, HHCR = adaptations of the Helkie-Hooper model (see text); XGS = exports of goods and nonfactor services.

basis and 5.4 percent on a bilateral basis.[20] The real decline of the dollar by about 6 percent (average of multilateral and bilateral) from the 1987 baseline, combined with a current account improvement of some $5½ billion per percentage point for movement against the industrial-country currencies (as discussed above), meant an improvement of about $30 billion in the prospective external deficit. Together with $30 billion in current account improvement from slower US growth, the result was to shift the baseline projection down from a current account deficit of over $150 billion by 1992 to the plateau at around $100 billion.

The plateauing observed in the medium-term projections of table 3 raises two questions. First, where is the adverse trend one might expect from the Houthakker-Magee asymmetry? Second, why doesn't the well-known gap factor bring about an eventual rise in the deficit? The answer to the first question is that the HHCR model has symmetrical export and import income elasticities, and the modest asymmetry in the EAG model is offset by the excess of foreign over domestic growth (even after the United States resumes steady 2½ percent growth).[21] As for the gap factor, in the initial years there are lagged benefits from the decline of the dollar in 1990 and slow US growth. By the later years, the steady-state growth of export earnings (about 11 percent) is just enough higher than that of imports (10 percent) to permit a declining trade deficit that compensates for the rising factor services deficit, again because the growth differential slightly outweighs the elasticity asymmetry.

If one set a medium-term target of $50 billion for the current account deficit, further correction would still be required. Simulations with the EAG and the HHCR models show that a further decline of about 6 percent in the dollar against all other currencies would reduce the current account deficit to $50 billion by 1995. As developing countries would not generally be in a position to appreciate against the dollar, the depreciation against industrial-country currencies would be somewhat larger. As discussed below, the further decline of the dollar from the third quarter of 1990 to late October amounted to perhaps one-third or more of this remaining adjustment.

Even without this further dollar depreciation or changes in relative growth rates, however, table 3 suggests a quasi-stable path for the US external accounts. The current account deficit trends down to 1½ percent of GNP by 1995. Although still in excess of the 1 percent target suggested by John Williamson (forthcoming)

---

20. The decline from the second-quarter 1989 level to the third quarter of 1990 was thus about 17 percent on a multilateral basis and 10 percent on a bilateral basis against these currencies.

21. Note also that, in the HHCR projections, relative capital stock growth is continued at its 1985–87 rate. With capital accumulation more rapid in the less developed countries than in the United States but slower in Europe (from the 1985–87 experience), the average foreign rate equals that of the United States, and the variable is neutral.

and even further from C. Fred Bergsten's (1988) preferred target of zero balance, this level might not be incompatible with continued availability of financing. At the level of congressional politics, a current account deficit that lingers at a flat $100 billion seems far less likely to precipitate a new round of protection than would a path of deficits rising to $160 billion or even $200 billion over the next three to five years, as was the outlook before the post–1989 decline of the dollar and slackening of US growth.

Other features of the medium-term projections warrant discussion. First, the two models show a major divergence in the outlook for the factor services balance, even after the HHCR model incorporates adjustments to trim its ebullience on capital service earnings relative to payments. The HHCR model indicates that even though the nominal net external debt would stand at $1.2 trillion by the end of 1994, the capital services deficit would amount to only about $25 billion in 1995. The cause of this optimism is a higher rate of return on US assets abroad ($1.5 trillion at the end of 1994) than on foreign holdings in the United States ($2.7 trillion). In contrast, the EAG model places the factor services deficit at $79 billion in 1995, based on the simple application of a 7 percent nominal return to the cumulative current account deficit in 1988–94. The assumption is that, in economic terms, US assets were equal to liabilities at the end of 1987, despite the nominal net external debt of $377 billion in that year (largely because of understatement of US direct investment abroad by the use of historical book values).

The offsetting differences in the EAG and HHCR projections in other components of the external accounts do not answer the question of whether the United States truly faces the medium-term prospect of a relatively small capital services deficit despite a large net external debt. The HHCR projections continue to strain credulity, but then so does the prospective near-zero factor services balance already in store for 1990. The medium-term burden of net external debt is probably somewhere in between the EAG and the HHCR projections.

The other notable feature of the projections is the pattern of imbalances in global payments that they imply. The EAG model projections through 1995 show massive current account surpluses for Japan (rising from $80 billion in 1990 to $270 billion, or 5½ percent of GNP, by 1995). Even though the 1990 estimate would appear too high (the IMF places the 1990–91 results at about $50 billion for Japan), the magnitude of the trend suggests a serious imbalance and potential aggravation of US–Japan trade conflict. This profile is consistent with the lag in the real exchange rate adjustment of the yen. Thus, although the dollar has declined by 8.3 percent against the German mark in real terms since the fourth quarter of 1987, the US currency has actually appreciated in real terms by 1.2 percent against the yen.

Other relatively large imbalances in the new baseline include large deficits by 1995 for the United Kingdom (7 percent of GNP), Canada (10 percent), and

Italy (4½ percent). These features are persistent international distortions already identified in the earlier baseline projections through 1992. The major change from the pattern of imbalances projected earlier is in the case of Germany. In the earlier projections, German surpluses were projected to rise to even higher levels, but in the new baseline they decline to only about 1.5 percent of GNP by 1995, because of the higher domestic growth rate.

The Role of Exchange Rates

In the overview paper for this volume (chapter 1), Krugman addresses the issue of whether the exchange rate matters to the balance of trade. He first asks whether changes in the nominal rate can affect the real rate; the evidence is compellingly in the affirmative, as he shows. Krugman then asks whether changes in the real rate affect the trade balance. He formulates the issue in terms of a debate between John Maynard Keynes and himself, on the one hand, and Bertil Ohlin and Ronald I. McKinnon on the other. One might appropriately add the "elasticities approach" to the first camp, and the "absorption approach" to the second, and express the two views as KKE versus OMA.

The heart of the OMA argument is that economists must not forget the national accounts identity between saving and investment on the one hand and the external balance on the other:

(1) $\quad M - X = I - S = I - S_p - S_g = I - S_p - [T - G]$

where M is imports, X is exports, I is investment, S is saving, subscript p is private and subscript g is government, T is tax revenue, and G is government spending. Some international economists simply dismiss analysis of the exchange rate and activity levels and state that the external deficit is caused by the investment-saving imbalance, full stop, and that until private saving rises or government deficits fall the external deficit will not decline.

Most trade models, in contrast, tend to estimate trade equations driven by real exchange rates and activity variables:

(2a) $\quad M = a + bR + cY_h$

(2b) $\quad X = d - eR + fY_f,$

where R is the real exchange rate (units of foreign currency per unit of home currency), thereby incorporating the price of the exporting country's good relative to the price in the foreign market; Y is GNP (or, in some formulations, domestic demand) in the home country (subscript h) or foreign market (subscript f). In these models, the trade deficit is thus:

(2c) $\quad M - X = a - d + (b + e)R + cY_h - fY_f.$

The obvious resolution of the KKE and OMA debate would seem to be that this is a general-equilibrium problem requiring joint solution of both equations (1) and (2c). The implicit assumption of the OMA position is that equation (1) is wholly determinant, and that whatever goes on in equation (2c) is at worst irrelevant and misleading and at best endogenously determined by the forces stemming from equation (1). However, a more reasonable position would be that each equation can influence the other. In particular, changes in the real exchange rate can alter levels of investment and saving, as well as vice versa.

The line of causation from equation (1) to equation (2c) is well known. A drop in domestic saving such as occurred in the United States in the 1980s because of the decline in both S_p and S_g causes a rise in interest rates, as investors and the government compete for scarcer funds. Higher interest rates attract capital from abroad, which in turn bids up the exchange rate R. Both KKE and OMA seem to agree on this point.

Causation in the opposite direction is also reasonable to expect, however. Suppose there is an exogenous strengthening of the exchange rate, for example because of a boost in confidence by the election of a conservative president, or a "flight to security" because of political instability abroad. The incipient decline in the trade balance from equation (2c) will erode GNP through the net exports term in the national accounts. Falling real GNP will cause saving to decline in the Keynesian manner. The rise in R in equation (2c) will thus induce a decline in S_p in equation (1), as well as a fall in S_g because of automatic stabilizers.

In short, a general-equilibrium determination of the trade balance will flow from adjustments in *both* equations until they generate the same outcome. Consider figure 5. The vertical axis shows the magnitude of either the trade surplus or the excess of saving over investment. The upward-sloping line *S-I* reports the excess saving for each level of GNP (Y on the horizontal axis). In the Keynesian formulation, saving responds more than investment to a rise in income. The downward-sloping line *X-M* is the trade surplus for a given GNP level. Higher income increases demand for imports (and may divert exports to the home market). The trade balance is determined by the equilibrium point E_0 in the top panel of the figure, where the two lines intersect ($X\text{-}M = S\text{-}I$).

Suppose now an exogenous real appreciation of the currency occurs, shifting the exchange rate from R_0 to R_1. At the new exchange rate, the equilibrium will occur at point E_1, where the excess of saving over investment is smaller and so is the excess of exports over imports. Importantly, in the convergence to this equilibrium there will be a *change* in saving; variable levels in equation (1) will not remain unaltered, and that equation cannot be seen as sufficient in itself to tell the outcome. Hence the inadequacy of OMA.

In contrast, the KKE position essentially adopts the joint determination of equations (1) and (2c) and the equilibrium process depicted in figure 5 (or some similar process). Krugman formulates the difference in terms of the need to clear

Figure 5 Determination of trade and saving-investment balances

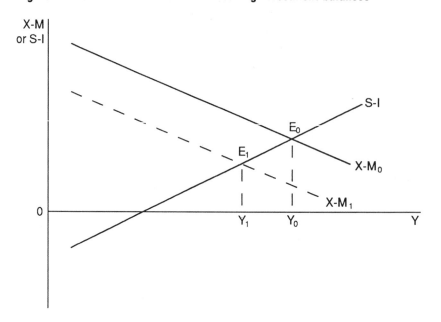

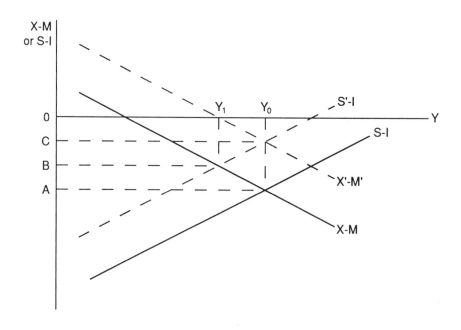

the domestic market; that need becomes evident in the bottom panel of figure 5. The OMA remedy to the trade deficit in this panel is to raise saving (for example, through higher taxes) so that the S-I line shifts to S'-I. The vertical shift in the saving-investment line will overstate the improvement in the external balance, however. With an unchanged X-M line, the equilibrium deficit will shift from level A to level B rather than all the way to level C. However, help from a currency depreciation that shifts the X-M line upward to X'-M' can move the equilibrium deficit to level C, permitting realization of the full potential increase in domestic saving. Krugman's point that otherwise the domestic market will be left with excess goods is evident in the fact that, without the exchange rate change, the equilibrium at deficit B involves a lower equilibrium GNP, at Y_1 and below the full-employment level Y_0.

Krugman raises one point that requires further consideration. He argues that unless the economy is below full employment, a fall in the exchange rate will generate inflation that will fully offset the initial depreciation and leave the real exchange rate and the trade balance unchanged. Experience from Latin America would suggest otherwise. Brazil and Mexico have amply demonstrated that sharp currency depreciation can be largely maintained in real terms and that the consequence is a sizable rise in the trade surplus, even when there is induced inflation. In terms of the top panel of figure 5, suppose Y_1 is the full-employment level of income. Suppose the exchange rate falls from R_1 to R_0. The result will be a boost in nominal income to Y_0, with inflationary consequences because income exceeds the full-employment level. There will be inflation, but there will also be some rise in the trade surplus, as indicated in the figure (from level B to level A).

In sum, the debate as to whether the real exchange rate can influence the trade balance would appear to be resolved clearly in favor of the affirmative. The argument that conventional models ignore the investment-saving identity is largely spurious; this identity is part of an equation system, not an independent imperative on its own. Far more meaningful is the question of *what* macropolicy conditions are implicitly or explicitly incorporated in particular projections of conventional trade models.

The projections of the EAG and the HHCR models in this study do not explicitly map the corresponding changes in the macropolicy variables: fiscal policy and monetary policy. However, the essential framework is that a depreciation of the currency in real terms will tend to be accomplished in the case of the United States by a correction of the persistent distortion of the 1980s when tight monetary policy was combined with loose fiscal policy. In particular, reduction of the fiscal deficit should permit an easing in monetary policy. The resulting decline in the interest rate should permit further easing of the dollar, which should stimlute exports and moderate imports, providing a positive contribution to growth. When the economy is at full employment, the objective is to have the additional stimulus from net exports just offset the contractionary effect of tighter fiscal policy. When the economy is below full employment, as is likely to be the case over the next year, there is some room for additional monetary ease that goes beyond merely offsetting the fiscal tightening.[22]

Appendix A presents a simple general-equilibrium model that formalizes the linkage between the investment-saving and the export-import equations and their relationships to the underlying monetary and fiscal variables. This stylized model provides a basis for examination of US fiscal and monetary policy in the context of the prospective US budget reform.

The Budget Deficit

It is widely recognized that the root reason for the failure of the US external accounts to reach balance in recent years has been the corresponding failure to close the fiscal deficit. Thanks to Mikhail Gorbachev, the United States is finally about to embark on fiscal adjustment. Largely because of the thaw in US–Soviet relations, in 1990 for the first time the administration was prepared to entertain the idea of sharp reductions in defense spending that application of the Gramm-Rudman-Hollings club would have required. As this threat became real, so did political negotiations on the deficit.

At this writing (November 1990) the parties remain engaged in last-minute conflicts (over how to tax millionaires), but the likelihood is that there will be an agreement to reduce the budget deficit from its baseline by $500 billion over five years. The exact terms are uncertain, but the timing of the cuts (if not their composition) seems likely to resemble the calendar established in the ill-fated 1 October summit agreement between the White House and negotiators from the Congress.

For purposes of this study, two central questions may be posed about the prospective budget agreement. Is it enough? And what will it do to the external deficit? Table 4 provides an initial basis for answering the first question. July 1990 projections by the Congressional Budget Office (CBO) indicated that the federal deficit (including the surplus from Social Security) was expected to rise from 2.9 percent of GNP in fiscal 1989 to 3.5 percent in 1990 and 4 percent in 1991 before declining to 2.9 percent by 1993 and about 2 percent by 1994–95. The unadjusted deficit figures include the large outlays for cleanup of the savings and loan crisis (through the Resolution Trust Corporation, or RTC). The great bulk of these outlays will serve merely to reestablish the capital of savings and loan organizations, or to permit the government to acquire assets it formerly did

---

22. For a discussion explicitly linking the monetary policy and fiscal policy instruments to the real exchange rate and growth variables in the EAG and the HHC projections, based on summary parameters from several macroeconomic models, see Cline (1989b, 288–90).

not possess (i.e., the savings and loans themselves). These expenditures should not be seen as comparable to most government spending in terms of (Keynesian) impact on the spending stream. Table 4 thus presents the CBO projections excluding the RTC outlays, as the more meaningful baseline trends in the deficit. On this basis, the baseline deficit hovers in the range of $165 billion annually over the medium term.[23]

Even under the baseline, the fiscal deficit (excluding RTC outlays) should decline relative to the size of the economy, from 2.9 percent of GNP in 1990 to 2.1 percent in 1995. The pending budget adjustment should reduce the deficit much further. Table 4 reports the timetable of deficit cuts originally agreed on at the domestic summit. Assuming that the final outcome resembles this schedule, there should be cuts of $40 billion in fiscal year 1991 and a total of $500 billion over five years. On this basis, the fiscal deficit (excluding RTC outlays) should fall to 1.6 percent of GNP by fiscal 1992, and to nearly zero by fiscal 1995.

The answer to the first question would thus appear to be in the affirmative: the prospective deficit cuts should be sufficient to achieve fiscal balance over a five-year horizon, if they are actually implemented. Although the deficit could be somewhat larger than projected in 1991 because of a weaker economy than assumed in the July CBO projections, that effect is cyclical and the trend by the mid–1990s should remain unchanged. This evaluation is at odds with the relatively common view that the budget negotiations have been a sham and will leave the fiscal accounts still woefully far from equilibrium. Moreover, to the extent that the picture is less favorable than shown in table 4 solely because of lower GNP growth, the qualitative judgment remains unchanged, because it is essentially the deficit for a given level of GNP (ideally, the full-employment fiscal deficit) that should be the criterion for adequacy of fiscal adjustment, not the actual outcome.

The second question—the impact on the external accounts—may be examined with the help of the simple general-equilibrium model developed in appendix A, as well as certain stylized macroeconomic parameters from existing models. The proper formulation of the question is probably to cast it in the reverse: what

---

23. Subsequent budget projections by the Bush administration raised the prospective fiscal 1991 deficit to $294 billion, up $60 billion from the July estimate, because of lower growth and higher cost assumptions for the savings and loan bailout. As the analysis that follows concentrates on the impact of the deficit reduction at the margin, the subsequent changes are of secondary importance. They do imply, however, that the baseline trend could be in the range of 1 percent of GNP higher than shown in table 4 (which is based on the July estimates), at least in the early years. Also, exclusion of the Social Security surplus would mean much larger deficits. Although exclusion is meaningful for some purposes, for the purposes of this study exclusion of the Social Security surplus would overstate the excess of domestic resource demand over domestic resource availability, and thus overstate the prospective external deficit.

Table 4 United States: fiscal accounts, 1989–95[a] (billions of dollars except where noted)

	1989	1990	1991	1992	1993	1994	1995
Revenues	991	1,044	1,123	1,188	1,260	1,337	1,417
Outlays							
Total	-1,143	-1,238	-1,355	-1,426	-1,455	-1,483	-1,555
Excluding RTC transfers	-1,134	-1,202	-1,285	-1,366	-1,443	-1,514	-1,574
Balance	-152	-194	-232	-238	-195	-146	-138
Excluding RTC transfers	-143	-158	-162	-178	-183	-177	-157
GNP	5,153	5,472	5,832	6,215	6,620	7,053	7,514
Deficit as a percentage of GNP	-2.9	-3.5	-4.0	-3.8	-2.9	-2.1	-1.8
Excluding RTC transfers	-2.8	-2.9	-2.8	-2.9	-2.8	-2.5	-2.1
Contribution from October 1990 budget package[b]	.	0	40	77	98	132	153
Adjusted balance							
Total	-152	-194	-192	-161	-97	-14	15
Excluding RTC transfers	-143	-158	-122	-101	-85	-45	-4
As a percentage of GNP							
Total	-2.9	-3.5	-3.3	-2.6	-1.5	-0.2	0.2
Excluding RTC transfers	-2.8	-2.9	-2.1	-1.6	-1.3	-0.6	-0.1

	1989	1990	1991	1992	1993	1994	1995
Memoranda:							
Real GNP growth (percentages per year)	3.2	2.1	2.4	2.6	2.6	2.6	2.6
RTC transfers[c]	−9	−36	−70	−60	−12	31	19
Social Security surplus							
Total		59	73	83	95	100	124
Excluding intrabudget transfers		37	45	49	53	59	65

RTC = Resolution Trust Corporation.

a. Data are by fiscal year.

b. The package was agreed at the budget summit but subsequently rejected by Congress.

c. RTC outlays other than interest and administrative costs.

Source: Congressional Budget Office, "The Economic and Budget Outlook: An Update," July 1990; *Washington Post*, 1 October 1990, x, xvii, 24, 32.

changes in the external sector would be compatible with avoidance of significant contraction of the economy from the program of fiscal austerity?

The fiscal adjustment envisioned in table 4 essentially amounts to reducing the deficit by 3 percent of GNP over five years, or an average cut of 0.6 percent of GNP annually. On the basis of equation (15) in appendix A, an annual fiscal cut of this magnitude might cause an annual reduction of GNP by about 1 percent.[24] However, the simple model essentially applies Keynesian multiplier analysis, and it is generally known that the actual multiplier tends to be below what would be expected from the savings, tax, and import leakage rates. A more realistic parameter is probably that identified by Bryant, Helliwell, and Hooper on the basis of a survey of macroeconomic models: a cut in the fiscal deficit by 1 percent of GNP causes a 1 percent reduction in GNP (Bryant et al. 1988). On this basis, the contractionary pressure from the fiscal adjustment currently planned amounts to about 0.6 percent of GNP annually for five years, for a total contraction of 3 percent of GNP.

A plausible scenario for achieving fiscal adjustment without net recessionary impact is to compensate fully through additional expansion of net exports, on the one hand, and domestic investment, on the other. For its part, gross private investment in 1989 was 14.5 percent of GNP,[25] substantially below the average of 16.2 percent of GNP in 1984–87 (Cline 1989b, 60). A lower fiscal deficit should permit "crowding in" by private investment, as the government preempts a smaller share of funds on the capital market. Suppose that private investment bore half of the demand stimulus required to offset the fiscal contraction. Then private investment would have to rise gradually from 14.5 percent of GNP in 1989 to 16 percent by 1995. This performance would seem not only feasible but relatively unambitious, even taking account of the dim prospects for construction investment (especially commercial) after the end of the tax shelter era and in view of the current bear market in real estate.

A formal presentation of the conditions for changes in policy variables required to offset the contractionary effect of fiscal adjustment is shown in equation (20) of appendix A. Essentially, monetary stimulus (perhaps combined with faster foreign growth and lower foreign interest rates) permits higher domestic investment and higher net exports (working through an induced reduction in the

---

24. $dY/dG = 1/B = 1/(s[1—t] + t + \alpha)$, where s is the private savings rate, t is the tax rate, and α is the marginal propensity to import. With s approximately equal to 17 percent, t approximately 0.3 (with the marginal rate higher and the average rate lower), and $\alpha = 0.2$ (as established in appendix A), $1/B = 1.6$. A fiscal cut of 0.6 percent of GNP would reduce GNP by about 1 percent. Note that the reduction in output would be somewhat lower if the adjustment were primarily from taxes rather than government spending (in the traditional Keynesian approach, but not in a supply-side approach).

25. US Commerce Department, "Gross National Product: Second Quarter 1990 (Final)," BEA 90-42, 25 September 1990.

exchange rate). Although the full set of parameters is not readily estimated, a truncated version focusing on the external sector provides meaningful implications about the feasibility of completing the task of offsetting fiscal contraction with investment and external-sector stimulus.

If the objective is to achieve a real expansion of net exports equivalent to 1½ percent of GNP over the next five years (which, added to a comparable boost in investment, would neutralize the fiscal contraction), the impact on the external accounts would be as follows. The real change in the trade balance would amount to 0.3 percent of GNP annually, or $15 billion. The nominal change that would appear after taking account of terms-of-trade effects would be about one-half as large (Cline 1989b, appendix F). Thus, this strategy would involve a reduction in the nominal trade deficit from baseline by about $38 billion at 1990 prices (or $47 billion at 1995 prices). The baseline current account deficit for 1995 would drop from some $110 billion (table 3) to about $60 billion, or from 1½ percent of GNP to about 0.8 percent of GNP—below Williamson's 1 percent of GNP ceiling.

As the purpose of the strategy would be to neutralize the contractionary effects of US fiscal adjustment, this reduction in the external deficit would have to come from dollar depreciation rather than a slowdown of US growth from already modest baseline rates. Appendix A provides stylized parameters (themselves derived from the EAG model) that permit evaluation of the extent of real depreciation that would be required. The target is to increase the real trade balance by $15 billion annually (at 1990 prices). From equation (2) in appendix A, a 1 percent real depreciation reduces real imports by $4.65 billion (parameter β). From equation (3) in appendix A, a 1 percent real depreciation increases real exports by $6.12 billion (parameter ϵ). The real trade deficit thus declines by $10.8 billion for each percentage point of real dollar depreciation. To obtain a $15 billion real trade balance increase annually, the dollar would need to decline by 1.4 percent each year.

Some of that decline has already occurred. From the baseline exchange rates applied in the projections of table 3 (end-September 1990 for the yen, 15 August for the other currencies), by 22 October 1990 the dollar had declined by another 3½ percent against the G-7 currencies as measured using multilateral weights, and by 4½ percent using bilateral weights. As the decline has been less against other countries (especially the developing countries), the overall real depreciation from the table 3 baseline has probably been on the order of 3 percent. Thus, out of a total of 5 × 1.4 = 7 percentage points real depreciation over the next five years required for the external sector to do its part to offset fiscal contraction (while bringing the current account deficit below the 1 percent of GNP mark), nearly half has already taken place since the third quarter of 1990. In terms of the appendix A equations, this decline may be attributed to a rise in foreign interest rates—i_f in equation (8)—and perhaps to a change in expectations, shifting the intercept term in the exchange rate equation (R_0) downward.

The Bryant-Helliwell-Hooper parameters suggest that the remaining 4 percentage points of real dollar depreciation would be forthcoming from a 4 percent increase in the money supply above baseline—in other words, an increase by about 1 percentage point in the annual money growth targets of the Federal Reserve. Monetary ease on this order of magnitude would seem consistent with avoidance of inflationary pressure, considering that it would be partially offsetting contractionary (and hence anti-inflationary) influences from the fiscal side. Monetary expansion would of course contribute to the objective of higher investment as well.

In summary, a consistent policy scenario for the next five years would read as follows. First, Congress enacts and implements the budget agreement to cut the fiscal deficit by $500 billion over five years. Second, the Federal Reserve increases its money growth targets by 1 percentage point annually over the same period. Third, the crowding-in effect permits private investment to rise gradually from its anemic 1989 level of 14.5 percent of GNP back to a more normal level of 16 percent, neutralizing half of the contractionary effect of fiscal adjustment. Finally, the recent real depreciation of the dollar, combined with modest additional depreciation associated with the easing of monetary policy, permits the real trade deficit to decline by $15 billion annually (and the nominal deficit by about half that amount), providing the remaining demand offset of one-half of fiscal contraction and leaving the external deficit at an acceptable long-term level relative to GNP by 1995. In short, equilibrium does not seem so unattainable after all.

Financial Markets and the Hard Landing

The financial markets could easily complicate the actual implementation of this seemingly well-behaved scenario. There are myriad concerns about a possible collapse in the dollar; the reasons for concern include scarcity of resources in the international capital market associated with German reunification, Eastern European investment, and reversal of Japanese capital flows to address bank reserve shortages and other needs at home. The easing of the dollar could turn into a rout; the hard landing might finally be around the corner.

There is no compelling reason, however, to expect these forces to implode in a dollar collapse. Consider the original scenario for the hard landing, circa the mid–1980s. Already in 1985 I wrote that I expected the decline of the dollar to follow a relatively orderly stairstep pattern rather than a roller-coaster path of downward overshooting (Cline 1985). It seemed to me at the time that market expectations were more likely to be stabilizing than extrapolative and destabilizing, and that a decline in foreign financing and the external deficit would be compatible with plausible adjustments in investment and the fiscal balance. In the event, fiscal adjustment was less than expected. But the exchange market did seem to demonstrate stabilizing rather than extreme bandwagon expectations, and after the dollar rose in 1988–89 (following G-7 intervention at the end of 1987) there was even more reason to expect investors not to have expectations based on one-way bets.

Nor does the lack of Japanese financing of the current account deficit in the first half of 1990 warrant much concern. It turns out that, according to US Department of Commerce data on foreign liabilities and assets, the Japanese had already stopped financing the US external deficit in 1989.[26] Yet there was no hard landing in 1989; indeed, the problem that year was an overly strong dollar.

Other papers for this conference consider the future of the hard landing in greater detail. It would appear, however, that the experience of the last five years indicates that the exchange markets are unlikely to take the dollar for a cataclysmic downward ride.

A more likely possibility is that there will be more limited overshooting of the dollar downward. Relatively high interest rates in Germany and Japan, anemic US growth prospects, and the simple consideration that the dollar overshot on the upside in late 1984 and early 1985 suggest that a further decline of some 10 percent or even 15 percent might not be unexpected. Such a decline would take the dollar to levels that would begin to eliminate the US external deficit rather than merely reduce it below 1 percent of GNP. That outcome would not be all to the bad; on the contrary, it would be favorable so long as the result were not an inflationary outbreak and an induced interest rate hike that caused (or prolonged) a recession.

For the time being, the proper policy stance would appear to be to permit the dollar to ease if the markets continue to pressure it downward. The centerpiece of policy still remains implementation of the fiscal adjustment package. With fiscal correction on track, inflationary risk from a weakening dollar will be substantially mitigated. A logical fine tuning of the policy package outlined above, however, would be that if the dollar has declined beyond the range suggested here (some 7 percent below the third-quarter 1990 baseline level), there should be somewhat less monetary easing to accompany the planned fiscal tightening.

Conclusion

The first task of this paper was to determine whether the still-large US external deficit confounds or confirms the expectations of the models and the policymak-

---

26. Whereas net US liabilities to Japan rose by $44 billion in 1988, they declined by $7 billion in 1989 (Cline 1990).

ers who stressed adjustment through dollar depreciation in the late 1980s. The analysis here finds that the 1990 current account deficit of approximately $100 billion conforms relatively well with what the models predicted, including those of Stephen Marris, a group of macroeconomic models surveyed by the Brookings Institution, and my own EAG and HHC models.

As a specific theme on this "no (or at least few) surprises" finding, the question of whether the dollar has fully given up its gains of the mid-1980s turns out to have a more ambiguous answer than the stylized view that the dollar is now back to where it was in 1980. The IMF's real exchange rates calculated by deflating by export unit values find the dollar still some 15 percent or more above its real level at the beginning of the decade. On a related specific theme, the analysis strongly suggests that "the dollar does matter": there was a clear relationship in the 1980s between the performance of exports relative to imports, on the one hand, and the real value of the dollar (after a two-year lag).

The analysis here does not give as much credence to the Houthakker-Magee income elasticity asymmetry as either Lawrence or Krugman (although he calls it by another name: competitiveness) would suggest. The HHC and EAG models track experience with little (EAG) or no (HHC) elasticity asymmetry. If a secular real decline of the dollar is required to compensate for such an asymmetry, it should be below 1 percent annually. This conclusion is reinforced if, based on the IMF unit value measures, the dollar has in fact fallen less than is generally believed.

The second task of the paper was to consider the outlook for the US external deficit. New simulations with the EAG and the (revised) HHC models show that instead of a rebound from the range of $100 billion to levels well above $150 billion by 1992 and after, the current account deficit now looks likely to plateau at a level not far from $100 billion annually over the next five years. The changed outlook stems from the significant decline of the dollar in 1990 and the shift in the prospects for US growth from a steady 2½ percent to at least 1 full percentage point below that rate in both 1990 and 1991. A flat $100 billion deficit is no great accomplishment, but it does mean that the external imbalance would continue to shrink in relative terms, from its peak of 3.6 percent of GNP in 1987 (and 2.1 percent in 1989) to around 1½ percent by 1995. Despite a slow-growth environment, this relative decline might be enough to stave off the higher protectionist pressure that would have been likely with a renewed upswing in the deficit.

The baseline outlook of a flat $100 billion deficit does not allow for fiscal adjustment. However, the October budget deal nearly in hand would reduce the fiscal deficit from about 3 percent of GNP to close to zero by 1995. After considering the general-equilibrium effects, and assuming that half of the contractionary effect is offset by a recovery in investment and the other half stems from increased net exports, the outlook for the external deficit would be a decline to about $60 billion by 1995, or less than 1 percent of GNP. The external sector would generate an annual real stimulus to demand of 0.3 percent of GNP during this period. This analysis comes close to suggesting that the long-awaited internal and external adjustment of the US economy is now at hand.

The discussion seeks to ease the minds of those economists who fear that the partial-equilibrium models of the external accounts based primarily on real exchange rates and activity levels have forgotten the basic income accounting identity between the trade deficit and the investment-saving gap. The analysis makes the simple point that the I-S equation should not be seen as hierarchically superior to the import and export equations, but that instead the equations are all part of a general-equilibrium system. Investment and saving can respond to changes in trade as well as vice versa. For the aficionados, appendix A presents a more formal general-equilibrium model along these lines, and goes part of the way toward making it operational by estimating stylized parameters.

Finally, the discussion notes that financial market instability and a plunge in the dollar could upset the seeming potential for external and internal adjustment. However, the relatively orderly behavior of the dollar in the last five years suggests that this outcome can be avoided. A more likely outcome is that the market will indulge in a modest degree of overshooting, which would drive the external deficit somewhat closer to balance rather than leave it near the 1 percent of GNP mark.

Epilogue: September 1991

In April of 1991 I reexamined the outlook for the US current account. By then the dollar had strengthened in the aftermath of the US military victory in the Gulf and in response to increasing perceptions of economic difficulty in German unification. Nonetheless, revised projections with the EAG and HHCR models indicated that the US current account deficit should decline to about $70 billion in 1991 and thereafter fall steadily to approximately zero by 1995 (Cline 1991). The recorded figure for 1991 is likely to be much smaller, perhaps as low as $20 billion, because of the "Gulf mirage" of some $50 billion in US transfer receipts from allied payments to help finance the Gulf war.

Three principal influences accounted for this shift from the outlook estimated in the October 1990 version of this paper. First, oil prices declined, and a revised projection of oil at $18 per barrel in real terms trimmed about $25 billion annually off the trade deficit. This revision left a medium-term plateau for the current account deficit at about $70 billion. Second, the revised estimates explicitly took account of the budget package. With a postulated 2 percent of GDP reduction in the full-employment budget deficit over five years, the effect was to remove the remaining $70 billion deficit. This calculation held up whether fiscal contraction was assumed to reduce domestic growth or whether instead half of the contraction was offset by more expansionary monetary policy (in which case the lesser reduction of imports was offset by the trade stimulus from greater dollar depreciation). Reassuringly, a $70 billion current account adjustment resulting from 2 percent of GDP fiscal adjustment (i.e., about $125 billion) was close to the 50 percent rule of thumb for the relationship of the two siblings suggested by Helliwell (1991) on the basis of several international macroeconomic models. Third, there was no further dislocation of the projections from the rise of the dollar, because it was offset by the weaker outlook for US growth.

By August of 1991 there were grounds for somewhat less optimism on US external adjustment. Trade data for the first half showed a deficit of only $30 billion, down from $48 billion in the same period in 1990, but the improvement was from recession-weakened imports (down 2.2 percent) rather than buoyant exports (up only 6.5 percent in nominal terms). The dollar had continued to rise until July, when the G-7 summit provided the occasion for massive intervention to knock it partway back (this correction was in turn temporarily reversed during the abortive coup in the Soviet Union). Although the most recent OECD forecasts (*OECD Economic Outlook,* July 1991) called for almost the same weighted-average growth of non–US G-7 countries as used in the April projections (2.0 percent versus 2.1 percent for 1991, and 2.8 percent versus 3.0 percent for 1992), the continuing uncertainty in the Soviet Union held greater downside risk than upside potential for European growth, in part from the danger of new pressures through immigration. Moreover, the stratospheric figures emerging in each reestimation of the US budget deficit made it seem a bit more heroic than before to assume that the full-employment budget deficit would fall by 2 percent of GDP by 1995.

In sum, it seemed likely that although the "true" current account deficit (removing the Gulf mirage) might be down to $60 billion or $70 billion for 1991, the prospects for its complete elimination by 1995 were beginning to dim. Of course, in relative terms a medium-term deficit in the range of, say, $30 billion annually would be modest: only about ½ percent of GDP, in contrast to the 3.6 percent of GNP peak reached in 1987.

These revisions to the outlook, as well as the successive changes in projections reviewed in the main text, do raise a problem for the policy forecaster. Increasingly, the path of the dollar since 1987 has taken on the appearance of a sine curve (or random walk). A trough occurred in the fourth quarter of 1987, a local peak in the second quarter of 1989, another trough in the fourth quarter of 1990, and a new phase of strengthening through the third quarter of 1991. The forecasting risk is to calculate a medium-term projection with the real dollar held constant at what turns out to have been either a trough or peak in the sine curve. The implication is that at any given time it may be more meaningful to project the real exchange rate as the average of the past four or even more quarters, rather than the current real rate.

Appendix A: A Simple Linearized General-Equilibrium Model of the External Sector

Let variables be designated as in table A.1. Then:

(1) $I - S_p - (T - G) = M - X$,

corresponding to text equation (1).

Let imports depend on foreign GNP and the real exchange rate as in text equation (2a):

(2) $M = M_0 + \alpha Y + \beta R$.

Note that the marginal propensities (α, β) and the intercept (M_0) can be chosen to be consistent with estimated elasticities, from the following relationship: elasticity = marginal propensity/average propensity.[27]

Similarly, exports depend on foreign GNP and the exchange rate:[28]

(3) $X = X_0 + \gamma Y_f + \epsilon R$.

---

27. Thus, in 1990 US imports stand at about $500 billion. Their income elasticity is 2.2 in the EAG model. Their ratio to GNP is 0.092. An estimate of α consistent with the desired elasticity is $\alpha = (.092)(2.2) = 0.2$, considering that marginal propensity (α) equals elasticity times average propensity (0.092). Similarly, the weighted price elasticity of US imports in the EAG model is -0.93. With R specified as foreign currency per dollar, a rise in R means a decline in the import price, so the absolute value of the elasticity applies. In this case, $0.93 = \beta/(100/500)$; $\beta = 4.65$ where the right-hand denominator in parentheses is merely the ratio of the exchange rate index (100) to imports (500).

With the marginal propensities α and β in hand, the intercept M_0 may be estimated for consistency with the base-year level of imports. Thus, from equation (1), in the base year:

$500 = M_0 + 0.2(5,450) + 4.65(100)$; $M_0 = -1,055$

where the first right-hand value in parentheses is GNP in billions of dollars; the second is the exchange rate index; and M_0 is in billions of dollars. Note that the device of applying a negative intercept permits an above-unitary elasticity of imports to GNP (marginal exceeds average) despite the use of a linear relationship between the two.

28. The parameters for equation (3) may be estimated as follows. US exports are approximately $400 billion. US GNP is approximately 30 percent of the world total, excluding countries that do not report to the World Bank (World Development Report 1989). Therefore Y_f is on the order of $12.7 trillion. The EAG income elasticity for US exports is 1.85. Applying the relationship between elasticity, marginal, and average propensities cited in the previous note, we have $\gamma = 1.85(400/12,700) = 0.058$. Similarly, the EAG price elasticity of US exports (including substitution effect) is -1.53. Again following note 28, $\epsilon = -1.53(400/100) = -6.12$. Applying equation (2) with $X = 400$, the intercept $X_0 = $275 billion.

Table A.1 Variable and parameter definitions

M	Imports
X	Exports
Y	GNP
R	Exchange rate (foreign currency per dollar)
I	Investment
S_p	Private saving
G	Government spending
T	Tax revenue
t	Tax rate
Y_d	Disposable income
H	Money supply
i	Interest rate
i_f	Foreign interest rate
Y_f	Foreign GNP

Let private saving depend on disposable income:

(4) $S_p = S_{p0} + sY_d.$

Disposable income depends on the tax rate:

(5) $Y_d = Y(1 - t).$

Let investment depend on the interest rate:

(6) $I = I_0 - \rho i.$

The interest rate depends on the money supply:

(7) $i = i_0 - \lambda H.$

The exchange rate depends on the domestic interest rate relative to the foreign interest rate:

(8) $R = R_0 + \phi(i - i_f).$

Tax revenue is:

(9) $T = tY.$

Substituting equations (2), (3), (4), (6), and (9) into equation (1):

(10) $(I_0 - \rho i) - (S_{p0} + sY) - (tY - G) = (M_0 + \alpha Y + \beta R) - (X_0 + \gamma Y_f + \epsilon R).$

Substituting equations (5) and (7):

(11) $(I_0 - \rho[i_0 - \lambda H]) - (S_{po} + sY[1-t]) - (tY - G)$
$= (M_0 + \alpha Y + \beta R) - (X_0 + \gamma Y_f + \epsilon R).$

Substituting equation (8):

(12) $\text{LHS} = (M_0 + \alpha Y + \beta[R_0 + \phi i_0 - \lambda Hi - i_f])$
$- (X_0 + \gamma Y_f + \epsilon[R_0 + \phi i_0 - \lambda Hi - i_f]).$

where LHS refers to the left-hand side of equation (11).

Collecting terms in Y:

(13) $-sY(1-t) - tY - \alpha Y = M_0 + \beta(R_0 + \phi[i_0 - \lambda Hi - i_f])$
$- (X_0 + \gamma Y_f + \epsilon[R_0 + \phi i_0 - \lambda Hi - i_f]) - (I_0 - \rho[i_0 - \lambda H]) + S_{po} - G.$

Representing the right-hand side of equation (13) by ψ:

(14) $Y = -\psi/(s[1-t]) + t + \alpha]).$

Thus, the system tells equilibrium GNP. There are three domestic policy instruments (t, G, H) and two exogenous foreign variables (Y_f, i_f). The marginal impact of each on equilibrium GNP is given by its derivative. Thus, for government spending,

(15) $dY/dG = 1/B,$

where $B = s(1-t) + t + \alpha$. This impact is the familiar multiplier, where leakages are to saving, taxes, and imports, respectively.

For the tax rate:

(16) $dY/dt = (-[-\psi][-s+1])/B^2,$

using the chain rule.[29]

For money supply:

(17) $dY/dH = (\beta\phi\lambda - \epsilon\phi\lambda + \rho\lambda)/B = \lambda[\phi(\beta - \epsilon) + \rho]/B.$

Increasing the money supply thus raises GNP through induced investment (ρ) and by the sum of lower imports (β) and higher exports (ϵ, keeping in mind that $\epsilon < 0$).

The impact of foreign growth on GNP is:

(18) $dY/dY_f = \gamma/B,$

---

29. $du^{-1}/dx = -u^{-2}du/dx.$

and the influence of foreign interest rates is:

$$(19) \quad dY/di_f = (\phi[\beta - \epsilon])/B.$$

If the economy is at full employment, the desired policy reform involves change in t, G, and H such that GNP remains unchanged but the external deficit declines. There should be a combination of an increased tax rate (t), decreased government spending (G), and increased money supply (H), such that this outcome obtains. Foreign cooperation can also help, if growth abroad is in a position to be accelerated (Y_f) and/or foreign interest rates can be increased (i_f). Thus:

$$(20) \quad \Delta Y = 0 = \Delta t(\psi[1-s])/B^2 + \Delta G/B + \Delta H(\lambda[\phi\beta - \epsilon + \rho]/B)$$
$$+ \Delta Y_f[\gamma/B] + \Delta i_f(\phi[\beta - \epsilon])/B.$$

More generally, considering the right-hand side of equation (12) along with equation (20), the trade balance responds to the policy and exogenous variables as follows:

$$(21) \quad \Delta X - \Delta M = \gamma(\Delta Y_f) - \epsilon\phi\lambda(\Delta H) - \alpha[k_1\Delta t + k_2\Delta G + k_3\Delta H + k_4\Delta Y_f + k_5\Delta i_f] + \beta\phi\lambda(\Delta H),$$

where coefficients k_1 through k_5 refer to the coefficients on the corresponding variables in equation (20).

Acknowledgment

Dorsati Madani provided research assistance for this study.

References

Bergsten, C. Fred. 1988. *America and the World Economy: A Strategy for the 1990s.* Washington: Institute for International Economics.

Bryant, Ralph C. 1988. "The US External Deficit: An Update." *Brookings Discussion Papers in International Economics* 63 (January).

Bryant, Ralph C., John F. Helliwell, and Peter Hooper. 1988. "Domestic and Cross-Border Consequences of US Macroeconomic Policies." Paper presented at a conference on "Macroeconomic Policies in an Interdependent World" sponsored by the Brookings Institution, Washington, 12–13 December.

Cline, William R. 1985. "Changing Stresses on the World Economy." *The World Economy* 8, no. 2 (June):135–52.

Cline, William R. 1989a. *American Trade Adjustment: The Global Impact.* POLICY ANALYSES IN INTERNATIONAL ECONOMICS 26. Washington: Institute for International Economics (March).

Cline, William R. 1989b. *United States External Adjustment and the World Economy.* Washington: Institute for International Economics.

Cline, William R. 1989c. "Impact of the Strong Dollar on US Trade." Washington: Institute for International Economics (mimeographed, June).

Cline, William R. 1990. "Japan's Trade Policies." Washington: Institute for International Economics (mimeographed, May).

Cline, William R. 1991. "The Dollar, the Budget, and US External Adjustment." Washington: Institute for International Economics (mimeographed, April).

Helliwell, John F. 1991. "The Fiscal Deficit and the External Deficit: Siblings but not Twins." In Rudolph G. Penner, ed., *The Great Fiscal Experiment.* Washington: Urban Institute, 23–58.

Lawrence, Robert Z. 1990. "US Current Account Adjustment: An Appraisal." *Brookings Papers on Economic Activity* 2:343–82.

Marris, Stephen. 1987. *Deficits and the Dollar: The World Economy at Risk,* rev. ed. POLICY ANALYSES IN INTERNATIONAL ECONOMICS 14. Washington: Institute for International Economics (August).

Williamson, John. *Equilibrium Exchange Rates: An Update.* Washington: Institute for International Economics (forthcoming).

A Sectoral Assessment of the US Current Account Deficit: Performance and Prospects

Allen J. Lenz

This paper provides partial, preliminary results from a larger, ongoing study of progress, problems, and prospects in reducing US current account deficits. Both this paper and the larger study focus on recent and prospective performance in individual manufacturing industries and product groups.

Specifically, the ongoing project seeks to shed light on the following questions:

- What basic changes, if any, have been occurring in world trade patterns?

- Which broad categories of trade—services, raw materials, energy, agriculture, manufactures—and which specific product groups are most significant in world trade? Which are growing most rapidly? Which are declining?

- Which types of goods and services dominated the decline of US trade performance in the early to mid–1980s? Which have contributed most to US deficit reduction?

- In light of potential world markets and the nature of the competition, which specific manufactures product groups offer the most significant opportunities for increased US exports?

- To what extent has a lack of adequate US–based production capacity constrained US exports or encouraged US imports?

- How much of any future improvement in US trade performance is likely to occur through export expansion and how much through import substitution, that is, by recapture of US markets by US–based production?

- Within product categories, what will be the major factors in improved US performance? Dollar depreciation? foreign direct investment in the United States? improved US productivity and competitiveness? other factors?

- What policy steps might facilitate further shrinking of the US trade and current account deficits?

Allen J. Lenz is a Visiting Fellow at the Institute for International Economics and Director of Trade and Economics for the Chemical Manufacturers Association. He was previously Director of the Office of Trade and Investment Analysis at the US Department of Commerce.

The first section of this paper describes the key role of manufactures trade in world trade, its part in the growth of US trade and current account deficits, and its role in the recent and prospective reductions of these deficits. The next section summarizes recent international trade performance and prospects for the next several years in one key manufactures product group—road vehicles—of the approximately 20 that will be examined in the larger study. These product group analyses are based on three types of data:

- **Historical Trade Data Base**   We constructed a World Manufactures Trade Data Base (Lenz, forthcoming) containing manufactures export and import data, at Standard International Trade Classification (SITC) one-, two-, and three-digit levels, for the 24 countries of the Organization for Economic Cooperation and Development (OECD) for the period 1979–87 and Taiwan for the period 1982–87. These data were supplemented by more detailed US Department of Commerce trade statistics in SITC format for the years 1979 through mid–1990.

- **Interviews**   We interviewed knowledgeable experts in government agencies, trade associations, individual companies, and elsewhere to obtain their assessments of past performance and of the outlook for the future, and to identify other relevant information sources and published materials.

- **Mail Survey**   A mail questionnaire survey conducted through 10 trade associations provided over 650 individual-company assessments of the prospects for and key determinants of exports, imports, and investment in plant and equipment.

Tentative conclusions from work to date are summarized in the concluding section.

The Key Role of Manufactures Trade

Manufactures trade performance will be the key factor in any significant narrowing and ultimate elimination of the US current account deficit. This part of the paper provides data and analysis to support this hypothesis.

Dissecting the Current Account

From 1981 to 1987 the US current account balance moved from a surplus of $8.2 billion to a deficit of $143.7 billion (table 1). Of that $151.9 billion deterioration, $131.5 billion was in merchandise trade; another $11.8 billion

Table 1 United States: current account by major component, 1981–89 (billions of dollars except where noted)

Account	1981	1982	1983	1984	1985	1986	1987	1988	1989	Change 1981–87	Change 1987–89
Total goods and services											
Exports	378.7	352.1	337.4	371.1	371.2	392.0	446.1	529.8	600.4	67.4	154.3
Imports	362.9	349.9	371.9	462.8	468.5	509.4	575.6	641.7	692.0	212.7	116.4
Balance	15.8	2.2	−34.5	−91.7	−97.3	−117.5	−129.5	−111.9	−91.6	−145.3	37.9
Merchandise trade											
Exports	237.1	211.2	201.8	219.9	215.9	223.4	250.3	319.3	361.9	13.2	111.6
Imports	265.1	247.6	268.9	332.4	338.1	368.4	409.8	446.5	475.1	144.7	65.3
Balance	−28.0	−36.4	−67.1	−112.5	−122.1	−145.1	−159.5	−127.2	−113.2	−131.5	46.3
Business services											
Exports	44.6	44.8	45.3	54.8	56.9	70.9	79.4	92.1	104.6	34.8	25.2
Imports	32.6	33.5	36.4	49.5	53.6	59.3	67.5	73.1	76.9	34.9	9.4
Balance	12.0	11.3	8.9	5.2	3.4	11.6	12.0	19.0	27.7	0.0	15.7
Other goods and services											
Exports	10.6	12.6	13.0	10.5	9.5	9.1	11.8	10.7	9.2	1.2	−2.6
Imports	12.9	13.9	14.3	13.4	13.9	14.8	16.0	16.6	16.3	3.1	0.3
Balance	−2.3	−1.3	−1.2	−2.9	−4.4	−5.7	−4.2	−5.9	−7.1	−1.9	−2.9

Account	1981	1982	1983	1984	1985	1986	1987	1988	1989	Change 1981–87	Change 1987–89
International investment income											
Receipts	86.4	83.5	77.3	85.9	88.8	88.6	104.7	107.8	124.7	18.3	19.7
Payments	52.3	54.9	52.4	67.4	62.9	67.0	82.4	105.5	123.7	30.1	41.3
Balance	34.1	28.7	24.9	18.5	25.9	21.6	22.3	2.2	1.0	−11.8	−21.3
Net unilateral transfers	−7.6	−9.2	−9.8	−12.5	−15.4	−15.8	−14.2	−14.7	−14.3	−6.6	−0.1
Current account balance	8.2	−7.0	−44.3	−104.2	−112.7	−133.2	−143.7	−126.5	−105.9	−151.9	37.8
As percentage of GNP	0.3	−0.2	−1.3	−2.8	−2.8	−3.1	−3.2	−2.6	−2.0	−3.5	1.2
Memorandum:											
US international investment position	140.9	136.7	89.0	3.3	−111.4	−267.8	−378.3	−532.5	−663.7[a]	−519.2	−285.4[a]

a. Preliminary.

Source: US Department of Commerce.

was in international investment income, reflecting the US change from the world's largest creditor nation to the world's largest debtor nation. In 1988 and 1989 the current account deficit shrank by $37.8 billion, as improvements of $46.3 billion in merchandise trade and $15.7 billion in business services trade (travel, shipping, and related transactions; royalties and license fees; and certain other services) were partially offset by a further deterioration of $21.3 billion in international investment income.

Merchandise trade thus provided the bulk of both the 1981–87 deterioration and the 1988–89 improvement in the US current account balances. What about the future? Can other elements of the current account provide major gains? Can business services continue to provide increasing surpluses? Analysis of the non–merchandise trade components of the current account shows that the prospects are dim. The unilateral transfers account consists principally of foreign aid and other external grants as well as payments to US pensioners living abroad. It is, therefore, always a deficit account, in which outlays are offset by very few receipts. Little change in these annual deficits is likely.

"Other goods and services" is a relatively small account, consisting mostly of military and US government services transactions. It consistently registers small deficits, and these will continue into the future.

Net international investment income is the difference between the income paid to foreign holders of US assets and the income received by US holders of foreign assets. The large positive balances of earlier years have eroded as the US international investment position has shifted from that of a large creditor to that of a large debtor. This erosion will continue as the US debtor position increases. Continued strong foreign economic performance may, however, slow this deterioration by increasing the foreign earnings of US direct investments abroad, and further dollar depreciation may increase the dollar value of these foreign earnings.

Business services trade is a relatively small factor in the current account. Exports of business services were less than 18 percent of total 1989 goods and services exports, but because imports have been considerably smaller, this account has provided sizable surpluses in recent years: $27.7 billion in 1989.

Business services trade is thus the only non–merchandise trade category in which current account improvement might occur. Further major business services gains, however, are unlikely. The bulk of the business services account is in three categories that do not fluctuate widely and do not offer the potential for major US gains (table 2).

Travel, shipping, and passenger fares summed in 1989 to a surplus of $0.8 billion, compared with deficits ranging up to $9.9 billion in other years of the decade. Marked further dollar depreciation would further improve the balances in these accounts by deterring US travel abroad, encouraging increased foreign visits to the United States, and increasing the dollar value of foreign-currency

Table 2　United States: business services trade by component, 1981–89 (billions of dollars)

Account	1981	1982	1983	1984	1985	1986	1987	1988	1989	Change 1981–87	Change 1987–89
Total business services											
Exports	44.6	44.8	45.3	54.8	56.9	70.9	79.4	92.1	104.6	34.8	25.2
Imports	32.6	33.5	36.4	49.5	53.6	59.3	67.5	73.1	76.3	34.8	8.9
Balance	12.0	11.3	8.9	5.2	3.4	11.6	12.0	19.0	27.7	−0.0	15.8
Travel											
Exports	12.9	12.4	10.9	17.8	17.9	20.5	23.5	29.2	33.9	10.6	10.3
Imports	11.5	12.4	13.1	22.7	24.5	26.0	29.2	32.1	34.2	17.7	5.0
Balance	1.4	−0.0	−2.2	−5.0	−6.6	−5.5	−5.7	−2.9	−0.4	−7.1	5.3
Shipping											
Exports	12.6	12.3	12.6	13.8	14.7	15.5	17.0	18.9	20.4	4.4	3.4
Imports	12.5	11.7	12.2	14.8	15.6	16.7	18.1	19.6	20.7	5.6	2.7
Balance	0.1	0.6	0.4	−1.0	−1.0	−1.3	−1.1	−0.7	−0.4	−1.2	0.7
Passenger fares											
Exports	3.1	3.2	3.6	4.0	4.4	5.5	6.9	8.9	9.9	3.8	3.0
Imports	4.5	4.8	6.0	5.9	6.7	6.8	7.4	7.9	8.3	2.9	0.9
Balance	−1.4	−1.6	−2.4	−1.9	−2.3	−1.2	−0.5	1.0	1.6	0.8	2.1
Royalties and license fees											
Exports	7.3	5.2	5.3	5.6	6.0	7.3	9.1	10.7	11.9	1.8	2.9
Imports	0.7	0.6	0.7	1.0	0.9	1.1	1.4	2.0	1.9	0.7	0.5
Balance	6.6	4.6	4.6	4.7	5.1	6.2	7.7	8.7	10.1	1.1	2.3
Other business services											
Exports	8.8	11.8	12.9	13.6	13.9	22.2	23.0	24.3	28.6	14.2	5.6
Imports	3.6	4.0	4.3	5.1	5.8	8.7	11.4	11.4	11.7	7.8	0.3
Balance	5.2	7.8	8.6	8.4	8.1	13.4	11.6	12.9	16.9	6.3	5.3

Source: US Department of Commerce.

earnings of US carriers. Very large additional gains, however, are most unlikely without either severe dollar depreciation or a persistently weak US economy.

The royalties and license fees account, which consists of income from the foreign sale or licensing of US technology, has long provided healthy surpluses. These have grown modestly in the 1980s, reaching $10.1 billion in 1989, reflecting in part the increased dollar value of foreign license fees denominated in foreign currencies. However, further major gains other than those generated by the currency translation effects of additional dollar decline seem unlikely, because the balance of trade in intellectual property rights is likely to turn gradually against the United States as it utilizes more and more foreign technology relative to its technology exports.

The "other business services" category includes a wide variety of tradeable business services such as income from communication services, construction contractors' fees, film rental income, financial and management services, and consulting services. The dollar value of many of these transactions is large, but the net return to the exporting country—the amount recorded as an export in the current account—is typically only a small fraction of the total transaction. For example, the return from very large insurance transactions is only a fraction of the total after claims and local administration costs are paid. Similarly, only a small portion of the very large gross amounts realized from US film rentals is reflected in the US current account.

Even so, total exports of other business services in 1989 were $28.6 billion, and imports were $11.7 billion, yielding a record surplus of $16.9 billion (table 2). The returns from other business services are thus significant, but with exports in this component comprising only about 4.8 percent of total 1989 US goods and services exports, and with foreign competition stiffening, there is little reason to expect further major gains. Recent increases in reported exports may in part reflect changes in the method of estimating exports of some services rather than a sustainable trend.

Nor is there any reason to expect that the United States will maintain whatever international competitive advantages in these kinds of services it presently has. International competition in many kinds of services is increasing rapidly; for example, the Japanese have become the bankers of the world. Moreover, US firms are now importing some kinds of labor-intensive services that they once performed for themselves or obtained domestically; for example, some data entry and computer services can now be handled in foreign countries and the results transmitted electronically to the United States. Korean firms have become very competent in handling major construction projects outside their own country. The United States is probably unmatched in the technological capabilities and low prices of its telecommunications services, yet it runs large telecommunications services deficits ($2 billion in 1989), partly because deregulated US telephone companies offer services at much lower cost from the United States than are available to callers in most foreign countries. This results in a much larger volume of calls from the United States to foreign countries than vice versa.

The nonmerchandise elements of the current account are relatively resistant to exchange rate changes. The unilateral transfers account is unaffected by exchange rate movements. Over the long term, dollar depreciation might raise the dollar amounts required to purchase some foreign services in the other goods and services account, but in the short term there is likely to be little effect from exchange rate changes. The effects of exchange rate movements on international investment income will be primarily of a currency translation nature, rather than causing changes in the foreign income itself. Thus, only in business services does there seem to be an opportunity for dollar depreciation to have a significant effect on US current account balances, and even in this account the potential is limited.

Within the business services account, a depreciated dollar will reduce US travel abroad and increase foreign tourism in the United States. Increased foreign tourism in the United States would also result from strong economic growth and rising affluence abroad. Conversely, foreign travel by US citizens will be reduced by poor US economic performance. With international air fares set by international agreements, dollar depreciation will not give American air carriers a price advantage over foreign carriers in the competition for passengers, although it will raise the dollar value of foreign earnings (but also the foreign costs) of US carriers in dollar terms.

A declining dollar will have favorable currency translation effects on royalties and license fees but is unlikely to have any significant effect on the volume of technology sales and licensing by US firms, and in fact it will raise the dollar cost of acquiring foreign technology. Similarly, the volume of exports and imports of other business services (insurance, film rentals, consulting, management services, etc.) is likely to be only slightly affected by relatively modest exchange rate movements.

To summarize, only one non–merchandise trade account, business services, offers the prospect of improving US current account balances as a result of changes in economic growth patterns, dollar depreciation, or changing competitive relationships. Even here further improvements are likely to be modest, and perhaps inadequate to offset continued deterioration in the international investment income account. The data thus lead to the conclusion that significant improvements in the current account balance must come primarily—and probably exclusively—from the merchandise trade component.

Indeed, the improvement in the merchandise trade account needed to achieve current account balance is likely to be greater in magnitude than the 1989 merchandise trade deficit. A balanced current account later in the 1990s will probably require a merchandise trade surplus to offset further deterioration in other segments of the current account, principally in the international investment income balance. For example, assuming a $20 billion further deterioration in the international investment balance from 1990 through 1992 and no significant changes in other accounts, a balanced current account in 1992—an unlikely prospect, but useful for illustrative purposes—would require a further improvement in merchandise trade performance of about $125 billion from 1989 levels. That would imply a merchandise trade surplus of about $12 billion. In contrast, the actual improvements recorded in the current account and the merchandise trade account from 1987 to 1989 were $37.8 billion and $46.3 billion, respectively (table 1).

Dissecting the Merchandise Trade Account

US merchandise trade has been in deficit since 1976, but the deficits were modest until a rapid deterioration began in 1983, which continued through 1987 (table 3). Analysis of recent performance in the four major categories of merchandise trade provides insights into their relative volatility and demonstrates the dominant role of manufactures trade in merchandise trade.

In 1989, manufactures trade accounted for four-fifths of US merchandise trade: 79.5 percent of exports and 80.3 percent of imports. Mineral fuels accounted for 3 percent of exports (mostly coal) and 11 percent of imports (mostly crude and refined petroleum). Agricultural products accounted for 11.1 percent of 1989 exports and 4.7 percent of imports.

"Other merchandise trade" is a group of miscellaneous items, including wood, hides, skins, and paper pulp. This category represented 6.5 percent of 1989 exports and 4.0 percent of imports.

From 1981 to 1987—the year that will probably stand as the low point in US trade performance—the merchandise trade balance declined from a deficit of $22.3 billion to a deficit of $152.1 billion, or by $129.8 billion. However, the decline in the manufactures trade balance during the same period was even greater: $146.8 billion. Performance also worsened in agricultural goods, as the surplus fell to $8.4 billion—an $18.2 billion slide. Movement in the "other merchandise trade" account was marginal, only $0.5 billion, while the mineral fuels deficit actually narrowed by $34.7 billion, from $71.1 billion to $36.4 billion. Thus, a major reduction in the oil deficit—a result of both reduced oil import volumes and lower oil import prices—prevented the US merchandise trade deficit from becoming even larger and to some extent masked the huge deterioration in manufactures trade performance.

The merchandise trade balance improved significantly—by $43.5 billion—from 1987 to 1989 (table 3). The manufactures trade deficit narrowed by $35.0 billion, and the agricultural surplus grew by $10.1 billion. The mineral fuels

Table 3 United States: merchandise trade by component, 1981–89 (billions of dollars)

Account	1981	1982	1983	1984	1985	1986	1987	1988	1989	Change 1981–87	Change 1987–89
Total merchandise trade											
Exports	238.7	216.4	205.6	224.0	218.8	227.2	254.1	322.4	364.3	15.4	110.2
Imports	261.0	244.0	258.0	330.7	336.5	365.4	406.2	441.0	472.9	145.2	66.7
Balance	−22.3	−27.6	−52.4	−106.7	−117.7	−138.2	−152.1	−118.5	−108.6	−129.8	43.5
Manufactures											
Exports	171.7	155.3	148.5	163.6	167.8	179.9	200.0	255.6	289.7	28.3	89.7
Imports	149.8	151.7	171.2	231.3	257.9	297.0	324.9	361.4	379.6	175.1	54.7
Balance	21.9	3.6	−22.7	−67.7	−90.1	−117.1	−124.9	−105.7	−89.9	−146.8	35.0
Agriculture											
Exports	43.8	37.0	36.5	38.2	29.6	26.6	29.1	37.6	40.6	−14.7	11.5
Imports	17.2	15.7	16.5	19.8	20.0	21.2	20.7	21.2	22.1	3.5	1.4
Balance	26.6	21.3	20.0	18.4	9.6	5.4	8.4	16.4	18.5	−18.2	10.1
Mineral fuels											
Exports	10.3	12.8	9.6	9.5	10.1	8.2	7.8	8.6	9.9	−2.5	2.1
Imports	81.4	65.4	58.3	61.0	53.9	37.3	44.2	41.0	52.6	−37.2	8.4
Balance	−71.1	−52.6	−48.7	−51.5	−43.8	−29.1	−36.4	−32.4	−42.7	34.7	−6.3
Other merchandise trade											
Exports	12.8	11.4	11.1	12.7	11.2	12.1	15.9	18.5	23.6	3.1	7.7
Imports	12.5	11.2	12.4	18.6	4.7	9.6	15.1	17.6	19.1	2.6	4.0
Balance	0.3	0.2	−1.3	−5.9	6.5	2.5	0.8	3.1	4.5	0.5	3.7

Source: US Department of Commerce.

deficit, however, increased by $6.3 billion, as oil import volumes grew and prices rose.

Through July 1990, US merchandise trade performance continued to improve, with the deficit in the first half of the year $8.0 billion smaller than at the same point in 1989. Manufactures trade showed a $12.1 billion improvement; however, the agricultural surplus was $1.5 billion smaller than in 1989 and the oil deficit $2.6 billion larger.

The first seven months of 1990 suggest, for the year as a whole, a merchandise trade improvement of about $10 billion or more, with a significant improvement in the manufactures trade balance of perhaps $20 billion offset by deterioration in the mineral fuels and agricultural accounts. Part of the improvement in manufactures trade performance may be temporary, however. Strong growth abroad increased US manufactures exports for the first seven months of 1990 by 10.1 percent over the same period in 1989, and a relatively weak US economy helped restrain growth of US manufactures imports to only 2.2 percent.

Looking to the longer term, it seems clear that further improvements in merchandise trade performance must come primarily from the manufactures trade account. "Other merchandise trade" will continue to be a relatively minor account. The 1989 agricultural surplus ($18.5 billion) was a significant improvement over levels of the mid–1980s, but was $8 billion short of the $26.6 billion record of 1981. Modest further gains above the 1989 level may be achieved in some years, but performance in the first seven months of 1990 is slightly behind that of 1989. More important, further major gains will be difficult to sustain in a world of agricultural subsidies and surplus stocks in many market economies. Moreover, increased market incentives in the communist countries that are moving away from collectivized agriculture are likely to increase global grain production. In all, the outlook is for supply-demand conditions that will preclude sustained US grain export bonanzas.

The oil import bill, on the other hand, may well increase. Import volume increases seem assured for the next several years, barring a severe US economic downturn. Import prices are difficult to predict, but medium- and longer-term levels above those of 1989 seem quite likely. Fluctuations in oil prices have a significant impact, with each one-dollar change in the price of a barrel of oil altering the US import bill by about $2 billion, assuming constant import volumes.

Wide fluctuations in manufactures trade have thus been dominant in recent US merchandise trade and current account performance, and improvements in the merchandise trade balance in the foreseeable future will almost certainly have to come about primarily in that sector.

The 1989 merchandise trade deficit was $108.6 billion; the manufactures deficit in that year was $89.9 billion. Thus, assuming no significant changes in the oil import deficit (i.e., no increase from 1989 import prices or volumes) and no major changes in the agricultural trade balance, a $125 billion merchandise trade balance improvement—projected earlier in this paper as that needed to achieve a balanced current account in 1992—would require a manufactures trade improvement of similar magnitude, to a surplus of about $35 billion. Increased oil import bills would, of course, raise the required surplus, as would any further delay in narrowing the current account deficit, which would likely be accompanied by a further slide in the international investment income balance.

The Global Role of Manufactures Trade

This dominant—and volatile—role of manufactures trade in external transactions is not unique to the United States. In fact, world trade to a substantial and increasing degree is trade in manufactured goods. From 1981 to 1989 total world exports grew from $1,664 billion to $2,757 billion (table 4)—a nearly two-thirds increase.[1]

The nonmanufactures portion of that trade (including fuels) decreased from $650.5 billion in 1981 to $549.1 billion in 1987—a 15.4 percent decrease. Manufactures trade, however, grew during the same period from $1,013.9 billion to $1,648.6 billion—a 63 percent increase. Thus, in 1981 manufactures exports were 60.9 percent of world exports, increasing to 75.0 percent in 1987. Setting aside mineral fuels trade, whose dollar value has fluctuated widely with oil price changes, manufactures exports were 78.5 percent of the total in 1981 and 83.3 percent in 1987.

A continued decline in the relative role (in dollar terms) in world merchandise trade of nonmanufactures, non–mineral fuel items (food, beverages and tobacco, raw materials, etc.) seems assured. Mineral fuels, on the other hand, has varied widely as a percentage of total world exports during the 1980s, from 22.4 percent in 1981 to 9.9 percent in 1987, mostly because of changes in oil prices. Oil prices will probably remain volatile, and oil could increase its share of trade in dollar terms.

Oil is a critical input for modern industrialized economies and is relatively price-inelastic, particularly in the short term. Oil trade volumes and prices thus can do much to determine international trade and capital flows. To the extent that the OPEC countries are able to set oil prices, they can alter trade and capital flows. Given the inelasticity of demand, a sustained increase in oil prices puts increased pressure on the manufactures trade accounts of individual oil-importing countries, which then have little choice but to try to pay their enlarged oil

---

1. Dollar exchange rate changes influence the values of the exports of other countries when translated into dollars. Time series from this data base thus include not only volume changes but the effects of inflation and dollar exchange rate movements.

Table 4 World and US trade, all commodities, 1981–87 (billions of dollars except where noted)

	1981	1982	1983	1984	1985	1986	1987	1988	1989	Average annual growth 1981–89 (percentages)
World exports to world[a]	1,664.4	1,556.2	1,529.9	1,630.9	1,676.9	1,855.9	2,197.8	2,571.9	2,757.3	6.5
of which:										
0 Food and live animals	152.8	139.6	137.4	142.3	138.3	162.2	180.9	207.1	215.5	4.4
1 Beverages and tobacco	16.2	16.3	15.5	15.4	16.6	19.5	23.5	26.0	28.2	7.2
2 Crude materials	101.2	89.5	90.5	98.5	94.0	99.8	119.0	145.2	153.2	5.3
3 Mineral fuels	373.0	329.8	297.7	298.1	294.0	203.3	218.4	205.1	241.5	−5.3
4 Animal, vegetable oils	7.4	6.6	7.0	9.5	8.9	6.9	7.3	8.9	8.6	1.9
5 Chemicals	123.5	117.0	122.1	131.2	136.9	162.1	195.9	238.3	246.8	9.0
6 Basic manufactures	258.5	239.1	236.0	250.0	255.0	298.3	354.5	438.3	469.0	7.7
7 Machines and transport equipment	465.7	454.7	456.6	501.2	535.1	654.3	781.9	932.9	990.0	9.9
8 Miscellaneous manufactures	144.1	142.0	144.4	158.5	170.4	217.5	269.4	310.6	334.7	11.1
9 Not classed by kind	22.1	21.6	22.8	26.2	27.7	31.9	46.9	59.6	69.9	15.5
Nonmanufactures (0–2, 4)[b]	277.5	252.0	250.4	265.7	257.8	288.4	330.7	387.1	401.0	4.7
Manufactures (5–9)	1,013.9	974.4	981.8	1,067.1	1,125.2	1,364.1	1,648.6	1,979.6	2,110.3	9.6
US trade										
Exports	225.8	206.0	194.6	210.2	205.2	204.7	243.6	304.9	347.0	5.5
Imports	271.2	247.8	268.0	338.2	358.9	381.4	422.4	459.0	491.5	7.7
Balance	−45.4	−41.8	−73.4	−128.0	−153.7	−176.7	−178.8	−154.1	−144.6	

a. World exports are calculated by combining OECD member exports to the world with OECD member imports from nonmember countries. A small amount of trade among non-OECD countries is therefore excluded.

b. Excluding mineral fuels.   *Source:* World Manufactures Trade Data Base.

bills by improving their performance in manufactures trade (enlarged exports, diminished imports, or some combination of the two). The result is stiffer international competition in manufactures trade.

Changes in net international capital flows are normally affected primarily by the monetary, fiscal, tax, regulatory, and other economic policies of nations. But whether they are caused by oil price fluctuations or by national macroeconomic policies, such changes impact primarily on the manufacturing sectors of the industrialized countries.

The foregoing data and analysis lead to the following conclusions:

- Within the current account, excepting merchandise trade, only tradeable business services offers any real prospect of improving US performance. However, business services is a relatively small portion of total US trade, is only modestly influenced by exchange rate movements, and does not provide a major means of improving US current account balances.

- Manufactures trade dominates US merchandise trade and the US trade and current account balances. It similarly dominates the balances of most industrialized countries.

- Manufactures trade is the major growth segment of world trade and one of intensifying competition. Competition for world markets is primarily a struggle for markets in relatively few key manufactures product groups.

- Major improvements in US trade and current account balances must come primarily from improved manufactures trade performance. Indeed, a balanced current account will require significant merchandise trade surpluses, which are likely to be achieved only through substantial manufactures trade surpluses.

- US monetary, fiscal, tax, regulatory, and other policy combinations that motivate net inflows of capital will inevitably be manifested in manufactures trade deficits and will adversely affect primarily the nation's manufacturing sector.

- Rising oil prices will put increased pressure on the manufactures trade accounts of individual countries as they attempt to compensate for rising oil bills primarily through increased manufactures exports, diminished manufactures imports, or both. Rising oil prices thus intensify international competition in manufactures trade.

Recent and Prospective US Manufactures Trade Performance

A detailed assessment of manufactures trade, focusing on major product groups, can provide important insights not only about US manufactures trade itself, but about the outlook for total US trade and current account performance. US manufactures trade performance declined rapidly during the 1980s. Balances fluctuated through 1982, but then performance worsened dramatically. In 1981 the United States enjoyed a manufactures trade surplus of $18.0 billion, but deteriorating performance resulted in a 1987 deficit of $132.7 billion. This slide of $150.8 billion was equivalent to 3.3 percent of 1987 GNP.[2] In part the decline was due to lagging US exports: the US share of world exports of manufactures to non–US destinations declined from 18.6 percent in 1981 to 14.5 percent in 1987 (table 5).

Table 6 ranks manufactures product groups by the amount they contributed to the overall change in the US trade balance over the 1981–87 period. Ranking product categories by export and import values, rates of change, and similar measures allows for a reasoned selection of those product groups meriting closer examination because of their importance in overall US trade performance.[3]

Table 7 summarizes the changes in individual product groups from 1987 to 1989 and from 1989 to 1990. The data show an overall improvement from 1987 to 1989 of $29.2 billion, or 19.4 percent of the $150.8 billion 1981–87 decline. Projecting 1990 performance by the simple expedient of doubling the first six months' exports and imports indicates a potential 1990 improvement of $25.4 billion. The manufactures trade balance will indeed show a large improvement when final data are in, but it is unlikely to be as large as $25.4 billion. Performance worsened in July, and there are reasons to believe that the first-half performance in some categories will not be sustained through the year. For example, although aircraft (SITC 79) will achieve major gains over 1989, the improvement will probably not be as large as the $7.6 billion projected in table 7.[4]

---

2. These data are on a domestic exports, imports customs basis that will be used in the analysis of individual product groups and may result in slightly different totals than those in table 3.

3. US trade data are available in SITC (Revision 2) format for the period through 1988. Revision 3 was implemented by the United States in 1989, and data for prior years through 1983 have been recreated by a concordance process. This study follows the general methodology of assessing change from 1981 to 1987, in most categories the low point of US trade performance, and then subsequent changes from 1987 to 1989 and 1990. Because at the two-digit level of detail the Revision 2 and 3 amounts may not correspond exactly, the general procedure has been to assess 1981–87 changes using Revision 2 data, and to use Revision 3 data in assessing changes from 1987 forward.

4. Assessing these changes is complicated by the fact that through 1989 exports to Canada were consistently underreported in individual product groups, but were summarized in a "Canada adjustment" figure (SITC 998). In 1990, however, the United States began using Canadian import data as a record of US exports and retroactively apportioned the $16 billion 1989 Canada adjustment figure among two-digit product groups. Deriving the most correct valuation of change in performance of a two-digit product group thus requires assessing the amount of the change from 1987 to 1989 using Revision 3 data that do not reflect the Canada adjustment, and separately assessing the change between 1989 data including the Canada adjustment and 1990 results, which are presumed not to require adjustment.

Table 5 World and US manufactures trade, 1981–87ᵃ (billions of dollars except where noted)

	1981	1982	1983	1984	1985	1986	1987	Average annual growth, 1981–87 (percentages)
World exports to world	999.7	974.4	981.8	1,067.1	1,125.2	1,364.1	1,648.6	8.7
World exports to non–US destinations	858.1	828.0	806.9	834.8	875.8	1,074.0	1,323.0	7.5
World imports from non–US sources	851.5	834.7	844.4	922.8	987.3	1,223.6	1,471.0	9.5
US exports	159.7	145.6	138.2	151.5	155.0	158.1	191.8	3.1
As percentage of world exports to world	16.0	14.9	14.1	14.2	13.8	11.6	11.6	
As percentage of exports to non–US destinations	18.6	17.6	17.1	18.2	17.7	14.7	14.5	
US imports	154.2	153.9	176.6	238.8	266.7	303.0	335.9	13.9
As percentage of world exports	15.4	15.8	18.0	22.4	23.7	22.2	20.4	
As percentage of imports from non–US sources	18.0	18.4	20.9	25.9	27.0	24.8	22.8	

a. World exports are estimated by combining OECD exports to the world (including other OECD countries) with OECD imports from nonmember countries. A relatively small amount of trade among non-OECD countries is therefore excluded.

Source: Organization for Economic Cooperation and Development, *Monthly Statistics of Foreign Trade,* SITC Revision 2, various issues.

Table 6 United States: commodity composition of trade, ranked by change in contribution to the trade balance, 1981–87 (millions of dollars)

SITC	Commodity	Exports 1981	Exports 1987	Imports 1981	Imports 1987	Balance 1981	Balance 1987	Change in balance
	Total all commodities	233,908	243,859	260,982	405,901	−27,074	−162,042	−134,968
33	Petroleum, petroleum products	3,710	3,958	75,589	41,555	−71,879	−37,597	34,282
34	Gas, natural and manufactured	577	361	5,526	2,496	−4,949	−2,135	2,814
28	Metal, ferrous ores, etc.	2,684	3,002	3,733	2,378	−1,049	624	1,673
06	Sugar, sugar preparations	650	230	2,407	841	−1,757	−611	1,146
12	Tobacco and tobacco manufactures	2,723	3,400	706	691	2,017	2,709	692
21	Hides, skins, and furskins	1,024	1,731	269	300	755	1,431	676
25	Pulp and waste paper	2,015	2,895	1,778	2,089	237	806	569
23	Crude rubber (including synthetics)	656	807	978	1,125	−322	−318	4
43	Animal and vegetable oils	85	77	23	32	62	45	−17
00	Live animals chiefly for food	270	405	332	540	−62	−135	−73
09	Miscellaneous edible products	584	767	146	408	438	359	−79
08	Feeding stuff for animals	2,744	2,694	132	209	2,612	2,485	−127
02	Dairy products and bird's eggs	407	359	359	444	48	−85	−133
29	Crude animal and vegetable meat	503	598	716	1,070	−213	−472	−259
27	Crude fertilizers and crude mineral	1,424	970	864	723	560	247	−313
41	Animal oils and fats	737	424	10	24	727	400	−327
42	Fixed vegetable oils and fats	953	536	449	519	504	17	−487
01	Meat and meat preparations	1,482	1,769	1,995	2,790	−513	−1,021	−508
24	Cork and wood	2,372	3,202	2,023	3,398	349	−196	−545
07	Coffee, tea, cocoa, spices	222	226	4,072	4,675	−3,850	−4,449	−599
11	Beverages	192	267	2,433	3,414	−2,241	−3,147	−906

SITC	Commodity	Exports 1981	Exports 1987	Imports 1981	Imports 1987	Balance 1981	Balance 1987	Change in balance
26	Textile fibers and their waste	3,402	2,552	371	548	3,031	2,004	−1,027
22	Oil seeds	6,863	4,617	435	58	6,428	4,559	−1,869
03	Fish, crustaceans, and mollusks	1,080	1,586	2,961	5,590	−1,881	−4,004	−2,123
05	Vegetables and fruit	3,299	2,949	2,556	4,449	743	−1,500	−2,243
32	Coal, coke, and briquettes	6,006	3,430	117	186	5,889	3,244	−2,645
04	Cereals and cereal preparations	19,441	8,034	245	596	19,196	7,438	−11,758
5–9	Total manufactures	167,803	192,014	149,757	324,730	18,046	−132,715	−150,761
98/99	Low-value shipments		15,112		2,334		12,778	12,778
56	Fertilizers, manufactured	1,694	2,261	1,094	794	600	1,467	866
67	Iron and steel	2,878	1,290	11,238	9,097	−8,360	−7,807	553
58	Artificial resins, plastic	3,758	5,395	733	1,893	3,025	3,501	477
96	Coins	2	6	0	14	2	−8	−10
57	Explosives, etc.	90	91	60	107	31	−17	−48
59	Chemical materials	3,423	3,856	755	1,264	2,668	2,592	−77
51	Organic chemicals	5,168	6,631	2,917	4,509	2,251	2,122	−129
61	Leather, leather manufactures	431	636	571	1,055	−140	−419	−279
54	Medicinal, pharmaceuticals	2,255	3,348	833	2,360	1,423	987	−435
53	Dyeing, tanning, coloring	538	641	339	1,068	199	−427	−627
55	Essential oils, perfumes	980	1,017	382	1,057	597	−40	−638
81	Sanitary, plumbing, heating	329	268	192	781	137	−513	−650
79	Other transport equipment	16,339	17,955	3,282	5,675	13,056	12,280	−776
52	Inorganic chemicals	3,203	3,131	2,094	2,865	1,109	266	−842
63	Cork and wood manufactures	600	688	1,237	2,172	−637	−1,484	−847
97	Gold	3,111	1,730	2,131	1,612	980	119	−862
83	Travel goods, handbags	83	49	802	1,903	−719	−1,854	−1,135

Table 6   United States: commodity composition of trade, ranked by change in contribution to the trade balance, 1981–87 (millions of dollars) (Continued)

SITC	Commodity	Exports 1981	Exports 1987	Imports 1981	Imports 1987	Balance 1981	Balance 1987	Change in balance
62	Rubber manufactures	1,197	1,363	1,573	2,942	-376	-1,579	-1,203
87	Professional, scientific	6,024	7,438	1,771	4,616	4,253	2,822	-1,431
73	Metalworking machinery	2,190	1,639	2,002	2,978	188	-1,339	-1,527
68	Nonferrous metals	2,803	2,179	6,950	7,957	-4,147	-5,778	-1,631
95	Armaments	2,132	58	101	107	2,031	-48	-2,080
88	Photographic apparatus	2,586	2,544	3,240	5,483	-654	-2,939	-2,284
64	Paper, paperboard	2,946	3,166	3,832	7,382	-886	-4,216	-3,330
82	Furniture and parts thereof	697	624	1,267	4,656	-570	-4,032	-3,463
65	Textile yarn, fabrics	3,619	2,933	2,875	6,131	744	-3,198	-3,942
66	Nonmetallic mineral manufacturers	2,245	2,332	4,887	8,972	-2,642	-6,640	-3,997
85	Footwear	141	186	3,146	7,236	-3,005	-7,051	-4,045
69	Manufactures of metal	4,297	3,131	4,251	8,158	45	-5,027	-5,072
71	Power-generating machinery	9,588	10,360	4,614	10,947	4,974	-587	-5,561
75	Office machines and computers	9,743	18,641	3,563	18,413	6,181	228	-5,953
74	General industrial machinery	11,884	8,380	4,855	10,568	7,029	-2,188	-9,216
89	Miscellaneous manufactures	5,286	6,542	8,064	19,292	-2,778	-12,750	-9,972
93	Special transactions	8,142	1,224	4,820	8,082	3,322	-6,857	-10,180
77	Electrical machinery	11,287	16,408	9,300	24,678	1,986	-8,270	-10,256
76	Telecommunications and sound	3,841	5,066	8,947	20,820	-5,106	-15,754	-10,648
72	Specialized machinery	14,602	9,243	5,244	11,459	9,358	-2,215	-11,574
84	Apparel and clothing	1,255	1,184	7,619	20,639	-6,363	-19,455	-13,092
78	Road vehicles	16,398	21,055	28,146	72,501	-11,748	-51,446	-39,698

Source: US Department of Commerce.

Recent US Trade Performance in Road Vehicles and Engines

Individual product groups vary widely in their role in international trade and in their contribution to US trade deficits and deficit reduction. Table 8 ranks manufacturing product categories (at the SITC two-digit level) by their contribution to total world manufactures trade. As the table shows, road vehicles (SITC 78) is by far the largest single manufactures product group in international trade. As table 6 shows, it was also by far the most important in the deterioration of US trade performance in the 1980s. This product group will continue to play a critical role in US trade performance during the 1990s.

Description of the Product Group

Road vehicles as identified in SITC data group 78 include motor cars (SITC 781), motor vehicles for the transport of goods (trucks) and other special-purpose vehicles (SITC 782), road motor vehicles not elsewhere specified (SITC 783), parts and accessories of motor vehicles (SITC 784), motorcycles (SITC 785), and trailers and semitrailers (SITC 786).

Motor cars and trucks are often lumped together, but it is useful to separate them for analytical purposes. Parts and accessories is a category of growing importance. Trade in internal combustion engines and engine parts (SITC 713) has also become important and is closely related to the globalization of car and truck production and assembly. For these reasons, we include it in the analysis of road vehicle trade here and in the larger study, rather than as part of the power-generating machinery group (SITC 71).

Role in US and World Trade

At $231 billion (table 9), world exports of road vehicles to all destinations by far exceeded those in any other single manufactures product group in 1987. Road vehicles constituted 10.5 percent of all 1987 world exports, up from 7.6 percent in 1981, and 14.0 percent of all 1987 manufactures exports, up from 12.6 percent in 1981.

US road vehicle exports grew only modestly, well below world rates, during the 1981–87 period, rising from $16 billion in 1981 to $22 billion in 1987. The result was a decline in the US share of world road vehicle exports to non–US destinations from 16.8 percent to 14.0 percent. US imports, on the other hand, played a key role in the growth of road vehicle trade, rising from $30 billion in 1981 to $75 billion in 1987, increasing the US share of world imports from non–US sources from 27.1 percent in 1981 to 36.5 percent in 1987.

Table 7 United States: commodity composition of manufactures trade, 1987–90 (millions of dollars)

	1987	1989	1990[a]	Change 1987–89	Change 1989–90[b]	Change 1987–90[b]
Total exports	191,729	276,037	299,841	84,308	23,804	108,112
Total imports	324,444	379,597	378,000	55,153	−1,597	53,556
Balance	−132,715	−103,560	−78,159	29,155	25,401	54,556
of which:						
51 Organic chemicals	2,209	3,567	2,890	1,358	−640	718
52 Inorganic chemicals	1,121	1,088	466	−33	−570	−603
53 Dyeing, tanning, and coloring	−314	−37	375	278	258	536
54 Medicinal and pharmaceutical products	1,209	1,574	1,736	366	133	499
55 Essential oils and perfume	−31	304	630	335	237	572
56 Fertilizers, manufactured	317	1,822	1,450	1,505	−262	1,242
57 Explosives and pyrotechnic products	2,920	4,040	4,187	1,119	−225	894
58 Artificial resins and plastics	333	572	891	239	49	289
59 Chemical materials and products	1,693	2,803	3,504	1,110	401	1,511
61 Leather and leather manufactures	−192	−171	16	22	192	214
62 Rubber manufactures, n.e.s.	−2,067	−2,132	−1,658	−65	13	−51
63 Cork and wood manufactures (excl. furniture)	−1,333	−1,060	−845	273	163	436
64 Paper, paperboard, and articles	−4,157	−4,354	−3,573	−197	387	189
65 Textile yarn, fabric, and madeup articles	−2,860	−2,197	−1,321	663	459	1,122
66 Nonmetallic mineral manufactures	−6,711	−6,967	−6,468	−256	135	−121
67 Iron and steel	−7,856	−7,311	−6,289	545	596	1,142
68 Nonferrous metals	−5,630	−6,199	−4,636	−570	1,250	680
69 Manufactures of metal, n.e.s.	−4,441	−4,357	−2,997	83	508	591
71 Power-generating machinery and equipment	−644	−83	1,291	561	186	747
72 Machinery specialized for particular industries	−1,868	685	2,304	2,553	887	3,440
73 Metalworking machinery	−801	−1,277	−650	−476	488	12

Table 7 United States: commodity composition of manufactures trade, 1987–90 (millions of dollars) (Continued)

	1987	1989	1990[a]	Change 1987–89	Change 1989–90[b]	Change 1987–90[b]
74 General industrial machinery and equipment	−3,090	−1,375	1,219	1,715	636	2,352
75 Office and automatic data processing machines	316	−2,495	−1,711	−2,811	−32	−2,843
76 Telecommunications and sound-reproducing equipment	−15,712	−15,513	−11,505	199	3,547	3,746
77 Electrical machinery, apparatus, and appliances	−8,482	−8,417	−4,376	64	2,531	2,595
78 Road vehicles (including air-cushion vehicles)	−51,679	−46,384	−39,845	5,295	4,176	9,471
79 Other transport equipment	12,024	17,899	25,702	5,875	7,608	13,483
81 Sanitary, plumbing, heating, and lighting fixtures	−586	−616	−507	−31	29	−1
82 Furniture and parts thereof	−3,979	−3,916	−3,498	63	127	190
83 Travel goods, handbags, and similar containers	−1,815	−2,024	−2,010	−209	2	−207
84 Articles of apparel and clothing	−19,276	−22,472	−21,396	−3,196	1,017	−2,179
85 Footwear	−7,276	−8,025	−8,660	−749	−651	−1,399
87 Professional, scientific, and controlling instruments	3,247	5,078	6,050	1,831	411	2,242
88 Photographic apparatus, equipment, and supplies	−3,052	−2,576	−1,863	477	623	1,100
89 Miscellaneous manufactures	−10,231	−9,451	−5,051	781	3,219	3,999
93 Special transactions, n.e.s.	−6,857	−8,000	−9,241	−1,142	−1,516	−2,659
95 Armaments	−48	−268	−157	−220	114	−106
98/99 Canada adjustment and low-value exports	12,778	23,778	5,761	11,000	1,922	12,922

a. Figures for 1990 are projected by doubling the results for the first half of the year.

b. These figures exclude the effects of the Canada adjustment.

Source: US Department of Commerce.

Table 8 World manufactures exports to all destinations by two-digit SITC category, ranked by value, 1987

SITC Category	Billions of dollars	Percentage of total
78 Road vehicles	231.2	14.0
77 Electrical machinery, apparatus, and appliances	115.4	7.0
75 Office and automatic data processing machines	84.5	5.1
89 Miscellaneous manufactures	79.8	4.8
72 Machinery specialized for particular industries	77.3	4.7
74 General industrial machinery and equipment	77.3	4.7
84 Articles of apparel and clothing	75.5	4.6
67 Iron and steel	70.0	4.2
76 Telecommunications and sound-reproducing equipment	68.6	4.2
65 Textile yarns, fabric, and madeup articles	67.8	4.1
79 Other transport equipment	53.4	3.2
71 Power-generating machinery and equipment	52.0	3.2
51 Organic chemicals	49.9	3.0
66 Nonmetallic mineral manufactures	47.0	2.9
58 Explosives and pyrotechnic products	45.0	2.7
68 Nonferrous metals	43.0	2.6
64 Paper, paperboard, and articles	42.2	2.6
93 Special transactions, n.e.s.	39.4	2.4
69 Manufactures of metal, n.e.s.	39.3	2.4
87 Professional, scientific, and controlling instruments	36.6	2.2
88 Photographic apparatus, equipment, and supplies	27.2	1.6
54 Medicinal and pharmaceutical products	23.7	1.4
59 Chemical materials and products	23.0	1.4
52 Inorganic chemicals	20.4	1.2
85 Footwear	19.9	1.2
73 Metalworking machinery	19.8	1.2
82 Furniture and parts thereof	19.5	1.2
62 Rubber manufactures, n.e.s.	16.7	1.0
53 Dyeing, tanning, and coloring	12.8	0.8
55 Essential oils and perfume	12.0	0.7

SITC Category	Billions of dollars	Percentage of total
63 Cork and wood manufactures (excl. furniture)	11.2	0.7
61 Leather and leather manufactures	9.9	0.6
56 Fertilizers, manufactured	8.4	0.5
95 Armaments	6.8	0.4
83 Travel goods, handbags, and similar containers	5.5	0.3
81 Sanitary, plumbing, heating, and lighting fixtures	5.4	0.3
57 Artificial resins and plastics	0.7	0.0
Total	1,648.6	100.0

Source: World Manufactures Trade Data Base.

At $126.7 billion, over half (55 percent) of the 1987 dollar value of world road vehicle exports was accounted for by passenger cars. Trucks, at $28.3 billion, comprised only 12.2 percent of the total, but parts and accessories at $63.4 billion had a 27.4 percent share.

As the globalization of production of cars and trucks has continued, world trade in internal combustion engines has also expanded rapidly, reaching $24 billion in 1987 (table 9). Over the 1981–87 period the US share of world exports of these engines declined from 31.8 percent to 23.5 percent, while the US share of world imports from non–US sources rose from 21.3 percent to 32.0 percent.

Given the relatively large share of road vehicles in world trade, strong performance in this group is clearly important in determining overall trade performance. To put it another way, a 20 percent share of 1987 world road vehicle exports would have generated $46 billion, the same export dollar value as a 54 percent share of office and computing machines (SITC 75). Thus, very large market shares and surpluses in several other product areas may be required to offset poor performance in road vehicles.

Globalization of World Automobile Production

The rapid rise in world exports of automobiles, trucks, and parts and accessories reflects the rapid increase in world automobile production and the increased role of exports in building a motor vehicle industry in some countries. Open US markets have provided much of the stimulus for this globalization, as evidenced by the 37.6 percent US share of world imports in 1985 (table 10).

Table 9   World trade in road vehicles and internal combustion engines, 1981–87 (billions of dollars except where noted)

	1981	1982	1983	1984	1985	1986	1987	Average annual growth 1981–87 (percentages)
SITC 78: Road vehicles								
World exports	125.7	123.7	127.6	140.7	156.6	195.1	231.2	10.7
of which:								
781 Passenger cars	57.8	59.7	65.7	71.8	82.4	108.0	126.7	14.0
782 Trucks	22.5	21.1	18.7	20.2	22.6	25.5	28.3	3.9
783 Other road vehicles	4.0	3.4	2.4	2.5	2.5	2.7	3.6	–1.6
784 Parts and accessories	32.5	31.6	33.8	39.1	42.0	50.9	63.4	11.8
785 Motorcycles	5.9	5.0	4.8	4.8	4.8	5.5	6.2	0.8
786 Trailers	3.0	2.7	2.2	2.2	2.3	2.6	3.1	0.5
World exports to non–US destinations	96.1	91.5	88.1	89.3	96.9	121.5	153.6	8.1
World imports from non–US sources	108.9	108.7	110.2	118.8	135.3	171.8	204.6	11.1
US exports	16.1	13.8	14.4	17.5	19.4	18.7	21.6	4.9
As percentage of world exports	12.6	11.1	11.3	12.4	12.4	9.6	9.3	
As percentage of exports to non–US destinations	16.8	15.1	16.3	19.6	20.0	15.4	14.0	

	1981	1982	1983	1984	1985	1986	1987	Average annual growth 1981–87 (percentages)
US imports	29.5	32.1	37.6	48.5	59.4	70.3	74.6	16.7
As percentage of world imports	23.4	25.9	29.7	34.9	37.6	36.2	32.6	
As percentage of imports from non–US sources	27.1	29.5	34.1	40.8	43.9	40.9	36.5	
SITC 713: Internal combustion engines								
World exports	14.9	14.5	15.3	17.5	17.8	20.5	24.2	8.4
World exports to non–US destinations	12.9	12.4	12.0	13.0	13.0	15.2	17.9	5.6
World imports from non–US sources	10.8	10.6	11.7	13.3	13.6	16.5	20.0	10.8
US exports	4.1	3.9	3.6	4.2	4.2	4.0	4.2	0.4
As percentage of world exports	27.6	26.9	23.5	24.0	23.6	19.5	17.4	
As percentage of exports from non–US destinations	31.8	31.6	29.9	32.2	32.3	26.3	23.5	
US imports	2.3	2.4	3.4	4.6	5.1	5.4	6.4	18.6
As percentage of world imports	15.5	16.6	22.2	26.3	28.6	26.3	26.5	
As percentage of imports from non–US sources	21.3	22.6	29.1	34.6	37.4	32.7	32.0	

Source: World Manufactures Trade Data Base.

The United States led the world in road vehicle production for many years. Total Japan-based production first surpassed that of the United States in 1980, as US production declined markedly, reflecting the US recession that year. But although US production was rising again by 1984, it did not reach earlier levels and remained below that of Japan. In 1988 the United States produced 11.2 million cars and trucks; Japan meanwhile produced 12.7 million, or just a bit over one-fourth of total world production of 48.1 million. With production of 4.6 million units, Germany was third in world production in that year, and France fourth with 3.7 million units.

There are great differences, however, between US and Japanese uses of domestic production. Apparent consumption (total output plus net imports) in the United States in 1988 was 15.6 million cars and trucks. US exports were 1 million (mostly to Canada), and imports were 5.4 million. In Japan, meanwhile, consumption was only 6.8 million, exports were 6.1 million, and imports only 200,000. Thus, US consumption was 139 percent of domestic production, whereas Japanese consumption was only 53 percent of domestic production.

The US market was important to Japan throughout the 1980s. In terms of units, however, Japan's exports to the United States peaked in 1986 at 3.4 million cars and trucks. The share of total Japanese car and truck production exported to the United States peaked that same year at 28 percent, and by 1988 had declined to 20.9 percent. The motor vehicle–producing nations together exported more than 19 million units in 1988, with Japanese manufacturers accounting for slightly less than one-third of the total.

US trade performance in road vehicles has long been dominated by deficits with Japan. Already in 1981 the bilateral deficit with Japan was 136 percent of the total US deficit in road vehicles and engines; in 1989 the $33.5 billion deficit with Japan was 60 percent of the total in these categories, and 51 percent of US passenger car imports were from Japan.

Germany is the world's second-largest car and truck exporter; its overseas sales of 2.7 million vehicles represented 13.9 percent of world road vehicle exports in 1988. The United States has played an important role in Germany's automobile production as well. Passenger car imports from Germany reached 366,543 units and $9 billion in 1987, and parts and accessories imports rose to $900 million. By 1989, however, US passenger car imports from Germany had declined to 221,000 units, and the bilateral deficit had narrowed dramatically.

The United States also provided the primary market for the growth of Korea's automobile industry during the 1980s. In 1988 Korea exported 53 percent of its production, the vast majority of that to the United States. US imports from Korea grew from only $6 million in 1985 to $2.5 billion in 1988 before declining significantly in 1989 and 1990.

The US and Canadian automobile industries have been integrated for years. Canada is by far the largest market for US exports in the SITC 78 group. However, the United States persistently runs road vehicle deficits with Canada: $5.5 billion in 1987, $8.3 billion in 1988, and $9.8 billion in 1989.

Each of the "Big Three" US automakers maintains significant production facilities in Canada, and there is specialization in production and a large cross-trade in vehicles and parts between the two countries. Canada is, however, a relatively small market. The great bulk of Canadian production is not to serve the Canadian market, but is exported to the United States. In 1989, for example, the United States exported 730,000 cars and trucks to Canada, but imported 1.65 million Canadian-produced units. Canadian Big Three car and truck production in 1989 was 1.83 million units, of which only 96,500 units remained in Canada.

US exports of parts and accessories to Canada are also large ($7.0 billion in 1989), but rising exports in this category do not necessarily signal an improvement in the overall road vehicle balance with Canada, because the increases usually reflect inputs for the increasing production of motor vehicles for export to the United States rather than rising production to serve Canadian or other export demands. US–Canada trade in internal combustion engines, however, is relatively balanced: US exports were $1.9 billion in 1989, while imports were $2.0 billion.

Growing Mexican production is also serving the US market. Each of the Big Three US producers has production facilities in Mexico, and part of their Mexican production goes to the United States. US car and truck exports to Mexico in 1989 were 4,500 units, but imports were 143,000, resulting in a $1.1 billion US deficit in cars and $87 million in trucks. As with Canada, rising US surpluses in parts and accessories ($880 million in 1989) largely represent inputs to production for reexport and do not necessarily presage a net improvement in the overall balance. The US deficit with Mexico on internal combustion engine trade in 1989 was $0.5 billion.

Overview of US Road Vehicle and Engine Trade Performance

The 1981–87 Slide

The deterioration in US trade performance over the 1981–87 period was larger by far in road vehicles than in any other single category of US trade. From 1981 to 1987 the United States moved from an already sizable deficit of $11.7 billion to a deficit of $51.4 billion—a $39.7 billion decline (table 11). Most of the change ($27.7 billion) was in passenger cars, but the truck deficit also increased, by $4.2 billion, and parts and accessories moved from a $4.9 billion surplus to a $2.8 billion deficit—a decline of $7.8 billion. Engine exports increased only marginally

Table 10 Geographic distribution of world trade in road vehicles, 1981–87[a] (percentages of total)

Country	1981	1982	1983	1984	1985	1986	1987	Change 1981–87
Share of world exports								
United States	12.6	11.1	11.3	12.4	12.4	9.6	9.3	−3.3
Canada	8.7	10.6	12.9	15.3	14.7	12.3	10.1	1.4
Japan	26.8	24.9	25.7	26.7	27.4	27.8	25.4	−1.4
European Community	49.1	50.3	46.9	42.1	41.4	45.9	49.4	0.3
Germany	20.7	23.0	20.9	18.7	18.9	21.1	22.4	1.7
France	8.7	8.0	7.6	6.7	6.3	6.9	7.3	−1.4
United Kingdom	4.9	4.4	3.7	3.2	3.2	3.0	3.5	−1.4
Latin America	0.5	0.6	0.6	0.9	1.4	1.0	1.5	1.0
NICs[b]	0.1	0.5	0.7	0.9	1.0	1.4	1.9	1.8
Other	2.2	2.0	1.9	1.7	1.7	2.0	2.4	0.2
Share of world imports								
United States	23.4	25.9	29.7	34.9	37.6	36.2	32.6	9.2
Canada	9.6	8.7	11.2	13.2	13.5	11.3	10.0	0.4
Japan	0.4	0.4	0.5	0.5	0.5	0.7	1.1	0.7
European Community	32.5	33.3	32.8	28.5	27.6	33.5	38.2	5.7
Germany	5.6	5.3	6.0	5.2	4.7	6.3	7.0	1.4
France	5.3	5.9	5.5	4.5	4.4	5.2	6.1	0.8
United Kingdom	5.5	6.4	6.9	5.8	5.6	6.0	6.3	0.8
Latin America	5.9	4.0	2.6	3.0	3.0	2.7	2.7	−3.2
NICs[b]	0.9	1.1	1.2	1.2	0.8	1.0	1.6	0.7
Other	27.3	26.6	22.0	18.7	17.0	14.6	13.8	−13.5

Country	1981	1982	1983	1984	1985	1986	1987	Change 1981–87
Export share minus import share								
United States	−10.7	−14.8	−18.5	−22.5	−25.2	−26.6	−23.3	−12.6
Canada	−0.9	1.9	1.7	2.1	1.2	1.0	0.1	1.0
Japan	26.4	24.5	25.2	26.2	26.9	27.1	24.3	−2.1
European Community	16.6	17.0	14.1	13.6	13.8	12.4	11.2	−5.4
Germany	15.1	17.7	14.9	13.5	14.2	14.8	15.4	0.3
France	3.4	2.1	2.1	2.2	1.9	1.7	1.2	−2.2
United Kingdom	−0.6	−2.0	−3.2	−2.6	−2.4	−3.0	−2.8	−2.2
Latin America	−5.4	−3.4	−2.0	−2.1	−1.6	−1.7	−1.2	4.2
NICs[b]	−0.8	−0.6	−0.5	−0.3	0.2	0.4	0.3	1.1
Other	−25.2	−24.6	−20.0	−17.1	−15.3	−12.6	−11.4	13.7

a. SITC 78.

b. Hong Kong, Korea, Singapore, and Taiwan.

Source: World Manufactures Trade Data Base.

Table 11 United States: trade in road vehicles and internal combustion engines by three-digit SITC category, 1981–90 (millions of dollars)

	SITC Revision 2			SITC Revision 3					
			Change					Change	
	1981	1987	1981–87	1987	1989	1990[a]	1987–89	1989–90[b]	1987–90[b]
SITC 78: Road vehicles									
Exports	16,397	21,054	4,657	20,906	25,479	32,171	4,573	6,692	11,265
Imports	28,145	72,500	44,355	72,584	71,863	72,014	−721	151	−570
Balance	−11,748	−51,446	−39,698	−51,678	−46,384	−39,843	5,294	6,541	11,835
of which:									
781 Passenger cars									
Exports	4,025	6,947	2,922	6,965	9,651	12,064	2,686	2,413	5,099
Imports	17,963	48,619	30,656	48,613	44,703	45,150	−3,910	447	−3,463
Balance	−13,938	−41,672	−27,734	−41,648	−35,052	−33,086	6,596	1,966	8,562
782 Trucks									
Exports	2,417	2,483	66	2,461	3,097	3,191	636	94	730
Imports	3,792	8,018	4,226	8,291	8,590	8,522	299	−68	231
Balance	−1,375	−5,535	−4,160	−5,830	−5,493	−5,331	337	162	499
783 Other road vehicles									
Exports	424	402	−22	402	420	586	18	166	184
Imports	401	697	296	700	650	647	−50	−3	−53
Balance	23	−295	−318	−298	−230	−61	68	169	237

| | SITC Revision 2 | | | SITC Revision 3 | | | | | |
	1981	1987	Change 1981–87	1987	1989	1990[a]	Change 1987–89	Change 1989–90[b]	Change 1987–90[b]
784 Parts and accessories									
Exports	9,177	10,925	1,748	8,295	11,708	15,380	3,413	3,672	7,085
Imports	4,258	13,771	9,513	13,375	16,365	16,323	2,990	–42	2,948
Balance	4,919	–2,846	–7,765	–5,080	–4,657	–943	423	3,714	4,137
785 Motorcycles									
Exports	98	147	49	1,224	270	442	–954	172	–782
Imports	1,696	1,301	–395	1,377	1,342	1,160	–35	–182	–217
Balance	–1,598	–1,154	444	–153	–1,072	–718	–919	354	–565
786 Trailers									
Exports	256	149	–107	1,557	333	507	–1,224	174	–1,050
Imports	35	94	59	228	213	212	–15	–1	–16
Balance	221	55	–166	1,329	120	295	–1,209	175	–1,034
SITC 713 Internal combustion engines									
Exports	4,113	4,241	128	4,082	4,806	5,933	724	1,127	1,851
Imports	2,268	6,389	4,121	6,321	7,923	7,601	1,602	–322	1,280
Balance	1,845	–2,148	–3,993	–2,239	–3,117	–1,668	–878	1,449	571

a. Projected figures were obtained by doubling the results for the first half of the year.

b. With correction for the Canada adjustment.

Source: US Department of Commerce.

from 1981 to 1987, but meanwhile imports grew rapidly, so that the balance declined by $4.0 billion, to a $2.1 billion deficit. For the road vehicles group as a whole, balances slid with every major trading partner (tables 12 and 13).

The 1987–90 Improvement

US trade performance in road vehicles improved markedly from 1987 to 1989. The US deficit narrowed by $5.3 billion, with the dollar value of exports up 21.9 percent and imports declining by 1.0 percent (table 11). The passenger car deficit narrowed by $6.6 billion but was partially offset by a $919 million worsening in motorcycles and a $1.2 billion worsening in trailers and semitrailers. The parts and accessories account also improved by $423 million, but internal combustion engines worsened by $878 million.

Exports of road vehicles in the first half of 1990 were up by 11.4 percent, and imports down by 4 percent, from first-half 1989 levels. Simply doubling first-half exports and imports indicates an improvement for the whole of 1990 of $6.5 billion (table 11). Allowing for a $2.4 billion Canada adjustment to the 1989 data, not reflected in table 11, would lower the projected gain to $4.3 billion. If sustained for the entire year, the reductions in imports of cars and trucks from Japan in the first half of 1990 could lower the deficit with Japan by $3.0 billion in 1990. Although the actual gains will probably not be quite this large, significant improvement seems assured for 1990.

The overall 1987–89 improvement was achieved primarily with Germany, where the US bilateral balance improved by $4.4 billion (tables 12 and 13). Germany's automobile exports to the United States shrank from $9.0 billion in 1987 to $5.1 billion in 1989.

From 1987 to 1989 the automobile deficit with Japan improved from $21.8 billion to $19.8 billion, and the truck deficit improved by $1.5 billion. The parts and accessories deficit expanded, however, from $3.7 billion to $4.7 billion, as did the deficit in internal combustion engines, from $1.8 billion to $3.1 billion. Overall, the US road vehicle and engines deficit with Japan improved by only $1.1 billion.

Performance Beyond 1990

Many factors will influence US trade performance in road vehicles and internal combustion engines during the 1990s. Modest increases in US exports of finished cars and trucks are possible, but it seems unlikely that the United States will become a major net exporter of road vehicles, other than to Canada. Significant favorable changes in the deficit with Canada are unlikely, since Canadian production is likely to be largely targeted at exporting to the United States, and because a large portion of US exports of parts and accessories to Canada tend to return to the United States in the form of finished automobiles and trucks. The size of the US deficit with Canada, therefore, is influenced primarily by the quantity of US domestic car and truck sales, not by Canadian sales levels or by modest changes in the US–Canada exchange rate.

Nor does Europe, with its highly competitive market, ample production capacity, on-the-scene production by US companies, and growing Japanese production, seem a ready market for US exports. Significant US penetration of the Japanese market, even through cars with Japanese nameplates made in the United States, will be even more difficult. There may be some increases in US exports to the less developed countries, although the depressed state of many of those economies is likely to preclude major expansions. With prospects for export expansion modest, improved US trade performance in this product group will necessarily occur primarily through enlarging the portion of the US market supplied by US–based production. US imports will not decline quickly, however. For example, without further significant dollar depreciation from mid–1990 levels, only modest further reductions in imports from Germany and other countries of the European Community are likely.

Also, modest increases in US imports from Mexico and in the bilateral deficit with Mexico seem likely as production there expands. Imports from Korea have declined since their 1987 peak, but a resurgence in Korean penetration of the US market remains a possibility if new Korean models prove successful.

Japan remains the key to narrowing US deficits in road vehicles and engines. At $31.1 billion, the 1989 US deficit with Japan in road vehicles and internal combustion engines remains the largest component and the key variable in US trade in these categories. Because the United States is unable to make significant inroads into Japan's markets, any narrowing of the deficit with Japan will have to occur principally through displacing imports from Japan with US–based production, by either US or Japanese companies. A more detailed examination of recent data and historical trends can provide some insights about likely future trends.

US–Japan Trade in Road Vehicles and Engines

The key factors that will determine US–Japan road vehicle and engine trade balances during the 1990s include the following:

- the strength of the US car and truck markets;

Table 12 United States: geographic composition of exports of road vehicles and internal combustion engines, 1981–89[a]

SITC Product	Millions of dollars			As percentage of total		
	1981	1987	1989	1981	1987	1989
78 Road vehicles						
Canada	8,567	15,029	15,891	52.2	71.9	62.4
Japan	166	325	852	1.0	1.6	3.3
European Community	1,131	1,292	2,087	6.9	6.2	8.2
Germany	238	379	724	1.5	1.8	2.8
Other	6,534	4,260	6,649	39.8	20.4	26.1
Total	16,398	20,906	25,479	100.0	100.0	100.0
781 Passenger cars						
Canada	3,168	5,776	6,252	78.7	82.9	64.8
Japan	49	92	431	1.2	1.3	4.5
European Community	95	321	821	2.4	4.6	8.5
Germany	38	114	331	0.9	1.6	3.4
Other	713	776	2,147	17.7	11.1	22.2
Total	4,025	6,965	9,651	100.0	100.0	100.0
782 Trucks						
Canada	520	1,831	2,157	21.5	74.4	69.7
Japan	17	12	25	0.7	0.5	0.8
European Community	101	50	78	4.2	2.0	2.5
Germany	15	15	28	0.6	0.6	0.9
Other	1,779	568	836	73.6	23.1	27.0
Total	2,417	2,461	3,096	100.0	100.0	100.0

SITC Product	Millions of dollars			As percentage of total		
	1981	1987	1989	1981	1987	1989
784 Parts and accessories						
Canada	4,657	5,588	7,013	50.7	67.4	59.9
Japan	90	145	317	1.0	1.7	2.7
European Community	894	677	999	9.7	8.2	8.5
Germany	175	155	298	1.9	1.9	2.5
Mexico	1,469	832	1,953	16.0	10.0	16.7
Other	2,067	1,053	1,426	22.5	12.7	12.2
Total	9,177	8,295	11,708	100.0	100.0	100.0
713 Internal combustion engines						
Canada	1,658	1,922	1,859	40.3	47.1	38.7
Japan	88	81	114	2.1	2.0	2.4
European Community	702	689	1,077	17.1	16.9	22.4
Germany	77	98	142	1.9	2.4	3.0
Mexico	345	367	472	8.4	9.0	9.8
Other	1,319	1,023	1,284	32.1	25.1	26.7
Total	4,112	4,082	4,806	100.0	100.0	100.0

a. Data for 1981 are from SITC Revision 2, those for 1987 and 1989 from SITC Revision 3.

Source: US Department of Commerce.

Table 13 United States: geographic composition of imports of road vehicles and internal combustion engines, 1981–89[a]

SITC Product	Millions of dollars			As percentage of total		
	1981	1987	1989	1981	1987	1989
78 Road vehicles						
Canada	8,928	20,520	25,725	31.7	28.3	35.8
Japan	13,476	30,647	28,918	47.9	42.2	40.2
European Community	4,585	13,500	9,487	16.3	18.6	13.2
Germany	3,119	9,923	6,026	11.1	13.7	8.4
Other	1,157	7,918	7,733	4.1	10.9	10.8
Total	28,146	72,585	71,863			
781 Passenger cars						
Canada	4,297	10,256	12,960	23.9	21.1	29.0
Japan	9,677	21,867	20,259	53.9	45.0	45.3
European Community	3,415	10,896	6,741	19.0	22.4	15.1
Germany	2,659	8,965	5,051	14.8	18.4	11.3
Other	573	5,594	4,742	3.2	11.5	10.6
Total	17,962	48,613	44,702			
782 Trucks						
Canada	1,974	3,725	5,492	52.1	44.9	63.9
Japan	1,809	4,243	2,762	47.7	51.2	32.2
European Community	6	178	115	0.2	2.1	1.3
Germany	4	23	23	0.1	0.3	0.3
Other	3	145	221	0.1	1.7	2.6
Total	3,792	8,291	8,590			

SITC Product	Millions of dollars			As percentage of total		
	1981	1987	1989	1981	1987	1989
784 Parts and accessories						
Canada	2,259	5,810	6,622	53.1	43.4	40.5
Japan	518	3,801	5,212	12.2	28.4	31.8
European Community	1,062	2,275	2,471	24.9	17.0	15.1
Germany	414	890	924	9.7	6.7	5.6
Mexico	202	645	1,073	4.7	4.8	6.6
Other	217	844	988	5.1	6.3	6.0
Total	4,258	13,375	16,366	100.0		
713 Internal combustion engines						
Canada	706	1,618	2,025	31.1	25.6	25.6
Japan	476	1,832	3,196	21.0	29.0	40.3
European Community	812	1,355	1,127	35.8	21.4	14.2
Germany	348	735	606	15.3	11.6	7.6
Mexico	101	966	824	4.5	15.3	10.4
Other	173	550	750	7.6	8.7	9.5
Total	2,268	6,321	7,922	100.0	100.0	100.0

a. Data for 1981 are from SITC Revision 2, those for 1987 and 1989 from SITC Revision 3.

Source: US Department of Commerce.

- Japan's penetration of the US market, both through exports from Japan and through units produced in the United States;

- the division of Japanese market share between production in the United States and imports from Japan;

- the US content of Japanese production in the United States;

- the unit value of imports from Japan.

A great many decisions and events that cannot be foreseen will determine the balance of US–Japan vehicle and engine trade during the 1990s. Some current trends favor continuation of the recent modest improvement in the US–Japan bilateral balance. US quality and competitiveness, for example, are generally improving, and major projects such as General Motors' new Saturn automobile could have important positive effects. There are, however, a number of reasons to believe that, absent further significant appreciation of the yen, there will be little improvement in the next several years in the US–Japan bilateral road vehicle and engine balance.

Table 14 reviews recent Japanese performance in the US market and projects 1990 and 1995 performance. The 1995 projection is not based on an econometric model. It is a best estimate based on research to date, assuming no further major depreciation of the US dollar against the Japanese yen from late 1990 levels of around 130 to 140 yen to the dollar. Key elements in the projection for 1995 are the following:

- The total 1995 US car and truck market in which Japan will share is forecast at 15.9 million units, somewhat larger than the projected 1990 level of about 15.0 million units.

- Car and truck imports from Japan do not decline but remain constant at the 2.0 million and 0.4 million units, respectively, expected for 1990.

- Japanese production in the United States rises by 1995 to 2.1 million automobiles and 0.4 million trucks.

- In effect, Japanese production in the United States supplements but does not replace exports from Japan, which remain essentially at 1990 levels.

The projected result for 1995 (table 14) is a significant increase in penetration of the US market by the combination of Japanese vehicles from US– and Japan-based production. Japan's market share from the two production bases rises to 39 percent of automobiles and 14.8 percent of trucks. Although this would be a substantial increase, it is below the projections of some other analysts.

Table 14 Japanese penetration of US car and truck market, 1988, 1989, and projected 1990 and 1995 (millions of units except where noted)

	1988	1989	1990	1995
Imports from Japan				
Cars	2.1	2.0	2.0	2.0
Trucks	0.6	0.4	0.4	0.4
Total	2.7	2.4	2.4	2.4
Japanese production in US				
Cars	0.8	1.0	1.3	2.1
Trucks	0.1	0.1	0.2	0.4
Total	0.9	1.1	1.5	2.5
Total Japanese sales in US				
Cars	2.9	3.0	3.3	4.1
Trucks	0.7	0.5	0.6	0.8
Total	3.6	3.5	3.9	4.9
Total US market consumption				
Cars	10.5	9.9	9.9	10.5
Trucks	5.1	4.9	5.1	5.4
Total	15.6	14.8	15.0	15.9
Japanese share as percentage of total consumption				
Cars	27.6	30.3	33.3	39.0
Trucks	13.7	10.2	11.8	14.8
Total	23.1	23.6	26.0	30.8

Source: US Department of Commerce estimates.

The projected increase is based on several facts and judgments, including the following:

■ Japanese production in the United States is very quality- and cost-competitive with production of the Big Three. Japanese plants in the United States are generally newer, and productivity is higher. Per hour labor costs are lower, partly because workers are younger, have less seniority, and impose lower health benefit costs.

■ Japanese nameplates can continue to increase market share, given US impressions of Japanese quality, style, and service. Japanese producers have demonstrated an ability to react to market trends and to translate new designs into production more rapidly than US producers. The quality of US automobiles is rising, but public perception lags reality. Also, Japanese marketing has not yet fully exploited several market categories (for example, sales to the US Midwest and fleet sales).

- To date, growth in Japanese market share has been achieved without extensive use of the price-cutting and other competitive practices employed by US automakers.

- US automobile companies will continue to import small cars produced in Japan.

- Except for GM's Saturn project, there is little evidence of price and capital investment policies by US companies directed at regaining market share.

- Conversely, taking their customary long view, Japanese companies will likely continue to make increased market share a primary objective, using a combination of US– and Japan-based production. To the extent economic and political constraints allow, however, Japanese companies will continue to give preference to Japan-based production to avoid cutbacks in Japan.

- Japanese companies have made very large capital expenditures in new plant and equipment in Japan for the purpose of improving productivity. There is no indication of similar heavy investments by US companies that would help to match, let alone exceed, Japanese productivity gains. Therefore, absent further major depreciation of the dollar, exporting from Japan to the United States will remain profitable.

Thus, freed from the prior constraints imposed by the US quotas, the combination of US–based production and exports from Japan can provide the basis for further expansion of the Japanese share of the US market. Absent any further major dollar decline that would make continued exporting from Japan a costly undertaking, there seems little reason to expect that the increased market share projected in table 14 will not be reached by 1995. In fact, it could well be higher.

Because the United States will remain a large net importer of cars and trucks for the foreseeable future, the 1995 US–Japan trade balance in dollar terms will also be a function of unit prices. From 1983 to 1988 the average value of automobiles imported from Japan increased by 46 percent, from $6,987 to $10,222. Truck prices rose from $3,531 to $5,380 per unit over the same period—a 52.4 percent increase. These kinds of unit price increases are likely to continue as Japan continues to upscale the production it exports from Japan.

US imports of parts and accessories and engines, for use as inputs to US–based production, will also be an important factor in the trade balance in the 1990s. The 1989 engine deficit with Japan was $3.1 billion. Imports of Japanese parts and accessories were $5.2 billion in 1989, yielding a US deficit with Japan in that category of $4.9 billion. US auto parts producers are, according to several

Table 15 United States: projected trade balance with Japan in road vehicles and internal combustion engines, 1995

Product	Billions of dollars
Automobiles	
2.0 million units imported @ $13,500[a]	27.00
Less 0.1 million units exported @ $13,500	1.35
	25.65
Trucks	
0.4 million units imported @ $7,500[b]	3.00
Parts, accessories, and engines	
US imports	10.00
Total 1995 deficit	38.65

a. Assumes annual price increases of 4 percent per year.
b. Assumes annual price increases of 4.5 percent per year.

sources, beginning to make some headway in supplying Japanese producers in the United States. Some observers believe that the tide is about to turn, as Japanese production in the United States begins to rely increasingly on parts, accessories, engines, and engine parts made in the United States. Japanese engine production in the United States is also increasing. Moreover, data for the first half of 1990 indicate that the 1990 engine deficit with Japan may not increase much from 1989 levels.

Nevertheless, as annual Japanese production in the United States doubles to well over 2 million units by 1995, and as the population of Japanese vehicles in use in the United States continues to cumulate, demand for parts and accessories and engines for Japanese automobiles will likely grow more rapidly than US–based production of these items for Japanese companies. Without marked dollar depreciation that would provide further incentive to move Japanese production to the United States, it seems likely that the deficit in these categories will rise modestly above 1989 levels, from $8.3 billion to perhaps $10 billion, and remain larger through 1995.

Obviously, no one can predict 1995 import, export, and balance levels with certainty. However, absent major further dollar depreciation, levels close to those in table 15 seem likely. The $38.65 billion deficit projected there compares with a 1989 deficit on these items of $31.1 billion.

Projections by several other sources are not markedly different (table 16). The forecast years vary, and where the trade balance is part of the forecast, price growth and other assumptions no doubt also differed. There is, nonetheless, a significant degree of agreement on the projected levels of US–based Japanese production, and, except for the Fuji Research Institute projection, all forecasters

Table 16 Alternative projections of US–Japan bilateral road vehicle trade

| Researcher and date of forecast | Forecast year | Millions of units | | | Nominal deficit (billions of dollars) |
		US–based Japanese production	US imports from Japan	Japanese imports from US	
Nomura Research, September 1989	1995	2.2	2.75	0.2	40.5
Fuji Research Institute, February 1989	1994	2.08	1.27	0.13	24.2
Robert Z. Lawrence, March 1990	1992	2.23	2.14	n.a.	30.2
Industrial Bank of Japan, June 1990	1995	2.29	2.06	0.34	27.6
Ariyoshi Okumura, Industrial Bank of Japan, June 1990	1995	2.35	2.2	0.1	n.a.
Michigan Report, September 1989	1993	2.32	2.8	0.13	35.7
Allen J. Lenz, October 1990	1995	2.5	2.4	0.1	38.6

n.a. = not available

Source: The data are drawn principally from Japan–US Business Council, "Views and Proposals Concerning the Michigan Report," 29 June 1990.

see Japan's exports to the United States—a critical factor in the bilateral trade balance—at above 2.0 million cars and trucks a year.

In summary:

- The deficit in road vehicles and engines has narrowed since 1989 by reason of a combination of economic and political factors. It is unlikely, however, to narrow much more without additional economic or political incentives and instead is likely to expand modestly, from $31.1 billion in 1989 to perhaps $39 billion in 1995.

- The improvement in the US trade balance in road vehicles that has occurred since 1987 does not appear to be due to declining US consumption of road vehicles. Rather, the share of imports in total US vehicle sales has declined modestly since 1987.

- Deficits have not been caused by lack of US capacity. On the contrary, many US–owned plants have closed while new Japanese plants have been opening.

- The improvement that has occurred appears to be in response to exchange rate changes, both actual and prospective. Political considerations may also have played a role, by motivating the movement of Japanese production to the United States more rapidly than economic factors alone might have accomplished.

- The strong appreciation of the deutsche mark has resulted in major price increases and significantly reduced sales of German automobiles in the United States. Dollar depreciation has also affected Korean competitiveness in the United States, but other factors—quality problems and domestic production difficulties—have probably also been important.

- Dollar exchange rate changes are unlikely to have major effects on US balances with Canada and Mexico.

- Export expansion is unlikely to be a major factor in improved US road vehicle performance. Rather, further significant improvements will have to come mostly at the expense of Japan, through the substitution of US–based production for Japan-based production.

- The appreciation of the yen has not been adequate to force Japanese production for the US market to shift mostly to the United States. Rather, Japanese production has moved to the United States largely as a hedge against future dollar declines and to temper political ill will that could lead to the reimposition of quotas.

- The production increases in the United States currently planned by Japanese firms will to a large extent supplement rather than replace Japan-based production for the United States. Japanese production in the United States in 1990 is likely to be about 1.5 million units, which will probably reduce the US deficit by around $10 billion from what it would be if the United States imported the same quantity from Japan.

■ Political considerations may motivate Japanese actions that will slow the tempo of increases in the Japanese share of the US market and maintain or moderately reduce the size of the US deficit in road vehicles and engines. However, major further appreciation of the yen will be required to achieve a major reduction in the US deficits by reducing US imports from Japan.

■ A critical—and difficult to predict—factor contributing to the size of the US deficit with Japan is the degree to which the assembly of vehicles in the United States will be supported by parts and components made in the United States, and the resulting balance on parts and accessories and internal combustion engine trade. Again, further dollar depreciation would provide economic motivation to Japanese producers to speed the transition to US–based production.

■ The additional dollar depreciation that will be required—to levels well below those of the early 1980s—to further reduce the road vehicle and engine deficits is a sign of long-term decline in the international competitiveness of the US road vehicle industry.

Summary of Group Analyses

The following are preliminary conclusions reflecting both the analyses in this paper and those of other products not included in this partial report, as well as our questionnaire survey.

■ Manufactures trade dominates world trade and US trade. The deterioration of US trade performance in the 1981–87 period was manifested in a manufactures trade balance decline that was larger than the decline in total merchandise trade. Similarly, any major recovery in US current account and merchandise trade performance must occur predominantly in manufactures trade. A balanced current account will require significant manufactures trade surpluses.

■ Fiscal, monetary, tax, regulatory, and other economic policies that cause large changes in net international capital flows inevitably impact primarily on the nation's manufacturing sector.

■ From 1987 to 1989 the US manufactures trade balance improved by $29.2 billion. A balanced current account would require an additional improvement in manufactures trade from 1989 levels of about $125 billion, to a surplus of around $35 billion. The actual improvement in 1990 will probably be about $20 billion.

- Disaggregating manufactures trade into 37 two-digit product groups identifies the "winners and losers" in US trade for the 1981–90 period and offers insights into likely performance during the 1990s.

- From 1981 to 1987, trade balances declined in 33 of 37 manufactures trade categories and improved in only 4. From 1987 to 1989, performance improved in 25 and declined in 13.

- The bulk ($104 billion) of the decline was registered in seven product groups: road vehicles, apparel, specialized machinery, telecommunications and sound reproducing equipment, electrical machinery, miscellaneous manufactures, and general industrial machinery.

- Road vehicle trade (automobiles, trucks, parts and accessories, and internal combustion engines) was a major factor in the 1981–87 trade balance decline, contributing $39.7 billion to expansion of the trade deficit.

- The road vehicles balance improved by $5.3 billion from 1987 to 1989 and is likely to improve by about another $4 billion in 1990 if reduced automobile and truck imports from Japan continue for the full year at first-six-months rates. Most of the 1987–89 improvement, however, was at the expense of Germany; the deficit with Japan was trimmed only minimally to $31.1 billion in 1989.

- Further major road vehicle and engine trade improvement will have to come at the expense of Japan. However, if exchange rates persist at mid–1990 levels, and given Japanese plans for production in the United States, the deficit with Japan in these products is likely to expand over the next several years. A further significant depreciation of the dollar against the yen from mid–1990 levels will likely be necessary to force more Japanese production for the US market to the United States.

- Another major loser during the 1981–87 period was apparel; the deficit in this product category widened by $13.1 billion, to $19.5 billion, from 1981 to 1987 and rose further to $22.5 billion in 1989. A modest $1.0 billion improvement may occur in 1990, but no major further reduction of this deficit should be expected in the 1990s.

- The aircraft industry has been the strongest US trade performer, registering a $17.9 billion surplus in 1989, up from $12.0 billion in 1987. A 1990 aircraft surplus of around $25 billion seems likely, and if oil prices return to more modest levels, the surplus could rise to around $29 billion by 1993. Opportunities for further large expansion are limited, however, by the size of the world market, which is only about one-fifth that of road vehicles, and by the already large US share of the world market.

- Another strong performer during the 1980s was the chemical industry, which posted a $17.2 billion trade surplus in 1989. Performance in 1990 has begun to slip, however, as new production capabilities begin to come on stream in several less developed countries. Absent further dollar depreciation, a modest decline in the industry's surpluses for the next several years seems likely.

- There is little prospect of major gains in a number of other categories, for example, footwear (an $8.0 billion deficit in 1989), several consumer electronic items not produced in the United States, iron and steel, textiles, and armaments.

- Modest further improvements may occur in several other product groups such as professional and scientific equipment and electrical machinery. There are, however, no evident "big winners" that, given world market sizes and US competitive advantages and disadvantages, can turn the tide in the next several years. This judgment includes aircraft, computers, and other high-technology products.

- These findings reinforce the conclusion that large gains will require both additional across-the-board gains and a very large improvement in the road vehicle and engine balance. Both will require additional dollar depreciation.

- The need for this depreciation, and the industry analyses on which it is based, support the hypothesis of a US competitive decline relative to other countries. In industry after industry US manufacturers face growing competition from foreign manufacturers with sophisticated technology and high-quality products.

- Evidence of hysteresis is strong in certain industries, particularly in areas with no US–based production capacity, such as some consumer electronics products. In the automotive sector, the exchange rate may need to undershoot its equilibrium value to stimulate the necessary response.

Acknowledgment

The research assistance of Hunter K. Monroe and Bruce Parsell is gratefully acknowledged.

Comment

Peter Hooper

I found both of these papers interesting, one in an informative way, the other in a more provocative way. My remarks will focus primarily on the more provocative macroeconomic analysis in the paper by William R. Cline.

There are three areas in which I can say I found room for agreement with these papers. First, the Cline paper nicely reviews the strong empirical evidence that exchange rate movements played a crucial role in determining the movement in the US external balance over the past decade. The importance of exchange rate changes in determining trade flows at the microeconomic level comes through in the paper by Allen J. Lenz as well, both in its review of recent history and in its projections. What I found particularly interesting about Lenz's analysis is the important role that exchange rates appear to play on the supply side in influencing the location of production facilities in such industries as chemicals and automobiles.

Second, I would agree that, contrary to popular misconception, at least as expressed in some newspapers, the observed performance of the US external balance in recent years has not fallen short of expectations, at least most model-based expectations. Cline argues that the Lawrence-Krugman paradox (continued external deficits despite a return to 1980 exchange rates and relative GNP levels) could be explained by the fact that the dollar has not returned to its 1980 level in real terms. I see some merit in this view, but I will also argue that there are enough alternative explanations for this paradox to suggest that US external adjustment to date has in fact exceeded model-based expectations by a significant margin.

Third, I fully agree with Cline's discussion of the theory of the determination of trade flows, as far as he goes with it. Trade flows are jointly determined with domestic savings and investment, and movements in relative prices or real exchange rates are a key endogenous linkage between the two sectors in the event of exogenous shocks to either sector. However, the theory as presented focuses only on Keynesian demand-side considerations; some of the effects can be quite different when aggregate supply is brought into the picture.

In his paper for the recent Brookings panel, Robert Z. Lawrence (1990) posed the paradox in these terms: given that for nearly three years now the dollar has been, in real terms, about where it was in 1980, and given that both US and

Peter Hooper is Assistant Director, Division of International Finance, Federal Reserve Board.

foreign GNP have grown at about the same rate on average over the past decade, why hasn't the partial trade balance (nonagricultural exports minus nonoil imports) returned to zero, where it was 10 years ago? Lawrence offered his update of the Houthakker-Magee result as the explanation. His conventional trade equations showed a much larger income elasticity for US imports than for US exports.

In contrast, Cline's explanation is that, if measured correctly, the dollar's real exchange rate has declined considerably less than we thought in recent years. Unfortunately, Cline's empirical measure of the real exchange rate, which is based on International Monetary Fund data on relative export unit values, has three strikes against it. First, his measure is based on unit values, not prices; second, as Cline himself notes, data compiled by the Organization for Economic Cooperation and Development (OECD) show a very different picture; and third, although Cline's measure may be relevant to US exports, it is not necessarily relevant to US imports (foreign exports do not compete with US exports in the US market).

Figure 1 shows several measures of US-Japanese relative prices. Relative export prices (defined as the ratio of US to Japanese export prices) have declined further since 1980 than have relative export unit values, although not as much as have relative consumer prices. This suggests that Cline's unit value data, at a minimum, overstate his case.

It may be more instructive, for assessing net changes in price competitiveness, to look at what has happened to the relative price terms that enter directly into the determination of trade flows in the models. The relative price terms in the Helkie-Hooper model's trade equations are shown in figure 2. The relative prices of US imports and exports have both declined on balance since 1980. In view of the lags involved in the response of trade flows to changes in relative prices, it makes more sense to compare the average levels of these relative prices during the past two years with their average levels during 1979–80. On this basis, the relative price of imports has fallen somewhat more than the relative price of exports, indicating that price movements have stimulated imports more than exports. However, this difference is not as great as Cline's relative export price chart would suggest.

Table 1 lists several factors that together can explain the Lawrence-Krugman paradox. First, the changes in relative prices that I have just discussed contributed, on balance, about $20 billion of the widening of the US trade deficit between 1980 and the first half of 1990. Second, while GNP grew at about the same rate in the United States and abroad during the 1980s, US domestic demand grew nearly ½ percentage point per year faster than did domestic demand abroad. A reasonable empirical case can be made for assuming that GNP and absorption share equally in determining import or export demand; on this basis, the difference in domestic demand growth added about another $20 billion to the deficit.

Figure 1   Alternative measures of US–Japanese relative prices, 1967–90[a]

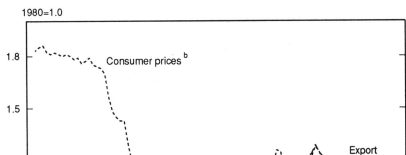

a. Defined as the US nonagricultural export price or unit value divided by the Japanese total export price or unit value, expressed in dollars.

b. As measured by the consumer price indices of both countries.

Sources: United States: Bureau of Economic Analysis, Bureau of the Census, Bureau of Labor Statistics. Japan: Bank of Japan, Economic Planning Agency.

Next comes what I have called the effect of changes in relative supply—what Lawrence would label the Houthakker-Magee effect. In the Helkie-Hooper model (the starting point for Cline's HHCR model), the difference in income elasticities is eliminated by the introduction of a relative supply variable: the ratio of US to foreign fixed capital stocks. This variable was included under the hypothesis that income elasticities in the conventional equations spuriously pick up shifts in supply that are not adequately reflected in available measures of relative prices. In principle, an increase in relative supply, *ceteris paribus,* should lead to a decline in the relative price. However, available price indices apparently do not adequately reflect actual movements in prices over time that are associated with the introduction of new products or of goods produced by countries entering international markets for the first time. That is, measured movements in the average price of a class of products generally will not reflect the introduction of a new product whose price is effectively below those of others in its class.

Figure 2 Relative prices of US exports and imports, 1967–90

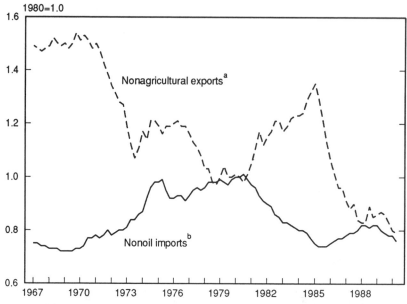

1980=1.0

Nonagricultural exports[a]

Nonoil imports[b]

a. GNP fixed-weight price index for nonagricultural exports divided by the weighted average of foreign consumer price indices, expressed in dollars.

b. GNP fixed-weight price index for nonoil US imports divided by the gross business product fixed-weight price index.

Sources: Bureau of Economic Analysis, Federal Reserve Board data base.

Table 1 Factors contributing to the Lawrence-Krugman paradox
(billions of dollars)

	Effect on US partial trade balance[a]
Changes in relative prices	−20
Changes in relative domestic demand	−20
Changes in relative supply	−60
Total	−100
Change in partial trade balance, 1980 to first half of 1990	−51

a. Nonagricultural exports minus nonoil imports.

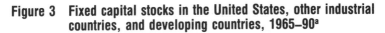

Figure 3 Fixed capital stocks in the United States, other industrial countries, and developing countries, 1965–90[a]

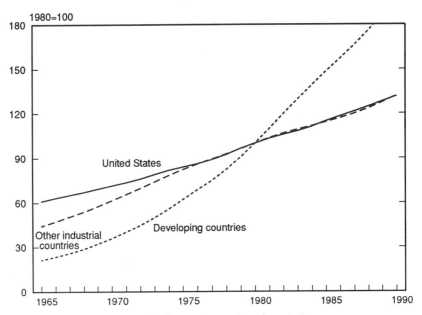

a. Calculated from total gross fixed investment minus depreciation.

Source: International Monetary Fund, *International Financial Statistics,* various issues.

The components of the supply proxy used to capture this phenomenon are shown in figure 3. The US fixed capital stock has risen by about as much as that in other industrial countries on average over the past decade, although its growth rate has fallen behind slightly in recent years. Meanwhile fixed capital in developing countries has grown considerably more rapidly. The ratio of the US capital stock to a trade-weighted average of foreign capital stocks is shown in figure 4. This ratio has declined over time, although at a decelerating rate over the past decade.[1]

The implications for the trade balance of the decline in the capital stock ratio during the 1980s, based on parameters in the HHCR model, are shown in the

---

1. In empirical analysis I did two years ago, I argued that the relative capital stock variable could begin to shift in favor of the United States if sufficient productive capital were attracted to the United States as a result of the low level of US labor costs compared with those in other major industrial countries. This shift has not taken place, evidently because investment decisions are based on many factors other than relative labor costs. Indeed, because of the investment booms in Japan and Europe over the past two years, the trend against the United States in the relative capital stock variable has accelerated somewhat.

Figure 4 Ratio of US to foreign capital stock, 1966–90

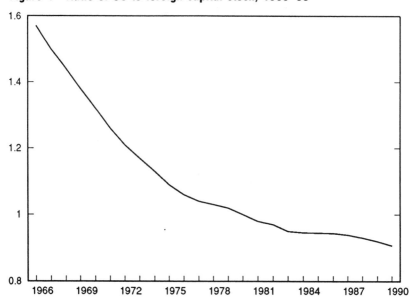

third line of table 1. By this estimate, the net effect of relatively faster growth in foreign supply was to widen the US trade deficit by $60 billion.

I should stress that this influence can be viewed as the result of an effective (although unmeasured) decline in the price of foreign goods relative to US goods. That is, if it could be measured in terms of the prices that actually influenced consumers at home and abroad, the dollar's real exchange rate rose more on balance over the 1980s than we thought. In brief, I agree with the thrust of Cline's observation on this point, even though the data he used may be deficient.

The sum of the effects in table 1 exceeds the actual widening of the US partial trade deficit over the 1980s (shown at the bottom of the table) by a factor of 2. This suggests that the paradox to be explained is just the reverse of what Lawrence and Krugman claim. That is, the trade deficit has narrowed more in recent years than might reasonably have been expected. But how do we reconcile this result with Cline's observations that the models have been about on track? I will argue that, in fact, many of the models have not been on track.

Our own revised version of the Helkie-Hooper model at the Federal Reserve has been overpredicting the trade deficit by an increasing margin for the past year and a half, with imports substantially overpredicted and exports slightly underpredicted. From his remarks at the conference on which this volume is based, I suspect that the model whose results David Mulford has been looking at has been underpredicting the progress in US external adjustment as well.

Lawrence's equations, too, have been overpredicting the deficit. The error in his nonoil, noncomputer import equation has widened steadily during the past two years to about 6 percent (or more than $20 billion) by the first half of 1990.

The Brookings survey of model projections conducted by Ralph C. Bryant (1988), referred to by Cline, appeared to be about on track if one adjusts for the recent unexpected decline in US growth. But that survey assumed that the dollar would remain at its level of late December 1987. Over the ensuing two-and-a-half years (through mid–1990) the dollar averaged about 7 percent above that level; from the third quarter of 1988 through the fourth quarter of 1989 (the period probably most relevant to the determination of the trade balance in 1990), the dollar was closer to 10 percent above its late-December 1987 level. Using the actual exchange rate and Cline's rule of thumb (a 1 percent change in the real dollar exchange rate changes the US trade balance by about $5 billion to $7.5 billion), the models would have been overpredicting the deficit recently by $50 billion or more.

Marris's projections for the trade balance may have been about on track, but as he notes (chapter 6, this volume), that result may have been fortuitous, inasmuch as his projections for the key components of the balance were off by a wide margin. Cline's External Adjustment with Growth (EAG) model also appeared to be on track, but I suspect this result was importantly influenced by a judgmental adjustment he made to narrow differences in income elasticities among countries.

Both Cline and Lenz offer projections for the medium term. Absent the effects of the budget package, Cline offers a relatively neutral outlook for the US current account, with little change in the deficit over the next five years. On the one hand, Cline's projection may be optimistic, inasmuch as he assumes in the HHCR model that the relative supply variable will be flat. Recall that, to the contrary, that variable has shown no sign of leveling off, and in light of the recent strength of investment abroad it seems likely to continue to trend down. This point is also made for several key variables in the Lenz paper. Cline's judgmental reduction of the elasticity differential in his EAG model achieves much the same effect as flattening out the relative supply variable.

On the other hand, in view of the recent growing errors in the models that I have described, some adjustment of the models in an optimistic direction, as Cline has done, may well have been justified. Figure 5 presents some further evidence on this point. The solid line shows movement over time in the estimated income elasticity of US nonoil, noncomputer imports, derived from a simple equation including income and a distributed lag on relative prices. The starting period for the estimation was 1969; the figure shows how the elasticity estimate and its 95 percent confidence bands evolved as the ending period for estimation was moved forward over time. The elasticity has been falling for several years now, in a manner consistent with at least the direction of Cline's adjustments.

Figure 5 Income elasticity of demand for US nonoil imports, excluding computers, 1980–90[a]

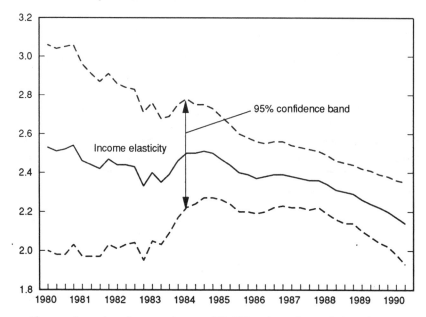

a. The equation relates import volume to US GNP and a poll on relative prices. It was estimated recursively beginning in the first quarter of 1969 and ending in the second quarter of 1990.

The reasons for this shift in income elasticity, and more broadly the models' recent tendency to overpredict the US deficit, are not immediately apparent. Some clues might be found on the supply side, particularly in the automotive sector. As both Lenz and Masaru Yoshitomi (chapter 3) note, automobile production by Japanese transplants in the United States has increased dramatically and has begun to displace imports, at least of finished units. In some tests with our own import equation we found that, when Japanese automobiles are removed from the equation, the recent overprediction of imports is reduced by as much as several billion dollars. However, as Lenz suggests, the prospects for further declines in imports from Japan may be limited, in light of planned further expansion of output capacity in Japan. Moreover, as Yoshitomi points out, the decline in US imports of finished units, to date at least, has been largely offset by increased imports of parts.

It is noteworthy that, according to Yoshitomi, the Japanese Economic Planning Agency's model has been overpredicting Japan's trade surplus by a growing margin during the past year and a half. His finding that the volume of Japanese exports has been overpredicted and the volume of imports underpredicted is at least consistent with what I have observed to be the recent tendency of models to overpredict the US deficit. Thus, more clues to the recent prediction errors might well be found in a closer examination of factors affecting US trade with Japan and competition with Japan in third markets.

Finally, the theoretical analysis in Cline's paper focuses on demand-side shocks. These results change, of course, when supply-side shocks are considered. The standard result Cline considers is an exogenous shock to saving or investment that increases aggregate demand. This raises interest rates and causes the home currency to appreciate and the external balance to fall. An increase in aggregate supply, on the other hand, resulting from a shock to productivity or the coming on stream of past investment, will lead to a depreciation of the home currency in the following sense: in order to sell the expanding country's increased supply of goods on the world market, the relative price of those goods must fall. That country's external balance need not rise, however, because the supply shock also raises income and demand for imports. It should be noted that, while the country's *real* exchange rate (measured in terms of tradeable-goods prices) will depreciate, both its nominal exchange rate and its real exchange rate measured in terms of relative consumer prices could very well appreciate. Moreover, the real depreciation envisioned here (coming as the result of a positive supply shock) does not imply a net decline in welfare for the home country. In brief, countries that experience positive supply shocks in their tradeable-goods sectors should experience real depreciations of their currencies.

This theoretical result is not altogether consistent with the data or with conventional wisdom. As Paul R. Krugman notes in his overview paper (chapter 1), there appears to have been a secular downtrend in the real equilibrium exchange rate of the dollar, and a secular uptrend in that of the yen associated with a faster pace of technological and productivity growth in Japan than in the United States. Indeed, over the past several decades, output capacity and productivity have grown much faster in Japan than in the United States. And, as figure 1 shows, the dollar's real exchange rate against the yen, when measured in terms of relative export prices, has exhibited a flat to slightly downward trend.

These empirical observations present a puzzle. In view of the large differences in productivity and output growth between the United States and Japan over the past several decades, theory suggests we should have seen more of an uptrend in the dollar's real exchange rate, when measured in terms of the prices of traded goods. I suspect that the explanation to this puzzle can be found in much the same reason we chose to include a relative supply term in our trade demand equations. That is, the measured relative price of Japanese goods has not declined as much as might be expected, because the price indices fail to capture the prices of new products. Robert Feenstra (1990) has been involved in a project to construct indices of US import prices that incorporate new products. His preliminary empirical results for a few disaggregated categories suggest that US import prices have risen substantially less than the published data show, which is consistent with the theoretical result.

To recapitulate the three main points I have made:

- US external adjustment appears to have exceeded our expectations, at least those based on model predictions. That is, the Lawrence-Krugman paradox can be more than explained by factors included in conventional trade equations.

- Given the first point, a good case may exist for adjusting the models in an optimistic direction for purposes of near-term projections.

- If it could be measured narrowly in terms of the prices of those traded goods that effectively influenced the decisions of consumers internationally, the underlying trend in the dollar's real exchange rate could well be positive.

Reference

Bryant, Ralph C. 1988. "The US External Deficit: An Update." *Brookings Discussion Papers in International Economics* 63 (January).

Feenstra, Robert C. 1990. "New Goods and Index Numbers: U.S. Import Prices." Davis: University of California, Davis (mimeographed, December).

Lawrence, Robert Z. 1990. "US Current Account Adjustment: An Appraisal." *Brookings Papers on Economic Activity* 2:343–82.

Comment

Robert Z. Lawrence

We have before us two papers that provide complementary approaches to the issue of US trade adjustment. William R. Cline argues that his macroeconomic models are able to track US trade behavior in the 1980s fairly accurately. He maintains that the trade deficit that the United States continues to have in 1990 reflects neither a fundamental erosion in competitiveness (which is captured in other models by differences in income elasticities for US imports and exports) nor hysteresis due to the strong dollar. Instead, it reflects that fact that in the late 1980s the dollar remained considerably stronger than it had been in 1980.

On the basis of a detailed microeconomic exploration, Allen J. Lenz tells us that the key to US external adjustment lies in the manufacturing sector. He concurs with Cline's judgment that additional devaluation is required to achieve balance, although unlike Cline he argues that there is widespread sectoral evidence of a serious erosion in competitiveness. I will comment on each paper in turn and give my own interpretation of what we know about the US adjustment process.

Cline claims that in terms of the real exchange rate the dollar has not fully reversed its appreciation of the early 1980s. Although indicators of relative US wholesale prices, consumer prices, and unit labor costs have returned to their 1980 levels, relative US export unit values as measured by the International Monetary Fund remain considerably higher than they were in 1980.

I disagree with Cline's claim at both a conceptual and an empirical level. Cline's discussion and his model are not consistent. To say that the failure of the dollar to decline sufficiently is an explanation for the persistent trade deficit involves treating the real exchange rate as exogenous. But the Helkie-Hooper model Cline uses actually makes relative export unit values endogenous. It treats unit labor costs and consumer prices as exogenous, but it includes equations that explain export prices. If, in fact, relative US export prices have not fully adjusted to the changes in these exogenous variables, this is evidence of hysteresis (or some other change in the structure of the trade equations). It is certainly not evidence that our models explain US trade performance relatively well. Accepting

Robert Z. Lawrence is Albert L. Williams Professor of International Trade and Investment at the John F. Kennedy School of Government, Harvard University. At the time of the conference he was a Senior Fellow at the Brookings Institution.

Cline's evidence, therefore, we should conclude that the equations explaining trade prices have performed poorly and that we may have hysteresis or a competitiveness problem, which shows up in prices rather than in the relationships between relative prices and trade volumes.

Indeed, in a paper written over a decade ago (Lawrence 1979) I argued that foreign productivity growth tended to be more rapid in export sectors than in the rest of manufacturing, whereas US productivity growth was not characterized by a similar dualism. I pointed out that this implied equal inflation in manufactured-goods prices in the United States and the rest of the world would be associated with rising US relative export prices.

This relationship does not appear to have continued to hold in the 1980s. Indeed, Cline's empirical evidence is questionable. First, he claims that relative export unit values are the most (or only) relevant price measure for explaining trade behavior. This is only partially correct. In fact, the equations in his own model explain export performance on the basis of *both* relative export prices and the ratio of US prices to foreign wholesale prices. I infer from Cline's discussion that the latter measure *is* actually back to its 1980 levels. Moreover, Cline ignores import prices. He rationalizes this on the grounds that foreign export prices are US import prices. But of course there could be compositional and behavioral differences between these variables. Indeed, many have argued that foreigners have been pricing to market, which implies precisely such differences. Surely the import price data (used in Cline's own model) are more relevant.

In fact, the relative unit value measure of the IMF is the only measure that supports his case. I have shown in my recent Brookings paper (Lawrence 1990) that, over the 1980s as a whole, US noncomputer, nonagricultural export prices increased by 30.2 percent and nonoil, noncomputer import prices rose 30.6 percent. Similarly, foreign export prices in dollars as measured by the Organization for Economic Cooperation and Development were up 29.5 percent and the US producer price index for finished goods was up 33 percent. Therefore, by the most relevant measures, even taking lags into account, the dollar was back to its 1980 levels, and the relative prices of US tradeables were likewise at 1980 levels. In my view, therefore, there is no mystery in the dollar-price relationships and no evidence of hysteresis. In my models, in contrast to Cline's, the residual trade imbalance is accounted for by the differences in US import and export activity elasticities—the Houthakker-Magee effect.

Cline claims, however, that his paper "does not give as much credence" to the presence of a Houthakker-Magee effect "as either Lawrence or. . .Krugman." In the most recent version of my paper, when I removed computer prices from US domestic prices, I obtained long-run activity elasticities for US imports and exports of 2.5 and 1.6, respectively. Actually these parameters are almost the same as those obtained from Cline's EAG model. My results, like Cline's, suggest that a real dollar depreciation of around 1 percent per year would have been required to maintain trade balance over the 1980s. This would imply, *ceteris paribus*, that a dollar at least 10 percent lower than in 1980 would now be required to achieve balance. Cline contends that the rise in the trade deficit over the 1980s is not due to the Houthakker-Magee effect. Yet surely if the dollar needed to be 10 percent weaker in 1990 than it was in 1980, the fact that it was not must account for a substantial share of the decline in the nonoil, nonagricultural trade balance over the decade. His paper would be more credible if he simulated both the price and volume equations in his EAG model over the decade using only his preferred exchange rate measures and activity elasticities. He needs to demonstrate, first, that dollar measures that can reasonably be considered as exogenous to a trade equation system can explain trade prices, and second, that using income elasticities of 2.2 for imports and 1.85 for exports one can in fact track US trade over the full decade of the 1980s.

In my view, US trade behavior can be predicted with reasonable precision by our econometric equations. There really are no great puzzles about either the pass-through of exchange rates into prices or the response of trade volumes to these prices. The equations ascribe the failure of the trade balance to fully reverse itself neither to the failed response of trade prices to real exchange rate changes, nor to failures in the response of trade volumes to trade prices. Instead, they "explain" the outcome mainly in terms of differential activity elasticities on US exports and imports. If hysteresis were important, functions estimated on data prior to the dollar peak should have trouble tracking behavior thereafter. But as several models and my own work has shown, they do not. The Bryant exercise and Cline's models were unduly pessimistic because they were too optimistic about US growth. Once the actual growth rates are taken into account, we can track trade behavior—with the possible exception of some weakness in recent import volume behavior.

We are left therefore with the Houthakker-Magee effect, which is really a shorthand way to capture the secular decline in the US real exchange rate required to maintain the trade balance at any given share of GNP. To be sure, the relationship between activity and trade volumes used in these specifications is not a well-specified structural equation. It should instead be seen as a statistical summary of the historical relationship between endogenous variables. Although some serious efforts have been made to specify supply and demand variables separately, these unfortunately have not been particularly successful or robust. In particular, Ellen Meade reported that once computers were excluded from the regressions in the Helkie-Hooper model their supply-side proxy was no longer significant. However, the fact is that, even if it has not been structurally well specified, the relationship between trade volumes and economic activity in the United States and the rest of the world appears to have been fairly constant over the past two decades. An econometrician estimating this relationship would find that the Houthakker-Magee effect has persisted in US trade behavior in the 1960s, 1970s, and 1980s.

In my most recent paper, I did find that over the past 18 months US imports have been growing more slowly than would have been predicted. This appears partly because US demand for automobiles and spending on capital goods have been unusually weak in this slowdown, and partly because the relationship between such spending and imports seems to have shifted. Although we can rule out hysteresis, therefore, we cannot rule out the view that there has been an improvement in the competitiveness of US import-competing sectors. Nonetheless, it would be dangerous to project, on the basis of this relatively short experience, that these effects will persist.

My comments about the paper by Allen Lenz relate to methodology rather than conclusions. I found much of the discussion interesting and informative. Clearly a lot of work has been done in obtaining a sense of what is happening across particular sectors. The problem I have is understanding how all the data hang together.

I think it was George J. Stigler who said that the plural of anecdote is data. This study gives us lots of numbers but it is not clear what one is to make of them. Many of the findings reflect the author's judgments, but how is one to evaluate them?

Much of the discussion is qualitative rather than quantitative. I felt while reading the paper much the same way I feel when reading a good piece of financial journalism. The paper provides interesting insights, but it is difficult to evaluate its claims. I would like to see many more of the individual claims backed up by harder numbers.

I also wonder if the discussions about the different sectors are mutually consistent. The paper is filled with interesting pieces of information taken from particular analysts, but it would be more convincing if some common disciplines were imposed in the discussions of each of the sectors. Are the discussions all premised on the same exchange rate and the same view of growth in the United States and the rest of the world? Some analysts could be forecasting weak US exports or strong imports because of their assumptions about growth or exchange rates rather than other particular competitive industry characteristics.

Finally, I am worried about a problem that results from the level of disaggregation in Lenz's analysis. One of the important aspects of US trade adjustment is that relatively large aggregate effects can result from quite small individual changes and indeed from changes in sectors that are often hard to treat as single industries. An analysis of this sort will be biased toward the large, conspicuous industries like automobiles and could miss changes in smaller, less obvious sectors that could be significant in the aggregate.

References

Lawrence, Robert Z. 1979. "Toward a Better Understanding of Trade Balance Trends: The Cost-Price Puzzle." *Brookings Papers on Economic Activity* 1:191–212.

Lawrence, Robert Z. 1990. "U.S. Current Account Adjustment: An Appraisal." *Brookings Papers on Economic Activity* 2:343–82.

Reply

William R. Cline

Neither Peter Hooper nor Robert Lawrence likes my IMF unit value of exports price index. I do not insist that it supplant the other measures, but I do maintain that it casts doubt on the stylized fact (reasserted by Lawrence) that by 1990 the dollar and relative tradeables prices were back to 1980 levels. Hooper apparently agrees with me, and he even puts a price tag on the shortfall in this return of relative prices: $20 billion of the annual trade gap.

Lawrence argues that even if relative prices are not back to where they started, the conclusion is hysteresis rather than that the models explain the trade deficit when the right prices are used. His argument is that a failure of the return of relative prices to their starting point would mean a structural shift in the relationship of trade prices to underlying economic variables. But hysteresis should be subdivided into a shift in the trade price equations (Lawrence) and a shift in trade performance *given* the trade prices. The close tracking of the EAG model (which *does* use exogenous trade prices, as translated by the exchange rate and operating with a lag) leaves little room for the latter. As for the former, the Helkie-Hooper equations do overpredict trade prices. However, their use of foreign consumer (rather than wholesale) prices as the explanatory variable, and even more importantly the computer price data pollution problem, make these equations an inadequate basis for judging structural shift.

Hooper argues that the mainstream trade models underpredicted US adjustment. The unrevised Helkie-Hooper model indeed did, but he probably overstates the case when he argues that the Bryant survey models would also have done so. He bases this conclusion on the strong dollar in 1989, but assuming a two-year lag the 1990 trade outcome was too early to show the 1989 dollar influence. Lawrence in contrast agrees with me that the Bryant model predictions (and mine) were on track after taking into account the divergence of actual from originally expected US economic growth.

Hooper argues that the EAG model tracks successfully because of my "judgmental" adjustment of US trade elasticities. This adjustment is not arbitrary: it is a simple averaging of US–specific and global-average elasticities. I interpret this process as similar to a Bayesian statistical technique, where the global average establishes a "prior value" on the expected value of the parameter. It is reassuring that Hooper's time series on annually reestimated import income elasticities shows a downward trend, suggesting convergence of the US parameter toward the Bayesian prior. Indeed, his 1990 value of 2.1 is almost identical to my global average (1.97; Cline 1989, 173). This trend line also shows why Lawrence's insistence that the EAG simulations should fully replay the 1980s is probably inappropriate, unless the EAG were respecified with a secularly declining import elasticity along Hooper's lines.

This same point helps resolve the puzzle that Hooper's decomposition more than explains the change in the US trade deficit. That excercise is already helpful at the outset, because it highlights the fact that the actual trade balance decline from 1980 to 1990 is not $100 billion (as loosely generalized in the stylized facts of what Hooper calls the Krugman-Lawrence paradox) but only $50 billion after the relatively unpredictable agricultural and oil sectors are removed. Hooper usefully explains $20 billion by relative prices (as noted) and another $20 billion by placing half weight on relative growth in aggregate demand (as opposed to GNP). That leaves little unexplained. His model explains too much, adding another $60 billion expected deterioration, after he adds the supply shift (relative capital variable); but his discussion also suggests that as this influence is essentially a substitute for Houthakker-Magee, and as the aberrant US import elasticity seems to be falling, this third component appears to be overstated. In short, to the extent that his conclusion that the models underpredicted adjustment is valid, it is not so for the EAG, and with some analytical justification rather than random luck.

Neither Hooper nor Lawrence explicitly deals with my suggestion that adjustment (to 1 percent of GNP external deficit) may be at hand after the budget deal, shifting the L-shaped curve (itself already an improvement from the U-curve) to clock hands at four o'clock. Lawrence implicitly calls for a one-time adjustment of another 10 percent in the exchange rate followed by 1 percent further devaluation each year to deal with the backlog and then the ongoing effects of the Houthakker-Magee effect; Hooper's prospective relative capital performance suggests something similar, but he implicitly moderates the needed decline by his discussion of the falling US import elasticity. He questions my projection of a flat relative capital variable, but that was the experience in 1985–86 (Cline 1989, 90), and Hooper's diagram of this variable strongly suggests long-term flattening. Overall, the discussants imply that the outlook I have presented is on the optimistic side, a comforting flank considering that Hooper feels that the models of this genre have under- rather than overstated US adjustment.

Reference

Cline, William R. 1989. *United States External Adjustment and the World Economy.* Washington: Institute for International Economics.

3

Japan

Japan

Surprises and Lessons from Japanese External Adjustment in 1985–91

Masaru Yoshitomi

The years immediately following the Plaza Agreement of September 1985 did not see any dramatic improvement in the Japanese external balance. As late as 1988, Japan's trade and current account surpluses stood at $95 billion and $80 billion, respectively, compared with $93 billion and $85 billion in 1986 (table 1)—hardly an impressive adjustment. Moreover, the yen had hit its peak against the other major currencies already in 1988 and began to depreciate in the course of 1989. Therefore, the general expectation was that a reversal of Japan's external adjustment would occur, probably in 1989 or 1990.

Then came a happy surprise. In 1989 the trade and current account surpluses fell to $77 billion and $57 billion, respectively (table 1), and declined further in the first eight months of 1990 to annual rates (seasonally adjusted) of $62 billion and $45 billion, respectively. Compared with their peaks in 1986, this represents a reduction in the trade surplus by 40 percent (or from 5.0 percent to 2.6 percent of Japanese GNP) and in the current account surplus by 60 percent (from 4.6 percent to 1.7 percent of GNP).

In 1986–88, when adjustment was slow and modest, one heard a lot of noise about Japanese economic policies and Japanese business behavior in both export and domestic markets. In 1989–90, when the extent of external adjustment has been quite impressive, further demand for changes in Japanese macroeconomic policies has virtually ceased. Instead a new critical view has emerged, namely, that too-easy monetary policy in the wake of the Plaza produced inflation in the prices of Japanese assets (stocks and real estate), which are now about to collapse

Masaru Yoshitomi is Director-General of the Economic Research Institute of the Japanese Economic Planning Agency.

Table 1 Japan: selected balance of payments accounts, 1986–90 (billions of current dollars)

Account	1986	1987	1988	1989	1990[a]
Current account	85.8	87.0	79.6	57.2	20.2[b]
Merchandise trade	92.8	96.4	95.0	76.9	28.0[b]
Nonmerchandise trade	−4.9	−5.7	−11.3	−15.5	−5.7
Travel	−5.8	−8.7	−15.8	−19.3	−9.8
Investment income	9.5	16.7	21.0	23.4	15.0
Long-term capital account (net)	−131.5	−136.5	−130.9	−87.9	−34.8
Direct investment (net)	−14.3	−18.4	−34.7	−45.2	−24.6
Securities	−101.5	−93.9	−66.6	−28.2	−8.4
Short-term capital account	58.9	92.7	64.7	41.3	9.0
Change in foreign reserves	15.7	39.2	16.2	−12.8	−11.2

a. First six months only.

b. Not seasonally adjusted.

Source: Bank of Japan, *Balance of Payments Monthly Statistics,* various issues.

in the face of the tighter monetary policy needed to counteract inflationary pressures.

After describing, in the section that follows, the dramatic changes in domestic saving-investment balances that are the counterpart of Japanese external adjustment, I will discuss in subsequent sections of this paper the effectiveness of the exchange rate change in bringing adjustment about; the role of absorption policy, particularly monetary policy; the factors responsible for the wide observed divergence between real and nominal external adjustment, namely, the pass-through ratio and the oil price decline of 1985–87; and the factors that account for the continued reduction of the external surplus in 1989 and 1990, including Japan's growing direct investment abroad. The concluding section will discuss where Japan now stands in its external adjustment process.

External Surpluses and the Domestic Saving-Investment Balance

Japan's current account surplus increased during the first half of the 1980s, eventually peaking at 4.5 percent of GNP. The main domestic counterpart of this rise was a nearly equal decline in the deficit of the general government (table 2). Hence the question became whether it was possible to unwind these current account imbalances without fiscal expansion in Japan (Yoshitomi 1986).

From 1986 to the first half of 1990, the main domestic counterpart of the reduction in Japan's current account surplus was a substantial increase in the excess of investment over saving in the corporate sector (table 2). Contrary to expectations, the general government continued to reduce its deficit and even moved into surplus during and after 1987. In the household sector, meanwhile, the excess of saving over investment declined, led by both a decline in saving and an increase in investment.

For the Japanese economy as a whole, the saving–GNP ratio remained more or less unchanged at 33 percent to 34 percent, while the investment–GNP ratio increased by approximately the same magnitude as the decline in the external surplus. External adjustment was thus facilitated not by a decline in national saving, such as a rise in the government deficit, but by an increase in national investment. In particular, as table 3 shows, business fixed capital formation relative to GNP increased by more than 4 percentage points, from 16.2 percent to 20.5 percent, and residential construction increased as a share of GNP by 1.5 percentage points, from 4.7 percent to 6.2 percent.

Helped by this buoyant investment activity and the booming national economy in the face of the appreciation of the yen, the government sector was able to improve its position during the period of adjustment. Measured by the cyclically adjusted change in the general-government financial balance, as calculated by

Table 2   Japan: saving-investment balances by sector in relation to nominal GNP, 1980–90 (percentages)[a]

Fiscal year	Household			Corporate			General government			Total		
	S	I	S–I	S	I	S–I	S	I	S–I	S	I	S–I[b]
1980	17.1	7.9	9.3	11.5	17.2	−5.7	3.1	7.1	−4.0	31.5	32.2	−0.6
1981	17.0	7.2	9.8	10.8	16.7	−5.9	3.3	7.0	−3.7	31.4	30.9	0.5
1982	15.6	7.4	8.2	10.8	15.6	−4.8	3.3	6.7	−3.4	30.5	29.7	0.8
1983	15.7	6.5	9.2	11.4	15.3	−4.0	3.4	6.3	−3.0	30.2	28.2	2.0
1984	15.2	6.3	8.9	11.2	16.2	−4.9	4.0	5.8	−1.8	31.3	28.3	2.9
1985	15.0	5.1	9.9	11.7	17.6	−6.0	4.9	5.6	−0.8	32.1	28.4	3.7
1986	14.9	5.3	9.6	11.9	16.9	−5.0	5.4	5.7	−0.3	32.5	28.0	4.4
1987	13.7	5.9	7.7	11.2	17.5	−6.3	7.2	6.2	1.0	33.0	29.6	3.3
1988	13.7	5.3	8.4	11.4	19.6	−8.3	9.0	6.1	2.9	33.7	31.0	2.6
1989[b]	13.0	(4.5)	8.5	12.0	(19.8)	−9.4	−8.5	(5.9)	2.5	(33.6)	(31.8)	1.9
1990[b]		(6.1)			(19.9)			(6.5)		(34.1)	(32.5)	1.5

S = saving; I = investment.

a. Figures in parentheses are preliminary estimates based on expenditure statistics alone.

b. Equivalent to net external lending.

c. First six months only.

Source: Economic Planning Agency, *National Accounts,* various issues.

Table 3 Japan: changes in composition of gross national expenditure, 1985–90 (percentages of total)

Component	1985	1986	1987	1988	1989	1990[a]
			At current prices			
Private consumption	58.2	57.8	57.7	57.0	56.3	55.7
Residential construction	4.6	4.7	5.6	6.0	6.0	6.2
Business fixed investment	16.2	16.1	16.2	17.5	19.4	20.5
Private inventory investment	0.6	0.3	0.3	0.5	0.4	0.3
Government consumption	9.7	9.8	9.6	9.3	9.3	9.2
Public fixed investment	6.8	6.7	6.9	6.8	6.5	6.4
Public inventory investment	0.1	0.1	−0.0	−0.1	−0.0	0.1
Change in foreign balance	3.8	4.4	3.8	2.9	2.1	1.6
Exports of goods and services[b]	16.4	13.1	12.7	13.0	14.6	15.9
Imports of goods and services[b]	12.7	8.7	8.9	10.0	12.4	14.3
			At 1980 prices			
Change in foreign balance	4.3	2.8	2.1	0.4	−0.5	−0.5
Exports of goods and services[b]	19.0	17.5	17.4	17.9	19.7	20.9
Imports of goods and services[b]	14.7	14.7	15.3	17.5	20.2	21.4

a. First six months only.

b. Includes investment income.

Source: Economic Planning Agency, *National Accounts*, various issues.

the Organization for Economic Cooperation and Development, the Japanese fiscal policy stance became expansionary in 1987 by only 0.3 percent of GNP, and turned restrictive thereafter.

The surprisingly strong rise of business investment, which continues as of this writing, cannot be attributed to the limited fiscal pump-priming undertaken in 1986–87, particularly given the prospect of an adverse impact on Japanese businesses of the sharp appreciation of the yen. Rather the main driving force has been technological innovation. (The role played by monetary policy will be taken up below.)

Effectiveness of Exchange Rate Changes

The counterpart of the dramatic upward and downward swings in Japan's external imbalance in the 1980s was the surprising asymmetry of the sectoral saving-investment balance alterations between the two swings. Can the effect of the exchange rate change consistently account for the external adjustment in terms of both the external account and its domestic counterparts?

The quantitative measurement of the effect of exchange rate changes is fraught with enormous problems, given that exchange rate changes impact not only on the relative prices of exports and imports but also on other prices and domestic incomes at more aggregate levels. This complexity can be illustrated using simulation results for the exchange rate change obtained using the World Econometric Model of the Japanese Economic Planning Agency (EPA).

Elasticity pessimism, or the belief that price elasticities of exports and imports are too low for exchange rate changes to be effective in changing the trade account, is unjustified as far as the partial-equilibrium effects of exchange rate changes on the volume of exports and imports are concerned. Many econometric studies confirm that the Marshall-Lerner condition (absolute values of the price elasticities for exports and imports must sum to greater than unity) is met for Japan, the United States, and Germany. Although the very short-run (less than one year) sum of the price elasticities of exports and imports is less than unity, giving rise to the J-curve effect, the long-run sum considerably exceeds unity. Thus, the simulation results of the EPA world model indicate that a sustained exchange rate change of 10 percent will reduce trade imbalances by more than 1.5 percent of GNP (annual average effect over six years) for Japan at constant prices. At current prices, however, the effect of the exchange rate change weakens—the trade account imbalance declines by only 0.7 percent for Japan. In other words, the value effect of the exchange rate change turns out to be about half of the volume effect, but is still reasonably large.

Of course, the initial large gap between exports and imports weakens the partial effect of the exchange rate change. In 1986, Japan's exports were nearly

Table 4 Japan: trade balance effects of exchange rate changes as calculated in partial- and general-equilibrium simulations (percentages of GNP)[a]

	Volume effect	Value effect
Partial equilibrium	1.52	0.70
General equilibrium	0.69	0.36

a. The numbers in the table represent the predicted effect on the trade account of a sustained 10 percent change in the yen exchange rate and are annual averages of simulation results for the period 1988–92 in terms of deviations from a baseline. The partial-equilibrium results are those obtained from simulations using only the balance of payments block equations of the EPA World Econometric Model; the general-equilibrium results are from simulations using the full-link world model.

Source: EPA World Model Group, "External Balance Effects of Exchange Rate Changes and Macroeconomic Policies—Main Issues on Simulation Results of the EPA World Model." Presented at the Fourth EPA International Symposium on Global and Domestic Policy Implications of Correcting External Imbalances, Tokyo, March 1988.

twice its imports. Even with this gap, the long-run Marshall-Lerner condition is satisfied.

However, the analysis of the effect of the exchange rate change does not stop here. The simulation results so far have been based on the assumption that only the prices of traded goods are altered by (and proportionately to) the exchange rate change, while other prices and incomes remain unaffected. It may be that the optimistic view about elasticities is supported only by the partial-equilibrium analysis of exchange rate changes.

Under the more realistic assumption that incomes and prices other than those of exports and imports are also influenced endogenously by the exchange rate shock, the outcome is much less favorable. The potential external account improvement due to export and import price changes alone is considerably offset by endogenized changes in incomes and other prices.

First, even the volume effect for Japan of a sustained 10 percent exchange rate change under fully endogenized equilibrium simulations is only 0.69 percent of GNP, or about half that obtained under the partial-equilibrium assumptions. It is now small wonder that the value effect under the full-equilibrium simulations becomes even smaller. The endogenized full-equilibrium outcome for the trade account improvement in terms of value is only 0.36 percent of GNP, or about half the partial-equilibrium outcome for Japan in nominal terms (these results are summarized in table 4).

Therefore, to evaluate the effectiveness of exchange rate changes in reducing external imbalances, it is extremely important to clearly distinguish not only between nominal and real but also between the partial-equilibrium effect and the full- or general-equilibrium effect. The differences between the volume effect in partial-equilibrium solutions and the value effect in general-equilibrium solutions are large.

The partial-equilibrium volume effect is defined as the trade volume effect exerted by changes in export and import prices alone that are directly caused by exchange rate changes. Incomes and prices other than those of exports and imports are assumed to remain unchanged. In contrast, the full-equilibrium value effect is defined as the full effect on the nominal value of the trade or the current account balance when all incomes and prices are influenced endogenously by exchange rate changes. In between these two extremes are two intermediate cases: one is the trade value effect in partial-equilibrium solutions. This effect is associated with the assessment of the efficacy of the exchange rate in terms of meeting the Marshall-Lerner condition. The other intermediate case is the trade volume effect in general-equilibrium solutions, which indicates the deflationary and depressive impact of exchange rate appreciation on external adjustment (table 4).

In sum, elasticity optimism (i.e., the expectation of reasonably large value effects under partial-equilibrium assumptions) may turn into overall pessimism about the adjustment effects of exchange rate changes (i.e., the expectation of relatively small value effects in a full-equilibrium solution). In other words, the actual effect of the exchange rate change may be only half the partial-equilibrium value effect, if incomes and prices other than those of exports and imports are endogenously determined.

The identity between external export-import balances and domestic investment-saving balances is a familiar one, but economic models designed to produce such an identity under an exchange rate shock tend to generate large gaps in external adjustment between constant and current prices and also between partial and full equilibrium.

These simulation results shed some light on the issue of how the initial exogenous shock to the *nominal* exchange rate change exerts a weakened effect on external adjustment, because of the induced endogenous changes in domestic incomes and prices, both of which tend to move in an offsetting direction. How much of the nominal exchange rate change is translated into a real exchange rate change? And how much is the effect of the nominal exchange rate change offset by the induced changes in domestic incomes and prices?

The simulation results indicate that a 10 percent initial change in the nominal exchange rate produces about a 0.5 percent change in the GNP deflator, resulting in a 9.5 percent change in the real exchange rate in the case of the Japanese economy. However, this is an extremely partial observation. If we take into account more general offsetting movements of both domestic prices and incomes, the effect of the nominal exchange rate change is halved, in terms of its effect on the *real* or the *nominal* external balance. This can be observed by reading down table 4 from the partial-equilibrium to the general-equilibrium effect.

In sum, the effect of the nominal exchange rate change cannot be measured by the induced change in the real exchange rate alone; much more important are the induced overall changes in domestic incomes as well as domestic prices. The effect of the nominal exchange rate change, although not totally nullified, is substantially reduced (by about half). In other words, sole reliance on expenditure-switching policy to achieve external adjustment via the exogenous change in the exchange rate will prove too costly for the domestic economy. Expenditure-absorption policy should be mobilized as well, to mitigate the offsetting movements of domestic incomes and prices induced by the expenditure-switching policy and thus keep the domestic economy in equilibrium.

Absorption Policy in Japan

The most important question for Japanese absorption policy under circumstances of exchange rate change is how to formulate monetary and fiscal policies to meet the medium-term goal of steady reduction of the external surplus, without violating the medium-term orientation of domestic macroeconomic policy. The simplest way would be to adopt expansionary macroeconomic policies, but excessively expansionary policies would not be sustainable over the medium run. The result could be acceleration of inflation or swollen budget deficits, which would force the reversal of the policies. Such a stop-and-go approach to policymaking would only destabilize markets and contribute little to adjustment. Fortunately, as already mentioned, strong private investment, not an increase in budget deficits, contributed to the reduction of the excess of domestic saving over investment in Japan after 1985.

What, then, about monetary policy after the Plaza Agreement? Was it too easy? Did it contribute to the the boom in business investment? Allegedly, easy monetary policy produced inflation in asset prices in Japan, leaving the Japanese economy vulnerable to a collapse of asset prices in the event monetary policy was reversed.

I have several doubts about this hypothesis. First, if Japanese monetary policy was too easy after the Plaza, the rate of inflation in the goods and services markets should have been very high. Yet on the contrary, the actual overall rate of inflation in Japan, as measured by the GNP deflator and the consumer price index, was 1.2 percent and 2.3 percent, respectively, from the second quarter of 1989 to the corresponding quarter of 1990. Why did the allegedly easy monetary policy produce inflation only in the asset markets, and not in the goods and services markets?

Second, if monetary ease can be gauged in terms of the money supply, the relative timing of the changes in the money supply and the rise in asset prices that occurred does not suggest any meaningful causal link. The money supply (as measured by M2 plus bank certificates of deposit) increased in each quarter by 8 percent to 9 percent on a year-to-year basis until the first quarter of 1987, and only thereafter accelerated to 10 percent to 12 percent per year. In contrast, price-earnings ratios doubled in the Tokyo stock market between the end of 1985 and the middle of 1987—a period in which growth in the money supply was relatively slow. After mid–1987, when the rate of money supply growth was relatively high, price-earnings ratios remained largely unchanged or even declined slightly. The price of land also saw its most rapid increases in 1986 and 1987 (by 25.2 percent and 32.9 percent, respectively), not in 1988 or 1989 (about 10 percent for both years).

Third, it is quite difficult to establish even a rough quantitative causal relationship between excess growth of the money supply and the asset price inflation that occurred. The underlying trend growth of nominal GNP in Japan is about 6½ percent per year (a combination of 4¼ percent real growth and 2¼ percent inflation). Meanwhile the underlying trend decline of monetary velocity is about 1.5 percent of GNP per year. Therefore, the recent rate of increase in the money supply of about 8 percent annually is appropriate and noninflationary. Actual money supply growth exceeded this standard by only 1 percent or so in 1986–87. This extremely small overshoot of money supply growth can hardly explain the extremely large rise in asset prices during the same period. Even in 1988–89, excess growth of the money supply was only 2 percent to 4 percent.

Finally, a too-easy monetary policy should have exerted a simultaneous, nationwide impact on asset prices, such as happened in the early 1970s. However, only in Tokyo did the price of land increase sharply in 1986–87; other areas saw hardly any increase. Only in subsequent years (1988–89) did land prices in areas outside Tokyo increase. This delayed spread of higher land prices beyond Tokyo suggests that the nature of the price increase was somewhat different from the more aggregate and macroeconomic nature of both the excess growth of the money supply and the rise in stock prices.

This analysis of Japanese monetary policy leads us to the question of the assignment of monetary policy in the context of absorption policy under a floating exchange rate regime. Under floating exchange rates, expenditure-switching policy (i.e., essentially the exchange rate change) is endogenous. Only a fixed exchange rate system enables the monetary authorities to utilize expenditure switching as a policy instrument. It is therefore meaningful to debate how to facilitate external adjustment by undertaking expenditure-switching policy, given the exogenously determined change in the exchange rate. A fundamental question is whether we can apply this theoretical framework of absorption versus switching policy to the floating exchange rate regime. Unless we treat exchange rate changes as exogenously determined even under a floating rate regime, such a framework cannot automatically apply, because the exchange rate is induced to change by the absorption policy itself, which consists of either fiscal or monetary policy or some mix of the two.

Fiscal policy can be consistent with both absorption and switching policy even under a floating rate regime. In a surplus economy, for example, expansionary fiscal policy would induce a rise in the value of the currency, as well as stronger domestic demand. However, monetary policy has an inconsistent impact on the direction of changes necessary for external adjustment. Expansionary monetary policy can indeed contribute to stronger domestic absorption, but at the same time the currency will depreciate, offsetting the contribution of stronger absorption to adjustment. In sum, if monetary policy is utilized as an absorption-increasing policy under a floating rate regime, the induced change in the exchange rate could run counter to the external adjustment, or at best its contribution will be near neutral.

To some extent, the acceleration of the Japanese money supply in 1988–89 may have induced the depreciation of the yen during the same period. Furthermore, domestic asset price inflation may have also encouraged Japanese capital outflow via the wealth effect, resulting in a weaker yen. At the same time, asset price inflation enabled enterprises to finance their business investment through equity financing as well as by using land and stock as collateral, thus contributing to stronger domestic absorption.

The assessment of such equity finance (including not only new stock issues but also convertible and warrant bonds) and collateral is difficult to make. It is indeed true that business investment must have been favorably affected both by low effective capital costs and by the availability of funds. However, large-scale enterprises, particularly in manufacturing, did not have to rely on external finance since their retained earnings were greater than their business investment. The extra funds obtained from external finance at effectively lower capital costs were used to finance their own financial investment (*zaiteku* in Japanese).

The sharp (about 40 percent) decline in stock prices after the peak in December 1989 caused equity finance and capital costs to rise, among other reasons because of difficulties in converting bonds into stocks. At the same time, new regulations imposed by the Bank for International Settlements on the own-capital ratio of commercial banks (8 percent to be satisfied by the end of March 1992) forced them to reduce their assets or to issue subordinate bonds (45 percent of the value of stock and subordinate bonds is counted as own capital). The decline in commercial bank lending and the higher capital costs expected to result from this consolidation will eventually weaken business investment, particularly that of small and medium-size enterprises. At the time of this writing, however, there are no indications that business capital formation, including that of small and medium-size enterprises, will substantially slow down in the coming several months.

Another important monetary policy issue is the determinants of long-term interest rates. The conventional theory of yield curve determination is hardly applicable to recent interest rate developments. It appears that long-term interest rates can indeed be influenced by the monetary policy stance, but equally importantly by developments in oil prices and expectations of exchange rate changes caused by nonmonetary factors. Since long-term financial assets are closer substitutes than short-term assets for stocks and real estate, the determinants of long-term interest rates are more important to understanding the asset price inflation of 1985–89 than the allegedly too easy monetary policy.

Real Versus Nominal External Adjustment

During the period up to 1988, when Japanese external adjustment was viewed as too slow and too modest, not only politicians but even economists sometimes spoke of the needed adjustment in nominal terms, or even in terms of absolute nominal values. Yet from 1985 to 1988, the ratio of net exports to GNP in real terms actually declined by 3.9 percentage points; in sharp contrast, the same ratio in nominal terms fell by less than 1 percentage point during the same period (table 3).

As discussed above, the ratio of real to nominal adjustment is about two to one if the exchange rate change is the only instrument used. However, the gap that actually occurred was much bigger than the simulation results for the exchange rate change suggest. Two factors help to explain why the actual gap was so big: pass-through ratios and the 1985–87 decline in oil prices.

Pass-Through Ratios

An extremely low pass-through ratio was once claimed to be the reason for Japan's modest external adjustment. However, the debate over the pass-through ratio is relevant only to the adjustment of exports in real, not in nominal terms, given the price elasticity, whereas the adjustment that was criticized as too slow was that measured in nominal values.

The EPA model can be used to shed some light on the allegedly low pass-through ratio. The yen actually appreciated against the dollar by 99.5 percent, from 255.5 yen to the dollar in the first quarter of 1985 to 128.1 yen to the dollar (annual average) in 1988. However, Japan's export price index, expressed in dollars, cumulatively increased by only 49.6 percent in 1988 from the first quarter of 1985. The pass-through ratio, defined as the ratio of the change in export prices (in the foreign currency) to the change in the exchange rate, is thus only 49.7 percent for this period (49.5 percent divided by 99.5 percent). Japan's export price function (in yen) is specified and estimated as follows in the EPA model (the estimation period is 1975–85, and all the variables are expressed as rates of change):

export price (in yen) = 0.42(exchange rate [yen per dollar])

+ 0.33(private inventory deflator)

+ 0.36(export price of foreign countries [in dollars]).

Thus, given yen appreciation of 99.5 percent by 1988, export prices in dollars should have risen by about 58 percent, according to the first term in this export price function, assuming the other variables remained unchanged. However, the private inventory deflator (the second term) declined because of the fall in the yen price of imported materials and a deflationary impact on aggregate demand, both of which are attributable to the yen appreciation. Judging from the third term in the export price function, some increase in the export prices of foreign countries due to the dollar depreciation should offset at least part of the dampening effect on export prices of the lower private inventory deflator.

The simulation results for exchange rate changes show that export prices in dollar terms would have increased by 60.4 percent in 1988 under the yen appreciation, resulting in a pass-through ratio of 60.7 percent (60.4 percent divided by 99.5 percent) in the year. This simulated pass-through ratio is about 11 percentage points higher than the actual figure. However, if we take into account the impact of the oil price decline on prices of Japan's exports (a 3.5 percent decline according to our simulations), the discrepancy between the actual and the simulated pass-through ratios narrows to 7 or 8 percentage points (detailed results are presented in Yoshitomi 1989).

Although this discrepancy is still subject to further examination, the low pass-through ratio actually observed is largely a result of historically observed "normal" pricing behavior of Japanese exports. US import price increases, which have been much lower than generally expected in the face of the large dollar depreciation, cannot be explained by Japanese exporters' pricing behavior in general, unless they have adopted a pricing strategy that grossly differentiates by export destination. Whether such a pricing strategy, if it exists, is unique to Japan or common to other countries is another question.

Effects of the Oil Price Decline

The roughly 50 percent decline in petroleum prices from 1985 to 1987 also widened the gap between the real and nominal measurements of Japan's external adjustment. Counterfactual simulation results based on the EPA World Econometric Model indicate that the sharp decline in the price of oil worked against the adjustment of Japanese current account imbalances in nominal terms. The oil price decline is estimated to have increased the ratio of the nominal current account surplus to GNP for Japan by 0.7 percentage point in 1988. In contrast, Japan's real domestic demand is estimated to have increased by 0.9 percent in 1988 with the help of the oil price decline, which in turn would have contributed to a decline in the ratio of real net exports to real GNP of 0.6 percentage point in 1988.

In real terms, therefore, the oil price decline helped Japan to strengthen its domestic demand and hence to reduce its external surplus. Thus, the oil price decline was one of the important factors that contributed to widening the gap between nominal and real current account adjustment in 1985–88. For Japan, nominal and real adjustments moved in opposite directions, feeding criticism of the slowness of Japanese external adjustment.

The Unexpected Reduction of the External Surplus: 1989–90

Just as the strength of Japanese domestic demand, led by private business investment, was a puzzle in the face of the sharp yen appreciation, so was the continued reduction of the external surplus in 1989 and the first eight months of 1990. Even well-performing export and import functions for 1980–88 cannot account for this development.

Figure 1 compares within-sample (1981–88) simulation estimates of trade imbalances with actual ones based on quarterly models of exports and imports. These simulations are conducted using only the block of equations relating to external trade in the EPA world model and treating major explanatory variables such as the exchange rate; domestic, import, and world competitors' prices; and domestic and world import demand as given exogenously. Endogenously determined variables in the simulations are the volume of exports and imports and export prices. The tracking ability of the equations is reasonably good: root mean square error is 2.58 percent for the dollar value of exports, 4.88 percent for the dollar value of imports, and 10.27 percent for the dollar value of the trade balance.

However, when we conducted out-of-sample simulations for 1989 and 1990 (but only for the first quarter), the estimated trade surplus in dollar terms exceeded the actual surplus by an extremely wide margin, as figure 2 shows. The root mean square error became 41.16 percent for the trade balance in dollar terms. The dollar value of exports was overestimated, while the dollar value of imports was underestimated. In other words, actual exports were much weaker, by about $6.8 billion per quarter (at annual rates), and actual imports much stronger, by $12.0 billion per quarter (at annual rates) than the out-of-sample

Figure 1   Japan: trade balance, actual results versus within-sample estimates, 1981–88[a]

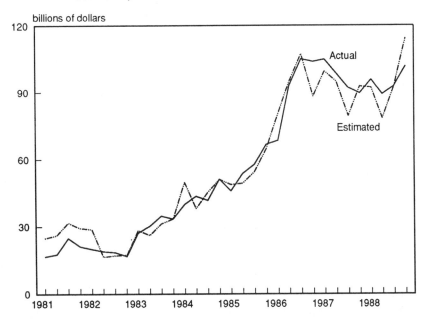

billions of dollars

a. Estimates were obtained using the Economic Planning Agency's World Econometric Model (see text for details).

Source: Actual data from Bank of Japan, *Balance of Payments Monthly Statistics,* various issues.

projection results. The actual ratio of the trade account surplus to nominal GNP was 0.68 percentage point lower than the estimated value.

What accounts for these projection errors? Does the effect of the exchange rate change have a longer lag than estimated? Does Japanese foreign direct investment exert a surplus-reducing effect that is not captured by conventional trade equations?

The parameter of relative prices in the export function in the EPA model has a 10-quarter distributed lag pattern with a summed price elasticity of -1.09. The lag pattern is heavily front-loaded, with elasticities summing to -0.78 for the first six quarters. Imports are estimated for three categories: mineral fuels, food and raw materials, and manufactured goods. The parameter for relative prices in the import function of manufactured goods has a five-quarter distributed lag, with a summed price elasticity of 0.82. Judging from the reasonably good tracking capability of both the export and the import functions, the lag pattern for the relative price parameters appears not to be grossly incorrect.

Figure 2   Japan: trade balance, actual results versus out-of-sample projections, 1988–90[a]

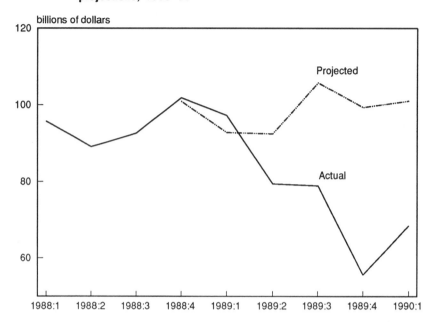

a. Projections were obtained using the Economic Planning Agency's World Econometric Model (see text for details).

Source: Actual data from Bank of Japan, *Balance of Payments Monthly Statistics,* various issues.

Reflecting the depreciation of the yen in 1989 and the first half of 1990, J-curve effects reduced the Japanese external surplus through a decline in export dollar prices. Our trade equations captured these effects well. Serious projection errors were made in the volume of exports and imports, however. The volume of exports was overprojected, while the volume of imports was underprojected, particularly for manufactured goods and mineral fuels.

Regarding manufactured imports, a large increase in imports of nonmonetary gold appears to account for the bulk of the discrepancy between actual and projected imports. The "gold investment account," in which investors reap gains from higher forward prices than spot prices of gold, increased by about $5.5 billion in 1989 over 1988 and further expanded by $7.5 billion in the first nine months of 1990. However, these are captured only on a balance of payments basis, not on a customs clearance basis. The increasingly large discrepancy in the course of 1989 and 1990 between actual and projected imports of manufactured goods shown in figure 2 corresponds to the continued rise in imports of nonmonetary gold by $13 billion (annual rate) in the two years from 1988 to 1990.

With regard to mineral fuels, there was an unexpected increase in the volume of petroleum imports despite a rise in petroleum prices. The EPA equation for petroleum imports carries a normal negative sign for the price elasticity of petroleum import demand. From 1988 to 1989, however, the volume of imported petroleum increased by 6.6 percent in spite of a 7.7 percent increase in the import price. As a result, the value of petroleum imports expanded by $2.7 billion in 1989 over 1988. (On a Japanese fiscal-year basis, the value of petroleum imports increased by $5.1 billion from FY1988 to FY1989.) Of course, since the short-run price elasticity of petroleum import demand is far less than unity (-0.2 in the EPA equation), any price rise in petroleum should cause the value of petroleum imports to rise despite a decline in the volume of imports. More than half of the actual increase in the value of petroleum imports is thus attributable to the unexpected increase in the volume.

In sum, the surge of imports of nonmonetary gold and the unexpected increase in the volume of petroleum imports appear to account for most of the underestimation of Japan's imports and the increasing discrepancy between actual and projected imports in 1989 and 1990. The alleged role of the Ministry of International Trade and Industry (MITI) in artificially encouraging Japan's imports, particularly from the United States, appears to be relatively small compared with the increased imports of nonmonetary gold and petroleum.

Still to be accounted for is the overestimation of the volume of Japan's exports in 1989 and 1990. Although world demand for Japanese exports is exogenously given for our export projections, the greater-than-expected slowdown of the world economy in 1989 and 1990, due to weaker economic activity in the United States and the East Asian countries, largely accounts for our overestimation. Comparison of the latest two issues of *OECD Economic Outlook*, which supplied the data from which our simulations were run, shows that projections for world import demand in volume have been revised downward.

Japanese FDI in the US automobile industry is often claimed to have had the effect of reducing Japan's trade surplus. From 1986 to 1989, foreign production by Japanese transplants in the United States increased to 1.1 million units from 0.3 million units, while Japanese exports to the United States declined to 2.0 million units. In nominal dollar terms, however, the value of Japanese car exports remained largely unchanged at $20 billion in 1989 compared with $21 billion in 1986, since the average price increased by more than 20 percent. Furthermore, the value of exports of auto parts increased from $6 billion to $11 billion during the same period. As a result, the total value of exports of both cars and parts actually increased, from $27 billion to $31 billion, during 1986–89 (table 5).

Table 5 United States: domestic production and imports of passenger automobiles, 1986-89

	1986	1987	1988	1989
US production (millions of units)				
Total	7.6	7.1	7.1	6.8
Big Three	7.3	6.4	6.3	5.7
Transplants	0.3	0.7	0.8	1.1
US imports from Japan				
Units (millions)	2.6	2.4	2.1	2.0
Average price (dollars)	8,040	8,810	9,360	9,750
Value (billions of dollars)				
Automobiles	21	21	20	20
Parts	6	7	9	11

Source: US Department of Commerce; *Ward's Automotive Reports,* various issues.

What More Needs to be Done?

From the Japanese point of view, external adjustment is nearly complete, since the primary current account surplus (the current account minus investment income) has fallen to only $11 billion (at an annual rate), or 0.4 percent of nominal GNP, in the first half of 1990. At the end of 1989, Japan's net external assets amounted to $293.2 billion, or 10 percent of nominal GNP. Given the relatively small surplus on the primary current account, the net external assets–GNP ratio will not expand very rapidly, unless the average rate of return on Japan's external assets exceeds the growth rate of nominal GNP in a common currency.

The issue of the sustainability of the US current account deficit has diminished considerably in importance. There are considered to be three potential undesirable outcomes to sustained US deficits: a severe outbreak of US protectionism, an explosion of the US net external debt and associated investment income payments, and refusal of the United States' creditors to continue financing the US external deficit. A study has shown that even if the US external debt position reaches a relatively large proportion of GNP (25 percent to 35 percent), net investment income payments would still amount to less than 4 percent of the net debt–GNP ratio in the year 2000. This result is due to the much higher rates of return on book value earned by US investment abroad (mainly direct investment) than by inward investment into the United States (Stekler and Helkie 1989).

The financiability of the US external deficit has been enhanced by the decline of the deficit itself in relation to increases in world savings available for financing it. Even if the share of dollar assets that investors seek to maintain in their portfolios remains unchanged, increases in portfolio size due to world growth of income and saving imply a sizable net demand for dollar assets, amounting to perhaps $60 billion in 1989, which is close to the most basic balance of payments (current account plus net foreign direct investment) calculation for the United States of $ − 76 billion for that year (OECD 1990; see also Dealty and Van't dack 1989).

In particular, Japanese institutional investors are in a position to transfer substantial Japanese domestic saving abroad. Investment in foreign securities by Japanese institutional investors increased by an annual average of ¥8,657 billion (or about $60 billion at ¥140 to the dollar) during 1985–89. The percentage shares of foreign securities in total assets vary among financial institutions; at the end of 1989, for example, Japanese life insurance companies held 15.4 percent of their assets abroad, compared with 2.3 percent for banks. The present shares are still well below the officially regulated upper limits, which vary from 30 percent for life insurance companies to 5 percent for banks.

US protectionist sentiment is at present associated not with its overall external deficit but with its bilateral trade deficit with Japan; hence its background is now much more political than economic. Contrary to widespread belief, US exports to Japan expanded by 65.9 percent during 1986–89, faster than US exports to the European Community, which increased by 60.2 percent. US imports from Japan increased at exactly the same tempo (14.3 percent) as US imports from the Community during the same period. Yet the US–EC bilateral trade deficit has been totally eliminated, whereas the US bilateral trade deficit with Japan remains largely unchanged at $40 billion to $50 billion, because of the initial gap between exports and imports in US trade with Japan, which was much larger than that in trade with the Community.

The bilateral trade imbalance between the United States and Japan will remain large unless US imports from Japan continue to decline as they did in the first half of 1990. Nearly all of the bilateral trade imbalance is now concentrated in only four categories of goods, all of which are R&D–intensive: automobiles and parts, videocassette recorders, computers, and semiconductors. Moreover, American industries have increased their dependence on Japanese capital goods since 1985.

Whereas Japanese external adjustment is nearly complete, with the ratio of current account surplus to GNP at about 1.7 percent, further reduction of the US external deficit is desirable, even though the issue of sustainability and financiability of the deficit has diminished in importance.

This leads us to the following policy issue. Japan does not need to undertake new macroeconomic policies in order to reduce its external surplus. The economy is at full employment and full capacity. Furthermore, the possibility of a world saving shortage and associated high long-term real interest rates suggests that fiscal consolidation is the most desirable macroeconomic policy the United States could now undertake. Such action would not only reduce its own undesirable external deficit but also mitigate any emerging world saving shortage. At the same time, the Japanese external surplus should decline further through the spillover effects of budget consolidation by the United States.

Epilogue: September 1991

In early 1991, Japan's current account surplus started once again to increase, led by two major components: an increase in the trade surplus and a decline in the travel account deficit. Since the latter is attributable to the dampening but temporary impact of the Gulf crisis on overseas travel, only the former raises the more fundamental question of whether the reexpansion of Japan's trade surplus again reflects the stubborn export bias of the economy. My conclusion is that Japan's surplus has been expanding largely because a mechanism is at work for making up for the emerging world saving shortage, which I touched upon at the end of my paper.

In the first six months of 1991, Japan's trade surplus on a customs clearance basis increased by about $20 billion (annualized) over 1990 when it registered $52.1 billion, or 1.8 percent of GNP. This expansion has nothing to do with decreased imports of nonmonetary gold associated with the gold investment account: customs clearance data, unlike the balance of payments data discussed above, do not include such imports. All of the increase in the surplus in the first half of 1991 was accounted for by Japan's trade with only two regions: the European Community and Southeast Asia (more or less evenly divided between them). There was little change in Japan's imbalances with the United States, the Middle East, and the rest of the world.

The surplus with the European Community surged largely because Japan's exports to the region, especially Germany, increased by 20.0 percent over a year earlier. Japan's exports to Germany expanded by 31.7 percent, and the increase in its surplus with that country alone accounted for more than half of the increase in the surplus with the Community as a whole. Japanese exports to the rest of the Community increased by 12.6 percent in the first half of 1991 over a year earlier; this rate of increase is nearly the same as that in 1990, when exports grew by 11.7 percent. Japan's imports from the Community declined by 3.2 percent ($2.5 billion). All of this decline was accounted for by a 78 percent drop ($2.6 billion) in imports of paintings from France alone, which was in turn caused by the collapse of capital gains in the asset market in Japan. Imports of luxury cars, particularly from Germany, were also adversely affected for the same reason. If one excludes paintings and automobiles, however, underlying Japanese demand for EC products remained reasonably strong, with an annual rate of increase of 7.5 percent. Likewise, Japan's exports to Southeast Asia increased by 24.5 percent from a year earlier, while Japan's imports from that region increased by 15.6 percent.

Why did these two regions absorb Japanese products so strongly? Since the Japanese economy remained at full employment and full capacity in the first half of 1991, during which its growth rate slowed to a more sustainable path, the surge of Japan's exports can be attributed to strong demand in the two regions rather than excess production capacity in Japan. In fact, strong investment demand in excess of domestic saving (i.e., a savings shortage) in unified Germany and Southeast Asia appears to have pulled Japanese exports of all categories of machinery: general, electrical, transportation, and precision.

A saving shortage in a particular country or region always causes two things to happen more or less simultaneously: a rise in real long-term interest rates and a deterioration of the trade balance. This parallelism was clearly visible in the United States in the first half of the 1980s when huge budgetary deficits emerged. Likewise, the unification of Germany has caused both a rise in real interest rates and a rapid decline of the German surplus from $60 billion to zero in 1990–91. Similarly in Asia, strong growth in domestic business investment has resulted in either a decline in the external surplus (in Taiwan) or an increase in the external deficit (in Korea, Thailand, Malaysia, and Indonesia), as well as in higher interest rates or a shortage of capital.

How did Japan accommodate this surge in net exports under conditions of full employment without undermining domestic price stability? As it happened, tighter monetary policy during 1990, aimed at preventing the acceleration of consumer price inflation, contributed to a slowdown in the growth of domestic demand. Such a policy contributed not only to the collapse of the Japanese stock market but also to weakening business investment as well as residential construction, which fell from extremely high tempos and levels, thus making room for net export expansion.

Monetary policy is essentially neutral in influencing the external accounts in real terms because the impact of policy-induced exchange rate changes offsets domestic absorption changes. During the period of tighter monetary policy in Japan, however, J-curve effects emerged. The yen appreciated to 138.22 to the dollar in the second quarter of 1991 from 155.25 to the dollar a year earlier, corresponding to which the average dollar price of Japan's exports rose by 6.2 percent, accounting for a large proportion of the 10 percent increase in the total dollar value of exports during the same period. The real effective exchange rate of the yen (at current nominal values of about 135 to the dollar and 80 to the mark) is still somewhat stronger than in the very early 1980s, when Japan's trade balance was near zero, according to calculations by the Organization for Economic Cooperation and Development (*OECD Economic Outlook*, July 1991, 33) using unit labor costs in manufacturing as the deflator.

In retrospect, therefore, three factors worked toward the reexpansion of Japan's trade surplus: a shortage of saving in Germany and Southeast Asia; restrictive domestic policy, and in particular, the resulting capital losses in the asset market; and J-curve effects. At the core, however, lies a world saving shortage. The great challenge now confronting international policymakers is how to reconcile this global shortage with Japan's external surplus, and which country actually can or should be allowed to be accommodate the shortage. This challenge will become more acute when the US economy recovers strongly without tackling its domestic saving shortage, and hence comes to exert stronger demand on both Japanese capital goods and Japanese savings than it has in the latest recession.

References

Dealty, M., and J. Van't dack. 1989. "The U.S. External Deficit and Associated Shifts in International Portfolios." *BIS Economic Papers* no. 25 (September). Basel: Bank for International Settlements.

Helkie, William L., and Lois E. Stekler. 1989. "Implications for Future U.S. Net Investments of Growing U.S. Net International Indebtedness." *International Finance Discussion Papers* no. 358 (July). Washington: Federal Reserve.

Organization for Economic Cooperation and Development. 1990. "The Net Dollar Positions of the Non–U.S. Private Sector, Portfolio Effects and the Exchange Rate of the Dollar." *Department of Economics and Statistics Working Papers* no. 76. Paris: Organization for Economic Cooperation and Development.

Yoshitomi, Masaru. 1986. "Growth Gaps, Exchange Rates and Asymmetry: Is It Possible to Unwind Current Account Imbalances Without Fiscal Expansion in Japan?" In Hugh T. Patrick and Ryuichiro Tachi, eds., *Japan and the United States Today: Exchange Rates, Macroeconomic Policies, and Financial Market Innovations*. Montpelier, VT: Capital City Press.

Yoshitomi, Masaru. 1989. "Evaluation of Actual Mechanisms Worked for External Adjustments in 1985–1988." *Rivista di Politica Economica* 6 (June).

Comment

Richard C. Marston

Masaru Yoshitomi is one of the leading experts on the Japanese economy, and so his analysis of Japan's recent trade adjustment is of considerable interest. Yoshitomi argues that Japan is on the right track in its external adjustment. Japan's trade and current account surpluses are falling. The current account surplus, for example, is down to $57.2 billion in 1989 from $85.3 billion in 1986, although just how much of this decline is due to a short-run investment boom is unclear. The remaining adjustment, if any is needed, must come as a result of policy changes in the United States and other industrial countries.

Although I agree with Yoshitomi that these figures show impressive gains, I would like to examine Japanese adjustment more closely, highlighting two key features. The first is Japanese pricing behavior in the United States and elsewhere. It is not possible to understand how Japanese exporters have absorbed the high yen without examining this pricing behavior. The second feature is the shift of production by Japanese firms from their Japanese base to sites elsewhere in East Asia as well as in Europe and the United States.

Yoshitomi reports that the dollar prices of Japanese exports rose 50 percent from early 1985 to 1988, while the dollar price of the yen rose 100 percent, so that the pass-through ratio was one-half. There are two possible reasons for this limited pass-through. First, as the dollar price of the yen rose, the cost of raw materials, including energy, fell, since most of the raw materials Japan imports are priced in dollars. So Japanese firms were able to limit increases in the dollar prices of their exports because their costs measured in yen were falling. Second, Japanese firms held down the increases in their dollar prices by "pricing to market," charging different prices in their export markets than in the domestic market. As the dollar price of the yen rose, Japanese firms lowered the yen prices of their exports in order to limit increases in the dollar prices of these exports.

Which of these two reasons is more important? I recently completed a study of pricing to market by Japanese firms during the period 1980–87 (Marston 1990). The paper compared the export prices in yen for 17 Japanese products with the corresponding prices charged in the Japanese market. The products included cars and other transport equipment as well as many consumer durables. The export prices are genuine price indices (rather than unit value series) pub-

Richard C. Marston is James R.F. Guy Professor of Finance and Economics at the Wharton School, University of Pennsylvania.

lished by the Bank of Japan. The domestic prices are wholesale prices at the primary wholesale level, also published by the Bank of Japan. The results of the study were quite definitive: after taking into account changes in raw material prices and other costs, the study found that Japanese firms lowered their export prices in yen relative to their domestic prices by about 50 percent of the change in the exchange rate. The reductions were larger for some products such as cars with engines over 2,000 cubic centimeters, and smaller for other products such as cameras. But the overall pattern of pricing to market was quite dramatic.

These results are not inconsistent with those of Yoshitomi. Indeed, pricing-to-market elasticities of 50 percent correspond to his pass-through elasticities of 50 percent if costs are constant (although the pass-through estimates are based on aggregate export prices rather than the prices of individual products). But my study establishes that it is primarily pricing to market, rather than lower costs, that accounts for most of the limited pass-through. I also agree with Yoshitomi that this limited pass-through is not just a feature of the post–1985 period. Pricing to market occurs when the yen depreciates as well. In only 5 of the 17 products was I able to find more pricing to market in the period after 1985, when the yen was rising, than in the pre–1985 period.

The second aspect of the adjustment process concerns the shift of production away from its Japanese base. One might view pricing to market as a temporary phenomenon designed to buy time until Japanese firms are able to shift production to offshore sites. This is a plausible view given that the rise in the yen was so steep. In that case, we should find pricing to market disappearing as new plants open offshore. We have no evidence that the pricing behavior we observed is temporary, but we cannot rule this possibility out.

Two types of production shifts by Japanese firms are taking place: to other developed countries where export markets are important, and to lower-cost countries in East Asia. The first type of production typically involves assembly operations or the production of final goods in so-called transplants located in the United States or Western Europe. There are two motivations for producing in such countries, one economic and one political. The economic motive must be important in the case of US production, since there was a 100 percent change in the dollar price of the yen within three short years. In contrast, the deutsche mark and the French franc prices of the yen were much more stable. But political factors must also play a role in both US and European production. Once Japanese firms establish plants, it is much more difficult to erect protectionist barriers to exclude Japanese products.

What evidence do we have on the role of transplants in trade adjustment? Table 5 in Yoshitomi's paper gives evidence on how new transplants have affected trade in cars between Japan and the United States. Production of foreign cars in the United States has risen from 0.3 million to 1.1 million units in three years, but imports of cars have fallen very little, at least in value terms. On the other hand, imports of parts have almost doubled. So the net impact of trade in cars and parts has been to raise US imports from $27 billion to $31 billion. How we view these figures depends on whether we consider what might have happened in the absence of Japanese transplants. In any case, Japanese transplants in the automobile industry have not helped to turn the trade balance around.

To assess the role of Japanese transplants as a whole, we need evidence for a variety of industries. We need to examine not only production from the new plants, but also the displacement of imports by local production and, just as important, the imports of components by the transplants.

The second type of shift typically involves the production of components in such countries as Malaysia, Singapore, and Thailand. Anecdotal evidence suggests that the shift to offshore sites is quite significant. The shift is also evident in the bilateral trade figures. Japanese imports from the Asian newly industrializing countries (Hong Kong, Korea, Singapore, and Taiwan) have more than doubled since 1986, from $12.6 billion to $27.0 billion in 1989.[1] Japanese imports from the ASEAN region (Indonesia, Malaysia, the Philippines, and Thailand) have risen 55 percent since 1986. Yet Japan still runs a big surplus with all these countries. In fact, Japan's exports to the newly industrializing countries rose so sharply (by 73.4 percent) that its surplus vis-à-vis those four economies rose from $17.7 billion to $25.5 billion during the same three-year period. So we have yet to see any significant adjustment in the trade imbalances between Japan and East Asia as a result of these production shifts. Adjustment may be delayed because of a temporary surge in Japanese exports of capital goods to this region, as the offshore plants gear up for production.

I have focused on the shift of production to overseas plants because I believe that Japanese trade adjustment may be achieved primarily through supply-side rather than conventional demand channels. The appreciation of the yen has not brought about a wholesale switching of US consumption demand away from Japanese products, at least partly because Japanese pricing to market has blunted the effects of the appreciation on Japanese export prices in the United States. Nor has the appreciation of the yen brought about a surge of US exports to Japan. Thus, perhaps the best chance for trade adjustment is on the supply side, through a shift in the locus of Japanese production.

So far there is little direct evidence that Japanese transplants have facilitated the adjustment process. But we are still in a transition period in which Japanese capital goods are being exported to the overseas plants and in which Japanese component manufacturers have yet to establish themselves overseas. Once new production is fully established, it will be possible to assess whether the shift of production has accomplished its task. We will then need to take a careful look

---

1. International Monetary Fund, *Direction of Trade Statistics*, various issues.

at the nature of trade flows to and from Japan to determine whether trade in manufactures has been altered by the high yen.

Reference

Marston, Richard C. 1990. "Pricing to Market in Japanese Manufacturing." *Journal of International Economics* 29 (November):217–36.

Comment

Peter A. Petri

The Japanese economy has again demonstrated its remarkable ability to adjust; it is the first of the three major "disequilibrium" economies of the 1980s to have returned roughly to its pre–1980s external balances. As Masaru Yoshitomi's very interesting paper shows, Japan's adjustment has combined large changes in absorption (in fact, an extraordinary economic boom led by investment) with intensified switching to imported products. What explains this outstanding record? As Yoshitomi modestly argues, the boom and the recent acceleration of imports are not well understood and have surprised even Japanese analysts. No red-blooded economist could help but rise to this challenge and try his hand at the puzzles of Japanese adjustment.

Let us consider first the nuts and bolts of expenditure switching. The details of Japan's import boom are truly remarkable. Nearly half of the change in Japanese imports plus travel[1] between 1986 and 1990[2] was due to consumer expenditures—purchases of durable and nondurable goods and expenditures abroad—even though these categories accounted for only 12 percent of imports at the outset of the adjustment process in 1986 (see figure 1). Consumer imports nearly tripled their share of GNP and now approach penetration rates in other industrial countries. In some products, such as automobiles, new distribution channels have been opened and may continue to bring results for years to come; in 1990 alone, automobile imports will increase by 81 percent, or $2.6 billion. In other products, too, there is evidence that distribution channels have become more receptive to imports. Overall, the adjustment may have permanently improved the access of consumers to foreign products and has demonstrated that Japanese consumers are not nearly as biased against imports as they were once claimed to be.

---

1. In order to better account for the role of the consumer in Japan's external adjustment, in the calculations below imports are augmented to include travel expenditures (measured as balance of payments travel debits).

2. Estimates of 1990 trade have been constructed from January-to-August data for 1990, taken from the Japan Tariff Association (1990), annualized by multiplying with the corresponding 1989 ratio of whole-year imports to January-to-August imports.

Peter A. Petri is Carl Shapiro Professor of International Finance at Brandeis University.

Figure 1 Japan: contributors to import growth, 1986–90

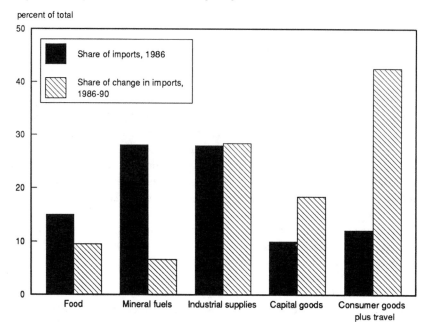

percent of total

Legend:
- Share of imports, 1986
- Share of change in imports, 1986-90

Categories: Food, Mineral fuels, Industrial supplies, Capital goods, Consumer goods plus travel

Source: Japan Tariff Association.

As the Japanese investment boom gathered strength in 1989 and 1990, consumer imports were joined by strong capital-goods imports. Of the $46 billion increase in imports and travel between 1989 and 1990, nearly half was in consumer goods and nearly one-quarter in capital goods. (The rest included special items, including increased imports of oil and gold.) The fact that vigorous volume increases in capital-goods imports began to appear only after the depreciation of the yen in 1989 has fueled speculation that the increase in industrial imports was triggered by administrative guidance. Of course, it may have been due instead to domestic capacity constraints. In any case, although consumer purchasing patterns have clearly responded to the strong yen, it is still unclear whether business and government procurement patterns have changed in any substantial way.

These developments have thoroughly upset the econometrics of Japanese trade (see figure 2 in Yoshitomi's paper). Equations estimated independently by the Japanese Economic Planning Agency (EPA), Robert Z. Lawrence (1991), and

3. This point is further supported by econometric evidence in Petri (1990).

myself (Petri 1991) all suggest structural changes in the Japanese import equations following the turnaround of the yen in 1986; starting in late 1987, manufactured imports began systematically to exceed the predictions of equations estimated on pre–1985 data. Through 1988, however, higher-than-predicted imports were matched by higher-than-predicted exports (the counterpart of US findings of a slow exchange rate pass-through). It is not clear whether the EPA's growing underprediction of adjustment is now due to still-stronger import behavior or weaker export behavior. Whatever the case, the composition of both imports and exports has changed enough so that aggregate trade behavior *should* be very different now from what it was a few years ago. Much new empirical work is needed—perhaps even with the "beachhead" models that have now become superfluous in the econometrics of US trade.

Concerning the absorption processes of 1985–90, the interesting questions are, What caused the investment boom of the late 1980s, given that yen appreciation should have made Japanese industry less competitive? And how did the policy mix affect adjustment patterns in the late 1980s? I will argue that the linkages between the asset price runup in the mid–1980s and the subsequent investment boom were stronger than Yoshitomi suggests, and that Japanese macroeconomic policy did in fact contribute to the asset price bubble.

The most rapid growth in Japanese asset prices occurred between 1985 and the second quarter of 1987, roughly in parallel with the collapse of the dollar, and well ahead of the investment boom that began in earnest in the first quarter of 1989. The runup seems to reflect a massive shift in portfolio preferences from US to Japanese assets in 1985–87. This shift may have caused the collapse of the dollar or may have been caused by it, but in any case it is not easily associated with changes in Japanese monetary policy. The runup almost certainly played an important intermediating role between the collapse of the dollar and the investment boom of the late 1980s. The causal linkages between asset prices and investment could have worked through various channels: high asset prices raised Tobin's q (making the market value of newly created assets attractive) and also reduced the cost of capital. According to this scenario, the seeds of the Japanese investment boom were sown in the mid–1980s, when investors frightened by the imminent or actual collapse of the dollar shifted funds toward Japanese assets.

Yet even if Japanese policies were not responsible for the shift in portfolio preferences that initially set the adjustment process into motion, Japanese policies after October 1987 provided strong support for asset prices and contributed to the fragility of the subsequent boom. Through administrative actions and easier monetary policies starting in late 1987, Japan essentially "delinked" its asset prices from foreign markets. The combination of relatively lax monetary and tight fiscal policies arguably set the stage for both the investment boom and the collapse of asset prices in 1990. Tighter monetary and more expansionary fiscal policies in 1988–90 might have produced a less-leveraged expansion. What is troubling in all this is that Japanese investors seem to have been caught in two bubbles in just five years: in dollar assets in 1985 and then in yen assets in 1990.

Whether accomplished by an optimal policy mix or not, Japan's adjustment to the imbalances of the 1980s is now complete—perhaps even too complete, given the potential demand for capital from Eastern Europe and the Soviet Union. As Yoshitomi argues, Japanese institutions have not yet hit regulatory limits on investments abroad, but the more general question is, What will happen to the economy's overall surpluses? Over the last decade, even before the asset price runup of 1986–87, private saving has declined steadily and has been replaced by government saving to the astonishing extent of 5 percent of GNP. Assuming that government saving will now level off or decline, national saving is also likely to fall. But investment will also decline below 1989–90 levels— certainly in 1990–91 but probably also permanently if long-term capital costs remain near global levels. Superimposed on these trends are expensive oil, growing foreign demands for Japanese assets (as the yen becomes an international currency), and stronger Japanese demand for foreign assets (for diversification in the wake of the bubble). The net effect of these contrary changes cannot be predicted with any confidence, and the Japanese surpluses are likely to fluctuate considerably in the near future.

References

Japan Tariff Association. 1990. *The Summary Report on Trade of Japan.* Tokyo: Japan Tariff Association.

Lawrence, Robert Z. 1991. "How Open Is Japan?" In Paul R. Krugman, ed., *Japanese Trade and Investment.* Chicago: University of Chicago Press for National Bureau of Economic Research (forthcoming).

Petri, Peter A. 1991. "Market Structure, Comparative Advantage and Japanese Trade Under the Strong Yen." In Paul R. Krugman, ed., *Japanese Trade and Investment.* Chicago: University of Chicago Press for National Bureau of Economic Research (forthcoming).

4

Germany

Germany

German External Adjustment Since 1985

Norbert Walter

Since 1985 the strategy of international cooperation in the management of trade and current account imbalances among the Group of Seven countries has been on the whole a success. One aspect of this success is the extent of mutual understanding that has been achieved: group members have been able not only to agree on the nature of the problems facing them, but in addition to adopt joint measures to address those problems and—often—to implement them. Pressure from outside in the form of international commitments has proved extremely helpful in getting measures passed at the national level that would otherwise have become bogged down in the morass of opposing domestic interests.

Cooperation has also been successful in achieving the goals for which these coordinated measures were intended, in particular in influencing the level of exchange rates. Exchange rates respond to news where this is important enough, and joint statements have proved to be effective where they are supported by coordinated intervention by all the major players and backed by appropriate economic policies.

Yet with regard to the fundamental problem that gave rise to the demand for enhanced international economic cooperation—that of reducing trade imbalances—the jury is still out. Some progress is evident since 1985 (table 1), but it is still too soon to talk of having achieved this goal.

In the United States the current deficit continued to rise, both in absolute terms and as a percentage of GNP, despite marked success in bringing the dollar down, until 1987. The improvement in US competitiveness due to the dollar's devaluation emerged in the trade figures only after a two-year lag. In addition

Norbert Walter is Chief Economist at the Deutsche Bank. He was formerly Professor and Scientific Director at the Kiel Institute of World Economics and John McCloy Distinguished Research Fellow at the American Institute for Contemporary German Studies.

Table 1 Current account balances in the G-3 countries, 1985–91

Country	1985	1986	1987	1988	1989	1990	1991[a]
United States							
Billions of dollars	−122.3	−145.4	−160.2	−126.2	−106.3	−92.1	−25.0
As a percentage of GNP	−3.0	−3.4	−3.6	−2.6	−2.1	−1.7	−0.4
Japan							
Billions of dollars	49.2	85.8	87.0	79.6	57.2	36.0	45.0
As a percentage of GNP	3.6	4.3	3.6	2.8	2.0	1.2	1.3
Germany							
Billions of dollars	16.4	39.5	45.7	50.2	55.3	47.8	−15.0
As a percentage of GNP	2.6	4.3	4.1	4.2	4.8	2.9	−0.9

a. Author's estimates.

Sources: Organization for Economic Cooperation and Development, national statistics.

to this one-shot boost to price competitiveness, the weak growth of US domestic demand has also helped shrink its external deficit.

In Japan the picture is more or less the reverse: the current account surplus as a percentage of GNP peaked in 1986 (table 1), and the revaluation of the yen that started in 1985 began to make itself felt in 1987. The downward trend in the yen in 1988–89 was a move in the wrong direction, but for the moment the sharp increase in demand for imports due to the rapid expansion of the Japanese economy is helping to eat into the external surpluses.

In Germany, in contrast, the surplus continued rising until 1989. Although the revaluation of the deutsche mark exerted a restraining influence, the product composition of German exports, with its preponderance of goods whose demand is relatively price-inelastic, caused the weaker dollar to have less of an impact than in Japan. German exporters also continued to benefit, well into the second half of the 1980s, from dynamic growth in many of Germany's trading partners, especially within the European Community.

Thus, whereas the United States and Japan have been making considerable adjustment progress in recent years, German surpluses have continued at an extremely high level until very recently. The next section looks at the reasons for this phenomenon.

A Detailed Look at the German Economy

In the second half of the 1980s, the German current account surplus continued to rise before stabilizing at a high level in 1989; it has only begun to decline in the period since then. The steep increase in the surplus in 1986 was primarily due to a drop in the value of imports of almost 12 percent. This in turn was mainly the result of falling prices: a combination of a sharp rise in the deutsche mark and the collapse in oil prices. This one-time effect was an important factor in the growth of the German surplus; it is also important, however, to note the sharply differing trends in Germany's bilateral trade with each of its major trading partners during the 1980s.

Exchange rate movements have had a visible effect on trade with the United States. Whereas German exports to the United States remained strong in the period up to 1985–86 and dropped significantly over the next two years, the reverse is true of German imports from the United States, which began to increase some two years after the peak in the dollar, responding positively but with a lag to the rise in the deutsche mark. Changing patterns in US trade with Germany accordingly account for a substantial portion of the global adjustment that occurred in the late 1980s, as Germany's surplus on current account with the United States fell from DM49.5 billion in 1985 (95 percent of its total surplus) to DM23.3 billion in 1989 (22.4 percent of the total).

In contrast, Germany's trade with Japan has grown steadily: with comparatively little change in the mark-yen rate (a slight downtrend in the deutsche mark up to the end of 1989, compared with its 1985 level), both exports and imports increased sharply. Although German exports to Japan (up just under 100 percent in nominal terms between 1985 and 1989) rose faster than imports (up almost 60 percent over the same period), they started from an adverse initial position: in 1985 Germany's imports from Japan were almost three times its exports. As a result, the German current account deficit with Japan has continued to grow over the past five years, from DM13.0 billion in 1985 to DM17.9 billion in 1989. However, the expansion of Germany's overall surplus over the same period has reduced the relative weight of this component from 27 percent to 17.2 percent.

Meanwhile Germany has had growing surpluses in recent years with other European countries both within and without the European Community. Exchange rate movements have played little part here, particularly within the Community, which accounted for over half of German imports and exports in 1989. In the period 1985–87 three major realignments resulted in a revaluation of the deutsche mark, but since the beginning of 1987 nominal rates have remained unchanged (except for the mark-lira rate, as the lira was downvalued in the course of the "mini-realignment" at the start of 1990). During this period of stable exchange rates, inflation was lower in Germany than in most of the other member states of the European Monetary System (EMS), leading to a real depreciation of the deutsche mark, which favors German exports. The key factor promoting growth in German exports, however, has been the relatively higher rates of growth in many of Germany's trading partners, particularly in the early years of this period. Overall, German exports to other EC countries averaged annual (nominal) growth in excess of 10 percent a year for the period 1985–89, well ahead of the 3½ percent annual growth in imports from those countries. Meanwhile the German surplus on current account with the rest of the European Community soared from DM2 billion in 1985 (4.5 percent of the total surplus) to DM64 billion in 1989 (61.6 percent of the total).

The rise in the overall German trade surplus that continued until 1989 thus obscures a wide diversity in the balances with individual countries and regions: a significant reduction in the trade and current account surpluses with the United States and an increase in the trade deficit with Japan have been offset by a sharp rise in the intra–EC surplus. This pattern in German trade in recent years is consistent with various theoretical concepts but also poses certain problems.

A current account surplus is synonymous with an increase in net claims on the rest of the world. In principle, the shifts in relative prices that occurred in 1986 meant that Germany benefited from increased investment income from abroad in addition to the boost to revenue from the improvement in the terms of trade. Of course, other parameters such as portfolio structures and interest rates played a role: a decline in the dollar reduces the deutsche mark value of income from investments denominated in dollars, and any decline in US interest rates further exacerbates this reduction. German net capital income in 1987 was down from its 1986 level, despite the higher level of assets, but rose significantly in 1989 under the combined influence of ongoing asset accumulation and an improved interest rate differential, reflecting the growing international diversification of private portfolios. On balance, the shifts in relative prices in 1986 increased German surpluses in nominal terms while shrinking the real surpluses (at constant prices). In volume terms, imports rose almost three times as fast as exports (table 2).

Besides the rapid "positive" impact—the direct boost to the surplus stemming from the revaluation—the slower "negative" influences resulting from a delayed response of trade flows to the shift in relative prices also made themselves felt. This "inverse J-curve" effect was particularly apparent in trade with the OPEC countries: whereas German imports from these countries fell by almost half in the period 1985–86 (lower oil prices had almost no stimulative effect on the volume of oil imports), exports to this group of countries fell more slowly, because of a substantial investment-goods component.

The shift in relative prices in 1986 was particularly marked with respect to the dollar region: the levels of trade between Germany and the United States in the following year confirm that substantial exchange rate movements do have an effect. Trade flows respond to such movements with a lag of up to two years. It takes time for these signals to be accepted as more than just temporary, for market reconnaissance and penetration to be completed, and for shipments to get rolling. Yet changes in relative competitiveness eventually have their effect.

However welcome the real impact of changes in relative prices, the allocation lag in particular emphasizes that the results are not without cost. Shifts in production and marketing consume resources, and if exchange rates overshoot or move in the wrong direction for extended periods, the result may easily run counter to the desired adjustment. The United States endured a significant revaluation of the dollar over a period of years, which put many producers under pressure and even out of business, and is now having to regain industrial ground laboriously in the course of an exchange rate correction. The question therefore arises whether flexible exchange rates are an unmitigated blessing—particularly since external price shocks, which are often accompanied by gyrations of exchange rates, tend on balance to boost inflation.

This is one of the reasons why, more than 11 years ago, the European countries established a zone of relative exchange rate stability within the EMS. The European experience is particularly relevant since the European economies are far more open than the US economy, with much higher shares of trade in GNP. Frontiers that are open and steadily losing their importance, a relatively homogeneous economic zone, and increasingly mobile populations together create a

Table 2 Germany: trade, exchange rates, and key prices, 1985–90

	1985	1986	1987	1988	1989	1990
Trade balance (billions of DM)	73.4	112.6	117.7	128.0	134.6	105.3
Current account balance (billions of DM)	48.3	85.8	82.5	88.7	107.7	77.4
Change in exports[a] (percentages)						
In nominal terms	9.6	-1.4	0.1	7.8	14.3	10.5
By unit values	3.9	-1.8	-0.9	2.1	2.8	-0.1
In real terms	6.8	0.0	0.9	5.8	11.1	9.7
Change in imports[a] (percentages)						
In nominal terms	5.9	-7.8	-0.2	7.7	13.6	11.7
By unit values	2.6	-15.7	-5.3	1.3	4.5	-2.4
In real terms	3.7	3.5	4.8	5.7	8.3	11.8
Change in terms of trade (percentages)	1.2	15.1	3.7	-0.1	-2.7	1.4
Exchange rates						
Yearly average (DM per dollar)	2.94	2.17	1.79	1.75	1.88	1.62
Percentage change over previous year	3.4	-26.2	-17.2	-2.2	7.0	-14.1

	1985	1986	1987	1988	1989	1990
Oil prices						
Yearly average (dollars)	27.5	14.4	18.4	15.1	18.0	23.5
Percentage change over						
previous year	−5	−48	28	−18	19	31
Yearly average (DM)	81	31	33	27	34	38
Percentage change over						
previous year	−12	−61	6	−20	28	12
Commodity prices						
Yearly average (1975 = 100)[b]	112.5	116.1	123.8	150.2	150.7	150.8
Percentage change over previous year						
In dollar terms	−10.1	3.2	6.6	21.3	0.3	0.1
In DM terms	−7	−24	−12	19	7	−14

a. Over the previous year.

b. Calculated in dollar terms by the Hamburgisches Welt-Wirtschafts-Archiv (HWWA).

Sources: Deutsche Bundesbank, Federal Statistical Office, HWWA.

favorable climate for a unified currency zone in the Old World, as indicated by the recent accession of the pound sterling to the EMS.

The EMS has evolved very well: the political will to cooperate is present, and after the painful recognition that isolated devaluations within a tight group mainly result in adjustment inflation rather than improving competitiveness, membership in the hard-currency bloc has grown steadily. Policy convergence is gaining ground, although not, admittedly, in every area. Coordination of economic policies still leaves something to be desired, and progress in reducing public-sector deficits varies widely from country to country, as not all the member governments are showing the necessary discipline over expenditure. Basically, however, attitudes toward stability as an economic goal have improved, as recent trends in inflation demonstrate: compared with the early 1980s, inflation has slowed in all of the EMS countries and is moving toward the German rate. The interval between individual currency realignments has also tended to increase: the last major adjustments were back in January 1987.

However welcome the growing adherence by the other EMS member states to German stabilization policy and the emphasis on maintaining exchange rate stability within the system, a problem—one hopes a passing one—remains. In the absence of complete alignment of stabilization policies in the other European countries, stable exchange rates mean a steady real devaluation of the deutsche mark (by some 5 percent since the beginning of 1987). This promotes German surpluses, as the Bundesbank in particular has repeatedly complained. Although the Bundesbank is primarily concerned about the loss of imported price stability, this is the price of progress in Germany's partner countries, and this success will probably ultimately outweigh the transitional loss of stability based on a beggar-thy-neighbor policy.

In recent years German industry has increasingly been earning its trade surpluses in Europe, benefiting not only from its price competitiveness but also from relatively weak growth at home and relatively robust growth in the rest of the Community (table 3). This pattern is changing, however, in the wake of the successful reduction of the high German budget deficits in 1982 and later. German fiscal policy has generally been only moderately restrictive, whereas monetary policy tended to be expansionary up to the summer of 1988. Short-term interest rates were then at their lowest point of the entire decade, and monetary growth overshot the Bundesbank's targets for three years in a row (1986–88). The Bundesbank has been able to tolerate this more easily in the light of the very relaxed inflationary situation, which is helped by the contractionary effect of the deutsche mark revaluation and the restraining effect of lower import prices.

Despite this loosening trend, Germany's major trading partners have been showing even more dynamic growth, with domestic demand in particular expanding at high rates (table 3). Strong domestic demand promotes imports,

Table 3 Economic growth and domestic demand in selected European countries, 1985–91 (percentages)

Country	1985	1986	1987	1988	1989	1990	1991[a]
Change in GNP[b]							
Germany	1.9	2.3	1.6	3.7	3.9	4.5	3
France	1.9	2.3	2.4	4.2	3.9	2.8	1½
United Kingdom	3.6	3.8	4.6	4.3	1.9	0.6	−2
European Community	2.4	2.6	2.7	4.0	3.5	2.8	1½
Change in domestic demand[b]							
Germany	0.9	3.3	2.6	3.6	2.7	5.1	3
France	2.5	4.5	3.3	4.4	3.5	3.2	2
United Kingdom	2.8	4.6	5.2	7.5	2.9	−0.1	−2¾
European Community	2.2	3.9	3.8	4.7	3.5	3.0	1½

a. Author's estimates.

b. In real terms over previous year.

Source: Organization for Economic Cooperation and Development.

which—under some circumstances—may be essential for overall growth. With certain differences from country to country, this has been the case for a number of Germany's major trading partners since 1985. In France, Germany's largest trading partner, domestic demand overtook GNP in the period 1985–88 following two years of successful restraint of consumption, which had soared after the Socialist government's U-turn in economic policy in 1982. Despite major progress in stabilizing prices and (particularly) unit labor costs, foreign trade—particularly in industrial products and trade with Germany in general—remains a problem for France, which is subject to recurrent scares that the nation is entering industrial decline. Given the otherwise good health of the French economy, these scares should not be taken too seriously, particularly since continuing strong growth in investment is offering good prospects for capacity growth in France, which in itself is productivity enhancing and anti-inflationary.

Germany's trade surplus with the United Kingdom has risen particularly strongly in the past five years. This trend is due to a minor extent to reduced UK exports to Germany (which were lower in 1989 than in 1985) and more to an increase in German exports to the United Kingdom. The UK economy maintained its vigorous growth right through to 1989, resulting in soaring imports (and the familiar result on the UK trade figures), which also benefited German exporters (1989 exports to the United Kingdom were up 30 percent in value terms from their 1985 level).

In 1989 Germany earned about one-third of its trade surplus from these two countries, up from somewhat over a quarter in 1985. There was a similar trend, although at a higher level, in the current account, where France and the United Kingdom now account for just under 50 percent of the German surplus. Although this confirms the importance of growth in domestic demand for a country's foreign trade position, relative growth patterns are only one aspect of the question: other, "softer" factors play a role as well.

For any given constellation of commodity prices and exchange rates, German exporters benefit from the reputation for quality their products enjoy. No one can seriously ask a surplus country to contribute to the international adjustment process by cutting back on ongoing product development, by lowering its standards of production, or by compromising its reliability on delivery deadlines. The logic of free competition demands instead that deficit countries catch up to the leader in these respects.

A Digression: Just How Serious Are Trade Imbalances?

Like other economic imbalances, surpluses or deficits on current account are automatically seen by many economists and economic policymakers as a problem that must be solved quickly, without stopping to look at the underlying causes, the likely duration, or the possible consequences of the imbalance. As closer analysis quickly shows, however, current account imbalances are by no means a bad thing in all circumstances.

One obviously innocuous case is where current account imbalances are temporary and cancel themselves out over the course of a single business cycle. In fact, foreign trade can be a cyclically stabilizing influence, as international differences in the timing of domestic expansion and contraction mean that countries at the top of a cycle incur a trade deficit while countries at the bottom earn a surplus.

Even where imbalances are more lasting they can still be a sign of an economically desirable trend. To give just one example, periods of rapid economic growth are often characterized by current account imbalances. It is irrelevant whether this growth is taking place in a relatively underdeveloped economy, or whether the emergence of previously unknown or inaccessible growth opportunities is creating what amounts to a new frontier. Countries seeking to switch to a higher growth path generally need resources from outside, both to build up their capital stock and to secure the supply of consumer goods to the population during the transitional phase. If the expansion is successful, and the economies involved increase their capacity, the deficits accumulated during the transition can be worked off later, although for this to happen the resources obtained from abroad must actually be used for economic development—that is, invested and not consumed. After showing trade deficits as late as the mid–1980s (with the exception of Taiwan), the "Four Tigers" of Southeast Asia today enjoy large trade surpluses and are a prime example of success with this process. Counter-examples are to be found abundantly in Latin America. The next test case may be Eastern Europe, where the outcome remains to be seen.

Demographic phenomena can also cause external imbalances, which only abate in the medium to long term. Recent developments in the United States, the United Kingdom, and Germany as well as evidence from earlier periods have shown that an immigration wave or a baby boom can result in a marked increase in a country's economic activity (the latter with a 20- to 30-year lag). The key factor here is the increase in the labor supply, and especially the fact that a large number of young people are joining the labor force. Young people are very flexible and mobile; those who have grown up in the country, if it is an industrialized one, are usually familiar with modern technology, whereas the competitive edge of immigrants is their willingness to adapt. In addition, young employees are typically highly motivated: they are at the start of their careers and are striving for higher incomes to satisfy their strong demand for consumer goods and to start and support a family.

All this means that the labor force in a country in demographic flux is not only growing but improving in quality as well. An increase in the number of young people in a country is accordingly followed by a productivity surge. As long as the proportion of young people in the labor force is relatively high compared to that in the overall population, production grows faster than domestic demand. There might be a temporary deviation from this general trend in the early years of a maturing baby boom, due to the high propensity of young people to spend, especially on consumer durables and housing. But eventually the result of the demographic shift is a current account surplus, and the country acquires a growing stock of foreign assets.

This, however, does not last forever. As the young workers age, the economy loses its momentum and the surplus shrinks. In the absence of a new wave of immigration or another baby boom, pensioners eventually become the largest group in the population and the situation changes completely: consumer demand now exceeds domestic production, which is constrained by the shortage of labor. The excess demand has to be covered by imports (paid for from the store of wealth previously accumulated abroad), and the result is a deficit on the current account.

There is, however, no such offsetting trend over the life cycle of a generation if the demographic change is a lasting rather than a transient shock, leading to a permanently shrinking or growing population. In contrast, where balance of payments problems last for longer than an economic cycle and are not caused by economic expansion or one-time demographic shocks, there is often good reason for concern: such problems indicate inadequate ability of an economy to adjust and tend to be self-reinforcing.

A deficit on current account can be interpreted as indicating competitive weakness: a developing reputation for uncompetitiveness will make it increasingly difficult for manufacturers in the deficit country to hold their own in international competition, and functions as a destabilizing factor. If, in addition, the deficit country fails to make the necessary effort to improve its competitive position, and the chronic import surpluses go mainly to support consumption, the result is a soaring mountain of debt that forces increasing diversion of income abroad. The eventual correction may make itself felt gradually or may take the form of a sudden crisis. Slow erosion of confidence in the currency forces interest rates above their natural level (insofar as foreign creditors remain willing to accept claims denominated in the local currency). This restrains investment, reducing future productive capacity. A risk of acute weakness in the currency emerges. If the situation continues to deteriorate, monetary policy faces the unattractive choice between pushing up interest rates, with adverse consequences for the economy and employment, and devaluing the currency, with imported inflation the result.

A country may also find sustained trade surpluses a problem. Trade originally designed to exploit the benefits of an international division of labor gradually becomes a process of unilateral transfer of assets. Difficulties emerge: deficit countries demand changes in the surplus country's policies, or turn to protectionism, and the adverse effect of rapid corrections in policies stops the flow of exports, making capacities obsolete. Foreign direct investments in deficit countries can create problems stemming from xenophobia in the deficit country. People are quick to react emotionally to obvious changes in the ownership of their country's firms and real estate and to clamor against a "sellout." The emotionally charged atmosphere may lead to extreme reactions, an example of which may be the Iraqi invasion of Kuwait—a surplus country rich in revenue and assets, which it was unwilling to relinquish voluntarily to its deficit neighbor.

Even long-term current account imbalances lose their importance when they come to be regarded as imbalances not between (mercantilist-dominated) nation-states but between entities in a larger political body in the process of evolving, such as the emerging single European market. From a major political concern at the focus of public interest, the deficits fade into just another statistic, without much news value. Intraregional trade attracts little attention, as the notion of community, of promotional measures and transfers for deficit regions, and even of interregional assistance gains increasing acceptance. In addition, there is a good chance that the leveling of the playing field in the course of economic integration will encourage expansion in regions that have lagged behind and incurred deficits because of shortcomings in their industrial base.

Finally, bilateral trade imbalances may persist over a longer period, without causing major distortions, simply as a result of differing national characteristics. This is the case where the population of one country has a greater preference for deferring consumption and a correspondingly high saving rate, whereas the population in the other country sets less store on accumulating assets for the future and more on current consumption. The two countries complement each other to the extent that the country with the population of savers has inherent excess supply that can be exported to the other country. Ultimately, however, the excess-savings country must be willing, at least occasionally, to forgive foreign debt.

Admittedly, in the real world it will probably become progressively harder for the importing country to finance the ongoing current account deficits and to service the resulting growing foreign indebtedness. At the point where the deficit country can no longer meet its interest payments, if not before, the exporting country will reconsider its role as creditor. It will generally be ready to waive repayment and continue exporting only if the importing nation is prepared to make structural adjustments—that is, to reduce its domestic demand. To argue that creditors will maintain their behavior and allow imbalances to continue, one has to assume that a high degree of amnesia makes them unable to learn from their losses.

Overall, then, it is premature at least to class all current account imbalances automatically as problems. The appropriate degree of concern depends on the individual case, with the size, duration, and causes of the imbalance the main criteria.

German Economic Growth: Appraisal, Lessons, and Recommended Measures

From 1982 through 1990 Germany enjoyed current account surpluses—a comparatively long period. Although there are countries that have maintained surpluses (Japan, the Netherlands, Switzerland) or deficits (Denmark, Greece) over longer periods, the scale of the German surpluses was unusual: the figure for 1989 was the highest in the OECD, with only Japan (table 1) and Switzerland reporting comparable surpluses recently.

One major reason for the continuing large German surpluses has been mentioned: the favorable shift in the terms of trade in 1985. The collapse in oil prices did not cause a reversal of the energy-conserving behavior already prevalent in the German economy. A greater challenge would have been a more timely signal to the markets not to keep pushing the dollar up. This certainly would have limited the extent of the overshoot and the subsequent dive. Naturally, this is easy to say with the benefit of hindsight, but much more difficult to argue in periods of turbulence. It is easier to identify a need for action on another important cause of the rise in the German surplus, namely, the low rate of German domestic growth compared with the rest of the world generally and in particular the other members of the Group of Seven, especially its European members.

The communiqués of the Group of Seven repeatedly note the need for policy measures to reduce external imbalances. The risks of a possible loss of confidence in deficit currencies, of a possible need to resort to enforced countermeasures, and of a hard landing all appear too great. A crucial part of the solution presumably remains a significant reduction in the US current account deficit through a higher rate of saving at home. As table 4 shows, US saving rates remain well below those in Japan and Germany. Here the first priority is a credible package of measures to reduce the budget deficit, but the prospects of this are poor, for various reasons. Even before the most recent Persian Gulf crisis, the state of the US banking system (in particular the savings and loans) and the sluggishness of the economy were seriously complicating efforts to reach a budget compromise and inexorably delaying achievement of the Gramm-Rudman goals.

A necessary complement to US budget reduction is for the main surplus countries to boost domestic demand. However, given the structure of US trade with Germany, increased German domestic absorption will have a very limited effect on the bilateral balance. Moreover, one possible drawback to this strategy is that additional consumption in Germany will come at the expense of saving: the resulting shortage of funds for investment could push up interest rates, reducing investment and thus future productive capacity. However, failure to tackle the present imbalances leaves the world economy exposed to the danger of a hard landing.

Table 4 Saving rates in the G-3 countries, 1985–90 (percentages)

Country	1985	1986	1987	1988	1989	1990
National saving as a share of GNP						
United States	15.8	14.7	14.5	15.3	15.4	n.a.
Japan	31.6	31.9	32.4	32.8	33.9	n.a.
Germany	22.1	23.9	23.7	24.6	26.2	n.a.
Net household saving as a share of disposable household income						
United States	4.5	4.3	3.3	4.2	4.6	4.6
Japan	15.6	16.1	14.7	14.3	14.2	14.3
Germany	11.5	12.4	12.7	12.7	12.6	13.4

n.a. = not available

Source: Organization for Economic Cooperation and Development.

Within Europe, a strategy of promoting German growth, particularly in investment spending, seems appropriate given the regional pattern of German surpluses and the product structure of German trade. Much has already been done in this direction: there has been a significant increase in domestic demand and in overall economic growth over the past three years. Basically, Germany has been following a policy of promoting investment since the autumn of 1982, when the liberal-conservative coalition under Chancellor Helmut Kohl came to power. The change in government was accompanied by a change in the paradigms of economic policy away from Keynesian demand management and toward supply-side policies, which in Germany have a domestic precursor in the initiatives taken under Ludwig Erhard in the 1960s. The present policies aim at creating a consistent economic environment by achieving stabilization in the medium term and restraining the public sector in favor of private-sector initiative. The main elements of this policy are a reduction in public-sector deficits, a reduction in the tax burden, privatization, and deregulation.

These measures have been implemented only very slowly over the last eight years. By the mid–1980s the only genuine progress to report was the reduction in the federal budget, although this achievement laid the foundation for the most important economic policy measure of the Kohl administration in the 1980s, namely, income tax reform.

This reform, implemented in three stages in 1986, 1988, and 1990, sought to introduce a linear, progressive income tax schedule that would reduce tax rates over the entire range and especially benefit middle-income groups. The new system will substantially improve supply-side conditions by reducing the discrimination against work and in favor of leisure and thus improving the motivation for individual effort. The net tax cuts during the reform period amounted to over DM50 billion (2.2 percent of 1989 GNP), with the bulk of the cuts (about DM38 billion) implemented in 1988–90.   The new tax policy thus marks an important contribution toward shifting the center of gravity of economic expansion from exports to domestic demand, although the investment climate will also benefit from the reform.

Supporting this trend will be a reform of the public-sector health insurance system. Since the beginning of 1989, the benefits paid out by the system have been subject to strict limits. This reform has succeed in stopping the long-established trend toward rising contributions (which are equally divided between employees and employers). On the other hand, the cuts in outlays by the public health insurance system—which covers the overwhelming majority of the work force—have had a restraining effect on private consumption, which is the main reason why tax policy overall had a deflationary impact in 1989.

Privatization was extensive in 1987 and 1988 as the German federal government sold all its remaining shares in Volkswagen and the public utility companies VEBA and VIAG. These transactions had a total value of just under DM5 billion.

Although this marked the almost complete disposal by the federal government of its industrial holdings, it did not complete the process of privatization, since the individual German states and municipalities still have investments in a large number of companies.

Germany has every reason to accelerate deregulation, as many international bodies (and particularly the OECD) have repeatedly complained about the extent of German government regulation. A number of steps have been taken in recent years, although much remains to be done, since some of the measures were implemented in a very half-hearted fashion, and some markets such as that in transport remain almost untouched. One positive development was the opening up of the financial markets in 1985 and 1989, which greatly enlarged the scope of permitted operations for domestic and foreign banks. However, there are still some financial innovations that are not yet allowed in Germany even though they are already licensed in the United States, the United Kingdom, and France.

Other countries also expected the German government to take a more decisive approach to liberalizing shop opening hours and reorganizing the federal postal service. A complete abolition of regulations on shop opening hours would have boosted private consumption far more than the arrangement actually introduced in 1989, under which shops are only allowed to open for an extra 2½ hours one day a week. The postal reforms also leave much to be desired: as the largest employer in Germany with 550,000 employees, the postal service remains entirely under state ownership, and its monopoly position has so far been abolished only in certain sectors. However, the market for terminal equipment—of particular importance for foreign manufacturers—was liberalized recently.

In the second half of the 1980s the German economy has received a boost from demographic trends: after the middle of the decade the number of Germans between 15 and 30 years of age reached a peak, both in absolute terms and as a proportion of the total population. This is a result of the postwar baby boom, which occurred in West Germany in the period 1957–69, some ten years behind the boom in the United States. The presence of a large number of young people in the German economy contributes significantly to economic recovery. Private consumption is boosted by their high propensity to spend, particularly on household investment goods. Demographic factors probably also played a role in the boom in the automotive industry, which has continued since 1986, and the same applies for other producers of consumer durables. Although young people often buy their first consumer durables (particularly cars) second-hand, the resulting higher prices in these markets stimulate purchases of new products by those selling used products at a good price. Demand by young adults is also one of the elements fueling the boom in the German housing industry since 1988.

Even more important for the growth of the German economy have been the supply-side effects resulting from the entry of these young people into the active working population. This development is particularly important given the impression, still widespread in the mid–1980s, that Germany is the sick old man of Europe, with little sign of economic or social revitalization even after the change in government. The entry of the baby-boom generation into the labor market creates the necessary flexibility; their education is good and generally matches the needs of industry. This opens up new potential for inflation-free growth in Germany, which is probably most evident in the late 1980s, since the supply-side benefits from the rising proportion of young workers make themselves felt only with a certain lag. While the young workers are training, growth in production lags behind employment—the full boost to productivity only emerges after the training phase is completed. Members of the baby-boom generation are also forming a large number of new companies, particularly in the service sector.

The baby-boom generation was still a recent arrival in the labor force at the end of the 1980s when a new demographic phenomenon emerged: massive immigration from Central and Eastern Europe. In the period 1988–89 over 1 million people migrated to West Germany. It is obvious that this growth in the population—some 1½ percent for the two years combined—will boost private consumption, even though the new arrivals generally have low incomes at first, as language problems prevent them from getting work immediately and they first have to complete several months of language and vocational instruction. For this reason, the impact of the immigrants is still far from complete at the beginning of the 1990s.

Faster economic growth in Germany is a fundamental prerequisite for correcting the current account imbalances. A higher rate of growth, with its accelerator and multiplier effects, supports the shift in focus from exports to the domestic economy, bringing an improved investment climate, higher employment, rising incomes, and ultimately a higher rate of domestic absorption. The recent demographic developments will tend to reinforce the imbalances after a lag of some three to five years, when the emergence of their full supply-side impact will outweigh the boost to demand. This will ultimately mean, simply for demographic reasons, that productive capacity in West Germany will grow faster than consumption by about the mid–1990s, which *ceteris paribus* would mean a rise in Germany's current account surplus. This makes it all the more important to continue with the policy of deregulation in order to strengthen domestic expansion, particularly by dismantling barriers in the service sector.

Germany's economic future is not being left to its half-hearted politicians: the plan to create a vast single market in Europe by the end of 1992 provides valuable help in the guise of external pressure. The 1992 project is in fact a deregulation program on a grand scale: the opening of markets is no longer a matter for individual governments to deal with at their leisure, but a common goal with an unambiguous deadline. This has already proved extremely valuable in the area of deregulation. In the past this process was often hampered by domestic interest groups; those groups are now losing their influence at the supranational, European level. Here many interests—often in conflict—come together and cancel each other out, or at least substantially reduce the impact of particular national lobbies. This is one reason why the achievements in the European Community since the start of the 1992 program are already much greater than many expected.

In the field of technical regulations and standardization, for example, nontariff trade barriers are being abolished through reciprocal recognition of national standards based on EC requirements. Much of the public-sector procurement market is also being liberalized. An important step toward the elimination of personal controls at the frontiers was taken in June 1990, with the signature of the Schengener agreement providing for free border crossings between Germany, France, and the Benelux countries.

Liberalization of capital markets has gone even further. Since mid–1990, capital is allowed to move freely between most EC member states. According to the Second Directive Coordinating Banking Law, banks registered in any member state will in the future be able to market their products in the other EC countries, either via cross-border transactions or through their own branches in these countries. Of course, there is still a lot to be done to make this a reality.

One area where progress has been slow so far is tax harmonization, which has been postponed, at least for the time being, until 1996. Yet there is good reason to hope that in these other areas the remaining steps in completing the single European market will be taken in time.

The Outlook for the 1990s

The 1992 initiative has reenergized Europe: there is no more talk today of the "Eurosclerosis" and lethargy so frequently complained of only a few years ago. In 1990 the European economy is outpacing the US economy for the third year in a row, and there is no sign of any reversal of that trend. The main source of European economic growth is vigorous investment, an indication that companies are preparing energetically both to exploit the opportunities of the European single market with its 340 million consumers, and to withstand the competitive pressures that will emerge with the full implementation of the program.

This strong growth should continue. In any event, the efforts to create a single European market will mean that Europe will gain in importance vis-à-vis the other major economic regions of the world. It would not be surprising if the positive European supply-side shock leads to a relative strengthening of the currencies in this region. A revaluation of the EMS currencies, particularly against the dollar, would probably further promote adjustment between the New World and the Old World, where much progress has already been made.

This is why it is important for the single European market to remain and indeed become more open to outside competition. The financial markets are already quite open: in 1992, institutions from non–EC states will operate under the same conditions as EC institutions, provided that EC institutions are likewise treated on the same basis as local institutions in the non–EC country. There will be no limitations on the operations of financial institutions along the lines of the Glass-Steagall Act in the United States, which separates investment and commercial banking functions.

In other areas the free trade position has not yet been accepted completely. At the moment it is still unclear what will happen to the remaining national import restrictions within the single European market. The EC Commission's program calls for the elimination of all national import restrictions and protective regulations by 1993, yet provision has been made for transitional measures covering vehicles, textiles, shoes, consumer electronics, and steel products. However, there is a lack of consensus on what level of trade protection is desirable: whereas the southern EC members tend to favor increased external protection as an accompaniment to increased competition within the Community, the northern members are firm advocates of a liberal trade policy. This is especially true of Germany, which is much more dependent on free world markets than the other EC countries. Since the aims of the 1992 program are incompatible with protectionism in trade policy, and given the encouraging developments in the financial services sector, the initiative is unlikely to lead to a "Fortress Europe." As of this writing there remains hope that the results of the Uruguay Round will support such an outcome.

The new mood in Europe is also making itself felt internally: EC institutions now enjoy a greater prestige than they did only a few years ago. One reason is that their work is promoting mutual understanding within Europe. The successful track record of the existing institutions and the gradual formation of new Community institutions are promoting acceptance of integration. Closer association within a group of nations once jealously concerned with maintaining their sovereignty, now growing together within a common framework linked by ties of partnership, is depriving bilateral surpluses and deficits of their former importance. "External imbalances" are turning into welcome "interregional flows."

German trade surpluses with the rest of Europe in particular are likely to fade in prominence as well. Advancing deregulation under the 1992 program will promote growth in Germany and facilitate the entry of foreign companies into the German market, or even (as in the insurance industry) make entry possible for the first time. The improved opportunities for foreign companies will undoubtedly be reflected in current account balances.

A new and crucial factor in the future course of the German current account is the changes in Central and Eastern Europe, and particularly the unification of East and West Germany, completed on 3 October 1990. The breakup and restructuring of the area of former Soviet domination, together with the continuing changes in the Soviet Union itself, have fundamentally changed Germany's economic and geopolitical position. From its status as a front-line country in the most dramatic sense of the term, Germany will in the future return to a central role in continental affairs. What could be more natural than for Germany to become an intermediary in and a focus for the growing trade with Eastern Europe, and a base for companies interested in the new markets there? This role will mean a constant stimulus for growth for Germany, although this will emerge only gradually as the Eastern European economies slowly make their way from convalescence to prosperity.

Events in Germany itself are having a much quicker impact: the unification of Germany is in effect a major medium-term stimulative economic program, benefiting not only the western part of Germany and its partners in the European Community but its other trading partners as well. The former East Germany has a tremendous amount of catching up to do in all sectors of its economy. It has only become clear in the last few months just how little the results of 40 years of Communist rule are worth. Except in a few industries such as mechanical engineering, East German manufacturing is unable to compete internationally. It is working with plants that are mostly obsolete, inefficient, and environmentally ruinous. The service sector is underdeveloped. Telecommunications, transport, and all other aspects of the infrastructure fall far short of Western standards. Everywhere in eastern Germany there are old buildings in need of renovation, and there is a shortage of housing. In addition there is the extra demand from 16 million consumers.

Although the western German economy still has substantial growth potential in most sectors, thanks to the massive investment effort of recent years and to continuing immigration from Central and Eastern Europe, additional demand in the East will be increasingly met by local suppliers. They will be able to meet a growing part of local demand for consumer and capital goods, thus accelerating the modernizing and reorganizing of eastern Germany's economy. Even so there will be, at the same time, spillover effects that create great opportunities for foreign companies. The scale of these opportunities will depend on how quickly the population of eastern Germany tries to bring its life-style up to western German standards. Such an alignment of living standards—which, it is fair to estimate, will take around seven years—will call for cooperation by partner countries to avoid inflation and the erosion of living standards in western Germany.

Developments in 1990 are showing that the massive pent-up demand in eastern Germany is capable of significantly affecting the German current account balance. Once the frontiers went down, extensive buying by East Germans significantly boosted demand for consumer goods in western Germany. However, with capacity utilization in many sectors of western German industry higher than it has been for a long time, imports rose sharply while recently exports have actually been declining.

The process of economic convergence of eastern and western Germany will probably tend to depress German current account surpluses for some years to come. Even when the eastern German economy has been modernized and reorganized, German current account surpluses will be, from a longer-term perspective, at worst a passing problem, quite apart from the progress to be expected by then in European economic, political, and monetary integration.

The long-term demographic trend in Germany is still toward a declining and aging population, indicating a slowdown in economic growth and a shift toward deficits on current account. The merger of East and West Germany has not fundamentally changed this situation: fertility rates in eastern Germany, as in the west, are below what is necessary to maintain the present population. Immigration by ethnic German groups is delaying the process of population decline and aging by several years, but this immigration will tail off in the mid–1990s when the reservoir is exhausted. Immigration by non-Germans in the second half of the 1990s on a scale that would prevent a slowdown in economic growth after the turn of the century seems very improbable at present, since most German politicians continue to reject the notion of Germany becoming a multiethnic society.

As these considerations show, the widespread fears that an excessively powerful Germany will emerge to dominate Europe and use its massive industrial power to overwhelm its partners are simply untenable. The newly unified Germany is facing an enormous developmental task in its eastern region, and its history and geography both impose a responsibility to cooperate in making a new economic beginning in Eastern Europe. In addition, there is Germany's growing integration into a European Community, which will eventually be augmented by the entry of new members, such as Austria or other countries of the European Free Trade Association. We will not see any German economic offensive increasing international imbalances—German current surpluses in coming years will not be a problem for the world economy.

Epilogue: Recent Developments in the German Current Account

Developments in the first half of 1991 have confirmed that German current account surpluses do not represent a problem for the western industrialized countries. The united German current account in the first half of 1991 posted a deficit of over DM20 billion, compared with a surplus of close to DM50 billion in the first half of 1990. It must be noted, however, that the present high deficit is partly attributable to the German contribution of about DM11 billion to the allied Gulf war effort.

One major reason for the swing into deficit was the deterioration of foreign trade, and first and foremost the import pull from the new states of eastern Germany. This pushed up western German imports in the first half of 1991 by 15 percent in nominal terms from the same period in 1990, with most of the imported goods being channeled to eastern Germany. High German demand represented a strong impulse to economic activity in Germany's trading partners. This impulse accounted for approximately ½ percent of GNP in the European Community, which enjoyed above-average benefits from its large-scale exports to Germany. German exports were dampened in the first half of 1991 by 5½ percent from the first half of 1990, mainly by the gap between economic activity in Germany and that in its western neighbors. This was due not only to the fact that the economic weakening in Western Europe that had already begun in 1990 is only gradually making itself felt in western Germany today, but also to the end of the investment cycle in Europe, which had greatly boosted German exports thanks to the country's strong position in world markets for investment goods. Both factors help explain why the growth rate for western German exports in 1990 lagged behind that of world trade—a trend that should continue in 1991.

For 1991 as a whole the united German trade balance is expected to worsen by around DM90 billion, from a surplus of DM105 billion to a deficit of approximately DM15 billion. Accordingly the current account will move into a deficit on the order of DM25 billion after posting a surplus of DM77.4 billion in 1990.

Provided that the anticipated recovery of the world economy actually takes place, the surplus on the German balance of trade could begin to increase moderately in the course of 1992. On the one hand, the economic cooling that is in the offing in Germany—partly due to restrictive monetary policy, partly due to tax increases that went into effect in July 1991—will dampen import growth. On the other hand, the recovery abroad should gradually make itself felt in German exports. Whether this expected revitalization of trade will also lead to an improvement of the current account, however, remains to be seen. Although the German balance on transfer account will register some relief from the fact that the contributions to the Gulf war will not be repeated, it remains highly uncertain to what extent Germany will have to step up its assistance to the Soviet Union and other Eastern European countries.

Comment

Richard N. Cooper

Norbert Walter's paper is comprehensive and full of useful information. There are, however, two important omissions, possibly excluded by his terms of reference but nonetheless important for understanding the role of the German economy and of German thought in framing German economic policy during the 1980s. The first concerns the fiscal consolidation of 1981. Why was this substantial fiscal contraction, covering many years, undertaken? The answer presumably lies in a desire to reduce the German budget deficit over the long term, with a view to slowing and possibly halting the buildup of public debt. But this fiscal stance exerted a major contractionary impact on the rest of Europe and the world economy during the first half of the 1980s. It also played an important role in the shift from domestic to external demand within the German economy, contributing in part to the very large German current account surpluses that had emerged by the mid–1980s. To say this is not to absolve fiscal and monetary policy in the United States, with its impact on the dollar exchange rate, from an important role in building up the large US payments deficits. But in the world economy as a whole, actions of all countries taken together, and of the major countries taken separately, play complementary roles in determining current account outcomes. One cannot sensibly discuss the US current account developments without also discussing developments in Japan, Europe, and the developing countries as a group.

During the 1980s, German officials advanced several analytical propositions, which were supported or at least largely unchallenged by most German economists, in response to international pressure, mainly from Washington and some other European countries, for fiscal expansion. The first of these propositions was that enlarging the German fiscal deficit would be inflationary (rather than expansionary) even though monetary policy was independently determined, and even though unemployment exceeded 8 percent and capacity utilization rates were relatively low. The argument for a price-increasing effect of fiscal deficits was grounded in alleged structural rigidities in the German economy, which was said to include a great deal of export capacity that could not be easily converted to satisfy increased demand by the government or by German

---

Richard N. Cooper is Professor of Economics at Harvard University and Chairman of the Advisory Committee of the Institute for International Economics. He was formerly Under Secretary for Economic Affairs at the US Department of State.

households (brought about, for example, through tax reductions). It would have been useful to have had a discussion about whether the German economy is in fact so rigid as to prevent substitution in productive capacity from satisfying various components of final demand. If it is, it suggests that the German economy is driven largely by demand elsewhere in the world; it also suggests that the German economy is in this respect structurally similar to certain Latin American economies, at least as alleged by the so-called structuralists in their discussions of inflationary pressures within Latin America.

A second proposition, not entirely consistent with the first, is that enlarging the fiscal deficit would lead to an offsetting reduction in German consumption and investment, because of public anxiety about fiscal deficits and the corresponding buildup of public debt, and so would not achieve the desired expansion. This proposition is a variant of the Ricardian equivalence theorem, which has lately received some attention in the academic literature but has found little empirical support where it has been tested. Again, does the German economy stand out as being markedly different from other industrialized economies in this respect? Of course, insofar as private reaction does offset any additional fiscal thrust, increased budget deficits are not likely to be inflationary unless the economy is exceedingly rigid.

These are both strong analytical propositions, and it would be desirable to have a serious examination of them. Germany may be running an unplanned experiment with its unification and the large prospective increase in its budget deficit. Will it be inflationary, as the first proposition above would suggest? Or will it not, as German officials currently insist? Will it lead to a rise in private savings in the western part of unified Germany? As is usual with unplanned experiments, various interpretations of any outcome will be possible. Still, the increase in the budget deficit will be so substantial that it should give some clue as to whether either of the two propositions frequently invoked during the 1980s in resistance to foreign pressures for fiscal expansion is valid.

Walter in passing makes two analytical statements on which it would be useful to have direct evidence: First, the statement that nominal devaluation leads to inflation, rather than to an improvement in the real exchange rate, seems to contradict Paul R. Krugman's observation (chapter 1) that real and nominal exchange rate movements track one another closely, at least for industrial countries. Second, Walter suggests that the gradual aging of the German population will lower aggregate saving. There are sound theoretical reasons for believing that this might be so, based on the life-cycle theory of household consumption behavior. But again, empirical issues are involved. Do older Germans in fact save a smaller portion of their income than younger Germans do? Similar arguments have been made for Japan, where the population is aging even more rapidly than it is in Germany. Yet the fragmentary evidence available suggests that saving does not vary in Japan with the average age of the household. Establishment of consumption patterns early in life, at much lower levels of income, may dominate life-cycle considerations when it comes to saving behavior by the aged. But it would be useful to have some empirical evidence on this, insofar as demographic factors continue to be evoked in support of an expectation that Germany's current account surplus can over time be expected to decline.

In a useful digression, Walter raises doubts about exclusive focus on a country's current account, in a world of high capital mobility. Should we worry about capital account imbalances at all? If the answer is affirmative, should we not also worry about the international mobility of capital, which supports and frequently leads to those imbalances? Walter does not exactly say we should not worry about current account balances, but rather that we should pay attention to the underlying reasons for any particular imbalance and gauge the current account balance accordingly.

I would go further and suggest that open industrial economies should not target their current account balances at all. I expect to see much larger current account imbalances in the future, for example within Europe, than we became accustomed to during the 1960s and 1970s. These should not be a source of special concern within a unified capital market.

An implication of this view is that the European Community should abandon its effort to continue to collect current account data on member countries with respect to intra-Community trade after the abolition of border controls in 1992. A substantial effort would be required to gather intra-European trade statistics once border checks are eliminated, and it seems to me that the gains are not worth the cost. Indeed the continued publication of current account imbalances may give rise to anxieties where none are warranted. We do not have current account figures for the states within the United States, and although such data would be useful for some analytical purposes, on the whole I believe it is beneficial not to have such figures.

It would have been nice if Germany had followed Walter's advice on the current account during 1980–81, when German officials panicked in the face of a large emergent current account deficit, despite a well-defined external reason for the emergence of the deficit, which Germany shared with many other industrial countries, namely, the sharp increase in world oil prices. Their concern led them to an excessively contractionary monetary and fiscal policy in 1981, which contributed to the European and world recession of the early 1980s, and to stagnation in Europe throughout the first half of that decade.

As to the United States, my main concern with the large US current account deficit in the mid–1980s was that it reflected a sharp increase in the competitive pressures on US manufacturing and other tradeable goods and services, and thereby contributed to strong protectionist pressures during that period. I felt that it was important to reverse the current account imbalance before an irreversible protectionist reaction set in. Fortunately, serious protectionist responses were largely avoided, but even so protectionist action has become much more respectable in 1990 than it was in the early 1980s. Thus, the large current account deficits of the mid–1980s, and the reasons underlying them, created an intellectual beachhead for government restrictions on foreign trade. It will take years to reduce the respectability of protectionist arguments back to the level of 1980. That is an unfortunate legacy of the strong dollar and large trade deficits of the mid–1980s.

Comment

Horst Schulmann

Norbert Walter has provided a very comprehensive overview of the German experience since 1985. There is little in his paper with which I seriously disagree, and it would be difficult to add to the wealth of information it contains. However, from a Washington perspective on policymaking in Germany and the United States, it seems useful to highlight some of the questions Walter has raised. In doing so, I will seek to relate German developments to the analytical points made in Paul R. Krugman's overview (chapter 1).

Let me start with a somewhat fundamental and perhaps pessimistic observation. I agree with Krugman that we have experienced greater variation in the time series of some key economic variables in the 1980s than economists are used to. But the experience of the 1980s is still a far cry from a controlled experiment. The number of observations is limited, and the number of parameters to be estimated is large, and therefore we are probably short of the degrees of freedom required for sound statistical inferences. For this reason, I am afraid it is too early to become complacent about our understanding of the adjustment process—about what works and what does not, what the role of exchange rates (nominal or real) is, what the relative contribution of domestic and external policies is, what role cyclical and structural factors play, and how important endogenous and exogenous variables are. There are some questions to which we will never know the answer because we do not know what would have happened in the absence of particular events. In addition, there are some serious measurement problems that may blur our vision.

To begin with the latter, according to the October 1990 *World Economic Outlook* (International Monetary Fund 1990, 143), the world current account imbalance, after declining in the mid–1980s, has increased sharply again in recent years, from $43 billion in 1987 to $98 billion in 1989. This means that some of the 1989 deficits in particular countries may indeed be smaller, but by the same token some of the surpluses may be larger. Unfortunately, we do not know what the swing in the world current account imbalance implies for the true deficit of the United States and the true surpluses of Japan and Germany. In absolute terms, the swing in the world current account balance between 1987 and 1989 is larger than the improvement in the US current account position between 1987

Horst Schulmann was State Secretary in the German Ministry of Finance and a personal representative of Chancellor Helmut Schmidt at the economic summits.

and 1989. Another measurement problem is the ambiguity of the real effective exchange rate, at least in the case of Germany. Three of the International Monetary Fund's six alternative definitions of the real effective exchange rate show a real effective appreciation of the deutsche mark that is greater than the nominal appreciation, whereas the other three suggest exactly the opposite.

One can cite several examples of extraneous events that may have hindered or expedited the adjustment process to an unknown and unknowable extent. The financial crash of October 1987 is one. There is even some question whether the Louvre Accord contributed to the crash. More important, however, is the question, What would have happened to the adjustment process in the absence of the expansionary monetary policies that were put in place after the crash, particularly in Japan? Would the dollar have strengthened as much as it did in the wake of the crash? Would inflationary pressures have increased as much as they did? Would we have had the great asset price inflation in Japan—and the subsequent asset price deflation? Could we still have a financial panic in Japan because the Bank of Japan pursued too-expansionary policies after exchange rate policies appeared to have failed?

It also happens that the years since 1985 have been years of increased central bank intervention in foreign-exchange markets. Two years stand out: 1987 and 1989. In 1987, net purchases in the US dollar market totaled $120 billion; in 1989 net sales totaled $75 billion. Applying traditional capital flows analysis, this means that in 1987 these purchases financed three-quarters of the US current account deficit. What would the dollar exchange rate—or dollar interest rates, or US investment and saving—have been in the absence of these interventions? We do not know. What we do know is that the United States now has, for the first time, a sizable stock of foreign-exchange reserves, totaling almost $50 billion—an interesting (albeit probably unintended) byproduct of the Louvre.

Another important extraneous factor was the collapse of world oil prices in 1986. That development had a pervasive effect on inflation, interest rates, exchange rates, exports and imports, and investment and saving. But this effect was not the same in all the major countries. In Germany, it was a multiple of the effect in the United States because of the concomitant appreciation of the mark. Whereas the dollar price of Brent crude oil declined by about 35 percent between 1985 and July 1990, the mark price fell by almost 70 percent. There is no straightforward way to assess the impact of lower oil prices on the adjustment process. The difference between the overall balance and the nonoil balance provides only a partial answer.

On a slightly lighter note: the beginning of the dollar's decline, which preceded the Plaza Agreement, coincided with Mikhail Gorbachev's assumption of power in the Soviet Union in the spring of 1985. This may not have had much of an impact on the dollar-mark exchange rate until the Berlin Wall was breached. But judging also by what has happened since 2 August 1990, when Saddam

Hussein invaded Kuwait, it can be argued that it took the dissolution of the "evil empire" to accelerate the adjustment process inside the G-3, at least if one believes that the disappearance of the "safe haven" premium on the dollar following the breach of the Wall has a real cause and is not simply a random event.

Finally, the advent of German unity has introduced yet another extraneous factor into the adjustment process. It is already obvious that German unification will absorb a good deal of the former West Germany's savings and will reduce Germany's current account surplus significantly. As it turns out, German unity is likely to do more for the adjustment process than any deliberate change in West German fiscal or monetary policy could have done.

Let me now turn to some of the reasons why Germany's current account position has behaved in the way it has in the wake of the Plaza and the Louvre. Inside the G-3, Germany seems to be the odd man out, with a current account surplus that has continued to increase—both in mark and in dollar terms— through 1989, while Japan's surplus has been shrinking (almost) according to plan. However, there are important differences in the two countries' trade structures. About half of Germany's foreign trade is with its partners in the European Community, whereas Japan's trade is, of course, much more oriented toward the United States and the newly industrializing economies in East Asia. The product structures of the two countries' imports also differ, with Japan importing a much higher share of raw materials than does Germany. Finally, relative to GNP, Germany's exports are almost three times Japan's. These differences have a bearing on the evolution of Germany's current account balance.

One of the implications is that the effective exchange rate of the mark has shown much less variation before and since 1985 than either the dollar or the yen rate. This is true for the nominal as well as the real rate. While the mark has appreciated against the dollar by almost 60 percent since February 1985, its nominal effective rate has risen by only 20 percent. A major factor in this regard has been the increased exchange rate stability within the European exchange rate mechanism (ERM). However, since prices and costs have risen faster in other ERM countries than in Germany, the mark has actually depreciated in real terms within the ERM since the last major realignment in early 1987. Together with the investment boom in the runup to Europe 1992, which fits well Germany's capital-goods-oriented export structure, this is a main explanation of Germany's exploding trade surplus. The ERM countries alone contributed close to 50 percent of Germany's trade surplus in 1989, and all the EC countries together contributed 70 percent (the numbers are 45 percent and 62 percent, respectively, in current account terms). At the same time, Germany's trade surplus with the United States, which peaked at DM28 billion in 1986, fell to DM8.4 billion in 1989, or a little more than 6 percent of the overall trade surplus.

(In current account terms, the US share of the German surplus was about 22 percent in 1989.)

Thus, even before the realization of Europe 1992, the German current account surplus has been internalized, in the sense that it is now largely an intra-European matter. It remains to be seen, however, whether intra-European disequilibria are easier to handle than those among the G-3. The disappearance of German surplus savings in the wake of German unification will provide an interesting test.

Already today the current account of the European Community as a whole is in balance, and so is the US trade balance with the Community. In this sense, the remaining payments disequilibria are largely a bilateral matter between the United States and Japan, not a trilateral problem. For this reason, the weakening of the yen between the end of 1987 and the spring of 1990 was a major impediment to a faster reduction of the US current account deficit.

The interaction among capital movements, exchange rates, and domestic and external adjustment is another much-debated issue. As we know, key exchange rates have been anything but stable since 1987 in spite of the Louvre Accord. Even the day-to-day percentage changes in the mark-dollar rate (as measured by the standard deviation) have only been about 25 percent smaller since the Louvre than before. More to the point, the last few years have shown that capital transactions are becoming more, not less, important for exchange rate fluctuations, and that financial markets and goods markets can have quite different perceptions of the equilibrium value of exchange rates. Presumably, the intention at the Plaza and the Louvre was to remove capital movements from the driver's seat and reinstate "fundamentals." That objective has not been met. It has been particularly frustrating for Germany, a low-inflation country, to see the currencies of high-inflation countries like Australia appreciate while the mark remained under downward pressure.

Politicians in particular tend to focus too much on the "goods market" equilibrium exchange rate. Financial markets have different requirements, and as we have seen in the 1980s the perception gap between the two markets can be quite considerable. Freely floating exchange rates react to several factors simultaneously: to inflation and productivity differentials, to supply shocks and demand shifts in the market for internationally traded goods and services, and—finally—to yield differentials in the financial markets. In these markets, exchange rate changes are needed to bring about yield equilibrium.

This task will grow in importance as net foreign asset and liability positions among key currency countries continue to increase. The German case is quite revealing in this respect, although I suspect that the Japanese case is even more impressive. The fact that both Germany and Japan have for years been running massive current account surpluses, whose accumulation now is measured in the hundreds of billions of dollars, could make for considerable exchange rate fluctuations in the future. Therefore we will continue to need freely floating exchange rates as a shock absorber if we want to avoid protectionism within the trilateral area.

Germany's net foreign assets have quadrupled since the end of 1985, from DM120 billion to DM500 billion. The gross reserves of the Bundesbank have increased by about DM20 billion to around DM100 billion. Net deutsche mark assets of foreign residents have actually declined during this period, from about DM180 billion to about DM140 billion. This means that net foreign-currency assets of German residents have increased from some DM200 billion to close to DM500 billion in a matter of four years. This does not bode well for exchange rate stability, because every time German residents shift their portfolio preferences, whether in favor of mark-denominated assets or in favor of foreign-currency assets, there will be pressure on exchange rates (bearing in mind that German households hold at least 70 percent of their foreign fixed-interest securities in non–ERM currencies). We are therefore dealing with a situation in which exchange rates, interest rates, domestic prices, exports and imports, and investment and saving are determined more or less simultaneously. Attempts to impose simple solutions will jeopardize either the freedom of capital movements or the freedom of goods and services movements. Needless to say, both have to be maintained.

In summary, although economists can draw some satisfaction from the observation that current account disequilibria among the G-3, and indeed within the trilateral area, have narrowed in the second half of the 1980s, they should not be sanguine about the future working of the international adjustment process. International policy coordination has largely been confined to the monetary area, and this has not curbed inflationary biases in the system. Fiscal policies in the G-3 countries have not been well coordinated, but remain very firmly embedded in the domestic politics in all three. And as obstacles to the free flow of capital have finally been removed, automatic forces pressing for current account adjustment have, not surprisingly, weakened. Gross capital flows have become a multiple of balance of payments financing requirements. In turn, pressure on central banks to compromise their commitment to price stability has increased. Finally, as of late 1990 there has been little change in countries' propensities to invest and to save.

Reference

International Monetary Fund. *World Economic Outlook.* 1990. Washington: International Monetary Fund.

5

The Great Exchange Rate Controversy:
Trade Balances and the
International Monetary System

The Great Exchange Rate Controversy: Trade Balances and the International Monetary System

Robert A. Mundell

The appropriate role of exchange rates in economic policy is one of the most complicated issues in international economics and public policy. The difficulty stems from the fact that the exchange rate is a ratio of two monetary quantities, whereas most targets of economic policy are real quantities. Solution of the problem requires specification of how nominal variables affect real variables. The same difficulty arises in relating nominal to real variables in closed-economy macroeconomic theory.

Much of the controversy in the literature has turned on differences relating to the mechanism for changing exchange rates in a flexible exchange rate system; the effect of devaluation on absolute and relative prices; the relation between the exchange rate and the trade balance; the relation between changes in the trade balance and relative prices; the role of exchange rates in general-equilibrium theory; the link between the international monetary system and exchange rate changes; and the relation of national currencies to the international standard (if any).

Models of international economic behavior are school-specific. This seems more true today than in the past because of the proliferation of models in closed-economy macroeconomic theory. Edmund Phelps, for example, identified "seven schools of macroeconomic thought" in a recent book of that title (Phelps 1990). These include the macroeconomics of Keynes, monetarism, the new classical school, the new Keynesian school, supply-side economics, real business cycle theory, and structuralism. The schools are distinguished by different assumptions about information, expectations, price flexibility, or disequilibrium-equilibrium methodology. It is possible to derive a distinct exchange rate theory corresponding to each of these schools.

Robert A. Mundell is Professor of Economics at Columbia University.

This paper sketches some important developments in exchange rate doctrine and analyzes some necessary links between theory and the international monetary system. The first part of the paper considers the theory of exchange rates and trade balances in the context of classical theory. The second part outlines 16 approaches to the balance of trade and considers alternative theories of the trade deficit. The third part analyzes "systemic deficits"—those deficits that arise out of the working of the international monetary system itself. Some concluding remarks about the current account imbalances of today complete the paper.

The Classical Theory of Currencies and Trade

Alfred Marshall could write, in 1912, that the most important thing that can be said about currency is that it is totally unimportant (Marshall 1925). In this way he summarized the attitude of a century dominated by the classical school and acclimatized to the monetary stability of the gold standard. Currency theory, incorporating the effects of exchange rate changes on real variables, had no place in the classical framework except as an offshoot of the quantity theory of money. Unlike in the preceding age of mercantilism and the succeeding age of Keynesianism, exchange rate changes were relegated to the realm of economic pathology.

The Gold Standard

The gold standard, like earlier bimetallic and silver standards, encouraged a fundamental conservatism in monetary and fiscal policy. It imposed financial discipline. The convertibility requirement pinned down the money supply to the level compatible with balance of payments equilibrium. Longstanding adherence to the gold parity ensured stabilizing, inelastic expectations. Future monetary policy was predictable from knowledge of demand and supply conditions for the monetary metal.

A government would tamper with the monetary standard only at its peril. Changing the standard would have a shock effect with reverberations on expectations for generations to come. Devaluation of a paper currency in terms of gold would result in a proportionate increase in the price level and a proportionate scaling down of the real value of debts; once this was tried, interest rates would adjust upward to allow for the cost of a possible repetition. On the other hand, belief in the standard—and in its restoration if a major, but infrequent, disturbance (such as a major war) had undermined it—was itself a resource that kept government credit cheap; stabilizing, inelastic expectations, resting on the assumption of early restoration of a broken standard, prevented the collapse of the bond market.[1]

The gold standard has been variously referred to as the golden rudder, the golden brake, and the golden umpire. As rudder, it gave direction to monetary policy; as brake, it inhibited excess monetary expansion (beyond that provided by fluctuations in supply of the precious metals); as umpire, it allocated the burden of adjustment fairly between surplus and deficit countries.[2] The classical economists did not believe that these functions could be adequately performed by any monetary system that was not tied to one of the precious metals. The consensus of the classical school rested on five pillars: the homogeneity postulate, Walras's law,[3] the quantity theory of money, purchasing power parity, and the assumption of flexible wages and prices. Together these assumptions made up

---

1. Several examples of this stabilizing element in expectations are afforded by the currency history of the United Kingdom and other countries. Instead of resorting to devaluation in the 1690s to finance the great recoinage, the British government harked back to Elizabeth I's recoinage of over 130 years earlier, which had been paid for out of taxes rather than through depreciation. Britain was able to compound its public debt to finance the several wars of the 18th century without devaluation; and when the Bank of England succumbed to inconvertibility in 1797, interest rates for two decades reflected the strong probability that Britain would restore the sacred parity after the war (as in fact happened in 1819). Again, the uninterrupted history of the gold standard in Britain in the 19th century, despite periodic crises, contributed to the belief, when payments were suspended during World War I, that after the war convertibility would be resumed at the old parity. This occurred in 1925, but it proved abortive when, for systemic reasons, the undervaluation of gold that had been a consequence of the war's inflation led to a liquidity crisis, tight money, and the great deflation. In the face of this external instability, Britain correctly opted out of convertibility.

In a recent paper, Bordo and Kydland (1990) analyze the gold standard as a contingent rule, meaning that the authorities could "temporarily abandon the fixed price of gold during a wartime emergency on the understanding that convertibility at the original price of gold would be restored when the emergency passed." See also Bordo and White (1990) for a recent discussion of British and French finance during the Napoleonic Wars.

2. If fiduciary monetary issues were permitted, they had to be kept within the limits of safeguarding the nation's central gold reserves. Gold also ensured that the domestic price level would remain, in the long run, basically constant relative to the world price level. The stability of the world price level would itself depend on the relation between world demand for and world supply of gold. When gold supply increased more rapidly than gold demand, the value of gold would fall and the world price level would rise; when gold supply increased less rapidly than gold demand, gold would appreciate and the world price level would fall. Although there were disturbing trends in the value of gold over the long period due to changes in supply, new gold production in any given year was a small proportion of the outstanding stock of gold, so that annual changes in the price level were comparatively small. Over the long run, relative changes in the real value of gold would affect supply and demand in a stabilizing way, with the result that periods of rising prices tended to be offset by falling prices.

3. I have argued elsewhere (Mundell 1968a) that John Stuart Mill at least, among the classical economists, did not confuse Walras's law (the sum of all excess demands, including that for money, is zero) and Say's law (supply creates its own demand for commodities).

the classical dichotomy. Changes in exchange rates engineered by monetary policy would result in equiproportionate changes in wages and prices, with no change in the underlying equilibrium of real wages, the real rate of interest, or the terms of trade. Devaluation—which in the classical world meant an increase in the national-currency price of gold—would increase prices and wages, improve the balance of payments, and increase the money supply until the initial real equilibrium was restored. Money was neutral, and there was no place for a theory of the exchange rate related to effects on the balance of trade or real variables.

The Transfer Debate

The classical consensus on exchange rates and the neutrality of money did not, however, imply unanimity on the nature of the international adjustment process. Specifically, there was disagreement over whether changes in relative prices are necessarily associated with changes in the trade balance induced by unilateral transfers. The subject can most easily be addressed in two parts: first, that applying to barter, and second, that applying to the international monetary economy. The first problem is to see how changes in transfers and the balance of trade affect changes in the terms of trade and the real exchange rate. The second problem is to determine how transfers affect the balance of payments (under fixed exchange rates) and the exchange rate (when the money supply is constant).

Analysis of the barter theory reveals two camps, the difference between which crystallized only during the Keynes-Ohlin-Rueff debate on the transfer problem in the 1920s. The debate that emerged therein pitted the income-expenditure approach against the relative prices approach, with John Wheatley, David Ricardo, Samuel Longfield, C.F. Bastable, J.S. Nicholson, Knut Wicksell, and Bertil Ohlin on one side and John Stuart Mill, Frank W. Taussig, and John Maynard Keynes on the other.[4] The Mill school argued that the generation of a trade surplus required a fall in relative prices of the transferring country, whereas the income-expenditure school denied that changes in relative prices were an essential ingredient in the adjustment process. As more sophisticated analysis by A.C. Pigou, Gottfried Haberler, James Meade, Paul A. Samuelson, and others subsequently showed, the income-expenditure school was vindicated.

---

4. See Mundell (1989a and especially 1989b) for a recent review of the literature on this subject and for detailed references. An excellent review of the literature up to 1937 is offered by Viner (1937).

The income-expenditure school got the better of the argument as far as the effect of transfer on the terms of trade is concerned; Viner (but not Keynes[5]) conceded the point. A revision of the literature became necessary to give credit to those classical writers who had fully incorporated expenditure effects into the analysis. Within the framework of the theory of exchange, a transfer of purchasing power produces expenditure effects that worsen the balance of trade of the receiving country and improve that of the paying country. The redistribution of world expenditure from the paying to the receiving country could leave global excess demand unchanged (if the expenditure effects cancel), or it could result in an excess demand for one country's goods, leaving room for changes in relative prices. The essential factor in the adjustment mechanism is the shift in expenditures relative to incomes in the two countries, the relative price changes being incidental to the process.

Mill and Marshall had investigated the stability question of whether a change in relative prices (a change in the terms of trade) would shift excess demand onto the good whose relative price has fallen. Marshall deduced that it depended on whether an elasticity criterion—the sum of the absolute values of the elasticities of demand[6] for imports minus unity—was positive or negative. There is no *a priori* way to determine that such a criterion will be satisfied. Economists in the postwar period came to be divided into two camps—elasticity optimists and elasticity pessimists—with the former stressing the advantages of relying upon the price mechanism, and the latter the need for direct controls. If, as is usually assumed, the stability condition is met, the direction of change in the terms of trade is determined by the expenditure effects, whereas the extent to which the terms of trade must move in order to correct any residual excess demand depends on the magnitude of the price elasticities. Because the elasticities fully incorporate supply effects, the latter play a role in determining the extent of any necessary changes in relative prices. The higher the elasticities, the more effective any given change in relative prices will be in eliminating a given excess demand. It should therefore be noted that even if the rearrangement of world demand creates excess demand, supplies might adjust to prevent changes in relative prices if one country incompletely specializes and produces both goods at constant costs.[7]

---

5. Keynes did not admit Ohlin's point in his reply to Ohlin's article in the *Economic Journal*, but later in correspondence with Ohlin he wrote, "As to your point that reparations cause a shift in the demand curve of the receiving country irrespective of any rise in the price level of that country, I do not think I disagree with you." This is quoted in Dimand (1988, 124) from Patinkin and Leith (1978, 162).

6. This assumes trade is initially balanced; a slight adjustment is required where this is not the case.

7. Constant costs and incomplete specialization imply that the elasticity of demand for imports is infinite. Meade (1950) produced the first algebraic formula for the change in the terms of trade explicitly integrating expenditure and price effects. Note that because expenditure propensities and price elasticities are related by the Johnson-Slutzky condition,

It is necessary now to consider the role of nontraded goods. The discussions of the 1920s had been couched in the framework of a two-good, two-country model, with primary focus on the terms of trade. But writers of both schools, going as far back as Richard Cantillon and David Hume, and including Ricardo, Taussig, and Keynes, had given some consideration to domestic (nontraded) goods. The existence of domestic goods brought into consideration not only the terms of trade, but also the ratios of the prices of domestic and import goods and the ratios of the prices of domestic goods and export prices in each country. One convenient definition of the real exchange rate is the ratio of the prices of home-produced goods at home and abroad. For a small country, in which the terms of trade are constant, the real exchange rate is sometimes defined as the ratio of the price of domestic (nontraded) and international (traded) goods.

The introduction of domestic goods into the transfer debate seemed to qualify the victory of the income-expenditure school somewhat, giving the Mill-Taussig school a second line of defense. Changes in relative price levels can take place even if the terms of trade are constant. In his little treatise *Capital Imports and the Terms of Trade,* Roland Wilson (1931) argued that an income transfer would shift demand onto domestic goods in the receiving country and away from domestic goods in the paying country. The effect on the relative prices would then depend on cost conditions. Under the assumption of increasing (opportunity) costs, the price level will tend to rise in the receiving country and fall in the paying country.

Increasing costs, of course, represent only one possibility. If opportunity costs between domestic and international goods are constant, no change in the real exchange rate will result. And if there are decreasing costs, the relative price of domestic goods will tend to move in the opposite direction from that postulated by the Mill-Taussig school. The result will depend upon the conditions of supply.

An interesting case involving domestic goods, which lends some support to Mill's conclusion that the terms of trade of the paying country worsen as a result of transfer, was recently analyzed by John Chipman (1989). If each country produces export and domestic goods (but no import-competing goods), there will be a tendency for the terms of trade to change in the Millian direction. This conclusion follows because resources are shifted from export to domestic industries in the receiving country, and in the opposite direction in the paying country, restricting the supply of exports in the receiving country and augmenting it in the paying country. Note that in this case it is the relative price of domestic and export goods that will be constant in both countries, but the relative price of domestic and import goods will rise in the receiving country and fall in the

import propensities high enough (greater than one-half on the average) to shift demand onto the goods of the paying country (the anti-Mill direction) are sufficient to ensure that the elasticities of demand are large enough (greater than one-half on the average) to ensure stability of exchange equilibrium. See Mundell (1960 and 1968b).

paying country; the real exchange rate will thus also improve along with the terms of trade in the receiving country and fall in the paying country.

Chipman's result depends partly on the supposition that there are no import-competing goods in the two countries. To complete the analysis it is worth considering the results from a two-factor, three-commodity Heckscher-Ohlin model under conditions that permit factor price equalization in the two countries.[8] In this case it can be shown that a transfer may have no effect on relative prices despite the increase in the output of domestic goods in the receiving country and the decrease in the output of domestic goods in the paying country. Let us consider first the condition of a receiving country that faces fixed terms of trade, given by the rest of the world. This fixes factor prices in the import and export industries of the receiving country and therefore the costs of production in the domestic goods industries. The receiving country's increase in expenditure (financed by the financial transfer) on import and export goods can be supplied by a decrease in its trade balance, but the increase in spending on domestic goods (assuming no inferior goods) must be supplied internally, by a shift of labor and capital out of the export and import-competing goods industries. It is possible to reduce the productions of the two international goods in exactly that proportion needed to release the factors—along the lines of the Rybczynski theorem—required to produce the additional domestic goods at constant factor prices. The conclusion does not, however, depend on the small-country assumption, provided that expenditure effects cancel. If marginal tastes for commodities are the same in the two countries, there will be no change in the global demand for factors and therefore no change in relative factor or commodity prices. But even if expenditure effects cancel, there is no presumption (given, as always, incomplete specialization) that the real exchange rate will change in the Millian direction.

Transfers, Gold Flow, and the Exchange Rate

Now consider the equilibrium after unilateral transfers in a monetary economy. Consider first the case where there is a single money—call it gold—in the world economy so that changes in monetary conditions will be reflected in the balance of payments rather than exchange rates. In the absence of transfers, equilibrium will prevail when the trade balances and the excess demands for gold are zero. Now let the equilibrium be disturbed by a unilateral transfer. How will this affect the balance of payments of the two countries? Will gold move to the receiving

---

8. This paragraph was part of my comment on Chipman's Baltimore paper.

or the paying country?[9] The answer to this question derives from the monetary approach to the balance of payments: money will flow to the country in which the transfer creates an excess demand for money. Of course, the demand for money in each of the two countries will depend partly on how demand shifts affect price levels. Money will normally flow to the country in which the price level increases. But there are also important independent effects that do not depend on changes in price levels. To isolate these effects, let us suppose that expenditure effects cancel.

The direction of change in the excess demand for money will depend on the arguments—apart from prices—in the demand-for-money function. To the extent that liquidity requirements depend on transactions, there will be an increase in demand for money in both countries to satisfy the additional transactions involved in arranging the transfer.[10] The extra transactions will therefore imply that domestic expenditure in the receiving country will rise by less, and in the paying country fall by more, than the transfer itself until the additional monetary requirements are met. If the stock of monetary gold in the world is constant, the increased world demand for money will result in a once-for-all decline in the world price level in order to raise the real value of the world gold stock to that required by the higher level of transactions.

Over and above this once-for-all transactions effect affecting both countries, there will be a differential effect on the two countries in view of their different

---

9. Jacob Viner addressed this question in his *Studies* (1937), analyzing the issue on the assumption that what he called the "final-purchases velocity" of money was constant. Viner's analysis resulted in an exchange with Dennis Robertson (1938–39) in the *Quarterly Journal of Economics*, Robertson arguing that it was more natural to assume that the income velocity of money was constant. In the ensuing debate a compromise position was arrived at, with Viner conceding that the money balances required to service the increase in expenditure in the receiving country would be, while still positive, less than that required to service expenditure from income produced at home, with the result that gold would still flow in the direction of the receiving country—changes in prices being abstracted from—but by a smaller amount than he had initially concluded. Robertson, however, held to his view that the same amount of money would be required in the receiving country to service the additional expenditure as was required to service the payment of taxes that the inward transfer made unnecessary.

A correct analysis of the issue requires splitting the demand for money balances into sectoral demands by consumers, producers, and governments. Because production in both countries is assumed to be constant, there would not ordinarily be a change in producers' money balances. But the money requirements of consumers would rise in the receiving country and fall in the paying country on account of the expenditure shifts. Government spending, however, would rise in both the receiving and the paying countries in view of the transactions associated with the disbursement of the proceeds through (say) an income subsidy in the payee and the raising of the proceeds by (say) taxation in the payer.

10. I have noted this transactions effect in Mundell (1988). As observed in the preceding footnote, a detailed treatment of the increased transactions demands would require splitting national demands into household, producer, and government sectors.

positions after the transfer. The movement of gold between the two countries will depend on how the demand for money is affected by the increase in expenditure (absorption) in the receiving country and the decrease in the paying country.[11] If, as seems natural, the demand for money in the two countries depends partly on expenditure, the receiving country will require more and the paying country less gold. To accumulate the additional liquidity, inhabitants (including the government) in the receiving country will increase spending by less than the transfer, thus improving the balance of payments and attracting gold; similarly, the paying country will for a time decrease its expenditure by less than the transfer, generating a balance of payments deficit until the lower equilibrium quantity of money is established.

The three individual types of effects of a transfer on the demand for money must be added together to determine the direction of the gold flow. The changes in the demand for money in the two countries arising from expenditure shifts must be superimposed on the pure transactions effect of the transfer discussed earlier; both effects operate to increase the demand for money in the receiving country, but they have opposing tendencies in the paying country. To these two effects must then be added those additional effects resulting from any altered patterns of demand that induce changes in price levels. To the extent that there is a presumption that the real exchange rate of the receiving country rises as a result of the transfer, the price effect will combine with the other two effects to increase unambiguously the demand for money and therefore the balance of payments of the receiving country. The transfer will in this case result in a flow of gold from the paying country to the receiving country, in addition to some deflationary effect in the world as a whole in the absence of any increase in the global money supply.

An alternative monetary assumption is that exchange rates are fixed but that the central bank has some flexibility in its credit policy. Consider, therefore, two countries with gold-convertible currencies, but in which central bank assets are

---

11. An alternative formulation would make the demand for money a function of wealth. Insofar as we are restricting our analysis to unilateral transfers, wealth and therefore the demand for money are lower in the paying country and higher in the receiving country, resulting in a balance of payments surplus in, and a flow of gold to, the receiving country.

This formulation would have to be modified in the case of capital movements. Unlike unilateral transfers, capital movements do not imply a change in wealth but rather represent a geographical redistribution of wealth. The purchasing power (absorption) of the borrowing country is increased, and that of the paying country is reduced, by the capital transfer, but the GNPs, which take into account international interest payments, are only slightly affected (by the extra rent associated with differences in rates of return). On these grounds, therefore, the intertemporal pattern of consumption would not theoretically be affected by borrowing; most of the borrowed money should therefore be devoted to the formation of physical or human capital. This implies that the product mix of marginal expenditure effects will be influenced by the proportion of the transfer that is unilateral and the proportion that is merely a loan.

composed not only of gold but of government or private-sector assets. Because it raises the level of transactions, the transfer will now, as before, increase the demand for money. Now, however, the central banks in the two countries could prevent world deflation by open-market operations in government or private securities. Now consider the changes in the demand for money induced by the increase in spending in the receiving country and the decrease in the paying country. To preserve balance of payments equilibrium at fixed exchange rates, making a gold flow unnecessary, the central bank in the receiving country could expand credit, and the central bank in the paying country could contract credit. In these cases, however, the ratio of gold to total monetary liabilities of the central bank would be correspondingly altered.

Let us now consider the alternative monetary assumptions where the authorities hold the money supply constant and allow flexibility of the exchange rates. According to the monetary approach to the exchange rate, the transfer will create an appreciation or depreciation of the currency in those circumstances in which, under a common money or fixed exchange rates, the balance of payments would move into surplus or deficit. Given the requirement of purchasing power parity as an equilibrium condition, an appreciation of a country's currency implies either a fall in the domestic price of tradeable goods in the appreciating country or an increase in the price of tradeable goods in the other currency.

As a result of a transfer—with fixed money supplies and flexible exchange rates—there will be, as before, a transactions effect that increases the demand for money in both countries, leading, to some degree, to worldwide deflation. Superimposed on this tendency will be an excess demand for money in the receiving country and an excess supply of money in the paying country due to the redistribution of world expenditure; this leads to an appreciation of the currency of the receiving country and a depreciation of the currency of the paying country. Both effects therefore work to create some deflation in the receiving country, but there are opposing tendencies in the paying country. Changes in relative prices induced by the rearrangement of world demand will have additional effects. To the extent that the prices of home-produced goods rise in the receiving country and fall in the paying country, the appreciation of the currency of the receiving country will be reinforced.

Bickerdike's Breakthrough

Classical reasoning, as we have just seen, emphasized an equilibrium methodology, price flexibility, the neutrality of money, and the long run. This was in contrast to the methodology of the mercantilists, who stressed disequilibrium transitional effects, rigidities, and short-run solutions. The classical school's rejection of mercantilist theory seemed much too harsh after the monetary chaos and short-run problems, including mass unemployment, thrown up by the breakdown of the gold standard during World War I. The exchange rate theories developed in the interwar period—and they survived long after World War II—had a closer affinity to mercantilist than to classical doctrine.

Mercantilist writings have a modern flavor in their account of lags in price adjustments giving rise to real effects of devaluation. Early in the 17th century, mercantilist writers recommended devaluation as a means of stimulating the economy. Schumpeter credits Simon Clement (1695) with the best early statement of the:

> description of the sequence of events that devaluation will produce as long as domestic prices do not respond to it: bullion will flow, exports increase, imports decrease. He [Clement] was not the first to see that, but his is the first compact statement, so far as I know, of the particular piece of the mechanism, made with a full sense of its importance. (Schumpeter 1954, 365, n. 8)

In the following century, many writers, not the least being Hume, emphasized the importance of employment effects in the transition from a lower to a higher price level.

Even during the classical period, there was important dissent from conventional prescriptions. Dissent (as usual) emerged especially in times of stress, particularly after the dislocations of big wars. Thomas Attwood and other members of the Birmingham school, for example, advocated either devaluation (a higher price of gold) or flexible exchange rates in the deflationary period following the Battle of Waterloo in 1815. A century later these ideas found their echo in the works of Irving Fisher and John Maynard Keynes, who openly criticized the attachment to external rather than internal stability.

A breakthrough in the theory of exchange rates occurred with the publication of C.F. Bickerdike's analysis (1920) of the "instability of foreign exchange." In a few short pages this landmark contribution[12] established the so-called elasticities approach to the balance of trade—defects and all! Bickerdike starts out with an additional payment of Z dollars "conceived of as an old loan falling due." He then differentiates the balance of payments equilibrium equation (inclusive of the transfer) to arrive at the elasticity expression, later made more famous by Joan Robinson and Lloyd A. Metzler.[13] He arrives at the effect of a transfer payment on the exchange rate, thus answering the question, By how much must

---

12. Among a number of other important contributions to theory and policy, Bickerdike (1907) originated the theory of the optimum tariff. Edgeworth (1908), following along the lines of Bickerdike's optimum tariff work, had explicitly developed the criterion for stability of the real exchange equilibrium. Bickerdike was the first, however, to relate the elasticity formula to changes in exchange rates, using the device of two inconvertible currencies.

13. Bickerdike's formulation uses the inverse of elasticities, which he calls "inelasticities."

the exchange rate change in order to equilibrate the balance of payments after a transfer? Bickerdike also develops the special case—usually identified with Abba P. Lerner—for the change in the exchange rate when supply elasticities are infinite.[14]

It is ironic that the elasticity condition came to be called the Marshall-Lerner condition. Marshall repudiated the notion that his real equilibrium could be applied to the analysis of devaluation, whereas Lerner added nothing new to Bickerdike's formulation. It would be more appropriate to call it the Bickerdike-Edgeworth condition.

There are, however, defects in Bickerdike's analysis, which have not usually been corrected in subsequent expositions. It is not in general valid to assume, as Bickerdike did, that "the shape of the demand and supply curves for commodities remains unaltered." Bickerdike's approach is not valid for comparing the *equilibrium* positions before and after an exogenous change such as "an old loan falling due." A payment cannot be made unless it is first financed, whether by money creation, taxation, or a voluntary act of saving. If there is an excess demand for foreign exchange, there must be an equal excess supply of the quid pro quo offered in exchange.

Although Bickerdike's analysis is not correct for analysis of a transfer, starting from and ending with an equilibrium position, it is valid for the study of the transition from a disequilibrium position to an equilibrium position. Starting from a position in which the expenditure effects of "an old loan falling due" have already been exhausted, Bickerdike's analysis gives us the answer to the question, By how much must the exchange rate fall to restore equilibrium?

Bickerdike is, at least in the short run, an elasticity pessimist. He worries that:

> if the Americans have not purchased British goods or stocks, or services to an extent sufficient to create a supply of dollars payable at the rate of exchange previously existing, the situation is not necessarily remedied by a further fall in the value of pounds in dollars. Prima facie, indeed, that fall makes the gap wider. If four million dollars are due to be paid, and Americans are due to pay one million pounds, if the exchange rate were four dollars to the pound, that would clear the market. If the exchange rate is three and a half dollars to the pound, however, there are not enough dollars obtainable with the million pounds, and competition does not tend to drive the rate up to four dollars, but, on the contrary, forces it lower and makes the impasse worse. It is like a "bear squeeze" on a stock market, when bulls have been caught short. (Bickerdike 1920)

There are, fortunately, mitigating factors "which may generally be reckoned upon to prevent the rate falling away indefinitely; but it is important to note that the mitigations do not act as promptly as might be desired, and the fundamental

---

14. That is, Bickerdike's "inelasticities" are zero.

instability is the dominating fact." Bickerdike then goes on to discuss the factors that help, including the cheapening of stocks in terms of dollars, loans that the British can make, and the cancellation of some new business. But he correctly notes that, insofar as stocks and bonds pay dividends and interest in pounds, they must fall in dollars more than the exchange rate "unless the lower rate is expected to be temporary" (Bickerdike 1920, 119).

Bickerdike thus emphasizes capital market transactions and financial payments as dominating factors in the short run, and reserves his mathematical analysis for consideration of the adjustment of the trade account in the long run. Thus:

> In the longer period, such as a year or two years, the influence of relative demands for goods and services will tell, but still it is comparatively short-period demands and supplies with which one is concerned. Large changes in the sources of supply can be effected over periods of many years, and the degrees of inelasticity may be considerable over periods of one or two years. (Bickerdike 1920)

All that is needed for the J-curve is a graph!

Bickerdike's contribution founded the elasticities approach that would come to occupy such a prominent place in subsequent literature. His framework, however, had the defect that it analyzed the nominal exchange rate outside a framework of full general equilibrium. Its omission of macroeconomic relationships created the opening for the "absorption approach," and its omission of conditions of money supply and demand left it vulnerable to the monetary approach.

Alternative Theories of the Balance of Trade

A correct analysis of the relation between the balance of trade of a country and other variables must take into account all the factors that enter into the balance of trade. The literature has concentrated on three approaches to the balance of payments or trade: the elasticities approach, the absorption approach, and the monetary approach. The usual assumption made in the literature is that the capital account is either zero or exogenous, unchanged by the effects of exchange rates, so that the analysis applies indifferently to the balance of trade or the balance of payments. But in a complete analysis where capital flows are allowed for, the elasticities and absorption approaches are ways of analyzing the balance of trade, and only the monetary approach is a way of analyzing the balance of payments.

Sixteen Approaches to the Balance of Trade

There are exactly 16 ways of looking at the balance of trade (or balance of payments).[15] Eight of these approaches can be deduced from the application of Walras's law in the national and the international economy; the other eight derive from the application of intertemporal budget constraints.

General-equilibrium analysis requires analysis of the conditions of equilibrium in three broad aggregates: goods, securities, and money. Each sector, of course, could be disaggregated into domestic and foreign components, and subdivided further into the innumerable categories relevant in the real world. To illustrate the 16 approaches to the balance of trade or payments, however, it is sufficient to maintain the degree of aggregation implied by the threefold classification. For the sake of simplicity, I shall also bypass the difference between GDP and GNP, and the corresponding difference between the trade balance and the current account. However, this difference cannot be ignored when we deal with the eight intertemporal approaches to the balance of payments.

The first equation in the analysis is the identity utilized by practitioners of the elasticities approach, namely, that the balance of trade is equal to exports minus imports:

$$B = X - M.$$

By specifying the arguments of the functions determining supplies of exports and demands for imports we arrive at approach number 1 to the balance of payments. Approach 2 is in the same family; it results from specifying the functions determining the supply of exports and the demand for imports in the foreign country. From Cournot's law, the trade surplus of one country is the trade deficit of the rest of the world, due allowance being made for asymmetries in the treatment of reserve suppliers and gold producers.

Analysis of these factors owes much, as we have seen, to Edgeworth and Bickerdike, as subsequently elaborated by Robinson, Lerner, Haberler, Meade, Fritz Machlup, and Metzler. A more sophisticated development of this approach would incorporate into the demand functions for exports and imports not just exchange rates, prices, and output, but domestic expenditure, capital movements, and wealth; it should then not be called the elasticities approach (why not the income propensities approach?) but rather the "direct approach," because it examines directly the forces determining exports and imports. The lesson from the direct approach is that no policy variable, including the exchange rate, can improve the balance of trade without increasing exports relative to imports. The direct approach is no more and no less valid than the other seven pairs.

---

15. The next few paragraphs draw on and summarize the analysis in Mundell (1979). (See also Mundell 1989a and b.)

The next pair of approaches makes use of the absorption relations:

$$B = Y - E$$

where Y is income and E is expenditure (absorption). This relationship can be subdivided into separate sectors to yield the equation $S - I + T - G = B$, where S, I, T, and G refer, respectively, to saving, investment, tax revenues, and government spending. There are two equations of this type, of course, one for the country under analysis and the other for the aggregate of economies in the rest of the world. These approaches owe much to Isaac Gervaise, Metzler, Machlup, Chipman, Meade, Sidney Alexander (especially), and Harry Johnson. Alexander called "absorption" what Meade had called "domestic expenditure," and this inspired the name usually given to the approach. The lesson from this approach is that no policy variable, including the exchange rate, can alter the equilibrium balance of trade (current account balance) unless it increases output (income) more than expenditure. The next pair of approaches relies on the balance of payments identity. The accounting balance of payments is the external counterpart to Walras's law. The current account surplus is equal to net capital exports plus the balance of payments deficit. Put another way, the current account surplus finances an import of securities (which is a capital export) or an inflow of money (balance of payments surplus). This can be expressed as:

$$B = K + P$$

where K is the net capital outward flow and P is the balance of payments surplus. Similarly, any current account surplus of the rest of the world must be matched by net capital exports or an increase in the net reserve assets of the rest of the world.[16] The lesson from this approach is that no policy variable can improve a country's balance of trade unless it generates a reduction in its capital imports and a reduction in the capital exports of the rest of the world.

It is worth noting here a longstanding dispute about the direction of causation in the balance of payments identity. There are those who argue that the trade balance has an independent existence requiring external finance; on the other hand, there are those who argue that capital exports and other transfers induce changes in the balance of trade through the mechanism of financing changes in expenditures. It should be emphasized, however, that the identity itself says nothing about causation; there are merely two sides to the same coin. It cannot be inferred from the balance of payments identity whether the financial transfer determines the trade balance or vice versa.

The classical school, up until Mill, put the capital flow in the driver's seat. It emphasized the fact that the mere act of making a financial transfer automatically

---

16. This abstracts from asymmetries in the treatment of the reserve assets that result in a recorded nonzero balance of trade for the world as a whole.

implies the additional saving to finance it, so that the mere existence of an outward capital flow implies an excess of income over expenditure. But the Mill-Taussig-Keynes omission of expenditure effects in the adjustment mechanism opened the way for Keynes's idiosyncratic view of the trade balance as a given entity independent of financial transfers. Although this involves a false dichotomy—independence of spending from finance—Keynes's view has strongly influenced the modern literature (in my opinion to its detriment). It is easy to see why economists who write down equations specifying exports as a function of output and prices fall prey to the single-entry bookkeeping approach that ignores the mechanism though which capital inflows or transfers stimulate an increase in expenditures. Causation can in principle go in either direction. But it is unlikely that enduring changes in the balance of trade can be motivated other than by basic financial transfers. It is true that a shift of domestic expenditure from home to foreign goods will worsen the balance of trade and immediately force accommodating finance, a loss of reserves, or a change in the exchange rate. But accommodating finance is purely temporary and short-run. Major trade deficits and surpluses are nearly always not only accompanied by but induced by voluntary financial transfers of one kind or another.

Because there are two balance of payments equations—one for the home country and one for the rest of the world—we now have six approaches to the balance of trade.

Approaches 7 and 8 make use of Walras's law directly. The sum of all excess demands is zero, so that any excess supply of commodities must be matched by an equivalent excess demand for securities and money. Because the trade balance is equal to the excess supply of goods, it must also be equal to the excess demand for securities and money. Formulated in a different way, the excess supply of goods is equal to the sum of the budget surplus and the excess of saving over investment. Any budget surplus must be expended on money or securities; it implies an excess demand for money or government bonds on the part of the government. Similarly, an excess of saving over investment equals an excess demand for securities and/or money. We can therefore deduce the current account deficit solely by examining the markets for securities and money. This approach applies to both countries, so that we now have eight approaches to analysis of the balance of trade.

It is convenient at this point to pause to summarize these eight approaches in the form of a system of equations. These equations can be looked upon as identities after the fact or as equilibrium conditions when they are defined in terms of intentions and plans.

All the variables in the equations below are flows. A and Z refer to the supply and demand for securities, respectively, and G and H refer to money creation and hoarding, respectively. The plus signs between the lines are inserted to indicate that the rows can be added vertically to equal zero:

$$\text{(1)} \quad Y - E \;=\; B \;=\; -B^* \;=\; E^* - Y^* \qquad\qquad \text{(goods and services)}$$
$$\quad + \qquad\quad + \qquad + \qquad +$$
$$\text{(2)} \quad A - Z \;=\; -K \;=\; K^* \;=\; Z^* - A^* \qquad\qquad \text{(securities)}$$
$$\quad + \qquad\quad + \qquad + \qquad +$$
$$\text{(3)} \quad G - H \;=\; -P \;=\; P^* \;=\; H^* - G^* \qquad\qquad \text{(money)}$$
$$\quad \| \qquad\qquad \| \qquad \| \qquad \|$$
$$\quad 0 \qquad\quad 0 \qquad 0 \qquad 0$$

The other eight approaches incorporate the intertemporal dimension. Intertemporal conditions are implied when we say that a deficit is "unsustainable." If a deficit is unsustainable, the worry is not that it will endure but that it will disappear in an unpleasant way. The above equations do not reflect this fact because they have not as yet taken into account the intertemporal version of Walras's law. Trade deficits integrated over time yield net debt, and debt has to be paid back. We owe to Hume—who first stated the theorem that Charles P. Kindleberger called Hume's law—that exports equal imports. Hume meant that the balance of payments adjustment mechanism would eventually bring imports into equality with exports. This is emphatically not true in the short run; the United States has had a trade deficit for nearly a generation, as it had a surplus for two prior generations. But there is a sense in which Hume is right after all. Exports equal imports over long periods of time.

A country's net indebtedness is limited by its perceived export capacity. The United States can sustain a trade deficit because it has the productive power to service and ultimately repay its debts. If, on the contrary, it were perceived that the United States could not generate the future trade surpluses to service a growing debt, external finance would dry up and expenditure would be brought back in line with income, eliminating the deficit. No country, of course, can pile up debts indefinitely unless it is at the same time generating increased means for repaying them. A country borrowing to expand its capital plants and productive power has more credibility than a country borrowing to finance pure consumption spending. It is sometimes relevant to note which sectors are doing the borrowing or lending. If the private sectors do the borrowing, the responsibility for making repayments rests with individuals; households or firms might legitimately borrow to achieve a better intertemporal pattern of consumption along life-cycle lines.[17] Budget deficits, however, raise other questions, as they create the potential for mistaken shifts in the intergenerational distribution of income.

At some point diminishing returns will set in and a country will reach its debt limit, beyond which it can no longer finance current account deficits. Higher

---

17. Even where the intertemporal borrowing is legitimate, however, there might be externalities associated with changes in the terms of trade that may create a divergence between the private and the social benefits from external borrowing.

debts require larger interest payments, which at some stage require unattainable trade surpluses to maintain debt service. At this stage the risk of default soars. An example is afforded by many of the less developed countries that borrowed excessively in the negative-real-interest days of the late 1970s and early 1980s. When real interest rates rose and the future export capacity of these countries seemed insufficient to service their debts, the flow of capital dried up and they were left with a painful adjustment process that has since abated only moderately.

Each of the eight approaches to the balance of trade described above thus has its reverse counterpart in the intertemporal dimension, when surpluses and deficits have to be reversed. In the long run, therefore, we need to pay special attention to the difference between GDP and GNP, and to the equivalent difference between the trade balance and the current account balance. Expected future net outpayments to service the debt, or inpayments of debt service, like repayments, lower or raise disposable income and domestic expenditure. The larger the debt, the larger the gap between GDP and GNP, and between the trade balance and the current account.

We must also pay attention to the pall that heavy indebtedness casts over expectations about the exchange rate and bond prices, signaling decreased creditworthiness. In the long run, debts involve a subtraction from wealth that should affect our current propensities to save. Individuals pay attention to those negative factors pertaining to personal debts, but only superrational individuals correctly subtract from personal wealth the share of the national debt that implies future tax obligations.

Is There an Equilibrium Trade Balance?

The major difference between a creditor and a debtor nation is that the former is enabled (without borrowing) to consume more whereas a debtor must consume less (without further borrowing) than its income; corresponding differences develop (given balance of payments equilibrium) between the current account and the trade balance, and between GDP and GNP.

How can disequilibrium be distinguished from equilibrium? Is the balance of payments the criterion of equilibrium, or is it the balance of trade? When is a current account deficit or surplus a symptom of disequilibrium?

Attitudes on this subject have changed with the international monetary system. Under fixed exchange rates, the balance of payments occupied center stage. There were, to be sure, alternative definitions of the balance of payments, and there was some debate about which was the most useful definition for the United States. One important and widely used measure of the target variable was the "basic balance," the difference between the trade balance, on the one hand, and repetitive transfers plus "normal" capital exports, on the other. Another measure was the "official settlements balance," which recorded the change in net liabilities of the monetary authorities. Whichever of these measures was employed, little attention was given to the trade balance or the current account balance. The most important problem was to ensure that the balance of trade and the net capital account offset one another, not to achieve any particular level of the balance of trade or current account. In the Tinbergian language of targets and instruments, the exchange rate and the balance of payments (not the balance of trade) were targets, not instruments, of economic policy.[18]

To the extent that the level of the current account was analyzed at all, capital movements, combined with a corresponding trade balance, were thought to be a desirable way of allowing countries to optimize the intertemporal distribution of spending. By borrowing and running a trade deficit, a high-interest-rate country could accelerate its economic development and service the loan out of the augmented income; similarly, a low-interest-rate country could find an outlet for high saving by investing abroad and earning a higher rate of return than that available at home. Under fixed exchange rates the current account was expected to adjust itself to the optimum extent, provided capital moved from low-interest-rate to high-interest-rate countries. The function of capital imports was to enable a country to attain economic objectives at an earlier stage than would otherwise be possible.

What came to be called the "composition problem"[19] of determining the correct structure of the balance of payments was defined as follows:

---

18. It is true that some attention was paid to the impact of the trade balance on the level of employment, partly on the basis of errors in economic theory. Superficial mercantilist reasoning, arguing from the national income accounts, Keynesian equations, and the fact that exports are a source of demand whereas imports are not (except via repercussion effects), seems to imply that an improvement in the balance of trade increases employment. This conclusion may be correct if the disturbance to the balance of trade originates from an increase in export demand on the part of the rest of the world, but it is false if the improvement arises from a reduction in domestic expenditure. It is a fallacy to argue that measures that improve the balance of trade *ipso facto* increase employment.

In late 1971, after the breakdown of the Bretton Woods system, an improvement in the trade balance became, for a brief period, an explicit target of government policy. Then–Secretary of the Treasury John B. Connally made his famous assertion that the United States wanted a turnaround in its trade balance of $13 billion. Treasury officials naively hoped that the devaluation of the dollar negotiated at the Smithsonian Institution would bring about that turnaround in the trade balance.

The devaluation failed to make a dent in the trade balance. In fact the trade deficit severely worsened in 1972 to over $6 billion, the largest US deficit up to that time. Although the balance became positive in 1973, it worsened again in 1974, only to become positive again in the recession year 1975.

The year 1975 marks a watershed in the history of the international accounts. It was the last year in which the United States had a trade surplus. Deficits rose after 1976 to over $30 billion and after 1983 to over $100 billion.

19. At the 1966 Chicago Conference on International Monetary Problems. See Mundell and Swoboda (1969).

If the balance-of-payments statement is divided into a current account, a capital account and a reserve account, and if adjustment is defined as the correction of the reserve account, should adjustment be achieved by improving the capital account or the current account? What criteria should determine the appropriate composition of adjustment? (Mundell and Swoboda 1969, 38)

Put another way, what are the costs and benefits—the welfare implications—of a larger or a smaller current account surplus fully financed by corresponding changes in capital exports? Alternatively, at what rate should a country build up or run down its international equity? What is the optimum level of external equity or debt, and what is the optimum speed of adjustment of the equity or debt (i.e., the optimum current account surplus or deficit)? Unfortunately, beyond the general recognition that international capital movements were means of altering the intertemporal distribution of expenditure relative to income, there was no explicit criterion for determining the rate at which a country should import or export capital.

Concern over a country's long-run creditor position partly reflects concern over its power position. In an age of war, a country's creditor position would give it a potential source of finance for wartime imports, supplementing the "gold chest" to which every country sought access. Other things equal, a debtor country's power position is weaker than a creditor country's. What Hume called the jealousy of the balance of trade may just as aptly be applied to the jealousy of a country's creditor position.

The distribution of power is a function of the size and wealth structure of countries in the world economy. It has often been remarked that the world economy is an oligopoly; each country reacts directly to the actions of other countries. Japan has replaced the United States as the world's largest creditor.[20] If the rest of the world were composed of small economies that, singly or in combination, could never be a political or military threat to the United States, there would be little concern over the US trade deficits beyond the ordinary economic problem of servicing the rising level of debt.

The Stages Theory

Current account deficits can persist for long periods of time. The United States had a chronic deficit in the 19th century as it made use of capital imports to accelerate its development. From World War I to about 1975, the United States

---

20. There was a short period in which the decline in the US creditor position made Saudi Arabia the largest creditor country, before Saudi Arabia was overtaken by Japan and Germany.

had substantial surpluses. In every year since 1975 the United States has had substantial trade deficits, which rose sharply to over 3 percent of GNP in the 1980s. Other countries have experienced similarly long trends, and the phenomenon has given rise to theorizing about a standard pattern of "stages" of a country's balance of payments over time. According to this theory, these stages can sometimes be related to the level of development of a country. Because capital exports (according to classical theory) are determined by relative rates of return and international saving rates, with international capital flowing from low-profit to high-profit countries, the stages approach implies systematic developments in net saving rates or rates of return on capital at different levels of development.

The simplest framework suggests four stages of the balance of payments.[21] A young country passes through the positions of immature debtor to mature debtor to immature creditor to mature creditor. A debtor pays interest on borrowed capital; a creditor receives interest on capital invested abroad. A debtor is immature when its trade balance is less than its debt service (implying that it is still borrowing) and mature when its trade balance exceeds debt service so that the country is now repaying its debts. A creditor is immature when its trade deficit is less than its interest receipts (implying it is still lending) and mature when its trade deficit is at least equal to its interest receipts.

The stages approach is an optimistic one in that it suggests a reversibility of debt positions. It seems natural that some prominent European and Pacific countries—notably Germany and Japan—moved quickly through several stages after the end of World War II, passing, in a matter of only three decades, from an immature debtor to an immature creditor position. One would predict from the theory that, as their receipts from foreign assets increase, these countries will gradually increase their absorption until trade surpluses are transformed into trade deficits, leading eventually to the position of mature creditor.

The United States, on the other hand, has passed from an immature creditor at the end of World War II quickly through the position of mature creditor back to that of immature debtor, commencing the cycle again. It could be argued that the supply-side tax revolution in the United States in the 1980s rejuvenated the US economy, raising its marginal efficiency of capital and inviting capital from all over the world to partake in the largesse of reborn efficiency. This transformed the United States from the world's largest creditor to the world's largest debtor. According to the stages approach, the position will reverse only when either the

---

21. See Cairnes (1874) for the development of a pioneering version of the stages approach; see also Taussig (1927). Crowther (1957) elaborates six stages: immature debtor-borrowers; mature debtor-borrowers; debtor-repayers and debtor-lenders; immature creditor-lenders; mature creditor-lenders; and creditor-drawers and borrowers. Halevi (1971) develops a 12-fold classification (allowing for borderline cases). Other work in the modern analysis of stages includes Onitsuka (1970, 1974), Neher (1970), Fischer and Frenkel (1974a and b), Bazdarich (1978), Genberg and Swoboda (1988), and Manzocchi (1990).

rate of return on investment in the United States falls to foreign levels, discouraging further capital inflow, *or* when the US saving rate rises by enough to restore the export surplus of the earlier decades. With a reduction in absorption induced by the need to finance outward payments of interest and dividends, and a larger capital stock that lifts GDP above GNP, the trade balance will move again into surplus.

There is a grain of tautology in the stages approach: what is borrowed has to be repaid (if it is not defaulted). The agents contracting the loan are committed to repayments. In the absence of differential rates of return it is necessary to seek answers to chronic trade balances in differential saving rates. One possibility arises from demographic changes that create systematic biases in the levels of borrowing and lending.

How Demography Creates Trade Deficits

If succeeding generations have different propensities to save and invest, as posited by the life-cycle (with or without bequest) hypothesis, blips in the age distribution of the population will alter net national lending and, via the transfer mechanism, the balance of trade. In Mundell (1990, 1991) I developed a four-generation model designed to elucidate the trade balance effects of demographic blips. The four generations include not only the very young and very old dependent generations, but two working generations. The cutting edge of the model lies not so much in the ratio of the size of the dependent to that of the working generations—although that produced some of the usual effects—but in the different characteristics of the two working generations. Although the working generations have similar earning and saving potential, the junior working generation invests—mainly in consumer durables—more that it saves, borrowing the difference, whereas the senior working generation saves more than it invests, lending the difference. The balance of trade will thus be a positive function of the proportion of senior to junior members of the working generations, even though, as I assumed, each individual obeys his or her intertemporal budget constraint on life-cycle principles.

Empirically, the model would have predicted the big deficits of the 1980s, and predicts big surpluses in the late 1990s, taking into account two salient facts: a small cohort of births in the 1930s (the Depression babies) and a large cohort of postwar births (the baby-boomers). The small number of the former, followed by the large number of the latter, results in a small number of senior workers to do the lending in the 1980s and early 1990s, combined with a large number of junior workers who are chronic borrowers. The small number of grown-up Depression baby lenders is no match for the hordes of yuppie borrowers. The excess of borrowers over lenders leads to high real interest rates and a capital inflow that imposes a current account deficit on the country as a whole.

The demographically inspired deficit is benign because it is reversible. In the succeeding period, when the baby-boomers mature into the senior working-lending generation and there is a relatively small cohort of junior borrowing workers, there will be an excess of lenders that will swamp credit markets, create a substantial capital outflow, and produce a sharp turnaround in the current account.

The effect of this cycle will be more important the more asymmetrical US experience is compared with surplus countries such as Japan and Germany.[22] If the net saving rate theory, based on reversible age-distribution trends, is of sufficient importance, it is not necessary to alter the policy of benign neglect of the current account deficit. If left alone, the deficits will reverse as a result of structural-demographic adaptations in private saving.

The Fiscal Approach to the Deficit

Yet another possibility—not incompatible with the undersaving demographic theory—is that the US trade deficit has been dominated by the budget deficit and that a reduction of the budget deficit is a precondition for elimination of the trade deficit. The budget and trade deficits are of course connected by the national income identities of the absorption approach.

The budget deficit ranged from zero to 2 percent of GNP for many years up to 1974, but it suddenly jumped to 3.4 percent and 4.2 percent in the recession years of 1975 and 1976, respectively. From 1977 to 1981 it was consistently (except for 1979) above 2.5 percent of GNP: 2.6 percent in 1977, 2.6 percent in 1978, 1.4 percent in 1979, 2.8 percent in 1980, 2.6 percent in 1981. In this period, it will be remembered, the trade deficit lurched upward.

In the recession year of 1982, the budget deficit jumped to 3.97 percent of GNP. It then rose to 5.95 percent in 1983 before falling to 4.72 percent in 1984, 5.28 percent in 1985, and 5.01 percent in 1986. These were the peak years of the budget deficit. A remarkable turnaround came in the next three years, as the budget deficit fell to 3.26 percent of GNP in 1987, 3.17 percent in 1988, and 2.71 percent in 1989. The improvement in the budget deficit coincided with an improvement in the trade deficit, although both remained over 2 percent of GNP.

---

22. Note, however, that the model would predict a turnaround again after the first decade of the 21st century as the baby-boomers retire and are replaced as senior workers by another small cohort.

Figure 1 United States: trade and fiscal balances, 1953–89[a]

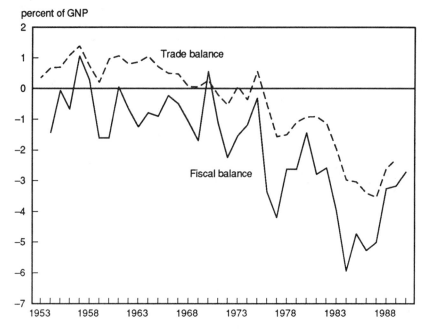

a. The denominator for the fiscal balance is GNP in the previous year.

Source: International Monetary Fund, *International Financial Statistics Yearbook* 1990.

More significantly, the changes in the budget deficit have been followed, usually with a one-year lag, by changes in the trade deficit. Figure 1 shows the budget and trade deficits as percentages of GNP, with the budget deficit advanced one year. The correlation is striking.

The future of the current account deficit will depend critically on net capital flows. Elimination of the trade deficit will depend on the United States resuming its position, which it maintained from 1915 until the 1970s, as a *net* capital exporter. There are several reasons, however, to expect the United States to be the recipient of continuing substantial gross capital and money inflows in the 1990s. Increasing global financial integration, the continued use of the dollar as a major international currency, and continuing advantages stemming from the tax reforms in the United States will be factors favorable to *gross* capital inflows. On the other hand, a rising saving rate due to demographic factors will act to lower interest rates and induce larger gross capital outflows. As the decade of the 1990s unfolds, the capital outflow factor will get larger relative to the capital inflow factor, and the current account deficit should gradually fall.

Exchange Rates and the Trade Balance

Exchange rate changes offer another possible explanation of the trade deficit. It is widely believed that dollar depreciation can correct the trade balance, and that depreciation since 1985 has started an adjustment process that is gradually reducing the trade deficit.

At the outset, however, a difficulty sets in. Under the present flexible exchange rate system, the exchange rate is an endogenous variable. Variations in the exchange rate represent the outcome of a solution of a system of general-equilibrium equations. The effect of a change in the exchange rate on the trade balance can only be determined in the context of the changes in the exogenous variables that brought about the change in the exchange rate.

In the case of wage and price flexibility, depreciation of a currency brought about by an increase in the money supply would probably not affect the trade balance at all. An increase in the money supply would bring about a proportionate increase in wages and prices, including the price of foreign exchange, and no change in competitiveness or relative prices Depreciation brought about by inflation clearly cannot be relied on to improve the trade balance.[23]

Another possibility is that the depreciation is brought about by monetary changes in the rest of the world. But if the dollar depreciates because of deflationary policies abroad, the deflation, or lower rates of inflation, will in the long run cancel the competitive advantages of the exchange rate changes. It can hardly be said that depreciation in a world of flexible wages and prices—whether brought about by inflationary policies at home or deflationary policies abroad—would have an ascertainable and predictable effect on the trade balance.

An alternative and widely adopted assumption, drawn from the Keynesian model, is based on rigidities. Monetary changes in an environment of price and wage rigidities have real effects. In the Keynesian theory of employment, it is usually assumed that wage rates are rigid. This assumption works best if there is unemployment. If the monetary authorities expand the money supply, the exchange rate will fall and prices will rise, lowering real wages and raising employment and output. Such a policy might well be in a country's interest regardless of its effect on the balance of trade. But that is not the issue. The issue under consideration is whether the exchange rate will improve the balance of trade.

---

23. It is, of course, possible that inflation would shift the distribution of wealth, resulting in a rearrangement of world demand and a change in relative prices. Inflation also has fiscal effects insofar as it reduces the real fiscal burden of the public debt. If saving increases (because of the wealth-saving relationship) and the budget deficit is reduced (because of reduced real interest payments), the trade balance will improve unless these changes are offset by increases in investment financed by increased capital inflows.

In a flexible exchange rate system, the equilibrium exchange rate is that rate which clears the foreign-exchange market. If there is no official intervention in the foreign-exchange market—as in the case of a freely floating rate—the exchange rate will equilibrate the current account and the capital account. Any reduction in the trade deficit must be exactly matched by an equal reduction in capital imports; similarly, any worsening of the trade deficit must be accompanied by an increase in capital imports. It is possible, therefore, to determine the direction of change in the trade balance by predicting the direction of change in capital imports.

The pure theory of international trade was mainly developed on the assumptions of either no capital movements or exogenously determined capital movements. But if there are no capital movements (and there is no change in reserves), exports must equal imports both before and after the disturbance that changed the exchange rate. In the absence of capital movements, even under Keynesian assumptions of wage rigidity, the exchange rate change—however it is brought about—cannot bring about a change in the balance of trade.[24] In the absence of capital movements, domestic expenditure and GNP must be equal.

But let us now relax the assumption that there are no capital movements and that the latter are unaffected by exchange rate policies. Assume that initial balance of payments equilibrium prevails with both a trade deficit and an equal capital inflow. We must now ask in what direction capital will move as a result of the policy change. Those who argue that a change in policy that brings about a depreciation of the dollar will improve the trade balance must also argue that the same change in policy will reduce the inflow of capital. If there is a decreased capital inflow as a result of the policy change, the trade deficit will be lower; but if there is an increased capital inflow, the trade deficit will worsen.

To answer this question we need to know how capital inflows are affected by the exchange rate.[25] There is a difference between classical and Keynesian assumptions. Under classical assumptions, the level of the exchange rate would not have an important effect on capital flows. It is true that financial assets are now cheaper under the depreciated dollar, but so is the income from those assets. The ratio of income to capital value, which is the rate of return on investment,

---

24. In offer curve analysis of the Marshall-Meade type there is no place for a balance of payments deficit. A price vector that differs from the equilibrium produces an excess demand for the foreign country's good, which can only constitute a transactions configuration if there is intervention: domestic commodity authorities must be selling foreign goods out of their own stockpiles, and simultaneously buying stocks of the domestic good. When official transactions are added to the private transactions, there is no deficit or surplus.

25. We might note that it is also necessary to determine the effect on net capital flows of the policy that creates the change in the exchange rate. If, for example, the central bank buys foreign exchange with newly printed money and invests the foreign exchange in a foreign security, the trade balance must improve by the amount of the capital outflow.

is unchanged. Under classical assumptions of price and wage flexibility, therefore, neither capital movements nor the balance of trade would be affected by changes in the exchange rate.[26]

In the Keynesian case of rigid wages, however, a different conclusion applies. Monetary expansion that brings about depreciation lowers real wage rates. The resulting increase in actual and expected profits amounts to an increase in the marginal efficiency of capital. Foreign companies now find it profitable to shift production facilities to the United States to take advantage of the lower wage costs, and this shift of resources amounts to a capital import. Even if exports increase as a result of the lower selling prices in terms of foreign currencies, imports must increase by an even larger amount in order to create an increased gap between imports and exports equal to the increased inward financial transfers. Paradoxically, the very factor that is often used to justify the effectiveness of depreciation in improving the trade balance—rigid wages—works against an improvement in the trade balance.[27]

Another possible rigidity is that of land prices. Unless the depreciation has been brought about by an increase in the US money supply, the price of land will not increase *pari passu* with the price of foreign exchange. Fluctuations in the dollar over the past few years have not been matched by equivalent fluctuations in the price of land. The depreciation of the dollar since 1985 has made the yen and mark prices of American land much lower relative to the corresponding prices of Japanese and European land. To the extent that real assets are only slowly affected by the exchange rate, they become a target for bargain hunting, for both investors and speculators. To the extent that this occurs, the capital inflow will finance a larger excess of expenditure over income and worsen the trade deficit.

Trade Balances as System Imbalances

Monetary problems frequently have their origin not in domestic policy mistakes, but in circumstances arising in the rest of the world over which the domestic authorities have no control. A typical example is a deterioration in a country's terms of trade due to outside factors; oil shocks are one such factor, but most raw material–producing countries have faced markets in which staple exports

---

26. As noted earlier, this was pointed out by Bickerdike (1920, 118–19).

27. A stronger case can be made for changes in relative prices in the manufacturing sectors of large countries than in small, open economies producing primary products for which there is a world market. The relative prices of basic commodities are determined by real variables, and it is unlikely that relative price changes play an important role in the process of adjustment.

can only be sold at disastrously low prices. We are not concerned here with problems of this type, important as they are in real life. We are concerned rather with problems that have their origin in the international monetary system itself. An outstanding example of this type of shock is the Great Depression, which had its origin in the breakdown of the gold standard in World War I and its unwise restoration at an undervalued price of gold in the 1920s. A second example is the balance of payments deficit of the United States in the 1960s, which developed as an inevitable outgrowth of the postwar gold exchange standard in the face of a recurrent gold shortage. A third example is the great inflation that occurred in the wake of the collapse of the Bretton Woods system and the severing of the gold link of currencies to the commodity world on 15 August 1971. Yet another example was the renewed outbreak of wild inflation in the late 1970s that produced negative real interest rates and a level of Third World indebtedness that could not be sustained in the disinflation of the 1980s.

Supply conditions have always played a key role in the selection of monetary metals. When countries fixed the legal prices of both gold and silver, an increase in the supply of one metal would result in a change in the standard, as the abundant metal was exchanged at the mint for the scarcer metal. In the middle of the 16th century, silver became dominant after the great discoveries in Potosì in Bolivia; that dominance was to last over two centuries. In the 18th century, new supplies of gold from Brazil enabled Great Britain to move toward a gold standard. In the middle of the 19th century, France, the bimetallic power of the first half of the century, exchanged its silver currency for gold following the great discoveries of the latter metal in Australia and California.[28] The great gold

---

28. Commodity standards were subject to instability arising from two main sources: fluctuations in the supply of the commodity, and shifts of demand. Although changes in supplies of the commodity were disturbing enough, it was possible to anticipate them, in view of long production lags. More disturbing were sudden and dramatic shifts of demand due to countries going from one standard to another.

From the 1820s to the late 1840s, when bimetallism in France and the United States gave the world a monetary unity, expanding silver supplies from Mexico were insufficient to make up for the shortfall in gold production. This position was reversed in mid-century, when the gold discoveries in Australia and California were sufficient to double world monetary gold stocks in a single decade; gold drove silver out of circulation in France, and world prices began to rise. The US currency became inconvertible during the Civil War, leaving France alone to bear the brunt of bimetallism; France too suspended convertibility during the Franco-Prussian War. By that time silver production had rapidly increased, forcing France to safeguard its gold currency by abandoning bimetallism for a limping gold standard; even earlier the new German Empire had dumped silver for gold, further lowering the price of silver.

The 1870s witnessed an explosion of silver production, leading to the abandonment of bimetallism and the march to the gold standard. This shift of standards created an excess demand for gold and an excess supply of silver, which led to deflation in the gold bloc and inflation in the remaining silver countries. Criticism at this time was directed at the shift away from bimetallism, which aggravated deflation in the gold brigade and inflation in the remaining silver countries. Objections to deflation led to agitation to restore bimetallism,

discoveries in South Africa in the 1880s ensured an easy trend to gold by most of the rest of the world in the 1890s. After World War I, countries could choose among gold, silver (rarely), the pound, or the dollar.[29] In 1936 a tripartite arrangement was adopted among three gold standard countries.[30] At the Bretton Woods conference in 1944, the choice was between gold and the dollar (except for a brief flurry of interest, prompted by the Mexican delegation, in silver). At the Smithsonian meeting in 1971, countries could choose either gold, the dollar, or the recently created Special Drawing Right (SDR) of the International Monetary Fund. When (or if) a European currency is created, the choice of international standards will be further widened.

The choice among monetary systems in recent history is elaborated below. The purpose is to investigate *systemic* problems that have a bearing on the relation between exchange rates and trade balances. Because of the major role that the dominant financial powers have played in the international monetary system, the solution of some their national problems lies in a change in the international monetary system.

The Gold Exchange Standard of the 1920s

A century of comparative stability under the bimetallic or the gold standard was shaken by World War I, when the major countries—except the United States

---

which, however, failed when South African gold arrived to prevent further deflation, and, indeed, induce a mild inflation for almost two decades before the outbreak of World War I.

29. Gold had become unstable after the outbreak of World War I when the belligerent countries engaged in inflationary finance, exporting gold to the few countries (including the United States and Japan) that remained on the gold standard. The commodity value of gold fell by half as US prices doubled. The immediate postwar deflation in the United States was insufficient to restore prewar gold prices. The stock of gold was sufficient to maintain the United States on the gold standard, but inadequate for an international gold standard of the prewar type. Nevertheless, the international gold standard was restored in the midst of a state of monetary uncertainty occasioned by wide fluctuations in exchange rates. Despite feeble attempts at international monetary coordination, the gold scarcity led to deflationary policies that inaugurated the great deflation, which was made worse by mass unemployment. Belatedly, some countries left the gold standard or devalued, leading to a revised system.

30. The new system relied heavily on the US dollar after its devaluation in 1934. The devaluation more than corrected the gold shortage (given the prohibition on privately owned gold in the United States), leading to an initially undervalued dollar (relative to gold). The dollar shortage, however, lasted only from 1934 to 1950. By 1950 wartime and postwar inflation had raised prices, creating a gold scarcity, which was concealed somewhat by the prohibition of gold holdings by US citizens and the disproportionately large gold holdings of the US government. Attracted by interest returns and confidence in the dollar, the rest of the world was initially content to use dollars in lieu of gold. But gold losses to European central banks eventually revealed the true nature of the global excess demand for gold.

and Japan—left the gold standard. Keynes (1923) warned against restoring gold at the old parity after the war, arguing that at current prices relative to the dollar the pound would be overvalued and that resumption would bring on tight money and deflation in Britain. More to the point, from the standpoint of the system as a whole, Gustav Cassel warned of an approaching deflation if the gold standard were restored at current price levels.

Britain did restore the pound at the historic parity, overvaluing it in terms of inflated postwar prices. This action has been universally condemned, not least by Winston Churchill himself, years later. Many of the subsequent ills of the world have been blamed on this unfortunate event. But the modern economist must be skeptical that such an apparently minor event as a mere overvaluation of (according to Keynes) 10 percent could have had such catastrophic consequences on the world as a whole. Notwithstanding that Britain was still the center of an empire, it seems merely silly, to observers in an age accustomed to wild gyrations of major currencies, to blame so many of the ills of the world on this little event.

The difficulties of sterling represented a symptom rather than a cause of the breakdown of the interwar gold standard. Whatever the inconveniences of adjustment Britain experienced because of the overvaluation of the pound against the dollar, they could have been managed if the system itself had been robust. Had the fundamentals of the international monetary system been sound, Britain's actions would have turned out to be right, and Britain would have gained long-run advantages for its short-run trouble. The fetish with Britain's short-run dilemma diverted attention from the fundamental systemic problem.

That problem was the undervaluation of gold. This had its origins in World War I when European countries left the gold standard, resulting in massive gold imports into the United States that were immediately monetized, doubling the dollar price level even though the United States continued to adhere to the gold standard. This overvaluation of the dollar against gold was only partly corrected by the postwar deflation, leaving gold undervalued by about 35 percent. In the 1920s, all currencies (including the French franc) were overvalued against gold; the pound was overvalued relative to the dollar; and the dollar (after 1927) was overvalued relative to the franc.

As already noted, Cassel (1925) was one of the few economists who spotted the systemic problem in the early 1920s; he warned that restoration of the international gold standard would bring on deflation (appreciation of gold). Even if Britain had restored the pound at an equilibrium parity vis-à-vis the dollar, world deflation would have resulted from the systemic problem of the undervaluation of gold.

Alternative policy steps could have prevented the disaster. The descent into deflation could have been averted as late as 1930. The solutions, however, were outside the intellectual framework of the times. One possible solution was an increase in the price of gold in terms of all currencies. Another possibility would have been a move to flexible exchange rates in 1930, before the onset of deflation instead of after it. A third solution would have been the creation of an alternative form of liquidity through a world central bank.

Despite some earlier indications of awareness of gold scarcity in the 1920s—witness the Genoa Agreement of 1922—the problem was not generally recognized as a systemic one. None of the needed measures were taken, or even discussed. The closest approximation to a solution—at least pointing in the right direction—was the creation of the Bank for International Settlements, which, although it provided a forum for discussion of international monetary matters, focused most of its attention on war reparations.

The Bretton Woods Problem

History repeated itself in a corollary mistake in the decades after World War II. From 1934 to 1945, gold appeared to be slightly overvalued as a result of dollar devaluation, the prohibition on gold holdings by US citizens, and the concentration of much of the world stock of monetary gold in the United States. The United States had ample gold for the backing of Federal Reserve notes after the reserve requirement was lowered from 40 percent to 25 percent in 1945. The apparent gold redundancy, however, concealed an incipient scarcity in the international monetary system. There was sufficient gold for US purposes, but not enough to permit a general redistribution of US gold to Europe. Although European countries pegged their currencies to the dollar, they nevertheless wanted to hold an important part of their reserves in gold.

The 1950s paradox of a strong dollar (measured against other currencies) coupled with a balance of payments deficit—as measured by gold losses and the increase in liquid liabilities to foreigners—can only be understood in the context of the new role for the dollar in the international monetary system.[31] Concurrently with the massive redistribution of monetary gold to Europe, the dollar was becoming the world's money. The acquisition of dollar liabilities abroad, combined with gold losses, was interpreted as a deficit in the US balance of

---

31. One of the problems associated with the confusion between systemic and national issues is the concept of the balance of payments deficit, conventionally defined as a loss of gold or an increase in liquid liabilities. This definition is inappropriate if deficits and surpluses are thought of as error signals, because it makes no distinction between desired and undesired changes in reserves. In Mundell (1965) I advanced a definition of balance of payments disequilibrium restricted to *undesired* changes in reserve assets or foreign liquid liabilities; I still believe this is the appropriate concept, despite its operational difficulties.

payments. Even in the heyday of what was called the dollar shortage, the United States developed a substantial balance of payments deficit.[32]

Robert Triffin (1960) posed the problem of the international monetary system as a dilemma: if the United States corrected its balance of payments deficit, the world would suffer a liquidity shortage and potential deflation; but if the United States failed to eliminate its deficit, gold losses would bring on a crisis of confidence in the dollar. Triffin's solution to the liquidity problem was to create a new source of liquidity through a world central bank; his plan was reminiscent of that proposed by Keynes two decades earlier.[33] However, it was an idea whose time had not yet come. The political ingredients of a solution along these lines did not exist: there was no political constituency for an international central bank.[34]

An alternative to the Triffin solution was an increase in the price of gold, as recommended by Sir Roy Harrod and Jacques Rueff.[35] But, as already noted, an increase in the price of gold could eliminate the undervaluation of gold but not the US balance of payments deficit. If the price of gold were set high enough to restore confidence in the dollar, the rest of the world would not only continue to accumulate dollars as reserve assets, aggravating the US balance of payments problem, but might even cash in their gold hoards for interest-bearing dollar assets. An increase in the price of gold without a reform of the system might have made the US balance of payments deficit permanent—that is, until the next crisis a couple of decades down the road.[36]

---

32. A dollar shortage is not, however, incompatible with a gold shortage. In the IMF, the dollar was the currency that was "needed to be drawn" even while countries with balance of payments surpluses were exchanging dollars for gold.

33. Keynes's proposal for an International Clearing Union was first presented to the public on 7 April 1943 (Cmd. 6437, His Majesty's Stationery Office). White's plan for an International Stabilization Fund was made public in the *New York Times* on the same day and published in full in the June 1943 *Federal Reserve Bulletin*. In 1968 I presented a Plan for a World Currency in a statement to the Joint Economic Committee of the US Congress; this plan combined features of both the Keynes and the Triffin plans but went beyond them in its currency features (see Mundell 1968c).

34. Certainly the Vietnam War did much to sour the trans-Atlantic climate. More important, however, the dominant power—always the country with, in the short run, the most to lose by powerful supranationalism—was not yet willing to demote itself.

35. There was a provision in the Articles of Agreement of the IMF for a change in the par values (specified in gold) of all currencies, so the founding fathers of the IMF anticipated the possibility. Note that this proposal would not necessarily involve any changes in exchange rates.

36. Other (often mutually contradictory) objections were that an increase in the price of gold would be inflationary; that it would create expectations of future gold price increases and lead to a gold shortage in the future; that it would tend to reinstate the gold standard; that it would unfairly redistribute wealth toward gold-holding countries; that it would penalize countries that had accumulated dollars rather than gold; that it would lower the

It is necessary, however, to distinguish between Harrod's and Rueff's proposals for increasing the price of gold. Whereas Harrod—always an advocate of elastic money—would condone the continued use of reserve currencies, Rueff advocated abolition of the gold exchange standard in favor of a full gold standard. Rueff's proposal thus took full account of the need to resolve the liquidity, adjustment, and confidence problems, albeit by means that would impose the discipline of automatic monetary adjustments of the gold standard. The necessary doubling of the price of gold, Rueff argued, would not be inflationary because the additional dollar value of gold liquidity would be used by the United States to extinguish reserve liabilities of the United States.

Many economists, arguing along traditional lines, believed that devaluation of the dollar was the correct remedy for the US balance of payments deficit. But this approach failed to distinguish between national and systemic problems. It failed to recognize the unique position of the US dollar in the world payments system. The economists who recommended devaluation of the dollar (as opposed to a general increase in the price of gold) were thinking in terms of devaluation against other currencies.[37] Besides the difficulty in bringing this about under the existing exchange system, it was not the right remedy to the problem.[38]

There was no indication that exchange rate changes would make US products more competitive or improve the US balance of trade. There had been, it is true, a gradual decline in the US share of world exports since the early postwar recovery period; European and Japanese goods were becoming much more important in world trade as their economies recovered from the devastations of war. The United States had been worried about its growth rate in the post-Sputnik years, but slow growth was not an exchange rate problem. Throughout the postwar period, the United States had enjoyed both current account and trade balance surpluses. (The United States had a trade surplus in each of the six decades from 1914 to 1974!) No systematic empirical study in economics had

---

gold value of existing contracts; and that it would help regimes in South Africa and/or the Soviet Union.

37. The difficulties attendant upon official devaluation of the dollar became clear in the debates at the Smithsonian meeting, where a political compromise was reached by which the United States devalued the dollar against gold and some other countries revalued their currencies against gold.

38. The devaluation of the dollar against other currencies could have been effected in either of two ways: by an increase in the dollar price of gold, with the par values of other currencies expressed in gold remaining constant, or by raising the gold values of other currencies, with the par value of the dollar remaining constant at 0.888671 gram (1/35 ounce) of gold. Either method would have required other countries to raise the price at which they bought dollars in the exchange markets. These difficulties were by no means insurmountable—they were resolved when exchange rates were changed at the 1971 Smithsonian meeting—but they indicated the great complications associated with the asymmetry of the dollar's position in the Bretton Woods system.

ever demonstrated convincingly that devaluation would improve the trade balance. The gap between theory and practice was even more apparent when devaluation of a key currency that constituted a major reserve asset was in question. The basic problem of the 1950s and 1960s was systemic, not national.

Devaluation of the dollar would not have been a solution to the problems of the Bretton Woods system. Only a substantial increase in the price of gold would have eliminated its undervaluation. On the other hand, an adequate increase in the price of gold would have restored confidence in the dollar and, in the absence of a change in the system, resulted in a reflux of gold to the United States at the higher price. The international monetary system based on the new price of gold would have lasted only until the ensuing great expansion of liquidity and inflation once again threatened the dollar.[39]

The dark horse among the solutions offered at Bretton Woods was a proposal for a system of flexible exchange rates. That proposal, initially advanced after the Napoleonic Wars, and advocated in modified form by Fisher and Keynes, had been supported by Frank Graham and others in the 1940s. It received extensive attention after James Meade and Milton Friedman advocated it for the world economy in the 1950s. It was one of the four proposals discussed in the G-32 meetings[40] in 1964. In 1966 sixteen prominent economists endorsed a proposal for a system of flexible exchange rates.

This solution was expected to give each country monetary independence. Fixing the national rate of monetary expansion would give each country the rate of inflation it desired, and international differences in inflation rates would be managed by changes in exchange rates in the free market. The liquidity problem would be solved under flexible exchange rates by dispensing with the need for international reserves; the adjustment problem would be solved by using exchange rate changes to offset rigidities in money wage rates; and the confidence problem would be resolved by a free market in international reserve assets.[41]

---

39. As always, systems have to be compared against the alternatives. Despite the arguments against such an arrangement, raising the price of gold might have been better than the alternatives, including the one actually adopted. There are worse systems than one that requires a change in the price of the international monetary asset every generation or so.

40. See Machlup and Malkiel (1964). The other three proposals that received detailed discussion were the gold standard, a world central bank, and a system of currency areas or large floating blocs.

41. The facts proved otherwise. National demands for international reserves did not abate with flexible exchange rates. On the contrary, as Harrod had predicted even in the 1960s, countries needed more rather than less liquidity under flexible exchange rates because of the increase in uncertainty. Moreover, a flexible-exchange-rate world without an official standard would naturally use the dollar as the most important reserve asset, imposing, in the absence of capital movements, a current account deficit on the United States equal to the secular demand for reserves in the rest of the world.

Another proposal, one that stopped short of a world central bank, was to create a new international reserve asset to supplement gold. Several plans were made along these lines, including those by Sir Maxwell Stamp, Edward M. Bernstein, and Valéry Giscard d'Estaing. But there was both doubt about what the right solution was and an inability to negotiate that solution if it had been found. A solution along these lines would have required a sufficiently large splash of paper gold to eliminate its undervaluation. The amount of paper gold required would depend on whether or not paper gold would be used to replace dollar reserves. If so, the creation of perhaps $35 billion of paper gold (in the form of SDRs) would have been necessary. If dollars were to remain in reserves—and some dollars would have been required for working balances—perhaps a once-for-all increase of SDR10 billion would have been sufficient, followed by continued growth along the lines that were actually enacted (about SDR3 billion per year).

A combination of these measures would have yielded a more balanced solution with a better chance of success. The dollar could not in practice have been replaced by either gold or SDRs, but limits could be placed on the rate at which dollar holdings were increasing. Disincentives or penalties could, at least theoretically, be imposed on countries whose deficits or surpluses exceeded predetermined limits.[42] Combined with both a modest increase in the price of gold and the annual creation of SDRs, a restricted form of dollar-gold standard could have preserved the essentials of the Bretton Woods system. The solution actually adopted—the SDR—did nothing to prevent the demise of the system.[43]

The Collapse of the Bretton Woods System

The gold scarcity, misread as a US balance of payments deficit, generated expectations that the dollar price of gold might be raised; gold was naturally preferred to dollars. The US Treasury sold hundreds of millions of ounces of gold before finally restricting further dollar conversions in the mid–1960s. Even though the United States was formally committed to buying and selling gold freely under a 1949 agreement with the IMF (which absolved the United States from interven-

42. Penalties in the form of asset conversions would have to be negotiated in advance rather than imposed. At the Copenhagen meetings of the IMF in 1970, IMF Managing Director Pierre-Paul Schweitzer proposed that the major reserve country accept some gold losses in view of the state of its balance of payments—a proposal that resulted in the withdrawal of US support for Schweitzer's reappointment.

43. The collapse of Bretton Woods was stretched out over three episodes: 1968, when the market price of gold was severed from the official price and the members of the IMF withdrew from the private gold market; 1971, when the dollar became inconvertible; and 1973, when flexible exchange rates were adopted.

ing in the exchange market to preserve exchange rates), other countries accepted dollars without converting them into gold rather than risk US action to dismantle the system. The gold pool, formed in 1961 to allocate scarce gold[44] in the private market, was abandoned when, in 1968, demand in the private market overtook supply.

With the famous communiqué of 17 March 1968, the market price of gold was detached from the official price, creating what came to be called a two-tier system.[45] Gold became immobilized: no country wanted to sell gold for dollars when the official price was much below the market price. Countries now needed dollars to fill the vacuum created by the immobilization of gold. After an initial stint of tight money in 1969, dollars became plentiful when the recession of 1969–71 unfolded. A so-called overhang of dollars developed in Europe,[46] bringing on the mark crisis in the spring and the dollar crisis in the summer of 1971. After the Joint Economic Committee of the US Congress explicitly recommended devaluation of the dollar, foreign central banks requested gold conversions, and the United States responded by closing the gold window.

Gold now became officially, as it had already been *de facto*, inconvertible after 15 August 1971. At the Smithsonian meeting in December of that year, the dollar was devalued, raising the price of an ounce of gold to $38. Because the price of gold was much higher in the market, no transactions would take place at that price. President Richard M. Nixon called the Smithsonian Agreement the most important monetary agreement in the history of the world. Ironically, it was the first general monetary agreement establishing an international monetary system in which no currency would be convertible into one of the monetary metals.[47]

---

44. The gold pool, organized at the initiative of the United States, with the central banks of Belgium, France, Italy, the Netherlands, Switzerland, West Germany, and Great Britain, was actually a gentlemen's agreement to divide the burden of stabilizing the price of gold in the London gold market, with the United States having a 50 percent share. The Bank of England acted as agent for the pool in its market operations.

45. The communiqué stated that the seven members of the gold pool (France had dropped out in 1967) "decided no longer to supply gold to the London gold market or any other gold market" and further asserted that in view of the prospective establishment of the SDR, the existing stock of monetary gold was sufficient.

46. The accumulation of dollars by the rest of the world was partly desired to compensate for the immobility of gold; but US monetary policy was more expansive over the period 1965–73 than the countries on the European continent desired. Those countries had an excess supply of dollars, which, however, disappeared with the rising price level in the early 1970s.

47. Gold was still, however, legally used as a numeraire. A few days before the Smithsonian Agreement of 17–18 December 1971, Nixon and President Georges Pompidou of France met in the Azores and agreed that the United States would devalue in terms of gold. The dollar was devalued by 7.89 percent, raising the price of gold to $38 an ounce. The mark was appreciated by 4.61 percent against gold (13.58 percent in terms of the old dollar parity); the yen was raised 7.66 percent against gold (16.88 percent against the old dollar

The economic theory that treated the US balance of payments deficit as a national rather than a systemic problem prevailed at the Smithsonian meeting. "Plausible" elasticities based on back-of-the-envelope intuition were substituted into the Marshall-Lerner condition to suggest an exchange rate change of about 10 percent to 15 percent against other currencies, accomplished by a rise in the price of gold in the United States and a fall in the price of gold in other countries.[48]

The full implications of the Smithsonian Agreement, in establishing a fixed exchange rate system without asset convertibility, were by no means fully realized at the time. With a continuing US balance of payments deficit—wanted or unwanted—other countries had to accumulate dollars with no prospect for asset settlement. Confidence in the dollar, previously the only currency with some pretense to gold convertibility, was shaken. More important, the link to gold—fictitious though it may have been in terms of operational convertibility—had been an important background factor maintaining confidence in money and the international monetary system. The breakdown of the system undermined confidence in money and abetted inflationary expectations.

Every country in the world could now inflate (provided all countries did it at the same rate) without experiencing balance of payments deficits. The absence of an anchor—asset convertibility—undermined the effectiveness of balance of payments discipline and led to monetary policies that accommodated inflationary wage settlements and price increases. No sooner was the ink dry on the Smithsonian papers devaluing the dollar than the OPEC countries raised the dollar price[49] of oil; this proved to be a foretaste of more important events two years later.

The Smithsonian Agreement was an exercise in futility, enacted by politicians with at best a shallow knowledge of its full implications. It set in motion a train of events that would lead the world into the greatest monetary inflation in its history. The tiny devaluation, far from improving the US balance of payments,

---

parity). The other G-10 countries, with the exception of Canada, whose currency was left floating, revalued against the dollar, but some devalued against gold.

48. Exchange rate changes could not, as we have argued, remedy the systemic problem of the undervaluation of gold against all currencies. The Smithsonian Agreement failed to correct the basic problem of the undervaluation of gold, and in 1973 a second dollar crisis emerged, with another equally futile devaluation of the dollar. Only a few months after this devaluation, in June 1973, the system broke down into one of flexible exchange rates, removing what little monetary discipline remained. The subsequent increase in oil prices was quickly ratified by inflationary finance and the explosion of credit in the Eurodollar market.

49. The connection between the two events was brought home to me in January 1972, before the Smithsonian Agreement had been fully ratified. Participants at two independent meetings—one of OPEC ministers and the other of the Bellagio group of academics and officials—were lodged at the Intercontinental Hotel in Geneva, simultaneously debating the agreement from entirely different directions. The OPEC group then and there decided to raise the dollar price of oil in reaction to the increase in the dollar price of gold.

worsened it. Little more than a year later, the dollar was confronted with another crisis of confidence, which led in February 1973 to an equally futile second devaluation of the dollar. With the official dollar price of an ounce of gold put at $42.22, still far below the market price, confidence in the dollar did not recover. The United States and its trading partners were still using national weapons to deal with a systemic problem.

The failure of the second devaluation of the dollar to resolve the US balance of payments problems stirred up interest in a joint European float. This attempt in the spring of 1973 failed, however, because Britain would not join the float unless the surplus continental countries agreed to unlimited support of sterling. Failure to organize a joint European float in the face of persisting US deficits in the spring of 1973 led to the abandonment of the fixed exchange rate system and the advent of flexible exchange rates.

Flexible Exchange Rates

Flexible exchange rates had for some time been more popular among academics than among officials.[50] In the early 1970s, however, they received the powerful patronage of US Secretary of the Treasury George P. Shultz. After the Committee of 20 failed to find a solution through international monetary reform, it approved a regime of flexible exchange rates, leaving responsibility for containing inflation to individual countries.

Flexible exchange rates represented the antithesis of an international monetary system. Its advocates had argued that the exchange rate was a price "like any other price" and that any attempt to fix it would lead to disequilibrium and the need for controls. If, instead of the monetary coordination that is necessary in a currency area, countries fix monetary targets and let the exchange rate float, the balance of payments will be maintained in equilibrium. If the rate of monetary expansion is fixed at about the rate of growth (after due allowances for secular changes in the demand for money), monetary stability, price stability, and balance of payments equilibrium will be simultaneously achieved. It was believed that surpluses would result in appreciation, and deficits in depreciation of a currency, until equilibrium was restored. Speculative capital movements would tend to be stabilizing. Floating exchange rates would solve balance of payments problems.

Events did not turn out that way. There was a large gap between the theory and the practice of flexible exchange rates. At the end of 1973 (the year floating

---

50. They had been, like devaluation, an "unmentionable" at US Treasury consultants' meetings in the 1960s.

began) international reserves were $102.9 billion. By the end of 1989 foreign-exchange reserves were $542 billion, an increase of 426.7 percent. Over the same period, world imports rose from $542 billion to $2,974.6 billion, an increase of 443.2 percent. In other words, international foreign-exchange reserves rose by about the same multiple as world imports. The ratio of reserves to imports was 18.8 percent in 1973 and about the same at 18.22 percent in 1989. World reserves were just as high under flexible exchange rates as under the system of fixed exchange rates.

If the increase in reserves had been evenly spread among countries around the world, there would have been no implications for current account balances. But this was not the case. The bulk of the increase in reserves represented an increase in liabilities of the United States, financing a corresponding deficit in the US balance of payments.[51] The prediction that flexible exchange rates would eliminate balance of payments problems has not been fulfilled. Most countries have found it necessary to intervene in foreign-exchange markets and accumulate huge levels of reserves.

Important relevant features of the real world were left out of the models relating exchange rates to the balance of payments. International trade theory had developed largely on the assumption of either a symmetrical gold standard, a system in which national money is only used inside the nation, or currency areas where satellite countries hold the mother country's currency. Little attention had been paid, up to the 1960s, to the explicit introduction into theoretical models of massive movements of portfolio capital. Exchange rate theory was largely based on long-run real models with emphasis on the balance of trade and the elasticities of demand for imports and exports.

The elasticities approach to adjustment under flexible exchange rates was based mainly on a theory that did not take account of capital movements.[52] In the absence of capital movements, the theory of the balance of trade and that of the balance of payments is equivalent. If devaluation improves the balance of payments, it must do so by improving the balance of trade. Now it is easily shown in monetary models that devaluation tends to improve the balance of payments (e.g., through real balance effects); it would therefore improve the balance of trade if there were no capital movements. However, that conclusion does not

---

51. The gross US deficit, measured by the increase in liquid liabilities of the United States to foreign countries, has amounted to over $1 trillion dollars since 1973; total liabilities rose over the period from $92.5 billion to $1,101.7 billion. Over the same period, liquid external claims rose from $26.6 billion to $658 billion. On an official settlements basis alone, US liquid liabilities to foreign central banks and governments have increased from $66 billion to over $300 billion.

52. Although Bickerdike pays close attention to capital movements, his elasticity formula is restricted to the trade account.

follow if there is capital mobility. All that can be proved by the monetary theory of the exchange rate when there is capital mobility is the tendency for devaluation to improve the *sum* of the trade balance and the capital account.

If devaluation induces a capital inflow in excess of the improvement in the balance of payments, it will also induce a worsening of the current account of the country with the depreciating currency. To the extent that currency depreciation is not offset by changes in wage rates, the marginal efficiency of capital rises and the resulting capital inflow increases absorption and worsens the trade balance. Depreciation can also temporarily underprice capital assets and land relative to the products produced from them; this too raises the marginal efficiency of capital, attracting capital imports and worsening the trade balance. Instead of increasing exports of ordinary goods and services, depreciation can lead to the sale of financial and real assets, a worsened trade balance, and an increase in net international indebtedness.

Market exchange rates have been dominated, in the short run, by capital transactions rather than trade. Global imports and exports amounted to $5 trillion in 1989. But transactions in the foreign-exchange market were more than 30 times that amount.[53] Instead of reflecting trade accounts and inflation differentials, exchange rates are dominated by sustained swings based on speculative capital market transactions. This has led to gyrations of exchange rates that for substantial periods of time result in sustained variations from purchasing power parity. From being worth DM3.2 at the end of 1972, the dollar fell to DM1.73 at the end of 1979, then rose to DM3.15 at the end of 1984, only to fall again to DM1.58 at the end of 1987; it rose to DM1.78 the following year, and then once again fell to DM1.5 in October 1990. The swings were equally large against other major currencies.

The demand for dollar reserves, both on the part of central banks and governments and on the part of private financial institutions, continues steadily. In every year from 1960 to 1990 liquid dollar liabilities have increased. This would in itself be sufficient to create a trade deficit in the United States if it were not offset by income transfers or capital movements. Neither devaluation nor the fall of the dollar under flexible exchange rates in the 1970s eliminated the US balance of payments problem. The US dollar was still the major world currency asset; neither the SDR nor any other currency has proved an adequate substitute. As long as the United States continues in that role, it will be saddled with a balance of payments deficit whatever the exchange system.

Flexible exchange rates can, it is true, eliminate excess demand in the foreign-exchange market; and zero excess demand in the foreign-exchange market is an

---

53. Estimates of foreign-exchange market volume put it at over $600 billion per working day, which implies total yearly transactions of over $150 trillion.

alternative definition of the balance of payments. But rather than solving the basic problem of equilibrium for the United States in its national role and in the international monetary system, it transformed the problem into another form. Instead of worrying about the level of reserves, government officials worried about the path of the exchange rate; instead of concern over the balance of payments, they worried about the balance of trade or the current account balance.

Flexible exchange rates have probably produced a less efficient international trading system, in view of the wide departures from purchasing power parity and the great gyrations in nominal and real exchange rates that have occurred. Flexible rates have also resulted in a breakdown of the monetary discipline that prevailed under the gold exchange standard and even under the Bretton Woods system. It has not, however, resulted in the chaos that some of its critics predicted.

Currency Areas

One reason why the movement to flexible exchange rates did not result in chaos is that countries protected themselves by joining currency areas. It soon became apparent that it was not practical for all countries to adopt floating exchange rates. Currencies differ considerably from one another in terms of their liquidity, marketability, stability, and market power. Market power is an increasing function of the size of the transactions domain of a currency, relative to typical market shocks. Because transactions domains are related to national income, the hierarchy of currencies reflects economic size. Other things equal—especially policy credibility—the currencies with the strongest monetary properties are the largest economies.[54] Countries in the economic hinterland of large and stable countries can improve the monetary properties of their own currencies by attaching them at fixed exchange rates to that of the hegemon. In turn, the attachment of additional currencies to the lead currency reinforce the latter's monetary properties.[55]

Another important factor is the monetary will of a country and the record and reputation of its central bank. As Karl Otto Pöhl (1987) has said, ". . .credibility

---

54. The comparative monetary properties of a currency are related to the slopes of the liquidity preference schedules in each country, the absolute value of which is normally proportionate to size. See Mundell (1974).

55. The cumulative improvement in the monetary properties of a currency area as it expands leads to the theoretical proposition that the optimum number of currencies in the world is one. Flexible exchange rates have usually been presented, by their major proponents, as a second-best arrangement, a necessary real-world adaptation to overcome nominal wage rigidities arising from the existence of labor unions. There is, however, no reason to expect the zones of labor bargaining power to overlap with the domain of currencies.

is the capital stock of any central bank" (quoted in Frenkel et al. 1989, 194). Over the centuries, of course, Britain has had the longest record of a stable currency without a currency conversion; the reputation of the pound has been damaged by inflationary policies and depreciation in the postwar period, however, and the transactions area of the pound has declined to below 5 percent of world transactions.

The dollar has stood out among currencies since 1914, with respect to both stability and the size of its transactions area. In recent decades, however, Germany, Japan, and Switzerland have established reputations for dynamic economies, stable monetary policies, and strong currencies, with the consequent benefit of relatively low interest rates on financial assets denominated in their currencies. In terms of both transactions area and reputation, the world community has three monetary leaders: the United States, Germany, and Japan. In 1975, almost 80 percent of official holdings of foreign exchange was in dollars, with less than 7 percent in marks and less than 4 percent in pounds sterling. By 1988, however, dollars accounted for only 63.3 percent of official holdings, while the mark share had risen to 16 percent and the yen share had risen to over 7 percent; the pound sterling was a not-so-distant fourth with 3.1 percent. The possibility of large currency areas centered on the dollar, the mark, and the yen emerged as a more realistic alternative to a universal system of flexible exchange rates.[56]

The planned movement to flexible exchange rates never occurred. The international system did not become a truly flexible exchange rate system. There are at least three reasons why this is so. In the first place, few countries proved willing to abandon their foreign-exchange markets to the winds of speculation that would have blown freely under a clean float. As we have seen, countries built up foreign-exchange reserves to offset private fluctuations judged to be against the interests of the community.

Second, and more important, most countries merged themselves into one of a few great currency areas. The IMF makes monthly lists of currency areas, among which the most important are, of course, the dollar area and the ERM (exchange rate mechanism) of the European Community. Smaller countries have found it desirable to stabilize their currencies into optimum currency areas. Currency areas give members a chance to coordinate monetary policies and share the same inflation rate at the expense of ceding their monetary independence to

---

56. See Tavlas (1991). The rise of the mark is accounted for by the growth in activity of the European Monetary System (EMS) and the use of European currencies for intervention purposes. Tavlas supplies, among others, the following figures: dollars accounted for 71.5 percent of EMS intervention in 1979–82, but only 26.3 percent in 1986–87; the mark accounted for only 23.7 percent in the earlier period but 59 percent in the later period. As far as US intervention is concerned, almost 90 percent was in marks in 1979–82, with virtually all the rest in yen; but in 1986–87 the mark share fell to 57.5 percent and the yen share rose to 42.5 percent.

a group solution. From an abstract point of view, currency areas are second-best in relation to a world system, but they may be the best that can be achieved in the absence of a coordinated currency area for the whole world. Currency areas are stimulated by the gains involved in exploiting, by internalizing, an externality: the larger the currency area, the less vulnerable a single currency will be to outside shocks.[57]

Third, and perhaps most important, the existence of the dominant superpower currency has imparted a natural stability to the currency organization of the world economy. Despite the weakness of the dollar from time to time, the huge US deficits, and the buildup of a huge international debtor position, the dollar remains at the center of the system. That position—especially now that Great Britain has opted for the ERM—could be dislodged if the European countries form a continental currency; that possibility is neither remote nor on the other hand highly probable. Until that event comes to pass, the dollar will play the leading role in the foreign-exchange markets.

The history of the international monetary system from 1973 to the present has not been dominated by a system of flexible exchange rates; its central theme has been the dollar against the mark (and its currency associates) and the yen; the exchange rates of these currencies are by far the most important in the world. The next most important exchange rate has been the dollar price of gold, changes in which are frequently looked to as a signal of changes in expectations about inflation.

The era of flexible exchange rates came to an end in 1985 when the United States and the other G-5 countries decided to coordinate exchange rates and allow, or induce, a depreciation of the dollar against the major currencies. This shift to coordinated rates at the G-7 Louvre meetings in 1987 reinforced the shift away from flexible exchange rates toward a system in which exchange rates are coordinated according to the goals of G-7 policy. It is interesting that, twenty years after the breakdown of the Bretton Woods system, the concern at G-7 meetings is still the relation between the dollar and the other currencies, with little attention paid to the other bilateral rates. In this respect the G-7 discussions have turned into dollar management sessions.

Instability of the Real Exchange Rate

Under the comparatively fixed exchange rates of the Bretton Woods system, real exchange rate fluctuations were minor. Under the flexible rate system, however,

---

57. There is nothing automatic about the advantages of a large currency area to a single country. It depends, among other things, on whether the prospective partner already has a more stable monetary policy than the existing members; or more exactly whether the new currency area will have a more stable monetary policy than the individual prospective member. The ERM system offers a good example of how some countries whose currencies

real exchange rates fluctuated a great deal. Substantial evidence suggests that changes in nominal exchange rates induced substantial changes in real exchange rates. To the extent that nominal exchange rates fluctuated excessively, that instability was transmitted to real exchange rates.

The dollar's episodes of overshooting have been followed by episodes of undershooting, with disequilibrium prices and efficiency losses in between. Taking 1985 = 100, the US real exchange rate, as measured by the IMF, was 79 in 1976, 68.1 in 1979, 100 in 1985, 64.1 in 1988, 67.8 in the third quarter of 1989, and 62.3 in July 1990. These fluctuations in competitiveness have had the effect of alternating profitability between domestic and international industries according to the whims of international capital movements that have little or nothing to do with international trade or even the balance of trade.[58]

Three observations can be made about the depreciation of the dollar, its effect on the real exchange rate, and the change in the balance of trade[59] since 1985: the real measured exchange rate of the dollar has closely tracked the nominal exchange rate; the real exchange rates of other countries have not followed their nominal rates as closely; and interest rates seem to have played a role in the direction of the discrepancy between real and nominal rates. Countries like Canada and Great Britain, where interest rates have been higher than in the United States, seem to have worsened their competitive position, judged by the real exchange rate, relative to countries like Germany and Japan, which have had lower interest rates.

With the exchange rate dramatically falling in the late 1970s, then rising in the first half of the 1980s, and then falling again in the second half of the 1980s, the trade balance seems to have been governed by forces other than exchange rates. In the early 1980s it was tempting to associate the rising dollar with the

---

previously experienced more inflation than the mark have been able to use the system as a political club for a more stable monetary policy.

58. The real exchange rate seems to have been an innocent victim of speculation and erratic monetary policy. After the 1979 oil price increase, the United States adopted an easy monetary policy to try to prevent the economy from falling into a recession in the 1980 election year; the result was too much inflation and an undervalued dollar. The rise of the nominal and the real exchange rate in the first Reagan term was motivated by five factors: a corrective of preceding inflationary policies; reflux into the dollar from foreign currencies as confidence was restored; an increase in capital imports as the Kemp-Roth tax cuts raised the marginal efficiency of capital in the United States; anti-inflationary overkill by an overzealous Federal Reserve Chairman (Paul A. Volcker) as a reaction against the presumed effect of the tax cut on the budget deficit; and an underestimation by the influential Friedman wing of the Republican Party of the increase in demand for money at home (reduction in velocity) due to a reduction in the rate of expected inflation. There was little or no attention given to the role of the real exchange rate in these deliberations, and little thought to the harmful consequences of arbitrary fluctuations in the real exchange rate.

59. The first two of these observations were made to me by Herbert Grubel.

worsening trade balance, and to expect a reversal of the exchange rate to correct the trade balance. That, however, has not occurred. Sharp-eyed economists claim to see an important reduction in the trade deficit, vindicating, they hope, the elasticities school. But a far more interesting observation is that the deficit has been remarkably stubborn.

Secular forces are at work. The trade balance has been in deficit since 1975. Three stylized facts stand out:

- The trade deficit jumped from a period of average balance in the period 1970–75 to a plateau ranging between $25 billion and $33 billion in the period 1977–82. As a percentage of GNP the balance was + 0.56 in 1975 and − 0.53 in 1976, but − 1.56 in 1977, − 1.51 in 1978, − 1.10 in 1979, − 0.92 in 1980, and − 1.15 in 1982.

- The trade deficit jumped again after 1982. As a percentage of GNP it stood at − 1.97 in 1983, − 2.98 in 1984, − 3.04 in 1985, − 3.42 in 1986, − 3.52 in 1987, − 2.61 in 1988, and − 2.16 in 1989. The figures for 1990 are not available as of this writing, but the deficit is not likely to be below 2 percent of GNP.

- The increase in the deficit, as a percentage of GNP, from the period 1977–82 to the period 1983–89 was slightly larger than the increase in the deficit from the period 1970–76 to the period 1977–82. It rose by 1 percent of GNP in the period 1977–82 from its level of the early 1970s, but by 1.8 percent of GNP in the period 1983–89 from the period 1977–82.

As already noted, the deficit has stubbornly resisted changes in both the nominal and the real exchange rate. The fluctuations in the dollar did not occur as a result of conscious policy aimed at changing the real exchange rate. The turnaround in the dollar came in February 1985 as a consequence of an earlier reversal of monetary policy, aimed at the domestic economy. In the summer and fall of the election year 1984, the recovery was petering out and a recession was widely predicted. As growth in the economy slowed, the Federal Reserve eased, first halting and then reversing the soaring dollar. The dollar had already fallen substantially by the time of the Plaza meeting in September 1985, from DM3.4 in February to DM2.5. The Plaza Agreement, designed to preempt growing protectionist pressure in the Congress, did not involve any major changes in policy in the United States beyond the comparatively easy money stance of the Federal Reserve enacted earlier. Most of the burden of lowering the yen-dollar rate fell on Japanese monetary policy. In the subsequent year, the fall in oil prices probably had greater impact on the yen-dollar rate than any further changes in policies.

If there is to be correction of the US current account deficit, there must be a decline in current account surpluses, or an increase in deficits, in the rest of the world. In a competition for reduced deficits or increased surpluses, which countries are likely candidates to give way by enough to match a substantial reduction in the US deficit?

It is not easy to find candidates for substantially increased deficits or reduced surpluses in the rest of the world. Countries must have assets to sell that other countries are willing to buy. From a welfare standpoint, it might be desirable to shift US deficits to the developing countries. But these countries lack sufficient creditworthy debt instruments that potential surplus countries are inclined to accumulate. Equity transfers have proved to have at best limited prospects.

There will probably be a continuing surplus of export capital from the Asian Four Tigers (Hong Kong, Korea, Singapore, and Taiwan), with North America as the main target. An improvement in the US balance would probably require some reduction in the export surpluses of these countries.

Another possibility is for needy Eastern European countries to "take over" the US deficits. But these countries have a creditworthiness problem similar to that of the developing countries. There is, of course, considerable scope for the surplus countries, and especially Germany, to shift surpluses to Eastern Europe, particularly to what was formerly East Germany. Some reduction in the German trade surplus can be expected on this account.

A correction of the US trade deficit therefore depends primarily on a reduction in Japanese and German surpluses. What are the prospects? The overall Japanese surplus was $56 billion in 1985, $92.8 billion in 1986, $96.4 billion in 1987, $95 billion in 1988, and $77.1 billion in 1989; because of the increase in the price of oil, it is probable that the Japanese surplus will be reduced in 1990. In Germany, the surplus was $28.5 billion in 1985, $55.7 billion in 1986, $69.9 billion in 1987, $79.4 billion in 1988, and $76.7 billion in 1989. Because of the expenses of absorbing East Germany, the German surplus, as already noted, will drop further in 1990 and thereafter. There are therefore some grounds for optimism that a reduction in the German and the Japanese surpluses will be achieved, making room for a further reduction in the US current account deficit.

Two other factors will play an important role. The budget deficit, which is increasing because of rising government expenditures and sagging growth, will be a factor worsening the trade deficit. On the other hand, the demographic factor, as the decade unfolds, will raise the net saving rate and reduce capital imports, perhaps creating a renewal of the net lending that was a US tradition from 1915 to the 1970s. Improvements in the trade balance due to demographics are sufficiently promising to make overt policies designed to improve the trade balance unnecessary.

References

Angell, James W. 1926. *The Theory of International Prices*. Cambridge, MA: Harvard University Press.

Bazdarich, M. 1978. "Optimal Growth and Stages in the Balance of Payments." *Journal of International Economics* 8:425–43.

Bergsten, C. Fred. 1975. *The Dilemmas of the Dollar*. New York: New York University Press.

Bickerdike, C.F. 1906. "The Theory of Incipient Taxes." *Economic Journal* 16 (December).

Bickerdike, C.F. 1907. "Protective and Preferential Import Duties." *Economic Journal* 17 (March).

Bickerdike, C.F. 1920. "The Instability of Foreign Exchange." *Economic Journal* 30 (March): 118–22.

Bordo, Michael D., and Finn E. Kydland. 1990. "The Gold Standard as a Rule." *NBER Working Paper* 3367 (May). Cambridge, MA: National Bureau of Economic Research.

Bordo, Michael D., and Eugene N. White. 1990. *A Tale of Two Currencies: British and French Finance during the Napoleonic Wars* (mimeographed, August).

Cairnes, J.E. 1874. *Some Leading Principles of Political Economy Newly Expounded*. London.

Cassel, Gustav. 1925. "The Restoration of Gold as a Universal Monetary Standard." In John P. Young, ed., *European Currency and Finance*, 205–06. Washington: Government Printing Office.

Chipman, John. 1989. "On the Concept of International Competitiveness." Paper presented at a meeting of the Eastern Economic Association, Baltimore, 4 March.

Clement, Simon. 1695. *A Discourse of the General Notions of Money, Trade, and Exchanges*.

Crowther, G. 1957. *Balances and Imbalances of Payments*. Boston: Harvard University Press.

Dimand, Robert W. 1988. *The Origins of the Keynesian Revolution*. Stanford: Stanford University Press.

Edgeworth, F.Y. 1908. "Applications of Mathematical Theories." *Economic Journal* 18 (December): 541–56.

Fischer, Stanley, and Jacob A. Frenkel. 1974a. "Economic Growth and Stages of the Balance of Payments." In George Horwich and Paul A. Samuelson, eds., *Trade, Stability and Macroeconomics: Essays in Honor of Lloyd A. Metzler*, 503–21. New York: Academic Press.

Fischer, Stanley, and Jacob A. Frenkel. 1974b. "Interest Rate Equalization and Patterns of Production, Trade and Consumption in a Two-Country Growth Model." *The Economic Record* (December): 555–79.

Frenkel, Jacob A., Morris Goldstein, and Paul A. Masson. 1989. "International Dimensions of Monetary Policy: Coordination versus Autonomy." In *Monetary Policy Issues in the 1990s*, 183–33. Kansas City: Federal Reserve Bank of Kansas City.

Halevi, Nadav. 1971. "An Empirical Test of the 'Balance of Payments Stages' Hypothesis." *Journal of International Economics* 1:103–17.

Host-Madsen, Paol. 1962. "Asymmetries Between Balance of Payments Surpluses and Deficits." *Staff Papers* 9:182–99. Washington: International Monetary Fund.

Keynes, J.M. 1923. *A Tract on Monetary Reform*. London: Macmillan.

Kindleberger, Charles P. 1985. *Keynesianism vs. Monetarism and Other Essays in Financial History*. London: Allen & Unwin.

Kojima, Kiyoshi. 1990. "Proposal for a Multiple Key Currency Gold-Exchange Standard." *Journal of Asian Economics* 1, no. 1: 19–33.

Machlup, Fritz, and Burton Malkiel, eds. 1964. *International Monetary Arrangements: The Problem of Choice*. Princeton: International Finance Section, Princeton University.

Manzocchi, Stefano. 1990. "Stages in the Balance of Payments: A Survey of the Neoclassical Theory." *Economic Notes* 397–416. Siena, Italy: Monte dei Paschi di Siena.

Marshall, Alfred. 1925. *Memorials of Alfred Marshall*. New York: Augustus M. Kelley.

Mundell, Robert A. 1965. *The International Monetary System: Conflict and Reform*. Montreal: Private Planning Association of Canada.

Mundell, Robert A. 1968a. *Man and Economics*. New York: McGraw-Hill.

Mundell, Robert A. 1968b. *International Economics*. New York: Macmillan.

Mundell, Robert A. 1968c. "A Plan for a World Currency." Paper presented at a hearing of the Joint Economic Committee, Subcommittee on International Exchange and Payments, Washington, 9 September.

Mundell, Robert A. 1974. "The Optimum Balance of Payments Deficit and the Monetary Theory of Empires." In P. Salin and E. Claassen, eds., *Stabilization Policies in Independent Economies*, 69–86. Amsterdam: North-Holland.

Mundell, Robert A. 1979. "Balance of Trade, Transfers, and Money: The Sixteen Approaches to Balance of Payments Analysis." Paper presented at the First International Conference on the Financial Development of Latin America and the Caribbean, sponsored by the Inter-American Institute of Capital Markets, Carabellada, Venezuela, 26–28 February.

Mundell, Robert A. 1988. "Latin American Debt and the Transfer Problem." In P. Brock, M. Connolly, and C. Gonzalez-Vega, eds., *Latin American Debt and Adjustment: External Shocks and Macroeconomic Policies*. New York: Praeger.

Mundell, Robert A. 1989a. "Trade Balance Patterns as Global General Equilibrium: The Seventeenth Approach to the Balance of Payments." *Rivista di Politica Economica* 79, no. 6 (June): 9–60.

Mundell, Robert A. 1989b. "The Global Adjustment System." *Rivista di Politica Economica* 79, no. 12 (December): 351–466.

Mundell, Robert A. 1990. "The International Distribution of Saving: Past and Future." *Rivista di Politica Economica* 80, no. 10:5–56.

Mundell, Robert A. 1991. "Fiscal Policy and the Theory of International Trade." In H. Giersch, ed., *Proceedings of the Sohmen Memorial Conference, Tegernsee, Bavaria.* Heidelberg: Springer (forthcoming).

Mundell, Robert A., and John McCallum, eds. 1990. "Global Disequilibrium in the World Economy." *Rivista di Politica Economica* 79, no. 12.

Mundell, Robert A., and Alexander Swoboda. 1969. *Monetary Problems of the International Economy.* Chicago: University of Chicago Press.

Neher, Philip A. 1970. "International Capital Movements and Balanced Growth Paths." *Economic Record* 46: 393–401.

Onitsuka, Yusuke. 1970. *International Capital Movements and Patterns of Economic Growth.* Unpublished doctoral dissertation, University of Chicago.

Onitsuka, Yusuke. 1974. "International Capital Movements and the Patterns of Economic Growth." *American Economic Review* 64, no. 1 (March): 24–36.

Patinkin, Don, and J. Clark Leith, eds. 1978. *Keynes, Cambridge and the General Theory.* Toronto: University of Toronto Press.

Phelps, Edmund S. 1990. *Seven Schools of Macroeconomic Thought: The Arne Ryds Memorial Lectures.* Oxford: Clarendon Press.

Pöhl, Karl Otto. 1987. "Cooperation—A Keystone for the Stability of the International Monetary System." First Arthur Burns Memorial Lecture at the American Council on Germany, New York, 2 November.

Robertson, Dennis H. 1938–39a. "Indemnity Payments and Gold Movements." *Quarterly Journal of Economics* 53 (February):312–14.

Robertson, Dennis H. 1938–39b. "A Rejoinder." *Quarterly Journal of Economics* 53 (February): 317.

Schumpeter, Joseph A. 1954. *History of Economic Analysis.* New York: Oxford University Press.

Swoboda, Alexander. 1989. "Global Disequilibrium and International Monetary Reform." *Rivista di Politica Economica* 79, no. 12:39–56.

Taussig, Frank W. 1927. *International Trade.* New York: Macmillan.

Tavlas, George S. 1991. "On the International Use of Currencies: The Case of the Deutsche Mark." *Essays in International Finance.* Princeton: Princeton University Press (forthcoming).

Triffin, Robert. 1960. *Gold and the Dollar Crisis: The Future of Convertibility.* New Haven, CT: Yale University Press.

Viner, Jacob. 1937. *Studies in the Theory of International Trade*. New York: Harper and Row.

Viner, Jacob. 1938–39. "A Reply [to Robertson]." *Economic Journal* 53 (February): 314–17.

Wilson, Roland. 1931. *Capital Imports and the Terms of Trade*.

Comment

John Williamson

The standard theory of how exchange rates influence trade is what Robert Mundell describes in his paper as the "direct approach." I strongly endorse his proposal to substitute this term for "elasticities approach," a nomenclature that may give the false impression that the mainstream model fails to incorporate income effects. I only wish that Mundell had continued to use his new terminology in the rest of his paper. This direct approach is what Paul Krugman lays out in his admirable background paper for this conference (chapter 1) and more formally in the concluding paper in this volume (chapter 8). Most important, it is this direct approach that is embodied in the macroeconometric models.

The attractions of the direct approach are perhaps most evident if one contemplates the problems involved in trying to put into practice one of the more indirect approaches among the 16 that Mundell describes. It would of course be possible to predict the Zambian balance of payments in 1991 by intitially estimating income and expenditure for every country in the world except Zambia for every year from 1992 until infinity. One would then take the differences between estimated income and expenditure to derive the implied set of trade balances, integrate these over time to get the implied net asset positions as of the start of 1992, subtract those from 1991 net asset positions to calculate the implicit 1991 trade balances, and add those trade balances up to get the Zambian trade balance for 1991 as a residual.

Although in principle possible, this procedure does have two disadvantages from the standpoint of the practicing forecaster. One is that because it repeatedly involves estimating outcomes as the small net difference between two large gross magnitudes, it carries a danger that the answer may not be very accurate. The other disadvantage is that it involves a lot of work.

The more promising direct approach specifies the trade balance as the difference between the value of exports and the value of imports:

$$TB = p_x X(Y^*/Q^*, RER)Q - p_m M(Y/Q, RER)Q$$

where TB = trade balance, p_x = export price, X = export volume, Y = real income (output or expenditure), Q = productive capacity, p_m = import price,

John Williamson is a Senior Fellow at the Institute for International Economics. He has served as Advisor to the International Monetary Fund and Economic Consultant to the UK Treasury.

M = import volume, RER = real exchange rate, and a starred variable denotes a world total.

There are two approaches to defining the real exchange rate. One approach specifies $RER = ep*/p$, where $p*$ and p refer to output prices (views differ on the index that should be used to measure output prices, which is why the International Monetary Fund's statistics give one a choice of five) and e to the exchange rate, measured as units of domestic currency per unit of foreign exchange. The other specifies $RER = p_t/p_n$, where p_t is the price of tradeables and p_n is the price of nontradeables. The first measure gives the relative price of two national outputs, the direct analogy to the definition of the nominal exchange rate as the relative price of two national monies, and is that found in the IMF statistics. The second stems from the "dependent economy model."

The first measure has usually been thought more relevant to explaining the trade of industrial countries, which consists predominantly of differentiated manufactures whose price is set by the producer, who then meets demand generated at that price. The second is more usually applied to the trade of primary producing countries, who sell in a perfectly competitive market and whose output is determined from the supply side. It would perhaps be worth trying to use both measures together rather than treat them as alternatives; indeed, such an approach might be one way of addressing Stephen Marris's complaints (during the conference's panel discussion) about the failure to incorporate profitability considerations into the standard analysis. On the other hand, this might not add much explanatory power, inasmuch as under most circumstances the one measure is a monotonic transformation of the other.

It is well understood that the trade balance equation is merely one equation in a general-equilibrium model. Most of us make the appropriate allowances for that fact most of the time when we apply the equation. We are, however, mortal, and so we occasionally slip up; but most economists are in my experience very willing to recognize their error and amend their ways when their error is pointed out to them.

One familiar criticism of the usefulness of exchange rate policy in contributing to adjustment is the charge that a nominal exchange rate change is unable to alter the real exchange rate. Monetary theory tells us that this is true under certain classic conditions: with no money illusion, in the long run, starting from a position of full equilibrium, with passive money or a gold-standard monetary policy, and with no other force (like fiscal policy) to curtail demand. The converse of those conditions defines when nominal exchange rate changes *will* influence the real exchange rate, and thus the division of spending between domestic and foreign sources of supply, and of output between the domestic and foreign markets.

The presence of money illusion is not usually judged a very interesting case. Neither is an influence that is limited to the short run. Of greater interest is the proposition that the real exchange rate will not necessarily return to its initial level if we start from a disequilibrium position: thus, a nominal exchange rate change may play a helpful role in accelerating adjustment and easing the transition by returning the real exchange rate to equilibrium more rapidly. Finally, most relevant of all, a nominal devaluation can be made to stick if it encounters an inelastic money supply (thus allowing a real balance effect to result from the devaluation-induced inflation) or an accompanying fiscal adjustment. The belief that exchange rate changes *must* be neutralized by induced inflation in the absence of money illusion is simply wrong.

The other traditional basis for questioning the potency of exchange rate policy is the charge that a permanent real devaluation may fail to lead to an improvement in the trade balance, given the dependence of the trade balance on both trade prices and quantities. It is well known that whether or not this is true depends on what most of us were brought up to call the Marshall-Lerner condition (although Mundell tells us it should really be called the Bickerdike-Edgeworth condition), with real income held constant. The condition is *a priori* satisfied for primary producing countries, which face an infinite demand elasticity for their exports. Much empirical evidence confirms that it is also satisfied for industrial countries (which face a finite export demand elasticity, so that the validity of the proposition is indeed an empirical matter).

All this is well known and consistent with what is incorporated in just about every macroeconometric model. I attach a great deal of significance to that consistency. Macroeconometric models are not perfect, and they are constantly being improved, but they do constitute a systematic assembly of such collective wisdom as the profession can muster. A recent Brookings study (Bryant et al. 1988) provides an invaluable summary of current consensus views. Assertions that exchange rate changes do not work, either because they are automatically neutralized by inflation or because the Marshall-Lerner condition is not satisfied, fly in the face of that consensus.

Moreover, the present conference has brought further evidence that the models are continuing to track payments balances reasonably satisfactorily. Yet essentially the only reason that Mundell gives for rejecting the conclusion of the models about the critical role that exchange rates play in achieving adjustment is that the US payments balance weakened on a decade-by-decade basis, moving into deficit after 1975, despite the depreciation of the dollar after 1971. Of course, lots of other things were happening in the world simultaneously, which the models attempt to sort out in a way that a casual historical comparison cannot hope to. The models imply that, after taking those other things into account, real depreciation does indeed have the expenditure-switching effect claimed by standard theory.

In recognizing that the evidence is that exchange rate changes work, there are certain things that are *not* being claimed. First, it is not being claimed that *any* depreciation will improve the balance of payments (or even the current account or the trade balance), even if the real exchange rate depreciates "permanently." In particular, a real depreciation engineered by monetary expansion will have a positive income effect that tends to offset the trade gain from a more competitive real exchange rate, and the empirical evidence is that typically the two effects are roughly offsetting. Second, it is certainly not being said that *only* depreciation can improve the balance of payments: recession, an oil price change, differential inflation, foreign growth relative to capacity—the list of alternative relevant variables is long. Finally, it is certainly not being claimed that the effect of a depreciation on the balance of payments can be judged independently of what caused it. Bryant et al. estimate, for example, that a 10 percent dollar depreciation will improve the US current account by about $7 billion if the depreciation results from a fiscal contraction, about $1 billion if it is caused by a portfolio shift, and zero if it is caused by a monetary expansion. The differences depend on how income is behaving, as a result of what is going on in the rest of the general-equilibrium model.

What one fundamentally means by saying that exchange rate changes work is that (in the absence of a fortuitous positive shock) an increased outward transfer with the maintenance of "full employment" (that is, unemployment remaining at some constant level like the nonaccelerating-inflation rate) will require a real depreciation. It is perfectly true that the literature contains patho-logical cases where a real depreciation is unnecessary, or even where a real appreciation might be required. Mundell's paper describes the most famous of these cases, namely, Ohlin's model where the sum of the marginal import propensities is greater than or equal to unity. But this does not correspond to what has been found by the econometricians when they have estimated macroeconomic models, which is why one has to label it a pathological case. The "victory" of the income-expenditure school was a victory only to those who are prepared to disregard empirical evidence.

The models do not say that adjustment would have been impossible at the exchange rates prevailing in February 1985. What they certainly do imply is that adjustment would have been so horrendously costly, in terms of excessive unemployment in the United States and the rekindling of inflation in Japan and Germany, that it is inconceivable that it would ever have happened without the return of the dollar to a realistic value.

In an interesting discussion, Mundell claims that depreciation may generate a current account deficit rather than a surplus, since greater competitiveness may be expected to increase the marginal efficiency of investment and thus stimulate investment spending and a capital inflow, which will tend to divert exports to the home market and suck in more imports. This may appear paradoxical, but in fact it constitutes no conflict at all with the standard analysis, provided one recognizes that the economy must either have been below full employment before the depreciation or be above full employment after the depreciation.

The standard analysis has strong policy implications for one current issue. Consider the hope that Germany will be able to draw on the resources that have been going into its external surplus in order to finance the reconstruction of eastern Germany. Can this be achieved by an "immaculate transfer," or must a real appreciation of the deutsche mark be a part of the process? A disproportionate part of eastern German demand is directed toward West German goods (45 percent of Austrian imports come from West Germany, and the figure is surely higher for the former East Germany). This is causing strong expansionary pressures in West Germany. But the West German economy was already operating at close to full capacity, so this increased demand is prone to generate a renewal of inflationary pressures. Some of the increased demand is currently spilling over into imports and so reducing the German surplus, but without a real appreciation of the deutsche mark to switch expenditure from German to foreign goods there will certainly be inflationary pressures in West Germany (unless the German government raises taxes after the December 1990 election, which would deny the hope of running down the external surplus to finance the reconstruction of the East).[1]

Since 1989 the deutsche mark has duly appreciated versus the dollar to help the adjustment process, just as the doctor ordered. But its appreciation vis-à-vis the other currencies in the European exchange rate mechanism is being blocked by its partners. This is confronting the Bundesbank with a choice between acquiescing in a corrective inflation that might threaten the very basis of the European Monetary System, namely, the anti-inflationary credibility of the Bundesbank, and imposing an increase in interest rates that would be excessively high for the rest of the ERM countries to match without creating a recession. One can be sympathetic to the aim of creating a monetary union in Europe and still believe that, until monetary union is actually achieved and the benefits are being reaped, it is silly to insist on paying the costs, of which the main one will be the inability to use exchange rate changes to facilitate adjustment to differential real shocks (European Commission 1990).

The case for European monetary union (EMU) has been argued partly on the ground that Europe is unlikely to suffer important differential real shocks in the future. It happens, however, that it *is* confronting one right now. A refusal to use the exchange rate instrument in this historically unique circumstance, where it is so clearly called for, just could discredit the very idea of EMU.[2]

---

1. The Kohl government did in fact raise taxes after the election, but not by enough to avoid inflationary pressures.

2. Of course, if the Europeans have the good sense to recognize the need for a realignment to facilitate adjustment to German unification, it will be important to emphasize that the reason for the realignment is a differential real shock rather than a revival of the differential inflation that has been responsible for almost all past realignments.

I see little to be gained by returning to the battles of twenty years ago and resuming the debate about whether it would have been necessary to raise the gold price, to create a supplement to gold, or to improve the adjustment mechanism in a manner consistent with the new reality of capital mobility, in order to save the essence of the Bretton Woods system (a goal that Mundell and I shared). It still seems to me crystal-clear that the first "solution" would have aggravated the confidence problem in anything but the very short run, and therefore that the need was for a combination of the other two approaches. Since the Special Drawing Right was created to address the second problem, the missing element was the third, which required adoption of a crawling peg (*not* a one-time dollar devaluation of 10 percent as actually happened). But obviously I am no closer to convincing Mundell of these truths than I was in 1970.

Let me conclude by returning from policy questions, present or past, to perhaps the most interesting of the theoretical issues raised by Mundell, namely, the determination of capital flows. This is a field where theory is not in the relatively satisfactory state that it is in regard to the current account. I was fascinated to discover that, in casting around for more basic explanations than interest differentials, Mundell focused on the same two ideas that I utilize in a forthcoming study (Williamson, forthcoming): the "stages theory" and demographic differences between countries. He also introduces fiscal factors as a third approach, which is again entirely natural in his context (although it would have been misplaced in my analysis, which was essentially normative). My only caveat is that he seems to treat these approaches as *competitive* with the role that exchange rates play in adjusting the current account. To my way of thinking they are complementary: the stages theory, demographics, and fiscal imbalances help explain capital flows, and exchange rate changes help the current account to adjust to transfer the capital flow.

References

Bryant, R.C., D. Henderson, G. Holtham, P. Hooper, and S.A. Symanski. 1988. *Empirical Macroeconomics for Interdependent Economies*. Washington: Brookings Institution.

European Commission. 1990. "One Market, One Money." *European Economy* 44 (whole issue, October).

Williamson, John. *Equilibrium Exchange Rates: An Update*. Washington: Institute for International Economics (forthcoming).

6

Why No Hard Landing?

Why No Hard Landing?

Stephen Marris

It is now five years since my book *Deficits and the Dollar: The World Economy at Risk* (Marris 1985)[1] was published, and I have been asked to write a postmortem. As such, however, postmortems can be pretty boring. So, in addition to reviewing the events of the past five years, I will try in this paper to pick out those aspects of my analysis—both those that turned out to be right and, more interestingly, those that unanticipated developments rendered obsolete or were simply wrong—that I feel would be especially relevant for someone sitting down today to write a book about the prospects for the world economy in the 1990s.

The central thesis of D&D was that ". . .on present policies, a hard landing has become inevitable for the dollar and the world economy. The dollar will, over time, go down too far and there will be an unpleasant world recession" (D&D, lv). More specifically, ". . .as confidence in the dollar ebbed, strong upward pressure on US interest rates would lead to a recession in the United States. This recession, combined with the weak dollar, would have a very negative impact on growth both in Europe and Japan, and in the indebted developing countries, and hence would spread out through the world economy" (D&D, xxi).

Obviously, the purpose of making such a dire prophecy was the hope that it might prove self-denying: that by influencing thinking in official circles it could help to promote a shift to policies that would produce the right answer, as set out in chapter 7 of the book. There are therefore two questions to be answered: How far did events conform to the analysis? And how far, when they did not, was this because policies were changed in the recommended direction?

---

1. The book originally appeared in December 1985. An updated version was published in September 1987. References in this paper are to the later version, using the abbreviation "D&D."

Stephen Marris is Senior Fellow in Europe with the Institute for International Economics. He is a former Economic Advisor to the Secretary-General of the Organization for Economic Cooperation and Development.

To summarize briefly: There was no hard landing. Instead, events over the last five years conformed in most major respects quite closely to the "cooperative" scenario set out in the book. Unanticipated events, most notably the sharp drop in oil prices in 1986, contributed to this favorable outcome. But so also did a significant shift in policies along the lines I—and many others—had recommended.

Today the United States' twin deficits, fiscal and external, no longer pose a major threat to the world economy. Indeed, if one looks beyond the current cyclical slowdown, the prospects for the real world economy in the 1990s look quite good. In the financial sphere, on the other hand, problems are likely to arise because the present ad hoc exchange rate regime for the major currencies is an unsatisfactory and fragile compromise between fixity and flexibility.

More worrisome, as we enter a decade in which, if all goes well on the political front, there should be a worldwide surge in investment, are some disquieting signs that the propensity to save in the developed countries may be being undermined by an unhealthy interaction between financial deregulation and financial innovation at the domestic and the international level. If so, and leaving aside the major geopolitical uncertainties, a shortage of world savings could, after several false alarms, prove to be the most serious threat to an otherwise moderately optimistic assessment of the prospects for the world economy in the 1990s.

Retrospect

The Dollar and the US Economy

Up to the end of 1987, both the timing and the magnitude of the dollar's decline followed quite closely the path set out in the hard-landing scenario in D&D, in terms of both the trade-weighted index and the bilateral rates against the major currencies. Since then the dollar has fluctuated around an average level nearer to the terminal level projected in the cooperative scenario than to that in the hard-landing scenario (figure 1).

There were two episodes of quite severe financial turbulence in 1987, but there was no financial crunch of a magnitude and duration sufficient to push the US economy into recession, as predicted in D&D. On the contrary, a sustained expansion continued for five years after the dollar began to go down, and only began to falter in the middle of 1990.

This soft landing for the US economy occurred despite the fact that the kind of decisive action recommended in D&D to eliminate the federal budget deficit was not taken. There was, however, a sharp decline in the structural deficit in 1987 (by 0.8 percent of GNP), which came, conveniently but coincidentally, just

Figure 1 Nominal effective dollar exchange rates: actual and in D&D, 1984–90

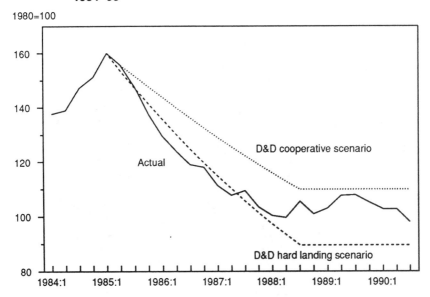

Source: D&D and International Monetary Fund, *International Financial Statistics,* various issues.

when the real trade balance began to improve sharply. Buoyant growth also reduced the cyclical component of the deficit by another 1 percent of GNP between 1986 and 1988.

Thus, between 1986 and 1989 the federal deficit fell from 4.9 percent to 2.8 percent of GNP, which certainly helped to ease the pressure on the US invest-ment-saving balance. Indeed, it could be argued that without this decline—especially the sharp drop in 1987 when confidence in the financial markets was very fragile—it would not have been possible to avoid a hard landing.

The dollar's decline, which halved its value against the yen and the deutsche mark, had a major impact on the US trade and current account balances. In the D&D baseline projection, in which the dollar was assumed to remain at its average level of the six months to March 1985, the current account deficit was expected to rise to $320 billion by 1990; the actual outcome should come in at under $100 billion.[2] This is still, however, $100 billion worse than projected in the cooperative scenario.

---

2. The final figure, released while this volume was in preparation, was $99 billion.

Figure 2 Economic growth in the United States, Europe, and Japan: actual and in D&D, 1985–90

percentage of GNP

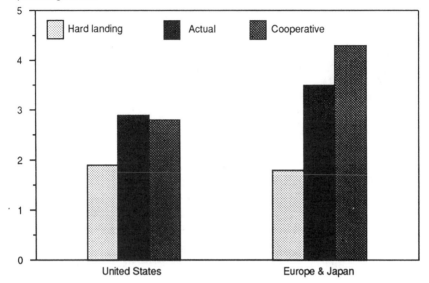

In part this outcome reflects the fact that growth in Europe and Japan was somewhat less than projected (figure 2), but on the other hand the dollar declined somewhat more than projected. In other words, the actual improvement was about 30 percent less than it should have been according to the D&D model, reflecting an overestimation of the benefits from devaluation (common to most models of the US trade balance extant at the time).

As anticipated, the dollar's decline developed into a bandwagon, which was only halted by massive central bank intervention in the spring and early summer of 1987. As also anticipated, the policy of benign neglect of exchange rates was abandoned, and a system of managed exchange rates has evolved very much in the ad hoc manner discussed in chapter 8 of D&D.

What came as a welcome surprise, however, was that under the strong leadership of the US Treasury the necessary cooperative arrangements between central banks and treasuries were put into place *before* the going got really rough, rather than having to be cobbled together in the heat of the crisis. This—plus a certain amount of luck—helps to explain how, by early 1989, the G-5/G-7 had acquired considerable credibility vis-à-vis the currency markets in their efforts to stabilize exchange rates. By the end of 1990, however, there were signs of systemic erosion (see "The Dollar and the Exchange Rate Regime" below).

Europe and Japan

As foreseen in D&D, the swing in the US trade balance had, during the course of 1986, a significant adverse impact on growth in Europe and Japan. In Germany, business confidence fell by 25 percentage points from the autumn of 1985 to February 1987, and orders for investment goods fell by 8 percent in the three quarters to the first quarter of 1987. In Japan, business confidence fell by 46 percentage points from late 1984 to early 1987, and in 1986 industrial production declined, on a year-on-year basis, for only the second time since World War II.

Subsequent events largely but by no means entirely conformed with the analysis and policy prescriptions in D&D. The initial response was mainly a sharp relaxation of monetary policy. In Japan, the discount rate was lowered from 5 percent to a historical low of 2.5 percent by early 1987, and was kept there until April 1989. In Germany, the growth of central bank money exceeded the Bundesbank's target during the three years 1986–88, averaging 7.3 percent per year against a target of 3 percent to 6 percent.

My concern that large-scale foreign-exchange intervention and excessive monetary ease would prove inflationary (D&D, 250) was, in the event, largely unfounded. In retrospect, the main reason was that inflation was held down not only by currency appreciation but also by the sharp drop in oil prices. Monetary ease did, however, contribute to the runup of asset prices and consequent financial fragility in Japan that became evident in 1990.

A fiscal stimulus was given in both countries, but on a much smaller scale than recommended in D&D. In Germany the boost amounted to 1.6 percent of GNP between 1986 and 1988.[3] In Japan it is more difficult to find evidence of a fiscal stimulus in the figures, partly for definitional reasons but mainly because the fiscal position benefited so quickly and so much from the fall in interest rates and the rise in asset prices.

Events very much confirmed the analysis that suggested that it should be possible to generate a domestic demand–led expansion, in which, with appreciating currencies and falling interest rates, a fiscal stimulus could lead to an *improved* fiscal position (table 1) without creating inflationary dangers. Subsequent events also validated the prescription in D&D that Europe should grow out of its real wage problem: "... the boost given to demand should be sufficiently strong to create some excess demand in product markets, enabling prices to be raised relative to wages, and at the same time providing a strong incentive to shift from capital-deepening to capital-widening investment" (D&D, 195). By 1989 Europe was enjoying a strong investment boom in new capacity, profit margins contin-

---

3. As measured by the cyclically adjusted budget deficit calculated by the Secretariat of the Organization for Economic Cooperation and Development.

Table 1   General-government fiscal balances in the OECD countries, 1984 and 1989 (percentages of GNP)

Country	1984	1989	Change
Japan	− 0.8	2.7	3.5
Germany	− 1.9	0.2	2.1
Total OECD excluding United States	− 3.5	− 1.2	2.3

Source: Organization for Economic Cooperation and Development, *OECD Economic Outlook,* June 1990.

ued to rise, and unemployment had at last begun to fall significantly. Europessimism had turned to Euroeuphoria.

In Japan, events showed even beyond my expectations that a combination of a strong boost to domestic demand and a "substantial and lasting appreciation of the yen" was the best, indeed the only way "to ensure that Japan invests and consumes more of the fruits of its remarkable productivity at home" (D&D, 231). Events also showed that it was both possible and desirable to correct the investment-saving balance via a rise in the share of private investment in GNP—from 21 percent in 1984 to 25 percent in 1990—rather than by a reduction in domestic saving (D&D, 227–32).

To sum up at this point, policies shifted quite significantly in the right direction both in the United States and in Europe and Japan. In itself, however, this shift would almost certainly not have been enough to prevent a hard landing, had it not been for the positive contribution made by three major unanticipated developments discussed below. These developments were very fortunate. Without them there would have been more pressure for fiscal restraint in the United States and for fiscal expansion in Europe and Japan. Whether this pressure would have led to enough additional fiscal restraint in the United States and fiscal expansion in Europe and Japan to muddle through without a hard landing is an unanswerable question, but it seems fairly certain that the overall outcome for the world economy would have been less growth and more inflation.

It was particularly fortunate that these unexpected developments reduced the need for fiscal expansion in Europe and Japan. A good deal of space was devoted in D&D to why an internationally coordinated package of fiscal and other action might be needed to break out of the "expectations trap"—the likelihood that fiscal expansion might precipitate adverse reactions in the financial and currency markets—which at the time made policymakers in Europe and Japan extremely reluctant to envisage a large-scale fiscal stimulus. True, the G-5/G-7 did try to coordinate monetary and fiscal policies along the lines suggested in D&D, but in practice the necessary policy shifts were only made tardily under the pressure of events. So it is particularly fortunate that they were lucky.

Unanticipated Developments

The sharp drop in oil prices in 1985–86 helped to avert the hard landing in two ways. First, despite the falling dollar, US inflation actually *fell* from 3.5 percent in 1985 to 2.0 percent in 1986, as lower oil prices more than offset the inflationary impact of the dollar's rapid decline. Second, lower oil prices gave an exogenous boost to domestic demand in Europe and Japan just when it was most needed.

Another major feature of the second half of the 1980s that was not foreseen was the dramatic rise in financial and real asset prices. This also helped to avert a hard landing in two ways. For most of the period, the rise in the price of dollar assets offset most of the exchange rate losses being incurred by foreign holders of such assets. The wealth effects generated by the rise in asset prices in Europe and Japan contributed to the adjustment process in another way, by giving a further exogenous boost to domestic demand.

Despite these favorable developments, there was, until the middle of 1989, one major flaw in the adjustment process. Although domestic demand had picked up in Germany, it was still lagging behind the rest of Europe. The consequent steady rise in Germany's current account surplus pointed to the need for a realignment of the deutsche mark in the European Monetary System of considerable magnitude. Unless carried out skillfully, revaluation of the mark threatened to hamstring the international adjustment process and the otherwise promising evolution toward closer monetary integration in Europe (Cline 1989, Marris 1989).

The quite unexpected events that led to German reunification went a long way toward solving this problem. Demand was boosted, first by the inflow of immigrants and then, after monetary union, by very strong demand from the former East Germany. By the end of 1990 the current account surplus was shrinking quite rapidly, and Germany had at last become—fortunately but inadvertently—the locomotive of Europe.

A Self-Denying Prophecy?

It would be immodest for an author to try to assess the influence of his own work. Nevertheless, it is true that the problem of the twin deficits was probably the single most discussed and researched economic phenomenon of the 1980s, and that the dangers of a hard landing were rehearsed at great length in books, the media, and official circles, both before and during the dollar's decline.

This may well, therefore, be a case where ideas did influence policies, and hence events. If so, it seems most likely to have been the case with respect to the behavior of the US Treasury, the Federal Reserve, and the other main central banks with regard to exchange rates and, to a lesser extent, interest rates. It may also have played a part in the generally sensible policy response to the dollar's decline in Europe and Japan. Where it clearly had little or no influence was in the US Congress.

Nevertheless, despite the imperviousness of the American budgetary process to economic reality, the fact is that the actual outcome over the last five years for the dollar, the United States, and the rest of the world was in the end quite close to the cooperative scenario set out in D&D. Unanticipated events played a positive role, but so also did a reasonably sensible policy response. I believe a good case can be made that the response would have been less sensible had it not been for the writings of myself and others, but since one cannot replay history, this can only be a matter of judgment, which I should leave to others.

Prospects

A Hard Landing Is Now Unlikely

The events of the last five years, as summarized above, have greatly reduced the risk of a hard landing—in the sense postulated in D&D:

- The remaining deficits and surpluses are, in relation to the GNPs of the countries involved, much smaller than in the mid–1980s and are generally moving in the right direction (regrettably this is no longer currently true for the US budget deficit).

- The US economy has had time to absorb the inflationary consequences of dollar depreciation.

- The dollar has been down long enough, and far enough, to put in train a reversal of the structural damage done to the manufacturing sector by the previous overvaluation.

- Europe and Japan have learned to live without a net stimulus from foreign demand, and have discovered that it is perfectly possible to generate a sustained expansion led by domestic demand.

- There has been a sea change in the behavior of the foreign-exchange markets. Five years ago, conventional wisdom in the markets was that central banks could have little or no influence on exchange rates. Yet for nearly four years now the G-5/G-7 have been able to keep fluctuations of the key rates more or less within reasonable ranges. As a result, they are now better placed to prevent a free fall of the dollar.

It follows that the weakness of the dollar in the second half of 1990 is unlikely to be the precursor of a Marris-like hard landing. That weakness was largely a cyclical phenomenon, with the causality running from slow growth in the United States relative to Europe and Japan, via narrowing interest rate differentials, to a weak dollar. In a hard-landing scenario the causality runs the other way, from a loss of confidence in the currency markets, via a *widening* of the interest rate differential, to a recession in the depreciating-currency country. Experience suggests that under normal circumstances the first type of problem is much easier for central banks to handle than the second.

Two qualifications are necessary, however. First, largely as a consequence of German reunification, the first half of the 1990s will see a significant shift in the international macroeconomic policy mix that is unfavorable to the dollar. In Germany, fiscal policy will be more expansionary and monetary policy more restrictive, with persistent upward pressure on interest rates; meanwhile in the United States fiscal policy will, one hopes, be more restrictive, with less upward pressure on interest rates.

Second, during the current phase of cyclical weakness, the dollar will move below the lower limits of the reference ranges set in December 1987. In itself this is quite sensible, given the fundamentals. Unfortunately, however, the G-5/G-7 have failed to develop any convincing procedure for realigning the reference ranges up or down in line with a rational assessment of changing fundamentals. Instead, they have already started squabbling in public about what should be done. It is thus quite likely that the dollar will overshoot downward, in which case the G-5/G-7 will be forced into another fire brigade operation. For the reasons given above, they should be able to limit the damage, but this is a rotten way to run an exchange rate regime.

The Dollar and the Exchange Rate Regime

Paradoxically, if one tries to look beyond this period of cyclical weakness, the problem may be that the dollar will be too strong on average during the 1990s, rather than too weak. One reason is the perverse feature of the present exchange rate regime whereby, so long as the authorities are thought to be targeting *nominal* exchange rates, money tends to flow into the higher-inflation countries with, normally, higher nominal interest rates. Once the present phase of cyclical weakness is past, this could tend to push the dollar up, since, as of now at any rate, US inflation seems likely to remain higher than in Japan and Germany.

A more fundamental factor pointing toward a strong dollar is the naturally high foreign demand for assets denominated in the world's leading currency. D&D contained estimates of the rest of the world's uncovered dollar portfolio. Updated estimates suggest that foreigners' "natural" demand for dollar-denominated assets (i.e., that operating when the influence of both interest rate and exchange rate expectations is neutral), to maintain the share of dollar-denominated assets in their total portfolios constant, is now more than enough to finance the US current account deficit at its present level. With the perceived reduction in the downside exchange rate risk in a system of managed rates, this automatic financing mechanism could—and probably has already at times—become a not-unimportant factor tending to push the dollar up.

There is a systemic issue here. History shows that strong worldwide demand for assets denominated in the currency of the richest and most powerful country at a given time leads to persistent upward pressure on that currency, which in time pushes the country into a trade deficit and eventually a current account deficit. To put it more bluntly, financial dominance leads in the end to deindustrialization, an overextended financial position, and relative economic decline. The United Kingdom in the 19th and 20th centuries provides perhaps the most vivid example of this sequence of events, but basically the same story can be traced in the economic history of the Netherlands in the 17th century, Spain in the 16th century, Northern Italy in the 15th century, and even the Roman Empire in the 3rd century.

The issue today is whether we still live largely in a "one-currency-at-a-time" world, in which case the long-term prospects for the United States could be bleak. Or are we moving sufficiently quickly—and for the first time in history—into a multicurrency world, in which the "burden" of having a sought-after currency will be spread around widely enough to save the United States from the financial and industrial fate of the United Kingdom? To an important extent the outcome will depend on how the exchange rate regime evolves. In a well-managed multicurrency regime it should be possible to resist, and where necessary offset, undue upward pressure on the most sought-after currency.

Unfortunately, both historical experience and recent events suggest that managed exchange rate regimes are subject to systemic erosion. The problem arises in the first place because, given the large margin of uncertainty about the sustainable equilibrium level of exchange rates, governments have a much greater power to influence exchange rates directly through announcement effects and sterilized intervention than many academic economists still seem to realize. The trouble is, however, that, possessing this power, governments nearly always end up by abusing it—and thus losing it.

In other words, managed exchange rate regimes can work *too* well, in the sense that as they acquire credibility it becomes too easy for governments to finance ultimately unsustainable surpluses and deficits, thus undermining the political will to take the necessary corrective action. This is how the Bretton Woods regime eventually broke down. Although it would be premature to predict the same fate for the Louvre regime, there are disquieting signs of complacency, and there is little evidence of the kind of leadership needed to develop

Figure 3   US budget deficit: plans and reality, 1980–95

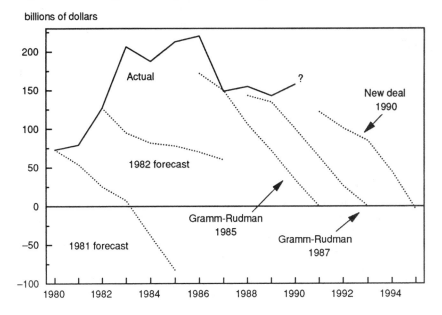

billions of dollars

the present regime into something sufficiently coherent, consistent, and constraining to be viable over the longer run.

Prospects for the US Economy

In another paper in this volume (chapter 2), my colleague William R. Cline sets out a "happy ending" scenario for America's twin deficits. In this scenario the October 1990 budget deal is carried out faithfully, and this frees up enough resources to raise the share of investment in GNP and reduce the current account deficit to a sustainable level (put at $60 billion), which requires only a further 5 percent depreciation of the dollar.

There are several caveats to this scenario. The first is that, if things go this well, then for the reasons just discussed the dollar could appreciate quite strongly rather than stay down at the sensible level postulated in Cline's scenario. The second is obviously the credibility of the budget deal itself. This is not the first time that Congress has legislated the demise of the budget deficit, and the history of previous efforts is dismal (figure 3). On this occasion expert opinion is moderately optimistic (see, for example, Penner 1990), in part because the deal incorporates a substantial peace dividend, which one hopes will stand. But the main reason for optimism is that the procedures for controlling the deficit have been tightened up: control will be exercised *ex post* rather than *ex ante* as under Gramm-Rudman, and nominal caps have been put on each of the main categories of expenditure over the next three years.

To the outsider, it is nevertheless difficult not to have doubts, in the light of past experience, about what will happen a year or two from now, when Congress and the administration find that this time they have really put themselves into a straightjacket, and when there will no doubt be many calls for additional expenditures and tax breaks.

There are some further question marks about the prospects for the US economy. One is how far the core rate of inflation will come down in what is generally expected to be a rather modest recession in 1990–91. Another is what will happen to private saving. More broadly, there is the question of how far, even with the twin deficits brought down to more manageable proportions, economic performance in the 1990s could be adversely affected by constraints coming from the massive buildup of foreign and domestic debt during the 1980s.

If, as is quite possible, there is a global shortage of savings in the 1990s, the external constraint could produce a "salami hard-landing" scenario. After the present recession, the US economy recovers quite strongly, stimulated by an intervening decline in the dollar and a renewed buildup of the domestic debt overhang. Interest rates and the dollar rise quite sharply. Later, as inflation picks up and the trade balance deteriorates, confidence in the dollar evaporates, and the stage is set for a mini–hard landing. Assuming that, although battered, the Louvre regime survives, this scenario could repeat itself several times (hence the salami).

Alternatively, the constraint coming from the buildup of domestic debt might produce a "Brookings" scenario. Several Brookings economists, notably Charles L. Schultze, have argued all along that, regrettably, there would be no crisis, that therefore nothing would be done to raise national saving, and that the consequences would show up "only slowly and imperceptibly as a steady erosion of US living standards," with the economy continuing to grow in line with potential output, but the growth of the latter gradually slowing down (Schultze 1988, 5). In an aggravated Brookings scenario, however, the growth of demand during the 1990s might persistently fall short of the growth of potential output (which would itself be declining). This could happen if demand is constrained by the domestic debt overhang and, on balance, by an overly strong dollar; if monetary policy is constrained by a stubbornly high core rate of inflation; and if fiscal policy is constrained by continuing large budget deficits.

The difference between the salami hard-landing scenario and the Brookings scenarios is not so much the end product, which would be much the same, but rather that in the first the binding constraint would come from the overhang of external debt, whereas in the second it would come mainly from the overhang of domestic debt (both private and public). In practice, each could play a key role at different times, or, in a worst-case scenario, they could feed on one another.

The bottom line is that, as a result of the excesses of the 1980s, the US economy has become more vulnerable to swings in sentiment in deregulated financial markets, at a time when these have become globalized. Given these developments, the outcome may depend as much on political and geopolitical developments as on straight economics, which is why, writing in November 1990 in the midst of the Persian Gulf crisis and the disintegration of the Soviet Union, I would want to hedge my bets.

Globalization, Deregulation, Asset Inflation, and Savings

One clear lesson from the last five years is that the globalization of financial markets has made it easier to finance persistent large current account deficits and surpluses than it was during the earlier postwar period. Apart from the United States, the United Kingdom provides a particularly dramatic example of this phenomenon.

In principle, mainstream economists should welcome this increased international mobility of capital on the grounds of improved allocative efficiency. In practice, one of the most disquieting features of the last five years is the extent to which, contrary to the textbooks, increased international capital mobility seems to have helped to finance *consumption* rather than investment. Equally disquieting is the fact that, although budget deficits were generally reduced where they should have been (and transformed into a surplus in the United Kingdom and Australia), there was at the same time a significant drop in private saving, so that the corresponding current account positions either improved only modestly (as in the United States), or were little changed (as in Australia), or deteriorated drastically (as in the United Kingdom).

In my view these developments pose a major challenge to our understanding of how the system is working, what the future holds in store, and what the policy response should be. One possible explanation—admittedly speculative and controversial—goes as follows:

■ Domestic financial deregulation and innovation has been a general phenomenon, but has gone furthest in some Anglo-Saxon countries, especially with respect to the ease with which households and companies can borrow (and spend) against unrealized capital gains on real estate and other assets. It is argued that this largely explains the runup in asset prices, the historically abnormal rise in debt-to-income ratios, and the drop in private saving rates in these countries.

- It is further argued that while the excess demand generated by asset inflation resulting from financial deregulation was one of the reasons for the shift to more restrictive fiscal policies, there was no direct causal relationship between reduced budget deficits and the fall in private saving (as suggested by some economists of the rational expectations school). In other words the apparent confirmation of the Ricardo-Barro equivalence theorem (with a coefficient of more than one for the United Kingdom!) is spurious.

- Adverse shifts in national investment-saving balances did not set off the corrective mechanisms that would have come into play in a closed economy (i.e., extremely high interest rates and recession in the savings-deficient countries), partly because of myopia in the financial markets, but mainly because, at the international level, financial deregulation and innovation have made it so much easier to finance current account deficits.

Whether this is or is not the correct interpretation of recent events is of considerable importance, because, looking ahead, the thesis that there will be a global shortage of savings looks much more plausible than it did five years ago. In the developed Western world the cushion provided by a margin of unused capital and labor has largely disappeared. In the European Community the dynamics of 1992 set off a strong surge of investment. In the rest of the world, both East and South, the end of the Cold War and the triumph of capitalism could also in time generate a sustained investment boom.

In this context, a key question is whether there could be a further sharp decline in private saving as the "Anglo-Saxon disease" spreads to other developed countries, where deregulation has proceeded more slowly and the financial system is still to varying degrees "repressed." This would in my view be a matter for great concern, because a global shortage of savings resulting from a decline in saving would be much more inflationary and less sustainable than one resulting from a rise in investment.

As of now, the verdict need not be pessimistic. The 1980s did after all demonstrate—in Latin America—that excessive external indebtedness can set off endogenous (and painful) corrective mechanisms. As we enter the 1990s, it can be argued that the constraints coming from both the internal and the external debt overhang are beginning to bite in the Anglo-Saxon countries, and that it may prove possible to wind the debt overhang down (with a fair amount of domestic pain) without inflicting too much damage on the rest of a generally buoyant world economy. It can further be argued that the demonstration effect of this process on the financial sectors and governments in the other major industrial countries will suffice to prevent them catching the Anglo-Saxon disease.

To sum up, if I were sitting down to write a new book today, my starting point would be that the prospects for the real world economy look pretty good. The main question marks (apart from the inadequacies of the US budgetary process) concern the observed tendency of managed exchange rate regimes toward systemic erosion, which could lead to chronic overvaluation of the dollar, and, especially, the decline in the private propensity to save in a number of countries, which may be the result of an unanticipated and disquieting interaction between financial deregulation and innovation at the domestic and the international level.

References

Cline, William R. 1989. *United States External Adjustment and the World Economy*. Washington: Institute for International Economics.

Marris, Stephen. 1989. "Whither the EMS?" *Amex Bank Review* 16, no. 4 (April):6–7.

Penner, Rudolph G. 1990. "The US Economy: Tattered But Not Torn." *International Economic Insights* 1, no. 3 (November–December):2–6.

Schultze, Charles L. 1988. *American Living Standards: Threats and Challenges*. Washington: Brookings Institution.

Comment

Herbert Stein

I did not believe the Marris scenario of five or three years ago, for very simple and general reasons. This goes beyond my usual skepticism about predictions and relates to the particular prediction Marris was making. It was not that he did not have the evidence that would be necessary to make the prediction probable. He was not making the garden variety of prediction that the United States would have a recession within a few years. He was predicting what he called a "hard landing," which sounded like quite a catastrophe, and he was predicting that it would come about in a specific way.

I am generally skeptical of predictions of hard landings, because I believe that, like hurricanes in Hertfordshire, they hardly ever happen. As I look back at what at the time seemed some of our hardest landings, for example the recessions of 1975 and 1982, they seem in historical perspective to have been mild adjustments. But I am especially skeptical of the kind of prediction that I understood Marris to be making. The prediction depended on the continuation of a development that Marris said could not go on forever. For some years I have been going around propounding Stein's law, which is that if something cannot go on forever it will stop. There is an important corollary to that. If something cannot go on forever, and everyone knows that it cannot go on forever, it will slow down and stop before it reaches the point beyond which it cannot go on. In general I am skeptical of predictions of endogenous catastrophes—catastrophes caused by the actions of private actors who would suffer in the catastrophe—if all the private actors have the same information as the predictor.

Marris's specific prediction, as I understood it, was that continuation of a large US budget deficit would cause a huge accumulation of dollar assets in foreign hands. At some point not very far off, foreigners would find that they had too much of such assets and would want to unload them. That would cause a decline of the dollar and a rise in US interest rates, and recession or inflation or both in the United States. This would spread to the rest of the world. Avoidance of this end would require cooperative measures, including reduction of the US budget deficit and joint action to stabilize exchange rates.

There were several specific reasons for my skepticism. First, foreign acquisition of dollar assets was voluntary, and done by people who knew what was going

Herbert Stein is a Senior Fellow at the American Enterprise Institute and a former Chairman of the President's Council of Economic Advisers.

on. I saw no reason to think that they would accumulate such assets beyond amounts that they would be reasonably willing to hold in circumstances that, if Marris could foresee, they could foresee also. Second, one can always observe trends, say of automobile production or of housing construction, whose sudden end could cause general disruption, but participants in those markets anticipate that possibility and the general disruption is usually avoided. I saw nothing unique in this respect in the trends in international finance. Third, I had no idea of where the limits to foreign accumulation of dollars were and thus no idea whether we were near the limits or far from them, and I didn't think that Marris had any idea either. Finally, I saw no peculiar problem in the foreign accumulation of dollar assets. It seemed to me that we would have the same troubles Marris foresaw if Americans rather than foreigners decided that they didn't want to hold dollar assets.

Marris now attributes the avoidance of the hard landing to the implementation of the kind of international cooperation that he originally prescribed. This explanation seems to me extremely doubtful. One of the main things I observe about the behavior of exchange rates is that no one has a very good story to explain it; in particular I have seen no evidence that cooperation, in the form of the various G-7 agreements, caused the decline of the dollar beginning in 1985. If there was cooperation to that end from the US side, it would have required a Federal Reserve policy aimed at that result. But Federal Reserve policy can, I believe, be explained by standard domestic considerations, and the Fed would probably deny that pursuit of some agreed-upon dollar exchange rate was an important factor in its decisions. To attribute US budget policy to international cooperation is even harder.

My reasons for doubting the Marris scenario were *a priori* reasons, based on assumptions about information and rationality that might not be true. If the Marris scenario had been validated, it might be taken as one more example of *a priori* assumptions being incorrect. But in fact the Marris scenario was not validated, and I take that as support for the thesis that it was improbable from the outset.

7

What Have We Learned About the International Adjustment Process?

What Have We Learned About the International Adjustment Process?

Peter B. Kenen

The papers in this volume have attempted to answer three questions about the substance of the international adjustment process: Is adjustment at hand? Do exchange rate changes work? And why has there been no hard landing of the dollar? I will attempt to summarize what the conference has said in answer to these questions and will address two additional questions: What has the conference said about the *conduct* of the adjustment process? And what has it said about the *study* of that process? My answers will cite some of the conference papers but will pay particular attention to some important comments made during the conference's panel discussion.

Is Adjustment at Hand?

If we take adjustment to mean the narrowing of current account imbalances, the answer is probably yes—or just plain probably. The Japanese surplus has been falling for some time and may continue to fall, even if the price of oil drops back quickly to the level prevailing before the Kuwait crisis. But three caveats are in order.

First, the sharp increase in Japanese domestic investment that has helped to shift the saving-investment and current account balances will presumably lead to import substitution and will also increase capacity in some of Japan's export industries. A few years ago, we were told that the US subsidiaries of Japanese automakers would start to export significant numbers of cars to Japan. Now we hear that they will not, because of the large increase in Japanese capacity.

Second, Japan will continue to upgrade its economy. By pricing to the American market, Japanese exporters held onto their market shares as the yen appreci-

Peter B. Kenen is Walker Professor of Economics and International Finance and Director of the International Finance Section, Princeton University.

ated, but they suffered cuts in profits. To compensate, they began to make direct investments in East Asia and the United States. This process has released resources in Japan, however, and those resources must be redeployed. They will probably be used in ways that raise Japanese exports of new high-technology products and hold down Japanese imports.

Third, Japanese households appear to be consuming more, and the saving rate has been falling, but we don't really know how the aging of Japan will affect the country in the long run. There are several uncertainties here: Does the life-cycle model really apply to Japan? How will the sharp fall in stock market values, compounded perhaps by a fall in real estate values, affect household behavior?

The German surplus will fall sharply in the next few years, but for reasons extraneous to the analytical issues examined by this conference. The huge sums that Germany must spend to rehabilitate what was formerly East Germany will be raised mainly in the capital market, not by taxation. Hence, Germany is about to engage in something startlingly similar to the American experiment with Reaganomics. There will be a big shift in the saving-investment balance, a capital inflow, and the need for a real appreciation of the deutsche mark. But Karl Otto Pöhl will play Paul Volcker. The Bundesbank will use monetary policy to combat inflation, so the real appreciation will have to take place by way of a nominal appreciation.

There is just one uncertainty, namely, whether the mark will drag along the other currencies of the European Monetary System (EMS) as it rises against the dollar and the yen, or whether there will be a realignment within the EMS. Hence, the ultimate outcome will depend in part on decisions made in Paris, not just Bonn or Frankfurt, and they will be heavily influenced by competing views about the benefits and costs of fixing exchange rates during the transition to European monetary union (EMU). In my view, the costs may be high and may rise quite steeply with the length of the transition. Therefore, it may be best to move quickly to EMU, even before complete convergence, and if that is impossible, to be more tolerant of realignments on the way to EMU. The prospects for Germany and its partners also underscore the need for Europe to find ways of making large quasi-endogenous transfers to offset asymmetrical shocks.

The US current account deficit has been trending downward, and William R. Cline (chapter 2) is quite right about the contribution of the US fiscal package to the prolongation of that process. The cut in the budget deficit attributable to that package should not be measured against the whole deficit, which reflects in large part the cost of the savings and loan crisis; it should instead be measured against the fraction of the deficit that affects the saving-investment balance. From this perspective, the reduction *is* significant. But there are caveats here as well: First, the supply of financing, measured at constant interest rates and constant (expected) exchange rates, may be falling faster than the current account deficit (see "Why No Hard Landing?" below). Second, it is impossible at this writing, in late 1990, to predict the evolution or the effects of the situation in the Persian Gulf.

Do Exchange Rate Changes Work?

To answer this question sensibly, we have to break it down. First, we must ask whether the real exchange rate matters and, if so, why it matters. Next, we must ask whether a change in the nominal exchange rate is an efficient way to change the real exchange rate. Finally, we must ask whether foreign-exchange markets, left to themselves, are likely to change nominal exchange rates in the right direction and at the right times.

Let's begin with the role of the real exchange rate. Robert A. Mundell (chapter 5) has given us a fascinating rerun of the Keynes-Ohlin debate. He is quite right: Ohlin won. A country that must transfer resources to foreigners will not necessarily suffer a deterioration in its terms of trade. But Mundell's case for fixed exchange rates drops one word from the previous sentence, which alters its meaning hugely. He leaves out "necessarily," as though it were an unimportant qualification rather than the core of Ohlin's contribution to our understanding of the transfer problem.

Edwin M. Truman went to the heart of the matter at the conference on which this volume is based when he asked us to consider how the history of the 1980s would have been different under fixed exchange rates. The United States, Japan, and Germany experienced large shifts in their saving-investment balances at the beginning of the decade, which should by themselves have driven the United States into current account deficit. But the size and nature of the deficit reflected in part the real appreciation of the dollar. The increase of absorption in the United States would have led to an increase of import demand and a decrease of export supply even in the absence of the exchange rate change, but the extent of import penetration, reflecting reductions in import-competing production, cannot be explained without reference to the appreciation of the dollar.

This brings us to a very important point made by Stephen Marris during the panel discussion at the conference concerning the ways in which changes in real exchange rates work. Some econometric models try to make allowance for supply-side variables affecting merchandise trade, but all of the trade equations derive fundamentally from our basic model of household behavior and thus focus on income and price effects. Marris wants us to look at the matter differently—to ask how relative prices and other variables affect producers' decisions to acquire, retain, or relinquish foreign markets as well as their decisions concerning the location of production. Instead of invoking these effects to explain why our trade equations don't always work, we should use them to reformulate the equations themselves. And when we do that, we should exploit as fully as possible the important analytical innovations of the last few years—the work by Avinash Dixit, Paul R. Krugman, and others that can help us to explain the puzzles of the 1980s. In brief, Marris and Kenen, a pair of plain-vanilla Keynesians, are telling Krugman that some of the exotica he described in his overview paper (chapter 1) may matter very much indeed.

Is a change in the nominal exchange rate a reliable way of changing the real exchange rate? I believe it is, because I agree with Paul Krugman: plain-vanilla Keynesianism is the right stuff. If I had to choose between a model with perfectly flexible prices and a model with perfectly rigid prices, I would take the one with rigid prices, even if its microeconomic foundations are faulty. It is the better representation of the real world. Unfortunately, Krugman has had to unlearn a lot of exotica in order to appreciate plain-vanilla Keynesianism, whereas I was so enamored of simple Keynesian models that I did not bother mastering most of the exotica.

It is not necessary, moreover, to be rigidly dogmatic about price rigidity in order to have confidence in the efficacy of nominal exchange rate changes. We can concede that supply curves slope upward, so that a country devaluing its currency will achieve some (but less than one-for-one) real devaluation, and it will therefore experience some improvement in its current account balance along with an increase in domestic prices. Nor is it so hard to explain how economies operating at high levels of activity "make room" for export expansion and import substitution when they devalue their currencies, thereby preventing prices from rising so much that they keep the real exchange rate from changing.

One theme running through our conference needs to be emphasized here. Macroeconomic policies are quasi-endogenous and usually go in the right direction, although they do not always go far enough. A not-so-simple Keynesian, James Meade, based his remarkable book *The Balance of Payments* (Meade 1951) on this supposition. He assumed that countries would follow a policy aimed at "internal balance" and would thus adjust absorption automatically when they had to make room for improvement in the current account balance resulting from a change in the nominal exchange rate.

It is rather easy for me to dispose of the final substantive question—whether freely floating exchange rates are likely to produce timely, right-signed changes in nominal rates—not because the question has been answered for all time but because there was remarkable unanimity at the conference. No one spoke up for floating rates. Horst Schulmann (chapter 4) said some wise things about the need to cushion national economies against exogenous shocks and policy errors. Marris reminded us that pegged-rate regimes tend to ossify. And none of us were terribly comfortable with our answers to Truman's challenge that we rethink the 1980s under a pegged-rate regime. Would the Reagan administration have been quicker to cancel its fiscal policy experiment? Would Paul Volcker have allowed the money supply to rise faster? Some of us thought we knew the answers but did not have very much confidence in them. Yet most of us seem to believe that floating was part of the problem in the 1980s, not part of the solution.

Why No Hard Landing?

Stephen Marris answers this question carefully in his conference paper (chapter 6), and I will not repeat his answer. Let me reflect instead on a pair of questions that surfaced in the course of the discussion: Do current account balances really matter? And is a hard landing still possible?

Richard N. Cooper (chapter 4) told us that current account balances do not matter very much—not even enough to warrant a major effort by the EC governments to find ways to keep track of intra–EC imbalances after the move to a single market deprives them of trade data. Yet most of the discussion at the conference was about the behavior of current account balances, which says that some of us must have some reason for believing that they are important. Two reasons surfaced in the course of the discussion.

First, there may be reason for concern about the evolution of a country's external debt—the integral of the current account balance. But C. Fred Bergsten and Shafiqul Islam in their forthcoming book (1992) argue persuasively that the external debt is not now and not likely to become a major problem for the United States. They choose to err on the prudent side and thus argue that the United States should reduce its current account deficit, but the amount of viewing-with-alarm is far below Bergsten's lifetime average.

Second, there may be reason for concern about the supply of financing available to cover large current account deficits. Some say that it is quite elastic, more than it was in earlier periods. After all, the United States has been able to finance huge current account deficits for several years. But this is not meaningful evidence. The capital inflow will always equal the current account deficit, whether the deficit is big or small. We have therefore to ask whether the supply of financing is stable and elastic at constant interest rates and constant expected exchange rates, and we have to distinguish between capital flows that reflect shifts in portfolio preferences and capital flows that represent balance of payments financing.

Shifts in preferences were important in the 1980s. Toyoo Gyohten, in a dinner lecture at the conference, reminded us that there were two distinct shifts in Japanese preferences in the 1980s: the shift in portfolio preferences at the start of the decade, linked with the liberalization of Japanese financial markets, and the shift in producer preferences later in the decade, which brought on the surge in foreign direct investment. The quasi-exogenous capital outflows associated with these shifts frequently exceeded Japan's current account surplus. The difference between them was offset by short-term capital inflows into Japan, induced by changes in interest rates and, more important, changes in exchange rate expectations, along lines suggested by Rudiger Dornbusch in his famous paper on exchange rate overshooting (Dornbusch 1976). The process can be traced, year by year, in the tables in Masaru Yoshitomi's paper (chapter 3).

These observations lead directly to my second question: Is a hard landing ahead? In my view, it may be happening now. The shifts in Japanese preferences have been completed, and the capital flows connected with them are falling off rapidly. But the supply of short-term capital is proving to be rather inelastic at constant interest rates and constant exchange rate expectations, and the dollar may have to depreciate sharply vis-à-vis the yen in order to coax out enough financing. The magnitude of the problem may not be fully apparent yet, because the rise in oil prices due to the Gulf crisis caused the OPEC countries to run big surpluses and absorb more dollars than usual. The problem will confront us squarely when we come to believe that interest rates should fall in the United States, to combat the recession and reduce the strains on the domestic financial system, but also come to believe that the dollar should not continue to depreciate. The problem will be mitigated, however, if the recession reduces the need for external financing by shrinking the US current account deficit.

What Have We Learned About the Conduct and Study of the Adjustment Process?

I do not claim to know what governments have learned from the 1980s, but I hope that they have drawn one conclusion, namely, that benign neglect is more expensive than exchange rate management. Toyoo Gyohten believes that the Louvre Accord was premature and that the G-7 governments had not thought their way through the long-run implications of the course they were charting. He is probably right. Yet the governments seemed to be coming out on top early in 1988, then gave the game away again when the dollar began to appreciate. They did not fully appreciate another point that Gyohten stressed. Once governments begin to make their views known, markets start to interpret government silences just as keenly as they interpret government declarations. When governments fail to contradict the markets' interpretations, they ratify the markets' views, and that is the story of the last two years. Governments have been indecisive and thus have damaged their ability to be decisive.

What have we learned about the study of the adjustment process? We appear to be learning that we have put too much effort into the fine tuning of our models. We should be investing instead in rather different approaches, including arithmetic. We need to look at what has been happening and allow the data to suggest new hypotheses. There is, of course, the danger that we will descend into storytelling of a sort that has no predictive value. But we are at risk of succumbing to another danger—that of refining our models after the fact to keep them from repeating old mistakes, only to have them make new ones.

Let us also remember the lesson implicit in Krugman's wry remarks about the exotica of the 1980s. We should pay more attention to stylized facts than to abstract axioms about rational, intertemporal behavior. Unfortunately, the imperatives of the academic profession will continue to get in the way. Because we must publish or perish, our need to produce new knowledge is bound to exceed the supply of new truth.

References

Bergsten, C. Fred, and Shafiqul Islam. 1992. *The United States as a Debtor Country.* Washington: Institute for International Economics (forthcoming).

Dornbusch, Rudiger. 1976. "Expectations and Exchange Rate Dynamics." *Journal of Political Economy* 84:1161–76.

Meade, James. 1951. *The Theory of International Economic Policy: The Balance of Payments,* vol. I. Oxford: Oxford University Press for the Royal Institute of International Affairs.

8

Has the Adjustment Process Worked?

Has the Adjustment Process Worked?

Paul R. Krugman

Introduction

The 1984 *Economic Report of the President,* published early that year but drafted in late 1983, correctly forecast that in 1984 the US merchandise trade deficit would for the first time in history exceed $100 billion. It also offered, in advance, a diagnosis of that unprecedented deficit. About $30 billion of the shortfall, the report argued, could be regarded as structural or normal, the counterpart of the US surplus in services. The rise in the deficit above that structural level could be attributed in part to the Third World debt crisis, which slashed US exports to Latin American nations after 1982, and to the relatively strong cyclical performance of the US economy, which had begun to recover from the 1982 recession, generating increased demand for imports. The lion's share of the prospective deficit, however, was explained by the strong dollar, which by late 1983 had risen some 30 percent from its low point (in nominal terms) in 1980. The strong dollar, in turn, could be explained by the collision between the federal budget deficit and a tight monetary policy; together these raised real interest rates in the United States, which in turn attracted foreign capital inflows.

It seems fair to say that the attitude toward international adjustment expressed in that report was shared by most mainstream international economic analysts at the time. It was an attitude of policy concern but analytical confidence: "We know how to cure this deficit," the report seemed to say; "All we need is the political will." In September 1985, finance ministers from the five leading market economies met at the Plaza Hotel in New York to coordinate a strategy for reducing current account imbalances among the leading industrial nations. Whether because of that meeting or coincidentally, the dollar (which had already

Paul R. Krugman is a Visiting Fellow at the Institute for International Economics and Professor of Economics at the Massachusetts Institute of Technology. This chapter was published separately as Has the Adjustment Process Worked? POLICY ANALYSES IN INTERNATIONAL ECONOMICS 34 *(Washington: Institute for International Economics, October 1991).*

Table 1 Current account balances in the G-3 countries, 1985–90

Country	1985	1986	1987	1988	1989	1990
United States						
Billions of dollars	−122.3	−145.4	−162.3	−128.9	−110.0	−97.0
As a percentage of GNP	−3.0	−3.4	−3.6	−2.6	−2.1	−1.8
Germany						
Billions of dollars	16.5	39.7	45.8	50.4	55.4	47.8
As a percentage of GNP	2.6	4.4	4.1	4.2	4.6	2.6
Japan						
Billions of dollars	49.2	85.8	87.0	79.6	57.2	47.5
As a percentage of GNP	3.7	4.4	3.6	2.8	2.0	1.7

Source: Organization for Economic Cooperation and Development, *Main Economic Indicators*, various issues.

begun to decline before the Plaza) fell massively from its 1985 peak and continued falling until early 1988.

The decline of the dollar, however, did not at first produce a corresponding decline in current account imbalances. Indeed, table 1 shows that through much of 1987 these imbalances continued to grow, leading to widespread assertions that the traditional international adjustment process no longer worked. Growing US trade deficits and Japanese surpluses created a political furor, while academic researchers turned their attention to a variety of models designed to show how uncertainty, strategic moves by oligopolistic firms, or other exotic factors might be frustrating trade adjustment.

Now the reconsideration is itself being reconsidered. Since 1987 the US trade deficit and the Japanese and German surpluses have shrunk, especially as measured against GNP. Correspondingly, the political heat has been turned down in the United States, where attention has shifted to other issues, notably foreign direct investment. Yet the questions raised during the initial period of disappointment over the results of the post-Plaza exchange rate realignments remain. Has the adjustment process worked?

As Herbert Stein has pointed out (in chapter 6 of this volume), taken literally this is a meaningless question. It is a fundamental proposition that things that cannot go on, like massive current account deficits, don't. The corollary is that things that must adjust, do. So of course the international adjustment mechanism has worked: we are where we are, and we got here from there.

When one asks whether the international adjustment mechanism has worked, however, what one is really asking is whether it has worked more or less as we thought it would, and whether it has worked in a way that we find acceptable.

That is, has the standard view of international adjustment been borne out by experience?

These are not only important questions but opportune ones as well. The 1980s were a difficult time for those who had to make policy, or a living, in the international economy. But the same volatility that whipsawed firms and nations provided a unique opportunity for economists to settle old controversies. From a scientific point of view, if not otherwise, the 1980s were a wonderful decade for the international economy—indeed, Robert Z. Lawrence (1990) argues that in the end we got virtually as good a controlled experiment on the effects of exchange rate changes as if it had been deliberately designed. This was not one of those stretches of history when everything is a smooth trend, all models fit well, and everything is too collinear to allow reliable estimation of anything. The decade's record of huge swings in exchange rates and trade balances gives us the best opportunity ever to sort out competing schools of thought in the economics of international adjustment, and perhaps even to get reasonably solid estimates of some key parameters.

In October 1990 the Institute for International Economics held a conference entitled "Has the International Adjustment Process Worked?" The purpose of the conference was to bring together leading researchers on balance of payments adjustment to discuss and evaluate the lessons of adjustment during the era of dollar decline. This monograph is an effort to pull together the insights gained from that conference.

The study is in five parts. The first part restates what we can regard as the mainstream view of international adjustment. The second part summarizes the three main intellectual challenges to that view that emerged during the period of post-Plaza frustration. The third part discusses the implications of these alternative views of international adjustment for exchange rate policy (and for trade policy as well, since the two turn out to be linked). The fourth part examines the lessons of recent experience in the United States, Japan, and Germany. The final part of the study draws some conclusions.

The Mainstream View of International Balance of Payments Adjustment

Most though by no means all international economists on the policy circuit carry in the back of their heads and on the backs of their envelopes a basic model of international adjustment that derives from the model devised by Robert A. Mundell and J. Marcus Fleming in the 1960s, with adjustments for expectations both of depreciation and of inflation. We might call this revised Mundell-Fleming model the "Mass. Ave." model, since its main contemporary adherents in the United States work on or near a Massachusetts Avenue in either Cambridge or

Washington.[1] Bergsten (US Congress 1981) had something like this model in mind when he offered an early warning of the trade consequences of the Reagan administration's emerging monetary-fiscal policy mix. A version of this model implicitly underlay Martin Feldstein's original statement (1985) of the "twin deficits" idea—the view that the trade deficit could be viewed as the sister of the budget deficit. More explicitly, essentially this same model underlay the assessment in the 1984 *Economic Report of the President*. Most major econometric models of the world economy, such as the Federal Reserve Board's MCM model and the Japanese Economic Planning Agency model, are also in effect elaborate versions of the model sketched out here.

I begin with a brief summary of the theory, then follow with a summary of the conventional wisdom about the corresponding empirical parameters.

The Mass. Ave. Model

The standard international macroeconomic model can be summarized in terms of a few key relationships (an algebraic statement is provided in appendix A). The first element of the canonical model is the Keynesian view that output is demand-determined at any point in time. Demand for the domestic goods of any individual country is the sum of that country's domestic spending plus net exports. Domestic spending depends at minimum on income and the real interest rate.

Net exports are assumed at minimum to depend on domestic income, foreign income, and the real exchange rate. This equation could easily have additional arguments—wealth and expected future income in demand, expenditure as well as output; in general these do not seem to add much explanatory power in practice, and a simple formulation in which imports and exports have constant elasticities with respect to domestic and foreign income respectively seems to work quite well.[2] It is crucial, however, to allow for lags in the effect of the real exchange rate. Without exception, empirical models of net exports find a substantial lag in the response of trade flows to relative prices. This is not surprising, since decisions by importers to change sources take time, and decisions by potential exporters to seek out new markets and step up production

---

1. In Cambridge, the main strongholds of this model are Harvard University, the Massachusetts Institute of Technology, and the National Bureau of Economic Research. In Washington, they include the Brookings Institution, the Institute for International Economics itself, and—a few blocks off Massachusetts Avenue—the staff of the Federal Reserve.

2. For an exploration of a variety of different specifications, see Helkie and Hooper (1988). Surveys of empirical evidence on trade may be found in Goldstein and Khan (1985) and Bryant et al. (1988a and b).

take even more time. At the same time, most empirical models suggest that a currency depreciation is fairly quickly passed through in a rise in import prices. As a result, most models indicate the presence of at least some J-curve, that is, an initially perverse response of the trade balance to the exchange rate change: although the *volume* of imports falls following a devaluation, their *value* (in domestic currency) initially rises because of higher prices, and the gradual rise in exports is initially insufficient to offset this adverse impact on the trade balance.

A third element in the standard model is an ordinary and fairly uncontroversial monetary sector. A supply of money (*M*) determined by the central bank must equal a demand for money balances that depends on income, the price level, and interest rates.

A fourth element is some kind of exchange rate equation. The typical formulation is something like the following: investors require that expected returns on domestic and foreign interest-earning assets be equal. They also see the real exchange rate as reverting gradually toward some long-run expected rate, say by eliminating a fraction of the gap every year. This implies that the real exchange rate is simply a function of the real interest rate differential: the higher are, say, US real interest rates relative to Japan's, the stronger the dollar.

To finish off the Mass. Ave. model, we need to determine prices. The typical formulation is one in which the price *level* is predetermined at any point in time. The rate of inflation is then determined by some expectations-adjusted Phillips curve in which inflation depends on the level of output relative to trend and on expected or core inflation; core inflation in turn is adaptive, adjusting slowly in response to actual inflation.

This standard formulation is essentially an updated IS-LM model, in which markets for goods are brought into equilibrium with those for money and financial assets. It is a dynamic model, with the dynamics arising from the lag in trade adjustment that results from sluggish export and import responses to relative prices, from the gradual adjustment of prices (from the Phillips curve), and from slow changes in the inflation expectations embodied in the core inflation rate. In discussions of adjustment, however, it is common to abstract from the dynamics, by thinking in terms of a medium run in which trade adjustment to the exchange rate is more or less complete but in which the other lags—the adjustment of prices and inflationary expectations—can be ignored. Whether such a medium run, which is implicitly the time domain of the Mundell-Fleming approach, is a useful shortcut is an empirical question. In estimated models, however, it seems to be.

It is straightforward in this shortcut model to think about the consequences of changes in monetary and fiscal policy for the external balance. Consider first the predicted effects of an expansionary fiscal policy. Such an expansion will raise demand for domestically produced goods and services, leading to an expansion in output. As output rises, however, the demand for money will also rise, pulling up the interest rate. This will lead to crowding out of private investment; in addition, the rise in domestic relative to foreign interest rates will produce a currency appreciation that leads to a fall in net exports at any given level of output. Thus, fiscal expansion leads to both an expansion of output and an exchange rate appreciation—and to a decline in net exports for both reasons.

Next consider the predicted effects of an expansionary monetary policy. The initial effect will be to lower the interest rate; this lower rate will stimulate investment and, since the domestic interest rate has fallen relative to foreign rates, lead to currency depreciation. Currency depreciation will in turn stimulate net exports at any given level of output, providing a second channel of expansion. The overall effect is a rise in output accompanied by a decline in the currency, with an ambiguous effect on the current account.

One could imagine combining a contractionary fiscal policy with an expansionary monetary policy just large enough to leave income unchanged. This would produce currency depreciation at a constant level of income. It is also possible to imagine a change in the exchange rate unconnected to any macroeconomic policy change.[3] Suppose, for example, that for some reason the long-run expected exchange rate falls—perhaps because of jawboning by G-7 ministers. The effect will be a downward shift in the exchange rate associated with any given domestic interest rate. Since this will have a stimulative effect on net exports, there will also be an expansion in the economy. This expansion will drive up interest rates, reducing but not eliminating both the depreciation and the increase in net exports resulting from changed expectations.

Empirical Conventional Wisdom

The Mass. Ave. model is not purely a matter of pencil-and-paper speculation. On the contrary, a large body of econometric work has attempted to fit elaborated versions of this basic model to real-life data, and to estimate policy multipliers. The relationships among output, exchange rates, and net exports in particular have been the subject of a vast empirical literature.

Table 2 offers some summary results aimed at giving a more or less standard view of the responses of imports and exports to income and exchange rate changes. It presents median estimates for US trade from seven trade models: six that were part of a model comparison conducted by Bryant et al. (1988), together with the recent work of Lawrence (1990).

---

3. Which is not to say that one can imagine the exchange rate changing for no reason at all: *something*, if only a change in expectations, has to change to move the exchange rate. Opponents of the Mass. Ave. view sometimes accuse proponents of treating the exchange rate as if it were not a determined as well as a determining variable; this charge is unfair.

Table 2 Representative elasticity estimates for US trade[a]

	Imports	Exports
Median income elasticity	1.8	1.2
Median long-run price elasticity	1.1	0.8
Median mean lag from exchange rate change to initial trade volume response (years)	0.6	0.8
Median exchange rate effect on price	0.9	0.2

a. Figures are median estimates of six independent econometric models surveyed in Bryant et al. (1988b) and the estimates of Lawrence (1990).

Sources: Bryant, Ralph C., Gerald Holtham, and Peter Hooper, eds. 1988. *External Deficits and the Dollar: The Pit and the Pendulum.* Washington: Brookings Institution; Lawrence, Robert Z. 1990. "US Current Account Adjustment: An Appraisal." *Brookings Papers on Economic Activity* 2:343–82.

The first line of table 2 presents estimated income elasticities for imports and exports. The main point to note here is that in general estimates for the United States find a higher income elasticity of import than of export demand, so that if United States and rest-of-world output were to grow at similar rates, the United States would need a persistent depreciation of the dollar in order not to have a steadily widening trade deficit. This observation plays a key role in one of the challenges to the standard view, what I call the "secularist" view, discussed below.

The second line of the table presents median price elasticity estimates for imports and exports. Basically, such estimates hover in the vicinity of one; this is large enough to ensure that a real depreciation will in fact increase net exports, but still much smaller than many economists might have assumed a priori.

The standard view also attributes substantial lags to the response of trade flows to relative price changes, as illustrated in the third line. The 7- to 10-month mean lag of trade *volumes* behind prices translates, as will be documented in a moment, into a substantially longer lag of trade *values* behind the exchange rate.

Finally, as the last line of the table shows, conventional estimates also strongly suggest that a dollar depreciation is reflected in a decline in the US terms of trade, albeit somewhat less than one-for-one. A depreciation of the dollar leads to some rise in US dollar export prices, but for the most part US exporters pass their lower costs measured in foreign currency on to their customers; similarly, while foreign exporters to the United States absorb some of the rise in their dollar costs, most of the rise is passed on to US consumers.

Table 2 by itself does not give a full picture of the conventional dynamics of the response of the trade balance to depreciation. Both because many models

Table 3   Estimated median response of the US current account to a 20 percent real depreciation of the dollar (percentages of GNP)[a]

Year	Change in current account
1	−0.21
2	0.51
3	1.32
4	1.43
5	1.45

a. Figures are the median values of six independent econometric models.

Source: Bryant, Ralph C., Gerald Holtham, and Peter Hooper, eds. 1988. *External Deficits and the Dollar: the Pit and the Pendulum.* Washington: Brookings Institution.

imply some lag in the response of trade prices to the exchange rate, and because the standard view implies that initial increases in real net exports will be largely offset by valuation effects, the improvement in the nominal trade balance following a depreciation takes much longer than the mean lags in table 2. Fortunately, Bryant et al. offer a table of simulated responses of the current account to a 20 percent dollar depreciation. Table 3 presents median values (unfortunately omitting the more recent Lawrence estimates). The important point here is that, by the conventional wisdom, it takes more than two years for the bulk of the response of the current account to currency changes to take place.

The Conventional Wisdom and the Adjustment Debate

I have taken some space to describe this more or less standard model for three reasons. The first is that this model represents the underlying text for much discussion of international adjustment, but it is often a hidden text, because economists are unwilling either to be excessively formal (if they are speaking to policymakers) or so brazenly ad hoc (if they are speaking to their colleagues).[4] This leads to much confusion. Even in conferences where speakers and audience are professional international economists, there are obvious moments when half the participants are listening to music that eludes the rest.

A second reason to restate the basic model is to clear the air of some common accusations leveled against international economists who focus on the role of

----

4. The Mass. Ave. model may not seem all that ad hoc to the lay public. In academic macroeconomics, however, it has become increasingly *de rigueur* to base all discussion on models with rigorous microeconomic foundations, and the criteria for what constitutes rigor have gradually narrowed to the point where virtually all policy-oriented macroeconomic analysis has become unacceptable in polite academic company.

the exchange rate. In particular, economists who ask how the exchange rate affects trade are often accused of a partial-equilibrium viewpoint—of failing to understand basic accounting identities or missing the point that whatever changes the exchange rate will also change other things. But the Mass. Ave. model does in fact respect the basic identities: the equation that sets output equal to aggregate demand can also be rewritten $S - I = NX$, or $NX = Y - A$ (where S is aggregate saving, I is investment, NX is net exports, Y is income, and A is domestic absorption). And the model is clear in allowing factors other than exchange rate changes to affect the trade balance. A fiscal expansion raises output as well as the real exchange rate; a monetary expansion, although it leads to real depreciation, has an ambiguous effect on net exports in principle (and little net effect in practice, according to the empirical studies surveyed by Frankel 1988). When mainstream international economists discuss international adjustment, implicitly they are discussing a scenario in which there is simultaneous contractionary fiscal policy and offsetting monetary expansion, which leaves output roughly unchanged while depreciating the currency.

The main reason for setting out a standard view, however, is as a vantage point from which to survey alternative views. The main alternative views can be summarized by contrasting them with what the mainstream view asserts about the need for dollar depreciation. In the mainstream view:

- a policy mix such as fiscal contraction *cum* monetary expansion that drives down the dollar in real terms without a large economic expansion will be *successful* in reducing the US external deficit;

- the real depreciation associated with such a policy mix is *necessary* in order to achieve that deficit reduction, or at least to achieve it without undesirable side effects such as recession;

- the extent of depreciation needed is more or less *predictable*, because there is a stable relationship between trade flows and real exchange rates.

The three main alternative views, all of which emerged in some form during the IIE conference, each deny one of these three assertions. The next part of this study examines each of their cases in turn.

Challenges to the Mainstream View

Is currency depreciation effective at raising net exports, or does it simply offer a fire sale of US assets to foreign investors? Is depreciation necessary, or is it irrelevant to an adjustment process driven by saving-investment balances? Is the appropriate exchange rate predictable, or are we chasing a moving (and receding) target as US competitive decline requires an ever-lower dollar? Amid the wide-spread dismay over the initial failure of the post-Plaza exchange rate adjustments to narrow trade imbalances, influential voices argued that exchange rate adjustment either did not work, was not necessary, or was an inadequate response to deeper competitive issues. For reasons that will become clear shortly, I will refer to the proponents of these three views as structuralists, shmooists, and secularists, respectively.

Do Exchange Rate Changes Work? The Structuralist View

A generation ago, it was common for economists from developing countries, especially in Latin America, to argue that for a variety of reasons the price mechanism in general and currency devaluation in particular did not work well in their countries. For example, they argued that there were institutional rigidities: a quasi-feudal agricultural sector would not expand production even if offered higher prices; organized urban workers would demand higher wages to offset the inflationary impact of a devaluation. They further argued that their countries' reliance on exports of primary products, which faced inelastic demand, meant that any attempt to increase export volumes would drive down the price received without increasing the foreign exchange earned. And they argued that the lack of domestic production competing with imports would prevent any fall in imports as a result of devaluation. Thus, they asserted, devaluation would not succeed at improving the trade balance, but would simply lower real incomes and/or lead to an acceleration in the rate of inflation.

This so-called structuralist view is now out of fashion among development economists, but it sometimes reappears in different contexts. During the 1970s, a form of structuralism achieved considerable policy prominence in the United Kingdom, where it was strongly pushed by the Cambridge Economic Policy Group (see, for example, Godley 1979 and other references discussed below). In the United States, a sort of neostructuralism emerged in 1986–87 amid the widespread disappointment over the continuing rise in the US trade deficit in spite of a sharply falling dollar.

Some of this revival of structuralism represented a crude failure to appreciate the role that relative prices play in economic decisions; for example, it was common for lay commentators to deny that a lower dollar would reduce US purchases of Japanese goods, asserting either that the United States produced no competing goods or that the quality of the Japanese products was so much better that no conceivable price differential would make any difference.

Politically motivated structuralism also gives foreign barriers to trade an exaggerated role as an explanation of persistent US trade problems: it was common in the mid–1980s to hear assertions that foreign protectionism would prevent any substantial increase in US exports. Proponents of a get-tough policy with Japan, including Fallows (1989), Prestowitz (1989), and Dornbusch (1989), still in effect assert that, in the case of Japan, implicit import restrictions are blocking trade adjustment.

More interestingly, however, during the 1980s a sophisticated version of neostructuralism emerged, which held not that relative prices were unimportant, but that the strategies of imperfectly competitive firms, especially in the face of uncertainty about future exchange rates, might frustrate the adjustment process.

The two most important concepts in this new literature were those of "pricing to market" and "hysteresis." Pricing to market occurs when firms, rather than pass on exchange rate changes into export prices, try to hold onto their market position by keeping prices in the importing country's currency stable. Such behavior was obvious in some consumer goods during the 1980s, especially when gray markets began to develop in some Japanese products reimported into Japan. A possible theoretical basis for pricing to market was suggested in an influential paper by Dornbusch (1987), and the extent to which it occurs in practice was documented more fully in several elegant empirical papers by Marston (1989, 1990) using Japanese data. Two key questions remain, however: Was pricing to market more widespread and severe in the 1980s than in the past? And did it in any important way frustrate the adjustment process?

Pricing to market is, in the light of Marston's work, undeniably something that really happens. More controversial is the idea of hysteresis: that markets lost when a country's currency rises in value may not be regained when the currency declines to its original level. This might occur if one thinks of market share as a kind of investment, achieved through costly creation of consumer reputation and of distribution networks. Once foreign firms have exploited a high dollar to establish new markets in the United States, they may hold onto them even at a less favorable exchange rate; once US firms have decided to abandon foreign markets for the same reason, they may not find it worthwhile to try to break back in even if the dollar falls to its original level.[5] Initially introduced as a hypothesis in Baldwin and Krugman (1989), the idea of hysteresis gained popularity as trade imbalances persisted, but despite efforts by Baldwin (1988) it has never really been firmly established as an important phenomenon.

In general, the empirical force of arguments suggesting that exchange rates are ineffective at correcting current account imbalances has fallen considerably since 1987. We will consider individual-country experiences in the next section, but by any measure the period since 1987 has seen a marked narrowing of deficits and surpluses, especially relative to growing world income (with the

---

5. Richard Baldwin has suggested the term "beachhead effect" for this phenomenon, with an implied military analogy. For example, it was a lot harder to get Saddam Hussein out of Kuwait than it would have been to stop him from getting in in the first place.

counterpart developments in the United States, Japan, and Germany of course dominating the picture).

It is also becoming embarrassingly clear that at least some of the apparently anomalous behavior of trade volumes and prices in the 1980s represents oddities in the data, rather than in reality. Lawrence (1990), in particular, has shown that if computers are excluded, the behavior of US trade in the 1980s looks more or less in line with pre–1980 expectations. Measurement of trade in computers is notoriously subject to difficulties: given the rapid improvement in technology, it is extremely difficult to establish reliable indices of either prices or volumes. The Bureau of Economic Analysis, the US Commerce Department agency that monitors US economic performance, attempts to adjust statistics on computers to represent the improvement in quality. Lawrence's evidence suggests that they have overcorrected, or at least that behavior in the computer market is wholly unrepresentative of behavior elsewhere.

This does not mean that the structuralist critique is completely groundless. There are at least two kinds of mild structuralism that remain reasonable sources of concern.

First, while crude structuralism is often characterized by misplaced concreteness ("America doesn't make VCRs—and can you imagine the Japanese buying Chevys?") that misses the complexity and flexibility of real economies, some degree of concreteness is not out of place. As Allen J. Lenz's paper for the IIE conference (chapter 2) reminds us, aggregate trade performance is the sum of trade performance in individual industries. While there is a great deal of commonality in industry experiences, there are also individual industry stories that matter. Telling the story of the subsidized rise of Airbus as a competitor to US aircraft exports, or of Detroit's competitive failures, is no substitute for macroeconomic analysis, but neither is it irrelevant.

Second, even if one believes that the effectiveness of the exchange rate in the long run has been vindicated, we nevertheless live in the short run. And one need not be a strong-form structuralist, believing in the complete ineffectiveness of exchange rates to alter trade balances, to share some short-run structuralist concerns. A weak-form structuralist would argue that at least in the very short run, and possibly for a little longer, the real exchange rate changes needed to achieve substantial trade adjustment are simply too large to be tolerable. Suppose, for example, that a country with a large trade deficit were suddenly to be deprived of foreign funding, and was thus compelled to reduce its trade deficit rapidly. If it tried to do so purely via depreciation, it would subject its economy to a severe inflationary shock. As a result, the adjustment process for countries in balance of payments crisis typically involves economic contraction as well as depreciation.

This is, of course, the celebrated hard landing scenario of Stephen Marris (1987). Despite Marris's warnings, such a hard landing never materialized in the United States. One should not conclude from this that hard landings are impossible—ask the Latin Americans.

Why, then, was the United States able to avoid one? Marris's paper for the IIE conference (chapter 6) suggests that the main reason lies in the forbearance of capital markets, which did not insist on a sudden reduction of the US trade deficit, but were instead willing to continue financing the United States through a prolonged process of gradual adjustment. As argued in appendix B, this patience of the financial markets was actually something that one should have expected, although Marris argues that it was aided to a significant degree by the cooperative guidance of policymakers. With occasional official intervention averting any free-fall in the dollar, the United States was able to continue to attract financing during the long wait before depreciation could bring the trade deficit down, and was therefore not forced into the devaluation-stagflation cycle that has produced hard landings in Latin America and elsewhere.

We will discuss country experiences below. To anticipate the conclusions, however, we can say that on the whole recent analysis has tended to confirm the old-fashioned view that exchange rates work. There are clearly significant lags, as there always were, and as a result every major exchange rate change will be followed by a period of agonizing over whether the change will eventually prove effective. There are some suggestions that the lags may be longer than we realized. With hindsight, however, we can see that reports of the demise of the exchange rate mechanism in the 1980s were premature.

Are Exchange Rate Changes Necessary? The Shmooist View

During the 1960s there was a bitter dispute between leftist economists in Cambridge, England (led by Joan Robinson and Nicholas Kaldor), and moderate economists in Cambridge, Massachusetts (led by Robert M. Solow), over the meaning and nature of capital. For reasons that remain slightly puzzling, the English Cantabridgians believed that the idea that a meaningful aggregate measure of capital existed was a crucial ideological prop for capitalist exploitation; anti-Solow modelers therefore ridiculed the MIT school of capital theory for its working assumption that economies produce a single homogeneous good usable either for capital or for consumption. Somewhere along the line, commentators took to referring to this all-purpose good as a "shmoo," after a cartoon creature (invented by Al Capp) that would obligingly turn into whatever food one wanted.

Shmoo-theoretic models are common in international monetary economics; it is often useful in thinking about monetary and financial issues to abstract from relative price changes by imagining a world in which all countries simply produce a single good. In such a world, changes in national saving-investment balances would translate directly into changes in trade balances, without the need for any accommodating adjustments in relative prices or output. (John Williamson [chapter 5] felicitously described this during the IIE conference as an "immaculate transfer.")

A shmooist would argue that this simplification is actually a reasonable description of trade adjustment in the real world. Of course, nobody thinks that we live in a one-good world; the question is whether trade adjustment can be accomplished without significant real depreciation on the part of the deficit countries. That is, the shmooist denies that real exchange rate changes are a necessary or a helpful part of the adjustment process.

This position is essentially that taken by Bertil Ohlin in his debate with John Maynard Keynes over the transfer problem (see Mundell 1989 for an account of this classic debate). If one country sends money to another—whether as a gift (or tribute) or to finance investment—the counterpart must be a trade surplus on the part of the donor, and a deficit on the part of the recipient. Correspondingly, narrowing or eliminating these imbalances is like ending a transfer. Keynes argued that, in order to generate the required trade surplus, a donor country would have to experience a real depreciation; Ohlin's position was that the transfer itself could generate the required trade surplus, without the need for price changes.

In its original version, Ohlin's position was based on the point that a donor country, by spending less, automatically reduces its demand for imports, while a recipient, by spending more, automatically increases its demand for the donor's exports. If the two countries have the same spending pattern at the margin, this will lead to exactly the right trade surplus, with no need for any price change.

Obviously this is not what the conventional wisdom asserts. The basis of the conventional wisdom was clarified by Dornbusch, Fischer, and Samuelson (1977): it rests essentially on the imperfect integration of markets for goods and services. Because many (most) goods and services are nontraded, most of a marginal dollar of spending in any large country goes to purchase domestic goods. As a result, there is a presumption that a reduction in, say, the flow of Japanese funds to the United States will reduce the demand for US goods and raise the demand for Japanese goods; this will require a rise in the relative price of Japanese goods, which is to say a real appreciation of the yen.

The leading contemporary defenders of the Ohlin-shmoo position are Robert Mundell and Ronald I. McKinnon; at the IIE conference (chapter 5), Mundell presented a wide-ranging essay on the history of thinking about the international adjustment mechanism, focusing largely though not exclusively on this question. Both Mundell and McKinnon have pointed out that the attempt to justify conventional presumptions about the effects of a transfer by appealing to the importance of nontraded goods is contingent on one's views about the structure of production—specifically the view that exports and nontraded goods are better substitutes in production than nontraded and import-competing goods. It is possible in principle to imagine a world in which much of output is nontraded, yet in which a transfer can take place with no change in relative prices—or even a real depreciation in the recipient country.

Again, we will turn to country evidence in the next section. To anticipate, however, we may argue that the apparent success of income-and-elasticity trade equations for the US and Japanese trade balances, as documented at the IIE conference in papers by William R. Cline and Masaru Yoshitomi (chapters 2 and 3), provides the empirical basis for asserting that while Keynes may have been wrong in theory, he was right in practice. The conference also, however, addressed a third case, that of Germany. As a paper by Norbert Walter showed (chapter 4), Germany's current balance with its Western European neighbors has showed highly variable surpluses, under a regime of more or less fixed nominal exchange rates, and little obvious correlation between trade flows and real exchange rate indices. Others have observed the same thing, and they use the European experience under the European Monetary System to suggest that a fixed exchange rate system can in fact easily accommodate necessary balance of payments adjustments.

A key question is therefore whether the apparent contrast between the experiences of Germany, on the one hand, and the United States and Japan, on the other, undermines the conventional wisdom that exchange rate changes are a necessary part of the adjustment mechanism.

Is the Equilibrium Exchange Rate Stable? The Secularist View

Ask noneconomists about the causes of the US trade deficit, and they are unlikely to mention the exchange rate. Instead, they will view the deficit as a symptom of a broader decline in "competitiveness"—in productivity, technological leadership, and product quality. Economists may dismiss this lay view, secure in their knowledge that $X - M$ always equals $S - I$, even if the X's are shoddy and the M's superb. The popular view does, however, point up a practical problem with the standard view of exchange rates, namely, the problem of secular change, of a shift over time in the trade balance associated with any given real exchange rate.

Let me label as secularists those who believe that the relationship between exchange rates and trade is unstable. Laypeople—for example, policy-minded engineers at MIT—are often both secularists and structuralists. That is, they see trade imbalances as the result of shifting technological advantage between countries, and they do not believe that exchange rate adjustment can offset such shifts. Few economists are such strong-form secularists. Weaker versions of the position, however, do emerge on several issues.

The most widely held secularist position among economists is the assertion that there is a consistent downward trend in the equilibrium real dollar, that the US currency needs to depreciate a little bit each year in order to keep the trade balance in the same place. The prime evidence for this is the observation that by most measures the real dollar ended the 1980s about where it began, yet the United States went from rough balance in its current account to a persistent large deficit. In his paper for the IIE conference, Cline calls this the Krugman-Lawrence paradox; it is a more recent version of the observation by Houthakker and Magee (1969) that the United States appears to face a foreign income elasticity of demand for its exports that is lower than its own income elasticity of import demand. That is, if income grows at the same rate in the United States and in the rest of the world, US imports will tend to grow more rapidly than US exports; thus, even at a constant real exchange rate, the US trade deficit will tend to rise, and over the long run a steady real depreciation of the dollar will be necessary in order to avoid an ever-growing trade deficit. Japan's experience offers a counterpart paradox: the yen ended the decade far stronger than it entered it, without any move into deficit.

Considerable effort has been devoted to explaining the apparent secular downward trend in the dollar. To secularists the answer seems obvious: it is the statistical counterpart of the decline in US "competitiveness," i.e., the declining relative quality and technological sophistication of US goods. Cline suggests, on the contrary, that it may be a statistical illusion, which goes away if one uses the right price index, but this view was not favorably received by most others at the IIE conference. Peter Hooper (chapter 2), who has long argued for the inclusion of supply-side variables (such as measures of productive capacity) in trade equations, argues that when this is done the paradox goes away, or even emerges on the other side: US trade performance has been *better* than we might have expected. Some support for Hooper's argument that US competitiveness has actually improved comes from the Japanese experience, where there was an unexpectedly rapid decline in the surplus in 1989–90.

The important point about this argument is that although there are some meaningful disputes among economists about the long-term trajectory of the dollar, in general they are pretty close in their views—at least as compared with lay views about competitiveness. There is general if not universal agreement that there has been a downward trend in the real dollar consistent with trade balance, at least by the usual measures, with the outstanding questions being why and whether that trend will continue. But there is also general agreement that the trend is fairly slow, on the order of 2 percent or less annually. This can amount to a lot over the course of a decade, but it does not make the short- and medium-run response of trade to the exchange rate either unpredictable or irrelevant. In short, most of us may be secularists, but of a very mild form.

We have now described the conventional wisdom with regard to the international adjustment mechanism and the main challenges to that conventional wisdom. We will turn shortly to the experiences of the three largest market economies, to see what light they shed on the process. First, however, we need to ask how the analysis of the international adjustment mechanism affects one's view of appropriate international economic policy.

Policy Implications of Alternative Views

The Mass. Ave. View

The conventional analytical wisdom about the role of the exchange rate in trade adjustment is generally associated with a conventional policy wisdom as well. The main purpose of this study is to discuss whether and how the adjustment mechanism works, rather than how it should be used; nonetheless it is important to place this discussion in a policy context.

The essence of the conventional wisdom about adjustment policy was expressed clearly in a classic paper by Harry Johnson (1958). Johnson argued that in order to adjust its trade account—say, to reduce a current account deficit— a country needs to pursue both expenditure-reducing policies, such as fiscal tightening, and expenditure-switching policies, such as devaluation. Expenditure switching without expenditure reduction would lead to inflation, but reduction without switching would lead to recession. Johnson then went on to assert that normally exchange rate adjustment would be an effective expenditure-switching policy.

Johnson's analysis, or something like it, underlies two basic mainstream propositions about international economic policy:

■ *The trade balance is a macroeconomic issue*: Trade deficits fundamentally reflect a disparity between spending and income, not a market failure. They are therefore not an appropriate subject for trade policy instruments such as tariffs and import quotas: a trade deficit can be dealt with by a combination of domestic expenditure reduction and depreciation, and trade policy should be based solely on microeconomic considerations.

■ *Exchange rate flexibility is a valuable policy tool*: The ability to change the exchange rate makes it much easier to deal with payments imbalances, and this piece of the adjustment mechanism should not be given up—for example by establishing immutably fixed exchange rates—lightly.

If we follow the implications of these propositions, we are led to a view of international economic policy that is basically an international extension of conventional wisdom about the relationship between macroeconomic and microeconomic policy. Since the 1950s most US policy economists (if not always most academic macroeconomic theorists) have believed that the government should take an active role in macroeconomic stabilization but otherwise leave markets mostly to themselves. In this conventional view of economic policy, macroeconomic tools—monetary and perhaps fiscal policy—should be used to maintain an appropriate level of aggregate demand. With the problem of aggregate demand allocated to macroeconomic policy, microeconomic policies can then be formulated on pure efficiency grounds; in general this means that an activist macroeconomics is combined with free-market microeconomics.

In the international extension, one adds to the problem of aggregate demand the problem of payments imbalances. This problem can, however, be solved either through deliberate adjustment of the exchange rate or through adoption of a regime of floating exchange rates in which payments problems do not limit a country's freedom to follow expansionary monetary policies. With flexible exchange rates, in turn, there is no need for other instruments to deal with payments problems; this leaves one free to advocate free trade. So one arrives at the same basic recommendation: activism on the macro side, but laissez-faire on the micro side.

Critics of the conventional wisdom on macroeconomics, naturally enough, attack this point of view from both left and right. Interventionists think that job creation should be pursued through microeconomic as well as macroeconomic means, for example through regional and industrial policies; monetarists and their even more free-market-oriented successors think that the government should be as laissez-faire about aggregate demand as it is about supply and demand in individual markets.[6]

Structuralists and shmooists are, in effect, the international equivalents of leftist and rightist critics of the conventional wisdom on domestic monetary policy, challenging the two basic policy propositions from opposite directions. Let us consider each in turn.

The Structuralist Case for Protection

Structuralists argue that exchange rates do not work as an adjustment mechanism, or at any rate work only at an unacceptable cost. Thus something else is

6. These two kinds of challenge to conventional wisdom have each had a peculiarly limited area of success in the United States. Government intervention to save particular jobs often wins out over the arguments of economists in practice, for example in the Chrysler bailout, but has virtually no intellectual respectability. Opposition to an active stabilization policy, usually based on equilibrium models of the business cycle, is widespread and perhaps on

Figure 1 The structuralist view of the exchange rate–trade balance relationship

Trade balance

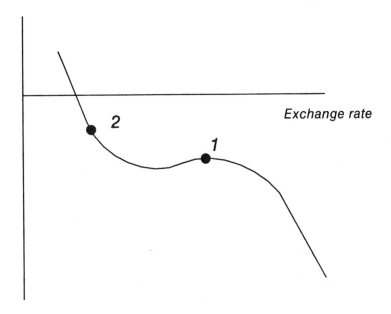

Exchange rate

needed. The something else is at best an industrial policy, at worst simple protectionism.

The argument may be schematically illustrated by a picture like figure 1. In that figure, the curve represents the relationship between the exchange rate and the trade balance as a structuralist might perceive it. Even structuralists generally agree that at some sufficiently low dollar the United States could balance its trade—if nothing else, at a very low dollar sheer lack of purchasing power would curb US demand for imports. What a structuralist like Robert Kuttner believes, however, is that the United States is currently at a point where modest dollar depreciation has only a small or even a perverse effect on the trade deficit, as represented by point *1* in the figure. Getting the deficit down substantially, say to the level at point *2*, would require a very large fall in the dollar; this would in turn imply large costs in the form of worsened terms of trade and domestic inflationary pressures. As Kuttner puts it (1991, 108) "the danger is that a

its way to being dominant in academic economics, but has had virtually no impact on policy.

cheaper dollar will only make the United States a poorer country, without making its products fully competitive."

It would therefore be greatly preferable to shift the entire curve up through some other means. Kuttner and other contemporary American structuralists are slightly evasive about what they propose, although skepticism about the effectiveness of exchange rates is generally followed in their writings by favorable discussions of managed trade. A nicely explicit discussion, however, was offered some years ago by the Cambridge Economic Policy Group (CEPG; Cripps and Godley 1976, 1978; Fetherston and Godley 1978; Godley 1979). The CEPG view was that UK growth was being constrained by the need to avoid running large current account deficits; that devaluation was ineffective as a way of reducing the deficits, both because of low elasticities and because of resistance by British workers to reductions in their real wages; and that tariffs or import quotas would therefore offer a superior alternative.

An extreme example may suggest the logic of such protectionist leanings. Imagine that at the current exchange rate a country faces a zero price elasticity of demand for its exports, and that its demand for imports is price-inelastic.Then depreciation would actually worsen the nominal trade balance, because while the volume of imports would fall, their value would actually rise. A tariff on imports, however, *would* improve the trade balance, because imports would fall but the price paid to foreigners would not increase.

The key to this example, of course, is that the country is assumed to have substantial market power in trade. In other words, the structuralist argument for protection is really a variant of the optimum tariff argument, which argues that large countries can use tariffs to improve their terms of trade. The economic case for an optimum tariff, however, has nothing to do with balance of payments adjustment: if the United States can successfully raise its welfare by imposing tariffs, there is no strictly economic reason to limit this policy to times when it has a trade deficit.

As a political matter, however, the structuralist case for protectionism may have something to it. There is not much question that large countries like the United States could in fact raise their welfare by imposing fairly substantial tariffs *if the rest of the world did not retaliate*. Indeed, quantitative models of trade like the computable general equilibrium model of Whalley (1985) suggest that the US optimum tariff rate is well above current levels, probably above 50 percent. An unprovoked US move to increase tariffs would, however, be seen as a beggar-thy-neighbor policy and would lead to retaliation or at least emulation. Protection undertaken to limit an intractable trade deficit, by contrast, might be much more readily accepted. Indeed, the existing rules of the international trade game embodied in the General Agreement on Tariffs and Trade make explicit allowance for special trade measures to deal with balance of payments problems.

The structuralist view of the adjustment process, then, gives at least indirect comfort to the idea of trade restrictions as a balance of payments tool.

The Shmooist Case for Fixed Exchange Rates

The essential moral of the shmooist view of the adjustment process, if that view is correct, is that exchange rate flexibility is of no value, and hence that the micro-monetary advantages of fixed exchange rates need not be weighed against macroeconomic disadvantages. In other words, the shmooist analytical view of the adjustment process is closely connected with the renewed popularity of fixed exchange rates as a policy recommendation.

The idea that there is a trade-off between the microeconomic advantages of fixed rates and the macroeconomic advantages of floating was first advanced in a classic paper by Ronald McKinnon (1963), in which he presented what has since become the standard theory of optimum currency areas. According to the McKinnon approach, flexible exchange rates are useful because they allow countries to adjust their balance of payments with minimal change in the domestic price level—implying in particular that deficit countries are spared the necessity of deflation and the associated unemployment. On the other hand, exchange rate fluctuations impair the liquidity of domestic money. For a fairly closed economy, the liquidity cost will be small and the benefit of not having to let the balance of payments dictate macroeconomic policy large; the more open the economy, the less valuable is monetary independence and the more costly the degradation that exchange rate instability imposes on the moneyness of money.

This analysis has been taken to imply that the appropriate structure of the international monetary system is one of regional currency blocs, with interbloc exchange rates flexible. Imagine a world composed of very small monetary areas. Since these areas would be very open, they would benefit from being combined for monetary purposes into somewhat larger blocs. If one then imagines grouping successively larger blocs into fixed exchange rate areas, however, one eventually arrives at a point at which the costs of further enlarging the blocs exceed the benefits; at that point, the world will have been organized into optimum currency areas.

Of course, the theory by itself gives no quantitative sense of the size of optimum currency areas. At one extreme, one might make the politically outrageous but by no means economically absurd suggestion that each major metropolitan area would be best served by having an independent currency. At the other, one might argue that while in principle the benefits of ever-larger currency blocs are at some point outweighed by their costs, in practice the world as a whole is an optimal currency area—i.e., that global fixed rates are the best system. At the moment there is widespread support for the idea that optimum currency areas are continent-sized—say, just about as big as the European Community. This is not an unreasonable guess, but it is a belief supported by essentially no evidence.

What the shmooist position on the adjustment mechanism does, however, is to deny that the whole optimum currency argument has any validity. If adjustment does not require changes in the real exchange rate, then there is no value to having nominal exchange rate flexibility as a way of facilitating real exchange rate changes. This leaves only the microeconomic benefits of fixed rates; the optimum currency area is as big as possible.

The foremost proponent of this view is, remarkably, the same Ronald McKinnon who is responsible for the optimum currency area argument. McKinnon (1984), in arguing against the need for exchange rate flexibility, has asserted that real exchange rate adjustment is necessary only for an "insular" economy with less than full mobility of capital—with mobile capital, changes in the saving-investment balance would be automatically converted into changes in current account balances. In some of their writings, McKinnon and others have seemed to suggest that this irrelevance of the real exchange rate is independent of the nature of world markets for goods and services; thus McKinnon wrote that *"With smoothly functioning capital markets, little or no change in the 'real' exchange rate is necessary to transfer saving from one country to another."* (McKinnon 1984, 14, italics in the original). As pointed out above, however, the shmooist view in fact does hinge crucially on how goods and services markets work. In particular, if conventional trade equations are right, then 1980s McKinnon is wrong.

This is not to say that 1960s McKinnon's belief in the benefits of fixed rates may not be right, and that even though exchange rate flexibility is valuable it is not valuable enough to justify flexible exchange rates for the United Kingdom or even the United States. The point is, however, that the shmooist view would make the case for fixed rates a closed one, where conventional wisdom leaves it very much open.

Policy Implications of Secularism

The secularist challenge to conventional wisdom about international adjustment is less directly relevant to policy than the other two. In principle it should perhaps have no exchange rate policy implications at all. Suppose, for example, that I am convinced that there is a secular downward trend in the equilibrium real dollar of 2 percent per year, directly as a result of declining relative US technology and quality, or indirectly as a result of poor US education, deteriorating infrastructure, or whatever. If I hold to conventional wisdom I will declare this to be a microeconomic problem, to be addressed with microeconomic instruments, such as education reform and increased government investment spending. Meanwhile, we should let the dollar depreciate. A shmooist (although he might have trouble accepting the idea that real exchange rates can show any trend) would prefer to allow the nominal dollar to remain stable, and would want the real exchange rate adjustment to take place via relative deflation. In either case, however, conceding the existence of a secular trend need not alter the policy conclusion.

In practice, however, secularism and structuralism are usually associated, and evidence of US secular loss of competitiveness is usually a key part of the arguments of advocates of an aggressive trade policy (such as Clyde Prestowitz's Economic Strategy Institute).

The logic of this association can perhaps best be appreciated by considering the typical dialogue between a mainstream economist and a group of opinionated laymen concerned about US competitiveness (like the belligerent engineers mentioned above). The laymen point to US trade deficits as evidence both that the United States has a major problem of competitiveness and that a direct response in the areas of trade and industrial policy is needed. The economist argues that the trade deficit is a macroeconomic problem, which can be fixed by dollar depreciation. When, as usually happens, the laymen express skepticism about the importance of exchange rates, the economist points to the role of a strong dollar in creating deficits in the 1980s. And at that point the laymen deny that the dollar was the cause of the trade deficit, pointing to US technological and quality failures instead.

As mentioned earlier, Kuttner (1991) is perhaps the clearest published example of how structuralism and secularism can reinforce one another. Arguing against relying on dollar depreciation to solve the trade deficit—and, implicitly, for managed trade as the alternative—he writes that:

> Even with a much cheaper dollar, the factors that have allowed America's competitors to adjust in the past to a cheapening dollar will continue to operate—the decline in input prices, the ability to outsource, to price to market, and the fact that some products just aren't made in the United States. To a few economists who emphasize structural factors, the danger is that an ever-cheaper dollar will only make the United States a poorer country, without making its products fully competitive. Even at 100 yen to the dollar, how many American-made Chevrolets will be sold in Japan and how many VCRs will be made in the U.S.A.? (Kuttner 1991, 108).

Secularism, then, need not have any particular policy moral. In practice, however, it generally reinforces the structuralist bias toward using trade policy for balance of payments adjustment. And thus even though it perhaps should not, evidence that secular change is modest in extent is in effect a result that supports the case for free trade.

We have now presented the conventional wisdom on the international adjustment process, described the main challenges to that conventional wisdom, and discussed the policy implications of those challenges. The next step is to ask what the experience of the 1980s tells us about how the international adjustment process really works.

The Record of Adjustment: 1985–90

The United States

The aggregate story of US external adjustment is simple and familiar, and is shown in figure 2. During the 1980s, the real exchange rate of the dollar went up the hill and came back down. The US current account deficit also went up, lagging behind the dollar. It too came tumbling after, but not all of the way.

Shown a picture like figure 2, neither economists nor the general public are likely to feel the kind of frustration over the United States' failure to adjust that they did three years ago. Nonetheless, US performance raises two major questions.

First, why did the adjustment take so long, with the US deficit continuing to rise for two years after the dollar began to fall? It was suggested above that the empirical consensus is for at least a two-year lag before the bulk of the impact of the exchange rate on the trade balance is felt, but this is not the same as saying that two years should pass before there is *any* impact. The question of the sluggishness of adjustment is connected with the structuralist challenge to conventional wisdom: such sluggishness is *prima facie* evidence for the presence of structural impediments to adjustment.

Second, since the dollar at the end of the 1980s was at about its level at the beginning of the decade, and had been fluctuating around that level for three years, why was the United States still running a substantial current account deficit? This question is, of course, associated with the secularist challenge.

At the IIE conference, William Cline addressed the behavior of US trade from an aggregate perspective. He found that a conventional set of equations actually accounted quite well for the data—there was, in retrospect, no anomaly to be explained. This is similar to the findings of Lawrence (1990); hence it is useful to consider the two papers in tandem.

The first point to consider is why the US trade deficit continued to widen for so long before turning down. The Cline-Lawrence answer is essentially that the United States did not carry out the textbook experiment of devaluing its currency from an initial equilibrium position, while holding all else equal. Instead, the dollar's decline followed a period of rise, and it took place against the background of continuing economic recovery. This stretched out the turnaround of the US current account, for two main reasons. First, not all the direct effects of previous dollar rise had worked their way through to trade volumes, so that some continu-

Figure 2 United States: real exchange rates and current account deficits, 1980–90

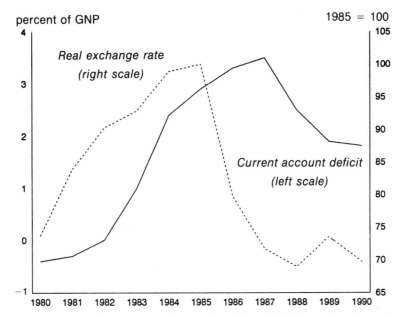

percent of GNP

1985 = 100

Real exchange rate (right scale)

Current account deficit (left scale)

Sources: International Monetary Fund, *International Financial Statistics,* various issues; Organization for Economic Cooperation and Development, *Main Economic Indicators,* various issues.

ing rise in the deficit was in effect in the pipeline. Second, because of the previous rise in the dollar, by 1985 US imports greatly exceeded US exports; this created a "gap factor," in which the growth in imports with economic recovery tended to raise the deficit unless offset by a significantly *faster* rate of increase in exports. To take an extreme numerical example, if imports are 500 and exports 200, and if imports are rising by 10 percent per year, then exports must grow by 25 percent just to keep the deficit from growing. These essentially commonplace factors, Cline's analysis suggests, delayed the turnaround in the US deficit by a few quarters relative to what the textbook case might have led us to expect.

The interesting question in that case is why analysts were so willing to call their own conventional wisdom into question. A major part of the answer is probably that official statistics showed what appeared to be very anomalous price behavior, particularly on the import side. Figure 3 makes the point. One line shows the ratio of the US import price deflator to the US GNP deflator, as reported in the national income accounts. Relative import prices fell as the dollar rose, as one might expect; but according to this measure they were very slow to rise as

Figure 3   United States: relative import prices, 1980–90

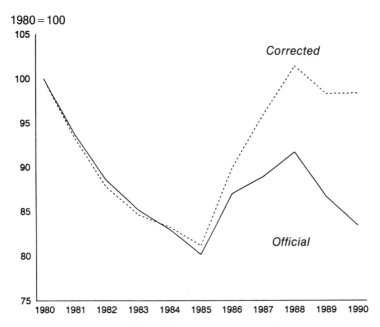

Source: Lawrence, Robert Z. 1990. "US Current Account Adjustment: An Appraisal." Brookings Papers on Economic Activity 2:343–82.

the dollar fell. This observation suggested to many economists—myself included—that something nonstandard was going on, with foreign (especially Japanese) firms showing a new strategic determination to hold onto the markets they had won in the first half of the 1980s.

It has become increasingly clear that the anomaly may have been more in the data than in the real world. Lawrence (1990) has shown that essentially all of the peculiarity in price behavior is associated with computers—and the creation of adequate price indices for computers, as noted above, is notoriously difficult. This point is also made in figure 3, which shows the contrast between the national income accounts measure of relative import prices and Lawrence's constructed index of nonoil, noncomputer relative import prices. Lawrence's measure behaves exactly the way the most conventionally minded economist would expect.

No one has ever claimed that conventional trade equations are highly precise, likely to track the behavior of the trade balance perfectly when projected out of sample. The important question for policy analysis is whether the predictions of such conventional equations are inside the ballpark, or whether the anomalies

Figure 4 Japan: real exchange rates and current account surpluses, 1980–90

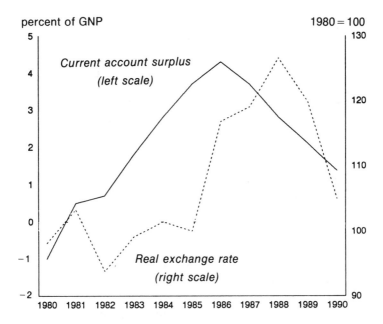

percent of GNP

1980 = 100

Sources: International Monetary Fund, *International Financial Statistics,* various issues; Organization for Economic Cooperation and Development, *Main Economic Indicators,* various issues.

are so great that conventional wisdom about the international adjustment process needs to be put aside. The fairly clear answer for the United States at this point is that the conventional wisdom has performed acceptably well, indeed better than we might have expected.

Japan

Japan's adjustment experience during the 1980s was not simply a mirror image of the US experience, but it follows a similar outline. As figure 4 shows, for several years after the 1985 Plaza meeting, Japan's effort at adjustment appeared to be a failure; then rapid adjustment seemed to occur, raising new questions about whether some more structural change was occurring.

Conventional models of Japanese trade, like the Economic Planning Agency model, find price elasticities of exports and imports comparable to those found for typical models of US trade: fairly low, but easily large enough to satisfy the

Table 4 Japan: current account, 1985–89 (percentages of GNP)

	1985	1986	1987	1988	1989
At current prices					
Exports of goods and services	16.4	13.1	12.7	13.0	14.6
Imports of goods and services	12.6	8.7	8.9	10.0	12.4
Current account balance	3.8	4.4	3.8	2.9	2.1
At 1985 prices					
Exports of goods and services	16.4	15.2	15.0	15.6	17.1
Imports of goods and services	12.4	12.5	13.0	14.8	17.3
Current account balance	4.0	2.7	2.0	0.8	−0.1

Sources: Organization for Economic Cooperation and Development, *Main Economic Indicators*, various issues; International Monetary Fund, *International Financial Statistics*, various issues.

Marshall-Lerner condition after an initial period of J-curve. At first glance, the behavior of Japan's current account from 1985 to 1988 seems flatly to refute any model predicting that exchange rate changes would produce international adjustment. From its trough in the first quarter of 1985, the yen nearly doubled in value against the dollar. Yet Japan's current account surplus in dollar terms was actually higher in 1988 than in 1985, and only slightly below its 1986 peak. Not too unreasonably, this apparent lack of adjustment provoked both political outrage and analytical soul-searching.

In retrospect, however, the stickiness of the Japanese surplus can be explained without much stretching as a consequence of a set of special factors. Masaru Yoshitomi's paper on Japan, like Cline's paper on the United States, shows that ordinary models worked better than many people imagined. The key point is that the stability of the nominal surplus masks a sharp change in real trade flows. As table 4 shows, in volume terms Japanese net exports fell sharply relative to GNP, while imports rose. In constant prices, the current account surplus fell by almost 4 percent of GNP.

This large real adjustment was, however, hidden by price changes. First, the 1985 worldwide collapse in the price of oil, a major import with inelastic demand, inflated Japan's nominal trade surplus. Second, the high initial ratio of exports to imports meant that the perverse valuation effect of a stronger yen via higher dollar export prices was unusually large, leading to an unusually large and prolonged J-curve. Also, as in the case of the United States, the fact that the yen was falling before it began rising, combined with the gap factor, helped to delay adjustment. Overall, the adjustment was not much different from what conventional models would have predicted.

After 1988, there was a reverse puzzle. Although the yen was stable or even rising in real terms after 1988, the Japanese current account surplus fell sharply. This raised speculation that some fundamental structural change had occurred or was occurring, perhaps tied to Japan's surging direct investment abroad: it was widely suggested that Japanese firms, like US firms a generation before, were shifting to overseas production for the Japanese market and local production for foreign markets. If this were the case, it would contribute both to raising Japanese imports and reducing Japanese exports.

Yoshitomi's paper suggests, rather prosaically, that the bulk of the explanation for the current account adjustment lies in more mundane factors. Most of the surge in imports is accounted for by increases in special categories, notably nonmonetary gold and oil, rather than ordinary manufactured goods. The export slump is tied more closely to the developing recession in Japan's export markets than to any large-scale shift of production overseas. The rapid adjustment after 1988, like the sluggish adjustment before it, seems to tell us more about the importance of getting the details right than about any fundamental need to revise our analytical framework.

In addition to the puzzles of overall adjustment, Japanese experience poses three specific questions. First is the question of export pricing. Pricing to market is a well-documented fact for Japanese exports. But was it more widespread in the post–1985 period than previously? The answer seems to be yes, but not dramatically so. Historical relationships between the exchange rate and Japanese export prices would have led us to expect the yen's doubling in value to be accompanied by about a 40 percent fall in yen export prices. In fact they fell about 60 percent. Much of the difference, however, can be attributed (once again) to special factors, notably the crash in oil and other commodity prices. Some residual is left unexplained, but on balance Japanese pricing behavior is not too different from what one might have expected. Yoshitomi argues that any anomalies in Japanese export pricing behavior were too small to explain the apparent anomalies in US import pricing behavior; this view is consistent with the evidence that those US anomalies represent data problems as much as real events.

A second question concerns the macroeconomics of Japan's adjustment. Whereas Japan's move into current account surplus was associated with a tightening of fiscal policy, the unwinding of that surplus was not accompanied by any comparable loosening. How was this possible? The accounting answer is a remarkable surge in domestic private investment demand. The reasons for that surge, however, remain an open question.

Finally, Japan presents its own version of the Houthakker-Magee-Krugman-Lawrence effect. Just as the dollar rose, then fell back to its original level, but left a seemingly permanently higher trade deficit, so too Japan's current account surplus surged and then fell back to more or less its original level, but at a far

Figure 5 Germany: real exchange rates and current account surpluses 1980–90

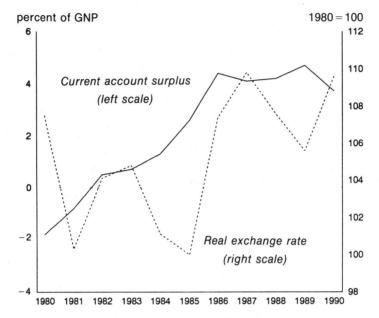

percent of GNP   1980 = 100

Sources: International Monetary Fund, *International Financial Statistics,* various issues; Organization for Economic Cooperation and Development, *Main Economic Indicators,* various issues.

higher real yen. Again, this apparent secular trend shows up in a difference in income elasticities of exports and imports (a very large difference given Japan's high rate of growth compared with its trading partners); presumably it reflects deeper supply-side phenomena that our models do not capture properly.

Overall, Japan's experience, like that of the United States, appears in retrospect to be far more in line with the standard view of international adjustment than initial reports suggested.

Germany

The Japanese and US adjustment experiences since 1985 have, in a rough sense, been counterparts. Germany, by contrast, has marched to a quite different drummer. While the mark rose against the dollar in tandem with the yen, Germany's current account surplus did not decline: in dollar terms it more than tripled from 1985 to 1989, and (as figure 5 shows) it rose from 2.6 percent to 4.6 percent of German GNP.

Does the German experience contradict the conventional wisdom on trade adjustment? It is not possible to offer as detailed an accounting for German trade as for that of the United States and Japan; for reasons to be discussed in a moment, it is more difficult to estimate German trade equations. Nonetheless, we can say for Germany as for the other two nations that the seeming contradiction of conventional wisdom is more apparent than real.

To some extent the failure of German surpluses to fall, like that of Japan, can be attributed to the fall in oil and other commodity prices. Germany is almost as dependent on imported raw materials as Japan, and in volume terms its imports grew consistently faster than its exports even as its nominal surplus was growing.

The main special feature of Germany, however, is that it is a very open economy, most of whose trade is focused on nearby European nations rather than on the United States and Japan. Indeed, the German trade surplus with the United States declined modestly in dollar terms and sharply in mark terms from 1985 to 1989, while the deficit with Japan widened. These movements were offset, however, by a surging surplus in German trade with the rest of Europe. (The effects of this surplus on the overall dollar surplus were, in yet another valuation story, exaggerated by the overall appreciation of European currencies against the dollar.)

Where the apparent nonadjustment of US and Japanese trade balances has provided ammunition for structuralist critics of orthodoxy, the apparent ease of trade adjustment within Europe provides the strongest empirical case for a shmooist view. As Norbert Walter's paper shows, Germany's current balance with its Western European neighbors has showed highly variable surpluses, under a regime of more or less fixed nominal exchange rates and little obvious correlation between trade flows and real exchange rate indices. Others have observed the same thing—and they use the European experience under the EMS to suggest that a fixed exchange rate system can in fact easily accommodate necessary balance of payments adjustments.

One should, however, be cautious in interpreting the evidence. After one starts to clean up the story by looking at the details, the German balance of payments experience begins to look less exotic.

First, as already mentioned, German trade with non-European nations, especially the United States, has in fact shown the kind of correlation with the real exchange rate that one would expect from the US and Japanese experiences—that is, if there is any evidence for a shmoo world, it ends in Europe.

Second, even the increase in Germany's surpluses with the rest of Europe can be explained in part by currency movements: the deutsche mark depreciated in real terms throughout most of this period.

Third, differences in short-term growth rates explain much of what happens in intra-European trade balances. Precisely because trade among European nations is so large, seemingly small differences in growth rates between countries can have a large effect on trade measured as a share of GNP. One way to put this is the following: since trade is three times as large a share of national income in Germany as it is in the United States, essentially because of intra-European trade, we would expect a difference in growth rates between Germany and its (mainly European) trading partners to have three times the impact on Germany's current account as a percentage of GNP. And in fact during 1985–89 German growth lagged that of other European countries: growth in domestic demand was more than a percentage point slower.

Finally, it is not too surprising that it is difficult to find a clear relationship between real exchange rates and trade flows within Europe, even if one is an unrepentant Mass. Ave. thinker. The reason is that when trade flows are as large as they are within Europe, the exchange rate changes needed to accommodate capital flows are small and easily obscured by growth effects, measurement error, and secular change.

This last point may need some enlarging. Consider a country whose saving rate rises, causing it to begin exporting capital at the rate of 2 percent of GNP. Suppose also that, as many estimates suggest, the price elasticities of both exports and imports are around 1. If the country starts with exports and imports of around 10 percent of GNP (as in the case of the United States), the currency will have to depreciate in real terms by a quite palpable 20 percent. If, however, the country starts like Germany with exports and imports of 30 percent of GNP, the required depreciation will be less than 7 percent. Now, our indices of real exchange rates are not perfect; movements in relative price indices may reflect not only actual changes but also differences in weighting schemes, in quality adjustments, and so on. Also, nobody thinks that equilibrium real exchange rates are constant. So the association between current account shifts and real exchange rate changes, obvious in US data, could easily be masked in German data by a variety of kinds of noise.

Also, while it may be difficult to establish any consistent relationship between real exchange rates and intra-European trade flows, the problems caused by German unification suggest that even Europe is far from being a shmoo economy. The cost of German unification has in effect forced West Germany into a Reaganesque fiscal expansion, which like the Reagan expansion is being offset by a tight monetary policy. Given German dominance of the EMS, the rest of Europe is in effect forced to emulate German monetary contraction. Under a shmooist view, this policy mix would not produce any conflict of interest: the fiscal expansion would offer a common European stimulus, so the same degree of monetary contraction would be appropriate everywhere. The only effect of the German fiscal expansion would be a reduction of Germany's current account surplus—Williamson's immaculate transfer at work.

In fact, however, matters are not working at all smoothly. The lion's share of spending in East Germany falls on West German products, so that a monetary policy tight enough to curb a German boom has produced a recession in the rest of Europe. This demonstrates both that German goods are less than perfect substitutes for those of other European nations, and that there is significant home bias in spending—precisely the combination of factors under which real exchange rate changes are a necessary part of the adjustment process.

Summary

As late as 1988, the trade experiences of the three largest market economies seemed to show that conventional wisdom about the international adjustment process was badly in need of revision. US deficits and Japanese surpluses were stubbornly persistent despite massive exchange rate adjustment, while German surpluses were growing in the teeth of a soaring mark.

The overall impression one gains from studying these experiences more closely is the extent to which apparently anomalous behavior is the result of special factors and annoying details. In all cases the peculiarity of the starting point distorted events. The dollar had been rising before it fell, and on the eve of the dollar's depreciation the United States had a massive trade deficit. The first fact meant that trade imbalances still had momentum behind them; the second that the sheer logic of growth and inflation (a.k.a. the gap factor) tended to push nominal imbalances up. The worldwide collapse in oil prices affected Germany and Japan more than it did the United States. Differential growth in Europe widened German local surpluses even as the surplus with the United States dwindled.

Peculiar price behavior, the subject of intense interest and speculation, looks less peculiar in retrospect: some of it was illusory, the result of bad indices, and much of the rest was the result of falling raw materials prices.

Even the rather sudden collapse of the German and Japanese surpluses in 1990 seems to have rather pedestrian economic (if not political) explanations. In particular, the suggestion that Japanese direct investment abroad has produced a fundamental change in Japanese trade patterns appears premature at best.

The International Adjustment Process: A Verdict

How the International Adjustment Process Works

The 1980s were a time of spectacular gyrations in the international economy. The deepest recession since the 1930s, the rise and fall of the dollar, the debt crisis, and the emergence of current account imbalances on a scale not seen since the 1920s amounted to a testing to destruction of our pet theories of international macroeconomics and finance.

Have the lessons of that experience invalidated traditional views of the international adjustment process? The surprising answer seems to be that they have not. Indeed, on the whole the standard view, what I have called the Mass. Ave. model, holds up remarkably well. In particular, my reading of the papers and discussion from the IIE conference is that, where the problem is one of reducing severe international trade imbalances:

- exchange rate changes work;

- they are necessary;

- the relationship between trade and exchange rates is stable.

Exchange Rate Changes Work

Before the 1980s, most economists concerned with the empirical modeling of US trade flows made use of simple equations that explained imports and exports by income and relative prices; the income elasticities in these equations tended to be about 2 (a little less for exports, a little more for imports), the price elasticities low in the short run but rising to 1 or a little more after two years or so.

During the 1980s, and in particular as the US trade deficit continued to widen after 1985, it was widely argued that this standard approach was misleading, because strategic behavior by foreign firms in general and Japanese firms in particular meant that exchange rates no longer worked to reduce imbalances. Yet two years after the dollar began its decline, the United States experienced an export boom; this happened just about when and in the magnitude that the traditional models would have predicted. There will always be some analysts who will assert that what works in practice does not work in theory. For the impure-minded, however, the evidence seems overwhelming that exchange rate changes do indeed work.

Real Exchange Rate Changes Are Necessary

During the 1980s a number of economists, most prominently Robert Mundell and Ronald McKinnon, questioned the need for real exchange rate changes as part of the adjustment process. It took a while before it was clear how the two RMs differed from the standard view, but eventually it emerged that their position was essentially a replay of Bertil Ohlin's side of the classic debate over the transfer problem—which has nothing to do either with monetary issues or with the integration of capital markets. And the question they raise is an empirical one: are world markets for goods and services sufficiently well integrated, or with sufficient substitution in demand and supply, so as to allow transfers to be effected with minor changes in relative prices?

As I read the evidence, the answer is a clear no for trade among the United States, Japan, and Europe. Within Europe a better case can be made for immaculate transfers that do not require real exchange rate changes, but even there the problems caused by German unification show that the inability to adjust exchange rates imposes some real costs.

The Relationship Between Trade and Exchange Rates Is Stable

Some of the most spectacular changes of the 1980s were of a kind that macroeconomic models are poorly equipped to capture. US leadership in technology and productivity was visibly eroded, while Japan surged ahead. The spread of microelectronics revolutionized a number of industries. Europe first seemed to sink into Eurosclerosis, then shook off its lethargy and boldly drove toward economic unity. One would not have been surprised to find that trade flows, stirred by all these changes, would be very poorly tracked by conventional equations.

The big surprise, then, is that there have been so few surprises. To a man from Mars or from the electrical engineering department, it is the apparent stability of the relationship between exchange rates, incomes, and trade flows, not the drift and errors in that relationship, that would surely seem most remarkable.

The general verdict, then, must be that the international adjustment process has worked, in both meaningful senses: that is, it has worked acceptably, and it has worked about the way conventional wisdom thought it would.

Implications for Economic Policy

The evidence on the international adjustment process essentially confirms conventional wisdom. That conventional wisdom, however, has been so much under attack of late that to reaffirm it is almost a radical act. Not surprisingly, the policy implications of that reaffirmation similarly confirm an embattled conventional wisdom, one that has perhaps been under even greater attack.

As pointed out earlier, the conventional wisdom on economic policy for open economies is an internationalized version of mainstream thinking on the respective roles of macroeconomic and microeconomic policy at the domestic level. Mainstream economists in general, taking their cue in the first instance from Paul A. Samuelson, have for decades advocated a combination of more or less laissez-faire microeconomic policy with an active use of monetary policy to manage the macroeconomy. These policies, though they may seem contradictory from an ideological point of view, are regarded by the mainstream economist as complements: because the use of monetary policy to control recession and inflation removes any need to use microeconomic policies to pursue macroeconomic goals, it frees the government to focus these policies on allocative efficiency instead.

Challenges to this mainstream point of view come from both the left and the right. Critics from the left would have the government intervene directly in markets to try to improve macroeconomic performance—for example, by using incomes policies to hold down inflation while pursuing expansionary monetary policies, or by using regional policies to try to generate jobs in high-unemployment areas. On the other side, monetarists and their successors would have the central bank forgo any active attempt to stabilize the economy, either because they regard the potential for error as greater than the potential benefits (the traditional monetarist view) or because they regard monetary policy as ineffective (the equilibrium business cycle view).

The policy debate in international economics runs along similar lines. Mainstream international economists—Richard N. Cooper (1971) provides a particularly clear example—have long advocated a combination of free trade and flexible (although not necessarily freely floating) exchange rates. Again, these policies are seen as complementary: exchange rate flexibility means that balance of payments problems are no longer an excuse for protectionism.

The two main challenges to the conventional wisdom about the adjustment process, those of the structuralists and the shmooists, lead directly to (and are largely motivated by) challenges to this policy position. Structuralists argue that exchange rate flexibility is ineffective, because exchange rate changes do not work; this assertion provides the basis for advocating import controls or other forms of managed trade to deal with payments imbalances. Shmooists argue that exchange rate changes serve no useful purpose, and they therefore assert that the benefits of a return to fixed exchange rates are not offset by any costs.

The evidence of the period from 1985 to 1990 allows us simply to dismiss the structuralist concern. Exchange rate adjustment did and does work. Because of the substantial lags in adjustment, all major exchange rate adjustments are followed by a period of confusion and doubt about the adjustment mechanism.[7] In the end, however, the depreciation of the dollar and the appreciation of the

---

7. For example, similar doubts were voiced following the 1967 devaluation of sterling and the 1971–73 depreciation of the dollar.

yen have had just about the effects that conventional wisdom would have predicted. There are intellectually defensible arguments for managed trade, and there are better arguments for domestic industrial policy; the assertion that exchange rates cannot solve payments imbalances is not one of them.

The only possible situation in which a balance of payments argument for import controls might be made is in the context of foreign-exchange crises like those faced by developing countries in 1982–83. Given the evident lags in the response of trade flows to exchange rates, we are all structuralists in the very short run. If a country is faced with an abrupt cutoff of capital inflows, one can therefore argue with some justification for supplementing currency depreciation with temporary import controls. Thus, if Marris's hard landing had in fact materialized in the United States, one could have made a reasonable case for supplementing currency depreciation with temporary import controls.

In fact, however, nothing of the sort happened in the United States. International capital markets proved quite willing to continue to finance the US current account deficit while the effects of dollar depreciation worked their way through the pipeline. One may be a pessimist about the effectiveness of the adjustment mechanism in the short run, but it works in the medium run, and financing has in fact been available to bridge the short-run difficulties. (The relationship between financing and adjustment in the United States since 1985 has puzzled many observers. An effort to provide a stylized description is provided in appendix B.)

While some politicians and a few economic heretics used the slowness of adjustment in the 1980s to argue for managed trade, the main challenge to conventional policy wisdom came from the other direction. During the 1980s there was growing disillusionment with floating exchange rates, and there were many calls for reestablishment of a fixed rate regime or at least for limits on the degree of permissible flexibility. These calls were based in large part on the perception that foreign-exchange markets had performed badly, leading to excessive and costly fluctuations and misalignments. The surprising success of the European Monetary System at stabilizing exchange rates also helped fuel the perception that fixed exchange rates are a more workable system than previously thought. An important part of the case for fixing exchange rates, however, has been the argument that flexible exchange rates do not perform a useful function—that exchange rate changes are not a necessary part of the adjustment mechanism.

What we have seen, however, is that experience since 1985 reconfirms the crucial role of real exchange rate changes in adjustment, and the facilitating role of nominal appreciation or depreciation in achieving such real changes. In other words, the conventional case in favor of exchange rate flexibility is as valid as ever.

Notice that this does not mean that freely floating exchange rates are necessarily appropriate. As pointed out earlier, even conventional wisdom, as embodied in the theory of optimal currency areas, agrees that there is a trade-off between the macroeconomic advantages of flexible rates and the microeconomic advantages of fixed rates. It is still possible to argue that the terms of this trade-off are such as to make a return to fixed rates desirable, or to invoke other factors, such as the need for inflation-prone countries to establish credibility by pegging their currencies. It is also possible to argue for systems of managed exchange rates, for example one based on target zones à la Williamson (1985). The shmooist position, however, is not that the costs of exchange rate flexibility exceed its benefits, but that there are no benefits at all; this is simply not a sustainable view.

What we have thus come to realize, after a decade in which the confidence of economists in the conventional wisdom—and of the public in economists—was profoundly shaken, is that the conventional wisdom was sounder than it seemed. The international adjustment mechanism does indeed seem to work more or less as understood a decade ago, and the policy views that were based on that understanding are still tenable.

This verdict does not deny that there are puzzles, or that much further research is needed. We are not, however, confronted with any great mystery—except, perhaps, the question of why not only the public but so many economists were so quick to declare the adjustment process a failure.

Appendix A: A Formal Statement of the Mass. Ave. Model

The text verbally described the standard model of open-economy macroeconomics, which I have called the Mass. Ave. model. This appendix offers a brief formal presentation in five equations.

The first equation of this model is the income identity. Income (which is determined by demand in this demand-side model) is the sum of domestic spending, which depends on income and the real interest rate, and net exports, which depend on domestic and foreign income as well as the real exchange rate:

(1) $\quad y = A(y, i - \pi) + NX(y, y^*, R)$

The second equation sets money supply equal to money demand, which depends on income and interest rates:

(2) $\quad \dfrac{M}{P} = L(y, i)$

The third equation determines the exchange rate. The typical formulation sets expected returns on domestic and foreign interest-earning assets equal, with

Figure A.1 Determination of the real exchange rate in the Mass. Ave. model

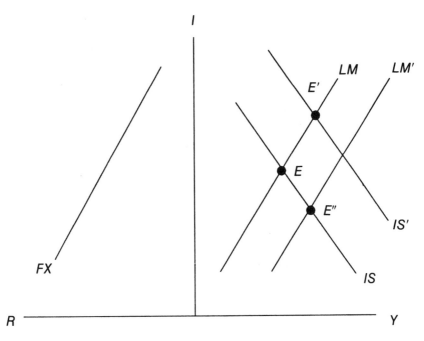

expected depreciation equal to the expected inflation differential plus some reversion of the real exchange rate to an expected long-run level:

(3) $i = i^* + \pi - \pi^* + \theta\, (R^e - R)$

Price determination completes the model. The rate of inflation is determined by an expectations-adjusted Phillips curve:

(4) $\dfrac{\dot{P}}{P} = g(y) + \pi$

Finally, expectations of inflation are adaptive, adjusting slowly toward actual inflation:

(5) $\dot{\pi} = \lambda \left(\dfrac{\dot{P}}{P} - \pi \right)$

This is, of course, simply an updated IS-LM model. Its short-run behavior can be represented by a two-panel diagram like figure A.1. On the left we represent the determination of the real exchange rate (in terms of the local-currency value of foreign exchange, *FX*), and on the right the determination of income; the *IS* curve shown there includes the effect of the interest rate on the real exchange rate and hence on net exports. From an initial equilibrium like point E, a fiscal expansion would move us to a point like E', raising income while appreciating the currency; a monetary expansion would move us to a point like E'', depreciating the currency.

In practice, even advocates of the Mass. Ave. model have in mind something a little more complicated, which takes into account the effects of lags in the adjustment of the trade balance to the exchange rate. The effects of such lags on the adjustment process are discussed in appendix B.

Appendix B: Financing and Adjustment

This study, like the conference on which it is based, has focused the bulk of its attention on the process of trade adjustment per se, and not on the macroeconomic background to that adjustment. Along with the controversies already discussed, however, the conference addressed two related questions about the context in which the decline of the dollar and of the US current account deficit has taken place. First, how is it possible for the US current account deficit to have declined so much when its supposed twin, the federal budget deficit, is headed for record highs? Second, why was the United States able to continue attracting foreign funds from 1985 to 1988 in spite of declining US interest rates?

Although a full treatment of these issues is a subject for another study, this appendix sketches out some answers.

The End of the Twin Deficit Era

The solution to the puzzle of why the budget deficit and the trade deficit have ceased to be twins is, like so many of the puzzles in recent US trade performance, a matter of details. For a variety of reasons, the numbers are not what they seem:

- A large part of the recent increase in the budget deficit consists of the cost of the savings and loan bailout. This cost, however, is best understood as the explicit recognition of a hidden government liability rather than as a new expenditure; depositors in thrifts are only being given money they thought they had in any case. Thus, the cost of the thrift bailout does not reduce national saving.

- For analytical purposes the remainder of the deficit needs to be corrected for both economic growth and inflation; as a share of GNP the deficit maintained a steady downward trend from 1985 to 1989.

- The 1990–91 recession has worsened the actual deficit, but not the full-employment deficit (i.e., the deficit that current policies would generate if productive factors in the United States were fully utilized).

- Finally, what matters for the current account is national saving as a whole, not just the federal component, and there has been some revival of saving in the private sector.

In a way it was a fluke that for much of the 1980s the uncorrected budget and trade deficits tracked one another as closely as they did. One would normally expect there to be enough nuisance factors complicating the picture to make the two deficits look quite different; we are now living in such normal times.

Financing the Deficit

A deeper conceptual issue is the question of how the United States was able to continue to attract capital inflows in spite of falling US interest rates in the second half of the 1980s. As pointed out earlier, this ability to continue financing the current account deficit until a low dollar could bring the deficit down was crucial to the United States' ability to avoid a hard landing. Was this success just a matter of luck, or was there a more fundamental mechanism at work? Without attempting a full accounting for US (and foreign) macroeconomic developments from 1985 to 1990, we can sketch out a stylized version of the adjustment process as it actually occurred; from this sketch it is possible to see that the ability of the United States to attract continued capital inflows was not an accident.

Imagine a country described by the formal model of appendix A, with the crucial addition of substantial lags in the response of the trade balance to the exchange rate. (A formal treatment is given below.) Suppose that this country combines a fiscal contraction with a monetary expansion just large enough to leave output unchanged. We have already seen that in the medium run this policy change will lead to a lower domestic interest rate; the lower interest rate will induce a currency depreciation; and the currency depreciation will lead to a fall in the current account deficit.

In the short run, however, currency depreciation will not reduce the current account deficit; rather, because of the J-curve, it will normally actually raise the deficit. Unless investors are willing to continue financing the deficit, the currency will fall without limit; yet the interest rate foreign investors are offered has fallen rather than risen. What keeps the capital flowing?

The answer is that the fall in the currency itself generates the necessary incentive. Suppose that investors were in fact unwilling to continue financing the country's current account deficit following a change in the policy mix. Then the country's currency would have to drop to a very low level to bring the current account into immediate balance, but it would recover from that low level once trade flows had had time to respond. Such a fall in the currency followed by a predictable recovery, however, would offer international investors the opportunity for large capital gains if they were to buy the currency during its period of weakness. These prospective capital gains would attract capital inflows—and these inflows would themselves limit the actual fall in the exchange rate. So, unless there is some additional reason for a collapse of capital inflows—for example, the fear of debt repudiation—capital inflows will be available to finance a transitional current account deficit following a policy change, even if that policy change lowers the domestic interest rate.

The actual extent of the currency decline is determined by the incentives required by investors. Following the policy change, the currency must fall to a level *below* its expected value in the medium run; this perceived undervaluation leads investors to expect it to *rise* in the future.[8] The size of the expected appreciation must be enough to offset the lower domestic interest rate, and thus assure the country of continued financing. Or, to put it another way, in the short run the currency must fall to a level that makes domestic assets look like good buys to international investors; the perceived cheapness of domestic assets is what attracts the financing needed to bridge the transition to a lower external deficit.

To see this more formally, consider a slightly modified version of the model of appendix A, in which trade adjusts to the exchange rate with a lag. A simple way to build such a lag into the algebra was suggested by Dornbusch (1976). We suppose that the *volumes* of exports and imports depend, not on the current real exchange rate, but on a "permanent" real exchange rate that is some distributed lag on past exchange rates. Net exports then depend both on this permanent exchange rate and on the actual spot exchange rate, with the spot exchange rate actually having a perverse effect because depreciation raises the relative price of imports. So we have:

(6) $NX = NX(Y, Y^*, R, R^P)$

where R^P is the permanent exchange rate. We suppose for simplicity that R^P simply adjusts gradually toward the current spot rate:

(7) $d(R^P)/dt = \lambda(R - R^P)$

---

8. Or, more strictly, the expected rate of appreciation must be greater, or the expected rate of depreciation less, than the expectation before the policy change.

Figure B.1 Temporary undervaluation and financing during adjustment

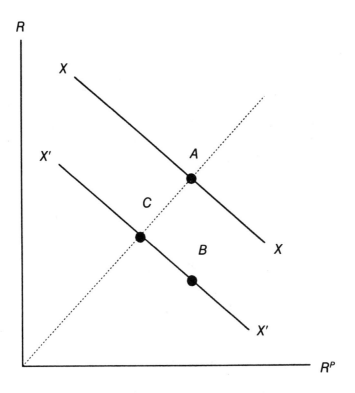

The process of adjustment can now be described in terms of figure B.1, which plots R^P against R. For any given monetary and fiscal policies, a higher value of R^P will have a contractionary effect on the economy, because it will lower net exports; this will lower the interest rate and lead to a lower valuation of the currency. Thus, the relationship between R^P and R at any given point in time is described by the downward-sloping curve XX. Also, at any point in time the permanent exchange rate is given; but over time this rate tends toward equality with the actual exchange rate, so that medium-run equilibrium lies on the dotted 45-degree line.

Suppose that the economy is initially in equilibrium at point A, and that there is a shift toward a contractionary fiscal policy offset by monetary expansion. At any given level of R^P this will imply a lower interest rate and therefore a lower value of R; thus, XX shifts down to $X'X'$, with an eventual equilibrium at C. In the short run, however, the permanent exchange rate is predetermined. So the economy initially moves from A to B. At point B the current account deficit is actually larger than at A, because of the J-curve. Over time, however, as R^P

adjusts, the economy will move from B to C; as it does, the current account deficit will be steadily shrinking. Rising net exports will also tend to pull up the domestic interest rate; hence, as we can see from the figure, the currency will be appreciating. It is the expectation of this appreciation that makes investors willing to finance the initially larger and slowly falling current account deficit.

This formulation is of course far too simplified and mechanical to capture the reality of the actual adjustment process after 1985. In particular, the behavior of the exchange rate is neither as predictable nor, in general, as rational as the model assumes. Nonetheless, this story helps to show how financing and adjustment are related, and why international markets will usually be willing to finance an adjusting country through the J-curve.

References

Baldwin, Richard. 1988. "Hysteresis in Import Prices: The Beachhead Effect." *American Economic Review* 78:773–85.

Baldwin, Richard, and Paul R. Krugman. 1989. "Persistent Trade Effects of Large Exchange Rate Shocks." *Quarterly Journal of Economics* 104, no. 4 (November): 635–54.

Bryant, Ralph C., Dale Henderson, Gerald Holtham, Peter Hooper, and Steven Symansky, eds. 1988a. *Macroeconomics for Interdependent Economies.* Washington: Brookings Institution.

Bryant, Ralph C., Gerald Holtham, and Peter Hooper, eds. 1988b. *External Deficits and the Dollar: The Pit and the Pendulum.* Washington: Brookings Institution.

Cooper, Richard N. 1971. "The Nexus Among Foreign Trade, Investment, and Balance-of-Payments Adjustment." In Commission on International Trade and Investment Policy, *United States International Economic Policy in an Interdependent World.* Washington: Government Printing Office.

Cripps, F., and W. Godley. 1976. "A Formal Analysis of the Cambridge Economic Policy Group Model." *Economica* 43:335–48.

Cripps, F., and W. Godley. 1978. "Control of Imports as a Means to Full Employment and the Expansion of World Trade." *Cambridge Journal of Economics* 2:327–34.

Dornbusch, Rudiger. 1976. "Exchange Rate Expectations and Monetary Policy." *Journal of International Economics* 6:231–44.

Dornbusch, Rudiger. 1987. "Exchange Rates and Prices." *American Economic Review* 77:93–106.

Dornbusch, Rudiger. 1989. "Give Japan a Target and Say 'Import'!" *New York Times.*

Dornbusch, Rudiger, Stanley Fischer, and Paul Samuelson. 1977. "Comparative Advantage, Trade, and Payments in a Ricardian Model with a Continuum of Goods." *American Economic Review* 67:823–39.

Economic Report of the President. 1984. Washington: Government Printing Office.

Fallows, James. 1989. *More Like Us—Making America Great Again*. Boston: Houghton-Mifflin.

Feldstein, Martin. 1985. "American Economic Policy and the World Economy." *Foreign Affairs* 63, no. 5 (Summer):995–1008.

Fetherston, M.J., and W. Godley. 1978. "New Cambridge Macroeconomics and Global Monetarism." In K. Brunner and A. Meltzer, eds., *Public Policies in Open Economies. Carnegie Rochester Conference Series on Public Policy* 9. Amsterdam: North-Holland.

Frankel, Jeffrey. 1988. "Ambiguous Policy Multipliers in Theory and in Empirical Models." In Ralph C. Bryant, D.W. Henderson, G. Holtham, P. Hooper, and S. Symansky, eds., *Macroeconomics for Interdependent Economies*. Washington: Brookings Institution.

Godley, W. 1979. "Britain's Chronic Recession—Can Anything Be Done?" In Wilfred Beckerman, ed., *Slow Growth in Britain*. Oxford: Clarendon.

Goldstein, Morris, and Mohsin S. Khan. 1985. "Income and Price Effects in Foreign Trade." In R. Jones and Peter B. Kenen, eds., *Handbook of International Economics*. Amsterdam: North-Holland.

Helkie, William L., and Peter Hooper. 1988. "The U.S. External Deficit in the 1980s." In Ralph C. Bryant, Dale Henderson, Gerald Holtham, Peter Hooper, and Steven Symansky, eds., *Macroeconomics for Interdependent Economies*. Washington: Brookings Institution.

Houthakker, Hendrik S., and S.P. Magee. 1969. "Income and Price Elasticities in World Trade." *Review of Economics and Statistics* 51:111–25.

Johnson, Harry. 1958. "Toward a General Theory of the Balance of Payments." In *International Trade and Economic Growth: Studies in Pure Theory*. London: George Allen and Unwin.

Kuttner, Robert. 1991. *The End of Laissez-Faire*. New York: Knopf.

Lawrence, Robert Z. 1990. "US Current Account Adjustment: An Appraisal." *Brookings Papers on Economic Activity* 2:343–82.

Marris, Stephen. 1987. *Deficits and the Dollar: The World Economy at Risk*, revised ed. POLICY ANALYSES IN INTERNATIONAL ECONOMICS 14. Washington: Institute for International Economics.

Marston, Richard C. 1989. "Pricing to Market in Japanese Manufacturing." *NBER Working Paper* 2905. Cambridge, MA: National Bureau of Economic Research (March).

Marston, Richard C. 1990. "Price Behavior in Japanese and US Manufacturing." Philadelphia: Wharton School (mimeographed).

McKinnon, Ronald I. 1963. "Optimum Currency Areas." *American Economic Review* 53:717–24.

McKinnon, Ronald I. 1984. *An International Standard for Monetary Stabilization.* POLICY ANALYSES IN INTERNATIONAL ECONOMICS 8. Washington: Institute for International Economics.

Mundell, Robert A. 1989. "The Global Adjustment System." *Rivista di Politica Economica* (December):351–466.

Prestowitz, Clyde V., Jr. 1988. *Trading Places: How We Are Giving Our Future to Japan and How to Reclaim It.* New York: Basic Books.

US Congress. House. Committee on Foreign Affairs. Subcommittee on International Economic Policy and Trade. 1981. *U.S. International Economic Influence: Agenda for the Future.* 97th Cong., 1st. sess., 1–25 (24 February).

Whalley, John. 1985. *Trade Liberalization Among Major World Areas.* Cambridge: MIT Press.

Williamson, John. 1985. *The Exchange Rate System,* 2nd ed. POLICY ANALYSES IN INTERNATIONAL ECONOMICS 5. Washington: Institute for International Economics.

Appendix

Appendix

Conference Participants
25–27 October 1990

Paul S. Armington
World Bank

Thomas O. Bayard
Institute for International Economics

C. Fred Bergsten
Institute for International Economics

Peter Bofinger
Baden-Württemburg Landeszentralbank

Ralph C. Bryant
Brookings Institution

William R. Cline
Institute for International Economics

Richard N. Cooper
Harvard University

Wendy Dobson
Institute for International Economics

Jonathan H. Francis
RHO Management

Jacob Frenkel
International Monetary Fund

Alberto Giovannini
Columbia University

Giorgio Gomel
Banca d'Italia

Toyoo Gyohten
Princeton University

William L. Helkie
Federal Reserve Board

C. Randall Henning
Institute for International Economics

Peter Hooper
Federal Reserve Board

Peter B. Kenen
Princeton University

Paul R. Krugman
Massachusetts Institute of Technology

Robert Z. Lawrence
Brookings Institution

Allen J. Lenz
Chemical Manufacturers Association

Stephen Marris
Institute for International Economics

Richard C. Marston
University of Pennsylvania

Paul R. Masson
International Monetary Fund

Warwick J. McKibbin
Brookings Institution

Ronald I. McKinnon
Stanford University

Nadine Mendelek
Princeton University

Lynn O. Michaelis
Weyerhauser Company

Hunter K. Monroe
Chemical Manufacturers Association

David C. Mulford
Department of the Treasury

Robert A. Mundell
Columbia University

Bruce Parsell
Chemical Manufacturers Association

Peter A. Petri
Brandeis University

Jacques J. Polak
International Monetary Fund

Lee Price
Joint Economic Committee

Hobart Rowen
Washington Post

Horst Schulmann
Institute of International Finance

Robert Solomon
Brookings Institution

Herbert Stein
American Enterprise Institute

Niels Thygesen
University of Copenhagen

Edwin M. Truman
Federal Reserve Board

Philip K. Verleger, Jr.
Institute for International Economics

David A. Vines
University of Glasgow

Norbert Walter
Deutsche Bank

John Williamson
Institute for International Economics

Masaru Yoshitomi
Economic Planning Agency

Index

Japan *(continued)*
  current account balances 11, 35,
    123–25, 137–39, 142, 145,
    156–57, 234, 278, 303–04, 309
  exchange rate movements 123, 128,
    251, 303
  fiscal policy 125, 128, 133, 151,
    251–52, 305
  household behavior in 268
  imports 127, 149–50
  liberalization of capital markets 271
  monetary policy 123, 125, 131–32,
    143–44, 151, 183, 233, 251
  private investment 125, 131, 150–52,
    252, 267, 305
  saving-investment balance in 125
  stock market decline 133, 143, 268
  trade balance 123–24, 137–38
  trade barriers in 287
  trade with European Community and
    members 142, 158
  trade with Southeast Asia 142–43,
    147
  trade with United States 35, 89–99
  withdrawal of financing for US deficit
    47
Johnson, Harry 6, 203, 293
Joint Economic Committee 224

Kaldor, Nicholas 289
Kenen, Peter B. 267–73
Keynes, John Maynard 6, 11–12,
  36–37, 189, 192-94, 199, 218, 222,
  290
Keynes-Ohlin debate 36–37, 192–95,
  269, 290
Kindleberger, Charles P. 205
Kohl, Helmut 170, 243
Korea
  current account surpluses 234
  demand elasticities 18
  private investment 143
  road vehicles trade with United States
    82, 89–99
  trade in services 61
  trade with Japan 147
Krugman, Paul R. 3–12, 18, 36, 39, 48,
  179, 181, 239, 270, 277–322
Kuttner, Robert 295, 299

Latin America 39, 165, 179, 260

Lawrence, Robert Z. 29, 30, 48, 98,
  103, 113–18, 150, 279, 288, 301
Lawrence-Krugman paradox 103–04,
  106, 112, 119, 292, 305
Lenz, Allen J. 56–103, 109–10, 113,
  288
Lerner, Abba P. 200, 202
Life-cycle theory 179, 205, 210, 268
Louvre Accord 183, 185, 231, 272
Lucas, Robert E., Jr. 7

Machlup, Fritz 202–03
Malaysia 143, 147
Managed exchange rate regime. *See*
  Exchange rates, managed;
  International economic policy
  coordination; Louvre Accord
Managed trade 15–16, 296, 299,
  312–13
Manufactures, trade in 57, 67–69, 100
Marris, Stephen 23–24, 48, 109, 240,
  247–63, 269–71, 288, 313
Marshall, Alfred 190, 193
Marshall-Lerner condition 128–30, 200,
  225, 241, 304
Marston, Richard C. 145–48, 287
Mass. Ave. model
  description 279–82
  empirical application 282–84
  formal statement 314–16
  policy implications 293–94
  role of exchange rate changes implied
    by 285, 293
  verdict on 310–11
Massachusetts Institute of Technology
  280
McKinnon, Ronald I. 5, 36, 290, 297,
  310
MCM model (Federal Reserve) 280
Meade, Ellen 115
Meade, James 192–93, 202–03, 222,
  270
Mercantilism 198
Merchandise trade 58–65. *See also* Trade
  balance
Metzler, Lloyd A. 199, 202, 203
Mexico 83, 89, 99
Michigan Report 98
Mill, John Stuart 191–93, 203

Road vehicles *(continued)*
    US trade in 83–100, 140
    world trade in 75–79, 85
Robertson, Dennis 196
Robinson, Joan 199, 202, 289
Royalties and license fees, US trade in
    62
Rueff, Jacques 220–21
Rybczynski theorem 195

Salami hard landing scenario 258
Samuelson, Paul A. 192, 290, 312
Saving, private
    formal determination of 51–52
    in Germany 144, 169
    in Japan 125, 152, 169
    in United States 37, 168–69, 317
    world shortage of 141–42, 144, 248,
        258, 260
Saving-investment balances 36, 49,
    125–26, 260
Savings and loan crisis, US 40, 168,
    268, 316
Schengener agreement 173
Schulmann, Horst 182–86, 270
Schultze, Charles L. 258
Second Directive Coordinating Banking
    Law (EC) 173
Secularism 10, 291–93, 298–99, 311
Semiconductors, trade in 141
Services, trade in 26–27, 35, 61, 277
Shmooism 289–91, 297–98, 307, 311
Shultz, George P. 226
Silver, as monetary standard 216
Singapore 147, 234
Smithsonian Agreement 217, 221,
    224–25
Solow, Robert M. 289
Southeast Asia 142–44
Soviet Union 50, 40, 152, 177, 183,
    259
Special Drawing Right (SDR) 217, 223,
    228, 244
Stages theory of external indebtedness
    208–10, 244
Statistical discrepancy, world 182
Stein, Herbert 262–63, 278
Stigler, George J. 116
Structuralism 189, 286–89, 294–97,
    301, 310

Supply-side variables in trade modeling
    10, 22, 103, 105, 269, 292, 306

Taiwan 18, 143, 147, 234
Target zones 314
Targeting of current account 34–35, 45,
    180, 207
Taussig, Frank W. 192, 194
Tax reform, in Germany 170
Telecommunications services, US trade
    in 62
Terms of trade. *See* Prices, relative
Thailand 143, 147
Third World debt crisis 216, 277
Trade balance. *See also* Current account
    as macroeconomic issue 293
    classical theory of 189–201
    determinants of 36, 103, 280
    imbalance as systemic problem
        215–17, 256
    in Japan 123–24, 137–38
    in United States 17, 64–67, 233, 275
    model-based projections 32–33,
        137–38
    lagged response to exchange rate
        changes 3, 9–10, 280, 283
    16 approaches to 202–06, 239
Trade barriers. *See* Protectionism
Transfer problem 6, 192–201, 290, 311.
    See also Keynes-Ohlin debate
Transplants, Japanese. *See* Foreign direct
    investment, by Japanese firms
Travel account 60, 124, 142
Treasury Department, US 23, 250, 253
Triffin, Robert 220
Truman, Edwin M. 269–70
Twin deficits 248, 253, 257, 280, 316.
    See also Fiscal policy

Unilateral transfers account, US 59–60,
    63
United Kingdom
    currency history 191
    current account 35, 259
    economic growth and domestic
        demand 163
    post–World War I return to gold
        standard 218
    reasons for decline 256
    trade with Germany 158, 164

Other Publications from the Institute for International Economics

POLICY ANALYSES IN INTERNATIONAL ECONOMICS SERIES

BOOKS

American Trade Politics: System Under Stress
I. M. Destler/*1986*
$30.00   ISBN cloth 0-88132-058-7   380 pp.
$18.00   ISBN paper 0-88132-057-9   380 pp.

Capital Flight and Third World Debt
Donald R. Lessard and John Williamson, editors/*1987*
(out of print)   ISBN paper 0-88132-053-6   270 pp.

The Canada-United States Free Trade Agreement: The Global Impact
Jeffrey J. Schott and Murray G. Smith, editors/*1988*
$13.95   ISBN paper 0-88132-073-0   211 pp.

World Agricultural Trade: Building a Consensus
William M. Miner and Dale E. Hathaway, editors/*1988*
$16.95   ISBN paper 0-88132-071-3   226 pp.

Japan in the World Economy
Bela Balassa and Marcus Noland/*1988*
$19.95   ISBN paper 0-88132-041-2   306 pp.

America in the World Economy: A Strategy for the 1990s
C. Fred Bergsten/*1988*
$29.95   ISBN cloth 0-88132-089-7   235 pp.
$13.95   ISBN paper 0-88132-082-X   235 pp.

Managing the Dollar: From the Plaza to the Louvre
Yoichi Funabashi/*1988, 2d ed. 1989*
$19.95   ISBN paper 0-88132-097-8   307 pp.

United States External Adjustment and the World Economy
William R. Cline/*May 1989*
$25.00   ISBN paper 0-88132-048-X   392 pp.

Free Trade Areas and U.S. Trade Policy
Jeffrey J. Schott, editor/*May 1989*
$19.95   ISBN paper 0-88132-094-3   400 pp.

Dollar Politics: Exchange Rate Policymaking in the United States
I. M. Destler and C. Randall Henning/*September 1989*
$11.95   ISBN paper 0-88132-079-X   192 pp.

Latin American Adjustment: How Much Has Happened?
John Williamson, editor/*April 1990*
$34.95   ISBN paper 0-88132-125-7   480 pp.

The Future of World Trade in Textiles and Apparel
William R. Cline/*1987, 2d ed. June 1990*
$20.00   ISBN paper 0-88132-110-9   344 pp.

Completing the Uruguay Round: A Results-Oriented
  Approach to the GATT Trade Negotiations
Jeffrey J. Schott, editor/*September 1990*
$19.95   ISBN paper 0-88132-130-3   256 pp.

Economic Sanctions Reconsidered (in two volumes)
    Economic Sanctions Reconsidered: History and Current Policy
      (also sold separately, see below)
    Economic Sanctions Reconsidered: Supplemental Case Histories
Gary Clyde Hufbauer, Jeffrey J. Schott, and Kimberly Ann Elliott/
1985, 2d ed. December 1990

$65.00	ISBN cloth 0-88132-115-X	928 pp.
$45.00	ISBN paper 0-88132-105-2	928 pp.

Economic Sanctions Reconsidered: History and Current Policy
Gary Clyde Hufbauer, Jeffrey J. Schott, and Kimberly Ann Elliott/
December 1990

$36.00	ISBN cloth 0-88132-136-2	288 pp.
$25.00	ISBN paper 0-88132-140-0	288 pp.

Pacific Basin Developing Countries: Prospects for the Future
Marcus Noland/*January 1991*

$29.95	ISBN cloth 0-88132-141-9	250 pp.
$19.95	ISBN paper 0-88132-081-1	250 pp.

Currency Convertibility in Eastern Europe
John Williamson, editor/*September 1991*

$39.95	ISBN cloth 0-88132-144-3	396 pp.
$28.95	ISBN paper 0-88132-128-1	396 ppp

Foreign Direct Investment in the United States
Edward M. Graham and Paul R. Krugman/*1989, 2d ed. October 1991*

$16.95	ISBN paper 0-88132-139-7	200 pp.

SPECIAL REPORTS

1   **Promoting World Recovery: A Statement on Global Economic Strategy**
    by Twenty-six Economists from Fourteen Countries/*December 1982*

(out of print)	ISBN paper 0-88132-013-7	45 pp.

2   **Prospects for Adjustment in Argentina, Brazil, and Mexico: Responding to the Debt Crisis**
    John Williamson, editor/*June 1983*

(out of print)	ISBN paper 0-88132-016-1	71 pp.

3   **Inflation and Indexation: Argentina, Brazil, and Israel**
    John Williamson, editor/*March 1985*

$12.00	ISBN paper 0-88132-037-4	191 pp.

4   **Global Economic Imbalances**
    C. Fred Bergsten, editor/*March 1986*

$25.00	ISBN cloth 0-88132-038-2	126 pp.
$10.00	ISBN paper 0-88132-042-0	126 pp.

5   **African Debt and Financing**
    Carol Lancaster and John Williamson, editors/*May 1986*

(out of print)	ISBN paper 0-88132-044-7	229 pp.

FORTHCOMING

North American Free Trade: Issues and Recommendations
Jeffrey J. Schott and Gary Clyde Hufbauer

A World Savings Shortage?
Paul R. Krugman

Who's Bashing Whom? Trade Conflict in High Technology Industries
Laura D'Andrea Tyson

Sizing Up U.S. Export Disincentives
J. David Richardson

The Globalization of Industry and National Economic Policies
C. Fred Bergsten and Edward M. Graham

The Economics of Global Warming
William R. Cline

Trading for the Environment
John Whalley

Narrowing the U.S. Current Account Deficit: A Sectoral Assessment
Allen J. Lenz

U.S. Taxation of International Income: Blueprint for Reform
Gary Clyde Hufbauer

The Effects of Foreign-Exchange Intervention
Kathryn Dominguez and Jeffrey A. Frankel

The Future of the World Trading System
John Whalley

Global Oil Crisis Intervention
Philip K. Verleger, Jr.

American Trade Politics, second edition
I. M. Destler

The United States as a Debtor Country
C. Fred Bergsten and Shafiqul Islam